# Mexico and Mexico City in the World Economy

# Mexico and Mexico City in the World Economy

Edgar W. Butler

James B. Pick

W. James Hettrick

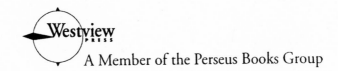

Westview
PRESS

A Member of the Perseus Books Group

Copyright © 2001 by Westview Press, A Member of the Perseus Books Group

Published in 2001 in the United States of America by Westview Press, 5500 Central Avenue, Boulder, Colorado 80301-2877, and in the United Kingdom by Westview Press, 12 Hid's Copse Road, Cumnor Hill, Oxford OX2 9JJ

Find us on the World Wide Web at www.westviewpress.com

A CIP catalog record for this book is available from the Library of Congress.
ISBN 0-8133-3542-6

The paper used in this publication meets the requirements of the American National Standard for Permanence of Paper for Printed Library Materials Z39.48-1984.

PERSEUS
POD
ON DEMAND    10    9    8    7    6    5    4

*To my wife, Leslie Hettrick*
*W.J.H.*

*To my wife, Rosalyn Laudati*
*J.P.*

*To my wife, Patricia M. Butler*
*E.B.*

# Contents

# Figures

# Maps

# Tables

# Preface

The idea for this book came from our observations that our prior studies of the internal structure of Mexican cities, states, and population may have been missing several major important trends of the late twentieth century. We observed that Mexico was undergoing a huge transformation, economically, in trade, and in business and society.

This book provides a more holistic and larger perspective than our previous books on Mexico. We utilize diverse data sources and examine trends and events not only for Mexico but also for Mexico related to many other parts of the world.

There are several overall observations we have at the end of this writing project. First of all, we perceive that globalization or the world economy process is highly complex, more so than we thought at the beginning. The many dimensions and large number of interrelationships we observe mean that simple generalizations about "globalization" are difficult. Rather, a developing nation such as Mexico has multifaceted processes occurring as it undergoes the world system transformation. Hence, multiple perspectives have been necessary. For instance, globalization impacts multinational giant firms in Mexico as well as small villages, but in quite different ways. We try to encompass and explain this complexity.

Another point about "globalization" in this book is that the perspective of economic globalization falls short of the true extent of transformation. On a strictly economy basis the U.S. looms as a northern "giant" that overshadows its southern neighbor in the world economy. However, we have attempted to balance that view by explaining other processes where there is more parity, such as in natural resources, people, migration, and culture.

We have been conscientious and careful in utilizing the available data. However, the information for this book was gathered by others and whatever deficiencies the original data have, were carried over into our analyses. However, we as authors are responsible for any deficiencies or errors in the subsequent analyses and conclusions.

# Acknowledgments

No book such as this is produced without the efforts and contributions of many people.

The one person most responsible for the production of this book is Katsumi Funakoshi and we acknowledge his great contribution. He has conducted geographic information systems analysis (GIS), developed tables and graphs, and always been a major contributor in moving this project forward. We have been fortunate over the years to have truly outstanding graduate students participating in our projects. Katsumi Funakoshi has lived up to that tradition by his technical skills, tenacity, knowledge, and superb contribution.

We acknowledge the many people who have contributed to this book over the past several years in the U.S. and Mexico.

At the University of California, Riverside, we thank the Department of Sociology's staff - Cathy Carlson, Robin Whittington, Anna Wire, Terry DeAnda, and Renee Deguire. Also, the staff of Rivera Library, in particular the Interlibrary Loan Department was very helpful.

At the University of Redlands, we acknowledge the office staff of the Department of Management and Business for excellence. We thank Susie Ahearn, Ann Bright, Sheryl Robinson, and earlier Karen Philabaum for their outstanding efforts and support. We also thank undergraduate student workers who provided assistance. We thank the Armacost Library staff and especially Linda Salem for their help.

Funding was provided by several sources. We thank the University of Redlands for several developmental research grants to James Pick from Whitehead College and from the Faculty Review Committee. We appreciate the research grant provided to James Pick by Universidad Iberoamericana during his sabbatical leave.

We thank the city of Loma Linda for technological support and interest.

In Mexico, we owe our largest debt of thanks to Dr. Carlos Jarque Uribe, who was President of INEGI for most of our project but is now Mexico's Secretary of Social Development. Since we first met him in the 1980's, he has been a strong and constant supporter of our work. At INEGI, we give special appreciation to Pilar Garcia Velazquez. We also thank present and former INEGI leaders including J. Arturo Blancas Espejo, Francisco J. Gutierrez, Enrique Ordaz, Mario Palma Rojo, Antonio Puig, and others. We also thank others at Banco de Mexico, BancoMext, SECOFI, and other federal government information offices for their help and assistance.

In Mexico, we thank Gerardo Mendiola at Grupo Editorial Expansion for assistance and ideas. We thank the managers and leaders at approximately fifteen Mexican companies and organizations, who responded to our interview case studies. We also thank Edgar Ortiz for reviewing parts of the book and to Carlos J. Navarette for discussions of several aspects of the book.

# 1

## Introduction

- **Introduction**
- **Corporate and Legal Historical Background**
  - Legal Background
- **Modernization and World Systems Theoretical Perspectives**
  - Modernization Theory
  - World Systems/Dependency Theory
  - FIRE
  - Worldwide Networks
  - National Networks
  - Local/ Regional Networks
- **Methodological Issues**
- **Remainder of This Book**

## Introduction

This volume is an outgrowth of previous research experiences on Mexico reported in our books on Mexico: *Mexico Megacity* (1997); *The Mexico Handbook* (1994); *Sucesion Presidencial: The 1988 Mexican Presidential Election* (1991); and *Atlas of Mexico* (1989), and reported by us in numerous articles on Mexico. As a result of our research, it became readily apparent that to understand contemporary Mexico, it was absolutely necessary to examine its level of development and its relationship with the world's economy. We expect the level of development to be related to the world system network but that they are not identical concepts. Accordingly, this book has as its primary *goal* determining Mexico's level of development, the level of development of its regions, and how Mexico fits into the world system.

Objectives of this book are:
1. To engender a hierarchical structure of development of world nation-states that is extended to include *internal nation dimensions;*
2. To place Mexico in this world hierarchy;
3. To construct a hierarchy of areas in Mexico using states utilizing the same or selected surrogate variables for the world cluster analysis;
4. To carry out similar analyses for municipios (i.e. counties) and delegations (i.e. city wards) within selected major metropolitan areas in Mexico, especially Mexico City (see Pick and Butler 1997).

A second set of objectives, dependent upon completion of those listed above are:
1. To generate the association of Mexico with other world nations;
2. To examine relationships of various regions in Mexico with each other and with world nation-states.

In this latter process, we utilize terminology of world systems theory and build upon world systems analyses. World systems theorists argue that the world consists of (1) core, (2) semi-periphery, and (3) periphery nations. In recent developmental research, Mexico has been classified as an upper middle-income nation in the global context (World Bank 1995). In world systems analysis Mexico has primarily, but not exclusively, been considered a semi-periphery nation.

The transformation of the world economy has impacted Mexico in a variety of manners, including its spatial dimensions. Transnational egress into Mexico is from all parts of the world. Spatial differentiation within Mexico is influenced by the oil industry, large-scale tourism, the maquiladora sector (sometimes known as in-bond industry), and transnational corporations (TNCs).[1] All of these economic enterprises, as well as the nationalized oil industry, in Mexico have clearly demarcated global spatial implications, both externally and internally. In addition to influencing the spatial contours of Mexico, the oil industry has a relationship with TNCs via its extensive international debt incurred as a result of selling petro-bonds (Cockcroft 1981: 275).

Changes in Mexico are inextricably linked to two countervailing trends in the world economy: (1) Concentration of management in transnational corporations and (2) dispersion – deconcentration – of the world's labor force. National boundaries are

---

[1] "TNCs are corporations with their base in one country but draw much of their income, raw materials, and operating capital from several other countries, through ownership of foreign subsidiaries, joint ventures with foreign governments or investors, and a host of other means" (Belshaw 1977: 620).

decreasingly effective as inhibitors to the flow of investments, production of goods and services, and communications.

The average annual net inflow of foreign direct investment to Mexico was 6.4 billion dollars in 1996 (United Nations 1997). New net foreign direct investment in the late 1990s should surpass four billion dollars per year. In subsequent years the government anticipates that 20 to 25 percent of total new investment will be from outside of the country. Some examples of recent foreign investment in Mexico during 1998-99 (González Lara 1999) are: (1) Chrysler (United States) one and a half billion dollars, (2) Ford (United States) one and a half billion dollars, (3) Volkswagen (Germany) one billion dollars, (4) Nissan (Japan) $800 million, (5) Labatt Brewing (in Participation with the Mexican Brewer Femsa) $731 million, IEP Global Development (Netherlands) (Electrical Energy Generation in Jalisco in Collaboration with the Mexican Firm Grupo Protexa), and Gaz de France (Distribution of Natural Gas in the Mexican Oil Region in Conjunction with the Mexican Firm Bufete).

## Corporate and Legal Historical Background

The emergence of *global corporations,* or TNCs, has occurred primarily since the 1950s (Taylor and Thrift 1982). TNCs have a fundamental objective of seeking locations in nations enabling maximal returns on investment. Increasingly, TNCs have sought countries in which there are uneven regulatory frameworks and ones in which monetary transfers can be made with minimum interference from and to the host country. The reasons for this are rather obvious – a TNC needs to produce a profit and it must be able to transfer funds rapidly from one country to another. The movement of money by TNCs has accelerated in recent years and individual corporations insist upon being able to transfer resources from one country to another, more profitable one, quickly (Wolfe 1977: 618).

Further, given the worldwide character of TNCs, they are able to react swiftly to prevailing political and fiscal conditions. One implication of this rapid reaction time to changing circumstances is that any given investment is continually checked against potentially more profitable locations in another countries.[2] This is apparently true despite the fact that a plant in any given location may be productive and profit making. (Thus, the question is one of whether a plant would be more profitable in another country and not if profit is currently being produced.) This has led TNCs being described as locationally 'fickle;' that is, when changing conditions warrant it, they can move without notice to a better location defined as one with greater profit potential (Taylor and Thrift 1982: 141).

Prior to World War II Mexico exchanged imported manufactured goods for primary exports with limited governmental regulation. President Cardenas in the 1930s stimulated foreign investment by providing tax incentives for private industry, state investments in the infrastructure, and the maintenance of a disciplined labor force receiving low wages with no social-welfare benefits (Cockcroft 1981: 262-263). Development over the next three decades focused on producing consumer goods rather than on the production of equipment for further industrialization. Foreign direct investment almost doubled between 1940 and 1960 and tripled between 1960 and 1970. Most of this investment was from the United States.

TNCs do not limit investments to one country but have increasingly diversified their investments to many countries, including the so-called developed nations. For example, the largest amount of direct investment by Japan is to the United States and continental European investment has been heavy to the United Kingdom (Taylor and Thrift 1982: 52ff). Implications of these trends for Mexico is that most jobs that will be developed

---

[2]  This ability is similar in some respects to 'program trading' on Wall Street.

under the terms of foreign investment are likely to be labor-intensive with labor that is cheap and untrained, such as in the tourist and maquiladora industries.

However, a more recent trend evolving in Mexico is that of capital-intensive industries such as automobiles and computer manufacturing, with an emphasis on robotics and consequently lack of jobs. The rationale for the emergence of more sophisticated industry is the ability to manipulate costs and taxes involving parts received from throughout the world and the completed product being exported, primarily to the United States.

## Legal Background

Fundamental goals stressed by former Mexican President, Carlos Salinas, involved controlling inflation, renegotiating the external debt, rationalizing foreign trade, and attracting foreign investment. In Mexico, as in many other countries, only advantages of foreign investment are mostly emphasized (Salinas 1989). Little attention is paid to potential negative impacts multinational corporations may have upon traditional values, spatial locations, and labor force. For example, the generation of jobs for women will undoubtedly weaken the traditional family, while developing tourism along the coasts engenders migration patterns, attracting primarily lower level manual labor positions, out does not develop a skilled labor force.

The preoccupation of the Mexican government in attracting foreign investment has resulted in legal changes making investment in Mexico more attractive. Decisions regarding foreign investment formerly were discretionary and administrative policies were unduly complicated. Generally, the law specified that foreign investors could not own more than 49 percent of a company.[3] These 1973 laws, until May 1989's Law to Promote Investment and Regulate Foreign Investment, controlled foreign investment in Mexico. The 1973 law divided economic activities in Mexico into those (1) reserved exclusively for the State, (2) reserved for Mexican citizens, (3) those subject to limits on foreign capital, and (4) all others, subject to general regulations.

The new guidelines established in May 1989 included the following requirements for the *automatic authorization* of up to 100 percent foreign ownership in every sector not specifically restricted by law: (1) a minimum of 100 million dollars invested in fixed assets, (2) direct external funding obtained through subscriptions of capital, external credit or foreign funds, channeled through Mexican financial institutions, (3) investment made in industrial establishments located outside of the three largest metropolitan areas – Mexico City, Monterrey, and Guadalajara, (4) the maintenance of an equilibrium in its foreign exchange transactions over the first three years of operation, (5) the creation of permanent jobs and establishment of training and personal development programs for workers, and (6) the use of appropriate technologies satisfying current environmental requirements.

New regulations required the government to: (1) Make a decision in 45 days, (2) Expand the duration ownership of real estate for tourism, (3) Allow foreign majority ownership in maquiladoras and other export oriented companies by registering with the National Foreign Registry, (4) Increase foreign access to the stock market, and (5) Give temporary outside control over sectors that under usual circumstances were reserved exclusively for Mexicans; that is, those with high export potential or facing financial difficulties.

The Mexican government began emphasizing foreign investment in the tourist sector by setting goals of doubling the number of tourists (Salinas 1989), and in the maquiladora sector by the expansion of in-bond plants. Leaders of both opposition political parties also went on record as encouraging foreign investments, the PAN via its party platform and the PRD in a speech by Cardenas (1989). In 1993, the Salinas Administration modernized the

---

[3]   Our analyses, however, suggest that some ownership in fact exceeded this mandate.

law on foreign direct investment making it much easier. The law on foreign financial investment was updated to be more encouraging. The emerging emphasis in Mexico upon privatization also allows foreign investors to gain access to economic sectors formerly prohibited to foreigners, e.g., the telephone industry (See Salinas 1989), national gas distribution, and banking.

Generally, the continuing Mexican position assumes the modernization perspective of development. The Zedillo Administration has continued the opening of foreign access and NAFTA has encouraged more direct foreign investment.

## Modernization and World Systems Theoretical Perspectives

*Modernization Theory*

Modernization theory assumes stages and phases of urbanization and that industrialization will take place in undeveloped countries mainly like it occurs in Western and U.S. cities. This approach emphasizes that less well developed areas will evolve through a progression of stages approximating Western urban growth and development. A further assumption is that urbanization is linked with industrialization. Cities are thus the foci of modernization, serving as conduits for information, innovation, and political transformation.

Mexico during the past several years has accepted wholeheartedly a positive view of foreign investment. Thus, Mexico is in concert with most other developing countries as their leaders accepted the modernization theoretical perspective. This positive view makes the assumption that foreign capital investment will generate jobs and income (other possible contributions are listed by Kissling 1978). Another assumption is that TNCs will enhance Mexico's ability to participate in the world's major commodity flows. Thus, more jobs, contributions to national income, increased government revenues and foreign reserves, and enhanced participation in world trade are all viewed as being advantages to Mexico. In addition, TNCs are assumed to contribute to local populations by offering training otherwise not available. Further, employees trained by TNCs may pass on or use their learned skills in other host country enterprises. Thus, the overall assumption is that poor nations are enhanced by foreign direct investments, and often by foreign investments and direct forms of foreign aid; that is by money and as well as by technical assistance.

There are possible disadvantages to foreign investment that are often neglected. A major criticism of modernization theory by social scientists is that it is out of concert with empirical facts. Emerging research has shown quite conclusively that Third World urbanization and industrialization have not followed the Western sequence. Further, there is substantial evidence showing that there has been uneven growth and extensive inequality in Third World cities. Inequality apparently exists at three levels: (1) between urban and rural regions, (2) among cities, and (3) within cities. This is typically coupled with the extensive urban concentration in one primate city in non-developed nations.

An explicit assumption of modernization theory is that there will be a convergence between developed and developing nations. Thus, this assumption means that nations that are not yet fully developed, in the Western sense, will pass through a transitional phase which will make them eventually become modern, i.e., like Western nations. Economic growth and urbanization are assumed to occur as an ordered sequence in which currently poor countries repeat strategies and experiences of wealthy nations (Snyder and Kick 1979).

Empirical evidence, however, illustrates the following:
1.  There has been little change in international economic stratification.
2.  Some change that has taken place results in nations regressing instead of following the Western mode.
3.  Rich nations continue to accrue wealth while poverty is endemic in Third World nations.

## World Systems/Dependency Theory

Differences noted between developed and developing nations undoubtedly influenced the emergence of what has been labeled world systems/dependency theory. The dependency perspective assumes uneven development and inequality are a result of uneven economic and urban growth.

It further assumes:
1.  There is a worldwide capitalist system.
2.  There are a variety of international network linkages, although at times they may not be specified.
3.  There are three 'types' of nations – core, semi-periphery, and periphery.
4.  Types of nations are more than descriptive; they denote an international division of labor that is dynamic, exploitative, and involves control by core nations.
5.  Peripheral economies within nations are poorly integrated because of production that is export oriented and raw material specialized.
6.  Some analyses suggest that domestic capital formation is positive and foreign investment negative on economic growth and reducing inequality; the locus of capital rather than investment per se is most important (see Chase-Dunn 1975).

From an economic point of view, a critical perspective of dependency theory implies that negative consequences may result from a country relying upon TNC investment (Moran 1978; Newfarmer and Topik 1982; Gereffi 1980). The potential influence of transnational investment in Mexico is especially important since benefits of direct investment in some instances may be "unequally" or "unfairly" distributed to the detriment of the host country in favor of the TNC (Enderwick 1985: 67). Johnson (1978) argues that over 80 percent of profits are removed from a country by TNCs. Also, in some countries, TNCs have created distortions in local economies by squeezing out local businesses, utilizing inappropriate technologies, worsening the distribution of income among the population, and distorting consumer patterns.

A criticism of world systems theory is that it is primarily based upon economic determinism to the neglect of the political (Bollen 1983: 471). However, another negative effect has been that foreign investors may subvert host country political processes. This is possible because some TNCs are larger economic entities than the host country. For example, in 1972 Mexico's economy ranked 14th in the world while if measured in a similar manner, General Motors would rank 16th (Newfarmer and Mueller 1975: 7). The economic power to TNCs then is great and their ability to obtain credit to build plants and facilities may be greater than a host country such as Mexico. Thus, economic resources available to some TNCs are at least as great as they are to Mexico and larger than many nations with smaller economic resources (Taylor and Thrift 1982: 142).

A further complication in some instances is that national and regional policies begin to reflect needs of TNCs rather than the host country and/or local populations (Gedicks 1978). When a government negotiates with a TNC, Plaza (1978) argues that the government is eroding its most important element – its sovereignty. Examples of foreign influence upon policy is the impact that the international financial community has had upon the periodic devaluation of the peso imposed upon Mexico and imposition of terms by the International Monetary Fund (IMF) to determine the "credit-worthiness" of Mexico (Cockcroft 1981: 275).

Perhaps the most critical comments regarding transnational was recorded by *The Economist* (1979), which noted the following:

It fiddles its accounts. It avoids or evades its taxes. It rigs its intra-company transfer prices. Foreigners run it, from decision centers thousands of miles away. It imports foreign labor practices. It does not import foreign labor practices. It overpays. It underpays. It competes unfairly with local firms. It is in cahoots with local firms. It exports from rich countries. It is an instrument of rich countries' imperialism. The technologies it brings to the Third World are old fashioned. No, they are too modern. It meddles. It bribes. Nobody can control it. It wrecks the balance of payments. It overturns economic policies. It plays governments against each other to get the biggest investment incentives. Won't it please come here and invest. Let it bloody well go home.

Thus, all the above suggests that one needs to keep an open, scientific mind in the research effort when the impact of the globalization of the economy on Mexico is examined from a world system orientation.

## FIRE

Sassen (1991) emphasizes the importance of finance, insurance, and real estate (FIRE) in evaluating the importance of global economies. Financial areas of particular importance are foreign direct investment and financial markets, as opposed to traditional banks.

In addition, there is a focus on services necessary for FIRE – advertising, computer and data processing, databases and other information, telecommunications, management and consulting, legal, accounting, and educational training services. Positive changes in employment in such service industries are good indicators of global importance of a country.

## Worldwide Networks

We present a number of case studies in this volume. Some of the case companies examined are large multinational firms that have major offices in most countries of the world, with manufacturing and distribution centers being scattered throughout many countries. In addition, there are a variety of other types of alliances and relationships.

Among them are (Kanter 1994):
- Investment capital
- Customers
- Suppliers (subsidiaries and/or outsourcing)
- Regulators (set policy)
- Competitors (sells similar products)
- Alliances (firm to firm, firm to government)
- Gatekeepers (to other relationships).

Other research has focused on flows of investments, people – especially managers, technical personnel, commodities and goods, and research and development.

## National Networks

Analyses similar to those carried out on a global scale can focus on comparable exchanges in a national economy such as Mexico. Similarly, exchanges within local and/or regions, cities, and areas within them also can be examined.

## Methodological Issues

What are the operational criteria for classifying a country in a developmental and structural position in the world system?    A corollary question is where do formerly communist nations and others belong in the system (see Shannon 1992: 117ff).

Another methodological issue, whether for modernization and/or world systems theory, is one of categorization.  How is a country, or one of its segments, to be classified into a category? Where are the breaking points to be established? Does *variation* exist within a category?  That is, are varying characteristics of different parts of categories substantively important?  Does this imply sub-categories?  Thus, it may be necessary "to explore national variations within particular positions in the system" (Snyder and Kick 1979: 1116).  Shannon (1992: 87), for example, divides the core into major core powers and minor core powers.

How does transmission from one category to another take place – ascent and decline (see Shannon 1992: 146 ff)? This is a question of movement across categories in the world system, i.e., Spain (Wallerstein) and Mexico (see Snyder and Kick 1979).    This is especially important for Mexico since it was formerly classified as periphery and we now designate it as semi-periphery.  So there has been transition from one category to another by Mexico; do other transitions exist?  When and on what basis does such change take place?  Is progression assumed for all countries, such as in modernization theory?  Where is the break; when and how does crossing the boundary take place?

Do countries similarly classified operate as theoretically classified – exert control or be controlled (Snyder and Kick 1979)?   How is control to be measured?   What are the exploitative links?

Should countries be viewed only in economic terms or should noneconomic dimensions such as population size, territorial size, military and political strength, cultural impact be examined?  What about trade flows, military interventions, diplomatic relations, and conjoint treaty memberships.  What countries should be included in the analyses; assume all?

The core should dominate the international trade network.  But who is linked to whom? Snyder and Kick (1979) suggest that periphery may not be linked to semi-periphery but only to core.  Where do investment flows (and other flows) come from and go?  There also is the question of magnitude of flows that so far has been systematically ignored in most world systems research. What variables should be used for analysis and are they really only binary as currently used or are they, or should they be, continuous? Are regions of countries viable as units to be classified as core, semi-periphery, or periphery? If so, what are the relationships between the regions? What flows occur and how dependent are the regions on each other?  These are only a few of the questions to be explored in this book.

While our theoretical perspective has been influenced by developmental and world systems theories, we, in contrast, first emphasize *internal* nation-state development dimensions.  We are doing this because we envision a number of deficiencies in the manner that levels of development and world systems analyses have become entangled.  In some analyses, there is a problem of conceptual tautologies; that is, there is the use of the same variables to define core, semi-periphery, and periphery as used in analysis of core to other nations.  Thus, imports/exports are used for defining nations in the system and then used in the analysis associated with the definitions.  It is, then, not too surprising that they are subsequently highly associated.

There are a number of other deficiencies in world systems analyses that have been identified:

1. There has been classification of nations with directionality missing – for example, sometimes equality is assumed in trade flows (Snyder and Kick 1997). However, while economic and trade relation flows may be highly correlated at a particular time, they may also vary across time in both directions (for example as shown later for Mexico and U.S.).
2. Relationships are often considered binary (0/1) (Snyder and Kick 1979).
3. The magnitude of interactions often is ignored (Snyder and Kick 1979: 1103).
4. There is geographic proximity built in via network analyses as currently examined (Van Rossem 1996: 510; Schott 1986). Increasingly geographic proximity is becoming problematic.
5. Non-relationships are excluded (Snyder and Kick 1979: 1107).
6. Often a limited number of network relationships are considered.

Our theoretical perspective substantially rejects modernization theory on empirical grounds. However, we also illustrate how world systems/dependency theory has some of the same weaknesses of modernization theory. For example, it can be shown quite conclusively that in "core" nations and their cities inequality exists at three levels: (1) between urban and rural areas; (2) among cities; and (3) within cities.

The question remains for both modernization and dependency perspectives: Are the processes similar or different in developed and developing nations? That is, how can differences between nations, urban and rural areas, among cities, and within cities be accounted for?

In this book, we utilize research showing that in core nations there are differences between urban and rural areas, among cities, and within cities that are in many respects similar to those in Mexico – here defined by our cluster analysis as a semi-periphery country. However, we cite evidence from other researchers illustrating that the relationships we are showing for Mexico also exist in so-called core countries, such as the United States.

We anticipate that our examination of the Mexican economy will give us ample opportunity to illustrate that 'world systems theory' is actually much more general than ordinarily assumed. Through illustrations by our own research, supplemented by others, on development in Mexico and on globalization of the Mexican economy, we illustrate that there are varying levels of the theory that apply at the world level, but simultaneously provides insights to urban and rural divisions within core nations and to areas within core cities and to divisions within semi-peripheral and peripheral nations. In this research, we illustrate that *Mexico is a semi-periphery country*, with respect to the nations of the world. We also make evident that Mexico can be viewed as a "core" nation in respect to other Latin American nations. We systematically examine Mexico's relationship to core, semi-periphery, and periphery countries via its domestic and multinational corporations.

In this research we show that *Mexico is a semi-periphery country* with respect to the nations of the world.

We assume the following within Mexico:

1. Mexico Megacity is a core area within Mexico; in Mexico there are, then, semi-periphery and periphery areas. An additional question examined is whether or not there are other core areas in Mexico, e.g., Monterrey.
2. Whether or not they are core cities within Mexico Megacity and other major cities.

We also assume that Mexico serves as a core country to some other Latin American countries and that within Latin American countries there are core, semi-peripheral, and peripheral cities.

Our research demonstrates and explicates that world systems theory may be more generally applicable than originally put forth, that it applies within all core, semi-periphery, and periphery nations, their regions, their cities, and within their cities. Thus, semi-peripheral and peripheral statuses will be shown to exist in the world system but also within a country, which has core cities, and then semi-periphery and periphery areas within these core cities. Further, the perspective may then be applicable to a country now defined as semi-peripheral or peripheral but which has "core" relationships to some other countries. Further, within these cities there are core, semi-peripheral and peripheral areas.

Another limitation in our view is that the role in the world system is determined by a nation's overall *pattern* of networks and not by the *identity* of its network. We, in contrast, argue that what country or countries a nation has relationships with and may be dependent upon is extremely important.

World dependency research typically involved some political, military, and economic indicators, as well as occasionally a cultural measure, i.e., motion pictures. Other researchers have included the presence of foreign troops (Van Rossem 1996). Neglected in most analyses is the possibility of temporal shifts in dimensions (however, see Shannon 1996; Snyder and Kick 1979). The time dimension is important because development as a concept implies change. In addition, an examination of world systems theory must assume that there can be change in the world system; that is, movement upward or downward among the basic categories of core, semi-periphery, and periphery.

Many world systems statistical analyses report little variance explained, even with tautological variables. One such analysis ostensibly reported nation-state *population size* as a key variable (Van Rossem 1996: 518-519). The argument presented was that China via its large population size, despite its low development level, was a core nation. Brazil, it was argued, also was a core nation because of its geographic size. Population and geographic size, of course, are not networked, world system variables, but are internal nation-state dimensions. On the other hand, in this same report, it was argued that such countries as Canada, the Netherlands, and Belgium obtained core status because of their level of economic development, e.g., internal state variables. Thus, there appears to be confusion over whether nation-state or network dimensions are most important.

In this book, we adopt the view that nation-state factors delineate level of development and then analyze their network relations. In this book, then, we first construct a developmental hierarchy of nations. We then examine within Mexico varying levels of development for regions, the state, municipio, cities, and the areas within cities levels. Our analytic strategy allows an intersection of global processes with nations, areas within nations, cities, and small areas within a city. In this instance we use Mexico as a case illustration but argue that the perspective and analytic strategy can be applied to all nations and areas within them.

## Remainder of This Book

The research presented in this book examines both the potential positive and negative consequences of globalization on the Mexican economy and its population. This project ties in with several other projects being carried out on Mexico. Future change in Mexico may be influenced more by transnational corporations than political parties. That is, as multinational corporations penetrate Mexico they are having a profound influence upon contact with the global economy and with foreign cultures, e.g., United States, Canada, Germany, England, and now with Asian countries, especially Japan, Korea, and Taiwan.

In summary, this research has primary goals.

1.  To place Mexico in the world systems theory framework of the global economy.
2.  To demonstrate that world system theory has utility for study of the economy of states, cities, and areas within cities.
3.  To analyze the economic demographic social, and business developments that occurred in Mexico in the late twentieth century.
4.  To explicate the domestic and international level of Mexico's development.
5.  To examine the processes of economic restructuring in Mexico and how it is adapting to the emerging global economy.
6.  To discuss Mexico's potential in the future global economy.

This book, then, focuses on the following flows:

1.  Financial, i.e., between Mexico and foreign countries or international agencies, between Mexican states and among and between Mexican-based private firms and government entities;
2.  Goods and Commodities;
3.  Personnel;
4.  Technology;
5.  Research and development;

Questions to be asked in meeting the above and goals and research on flows are as follows (Taylor and Thrift 1982: 139):

1.  What are the flows of investment and productive capital to and from Mexico?
2.  What form is foreign investment in Mexico taking; what is its degree of transience; is it creating inequality and competition with domestic enterprises; and what is its relationship with the source and Mexican government?
3.  Is foreign investment transforming the national, regional, and local labor markets through such processes as migration, de-skilling, and moving managerial loyalties from the state and private Mexican enterprise to the TNCs?
4.  How are export sectors such as petroleum, autos, tourism, and maquiladoras, growing and changing?
5.  Have Mexico's commercial and service sectors remain inward looking or have they been impacted by the international economy?
6.  What cultural alignment is being brought about in the outward looking economy sectors via more women entering the labor force and achieving higher educational levels?

We accomplish this by examining concentrations, flows, and dispersal of activities across time and by series of case studies of transnational and Mexican corporations. The focus on monetary and productive capital flows as they are related to Mexico and TNCs is particularly relevant as more countries and corporations become involved in the Mexican economy. Transnationals have influenced spatial changes and they may have engendered labor force stratification at the local level, in Mexico and worldwide. A variegated economy at the worldwide level implies that activities of TNCs will be spatially differentiated with substantial specialization by countries such as Mexico. Thus, within Mexico, not all regions are similarly effected by TNCs. For example, the border region with its tourism and maquiladoras, and international tourism in areas scattered throughout Mexico, mainly on the coasts, have been the location of substantial TNC activity. Corporate headquarters have been concentrated in Mexico City to the exclusion of most other areas.

The globalization of the economy has implications for worldwide production activities. In addition, TNCs via maquiladoras and tourist industry influence specific geographical locations by drawing migrants from other regions within Mexico (Butler et al. 1987). Given the prevailing investment climate in Mexico, there will be continued emphasis in three regions: (1) tourist areas, (2) maquiladoras along the U.S.-Mexican border, and (3) and certain areas within Mexico City (see Pick and Butler 1997). Research reported in the remainder of this book examines flows related to the globalization of the economy especially as it impacts Mexico – finance, commodities, personnel, technology and development, and research and development.

# 2

---

## Methodology

### Data Acquisition, Coverage, and Quality

- **Introduction**
- **Data Sources**
- **Methodology**
  - Descriptive Statistical Analysis
  - Cluster Statistical Methodology
- **Geographic Information Systems (GIS)**
- **Base Maps**
- **Conclusions**
- **Case Studies**

## Introduction

Data utilized in this book were acquired from a variety of sources. For the nation-state cluster analysis, most data were obtained from the *World Bank* (1995, 1997), INEGI (various years), with some additions from the *CIA Factbook* (1996). These are the same two international sources used by many others in examining development and world systems (Korzeniewicz and Moran 1997). Not all countries are covered by these two data sources; countries with limited data are generally those less developed. Similarly, less developed nations typically have lower quality data.

For the states of Mexico and cities of Mexico, the Mexico Database Project at the University of California, Riverside, and University of Redlands contained the necessary data; the Database has computerized information from 1895 through 1999.[1] For this book, more or less similar time periods are covered for all analyses. The Mexican censuses have varying quality of data. However, the 1990 census and Conteo Survey of 1995 are considered of good quality. They were undertaken under the direction of Dr. Carlos Jarque Uribe, who served for many years as President of INEGI, President of the UN's Statistics Committee, and he was appointed Mexican Secretary of Social Development near the end of the Zedillo Administration (Gane 2000). Available data on Mexico cover most social, economic, business, and global-local aspects of Mexico, including information that is necessary to determine Mexico's pattern of relationships with other nations of the world. These latter data are useful in tracing how Mexico fits into the world system.

While we view this project as developing methodology for additional developmental and world system case studies, we are well aware that data available for Mexico is superior to that of most countries, especially those at a lower level of development.

## Data Sources

Dimensions used in this volume are only a selected few of the multitude available from our database. This work uses data from a variety of international, national, and local agencies and groups, both private and governmental. In addition to variables and time periods presented in this work, the database project contains substantially larger computerized information. This volume, then, is only illustrative of the range of variables available and time periods actually contained in the database. The range of dimensions and time periods contained in this volume were constrained by cost and page restrictions rather than by database information.

In addition to INEGI, World Bank, and CIA sources, the following were accessed for data used in this book:

> *United Nations publications*
> *Mexican government population, housing, and other censuses*
> *Mexican economic census*
> *Mexican national accounts*
> *Mexican and U.S. International Exchange and Import/Export data*
> *The Journal Expansion, various years*
> *The Journal MB (formerly U.S./Mexico Business, various years)*
> *Corporate annual reports and publications*

---

[1]  The Mexico Database consists of geographic information on the states, municipios, cities, AGEBs, and corporations in Mexico.

*Banamex publications*
*Bancomext (Banco Comercial Exterior de Mexico)*
*International Monetary Fund publications*
*Instituto Nacional de Migracion*
*Mexican Secretary of Energy*
*Newspapers both in Mexico and the U.S.*
*Case study interviews with corporate leaders*
*Other sources, cited as appropriate*

After data were collected from a variety of sources they were processed for statistical and mapping purposes. Several different software packages were utilized in this process. For most mapping, ArcView or ArcInfo from ESRI were utilized. Microsoft Excel was used to develop some figures and charts while SPPS 8.0 was used for statistical analyses.

Data were entered and manipulated and maps created by the following steps:
(1) Data were obtained from CD-ROMs, diskettes, websites, and when necessary, data were input from hard copy.
(2) After input, data were tested for accuracy.
(3) Some raw data were used to calculate constructed variables such as rates, ratios, and percentages.
(4) Data were analyzed to determine the range of the distribution.
(5) Some spatially referenced data were entered into a Geographical Information System (GIS).
(6) For most spatial analysis, geographical areas were grouped approximately into quintiles; however, variables with unusual extreme values, or outlying values, were mapped with customized classifications assigning extremes to special thematic categories.
(7) Various statistical calculations were performed.
(8) A systematic set of files was developed to include all variables. Computerized documentation was maintained to keep track of variable definitions, names, data sources, and mapping codes; and
(9) A computerized codebook was generated and updated to keep track of the organization of data and information.

## Methodology

Various methodological techniques are used in this book. Among them are (1) descriptive statistical analysis, (2) cluster statistical analysis, (3) spatial analyses, and (4) case studies.

### Descriptive Statistical Analysis

The text emphasizes simple statistical interpretation and comparisons. Descriptive statistics often utilized are the mean, median, and mode, extreme values, percentiles, and standard deviation. For longitudinal data series, trends and changes over time are pointed out. At times the text refers to other maps and data scattered throughout the chapters showing similarities and contrasts.

Correlation analysis is used to clarify some relationships. Generally, correlation coefficients examine the relationship between two variables with a range from $-1.0$ to $+1.0$

(Afifi and Azen 1979). Finally to present some idea of relative homogeneity among variables, on occasions, the Coefficient of Variation (CV) is reported. The CV is defined as 100 times the ratio of the standard deviation to the mean. Thus, the CV allows a relative comparison of variation among all variables. In the text, a CV of less than 20 is treated as small or narrow; a CV between 21-99 is labeled as middle-range, while a CV of 100 or more is assumed to be large.

## Cluster Statistical Methodology

Cluster analysis may be applied to identify cases (nations, states, individuals) that are similar to each other based on a measure that averages similarity on many variables simultaneously (Hartigan 1975; Chatfield and Collins 1980). Cases are grouped starting with those two most alike. Once grouped, two or more cases are represented by average values for many variables. The averaged values are subject to further grouping just as an individual case is. The clustering process continues until all cases are in one large cluster. The clustering process can be stopped at any point of interest to an investigator or at a specially determined point, e.g, four, five or six clusters.

Clustering, in this book, is based upon Euclidean squared distance, as a measure of the closeness between the values of variables for any two cases and/or clusters. This means that the similarity between the value of variables and/or clusters is computed as the sum of differences squared, summing over all variables (Hartigan 1975; SPSS 1998).

The clustering process used is Ward's hierarchical clustering method (Chatfield and Collins 1980). In this method within groups sum of squares is calculated for each formed cluster. Then, the number of clusters is reduced by one. This process gives the smallest value for sum of within cluster group sum of squares. Euclidean squared distances are very appropriate and commonly used as the distance measure for Ward's hierarchical clustering.

Cluster analytic techniques involved developing a data matrix containing measurements on $m$ variables for each of $n$ units of observation (Chatfield and Collins 1980; SAS Institute 1985). In our cluster analyses, $m$ refers to various socioeconomic, population structure and economic variables, whereas $n$ identifies units of observations, i.e., nation-states, State of Mexico, municipios, and selected metropolitan areas.

The intent is (1) to reduce dimensions of $n$ units of observation into a smaller number of common units of observation, $R$, based on homogeneity of sets of variables within common units; (2) to describe and compare units; and (3) to interpret spatial patterns. It should be specifically noted that spatial patterns are defined by clustering of variables rather then geographic proximity, although similar types of areas may be located geographically near each other. Computer generated maps and graphics utilize the cluster analyses to illustrate more or less homogeneous areas.

The research framework calculated overall clusters for variables covering the dimensions used for all cluster analyses. Specific variables and cluster descriptions are given below. As previously cited, data for the nation-state cluster analysis were primarily derived from the World Bank and CIA. Data for the Mexican State cluster analysis were derived mainly from INEGI. Other data from these and other sources could have been included into the cluster analyses, e.g., energy (Rubinson 1976).

The primary variables used are presented below:
1) Population in 1994, log;
2) GNP/capita (Peacock et al. 1988; Kirman and Tomasini 1969);
3) Life expectancy, 1991;
4) Illiteracy, 1995 (Snyder and Kick 1979 use secondary school enrollment;

Boli and Thomas 1997 use both primary and tertiary school enrollments);
5) Population growth, 1990-1994 (Krozeniewicz and Mora 1997); and
6) Infant mortality, 1994.

Results of the various cluster analyses are presented at appropriate chapters in this volume.

## Geographic Information Systems (GIS)

The Geographic Information System is part of the Mexico Database, a larger project originally focusing almost exclusively on Mexico. However, the GIS is in process of being enlarged to encompass Mexico data into a form allowing the relationship of Mexico to the world system to be dissected. Thus, currently the GIS includes a section with information on most nation-states of the world.

Figure 2.1 presents a conceptual overview of the system that should be helpful in understanding the overall project design. Study attributes include demographic, social, labor force, economic, natural resource, international trade, and a variety of other dimensions from a host of earlier listed sources. Data were arranged on master spreadsheets and input for computerized data analysis. Attributes were keyed to geographic layers of boundaries such as nations, states, municipios, cities, etc., or what is known as *coverages*.

The most important coverages are base maps (shown in the next section). These are then linked to attributional data. Outputs from the GIS contain many attributes using various coverages. Figure 2.2 presents in more detail the process of obtaining information and boundary layers, analyzing the information, and producing spatial outputs using this database. The attribute information resides in a large database with a codebook detailing variables, their definition, source, and other miscellaneous information.

The GIS is suitable for many purposes beyond those used in this book, such as (1) computerized information to produce maps and statistical analyses for policy makers and businesses; (2) other academic studies; (3) for a variety of demographic, economic, and environmental research projects; (4) incorporation into a database with additional variables as they become available; (5) a variety of useful research and teaching activities in different disciplines, and (6) for longitudinal analyses as data becomes available.

## Base Maps

This section presents base maps essential in understanding subsequent text, statistics, figures, and other maps included in this volume.

Base Map 2.1 delineates world nation-states. Map 2.2 illustrates the states of Mexico, while base Map 2.3 shows delegations and municipios that make up the greater Mexico City area. Table 2.1 lists the names and key numbers of Mexico Cities' delegations and municipios. Map 2.4 illustrates the delegations of the Federal District. Map 2.5 shows the major cities of Mexico in 1990. Map 2.5 shows some of the major features of Mexico Megacity. These base maps, or coverages, were used for producing most other maps found in this volume. Other base maps are included in this volume at appropriate opportunities in the text, including the border region and cities, the cities of Monterrey (Map 2.6) and Guadalajara (Map 2.7), etc.

**Table 2.1 Delegations and Municipios in Mexico City**

| No. | Delegation/Municipio | No | Delegation/Municipio |
|---|---|---|---|
| 1 | Acolman | 36 | Magadalena Contreras * |
| 2 | Alvaro Obregon * | 37 | Melchor Ocampo |
| 3 | Amecameca | 38 | Miguel Hidalgo * |
| 4 | Atenco | 39 | Milpa Alta * |
| 5 | Atizapan de Zaragoza | 40 | Naucalpan |
| 6 | Atlautla | 41 | Nextlalpan |
| 7 | Axapusco | 42 | Nezahualcoyotl |
| 8 | Ayapango | 43 | Nicolas Romero |
| 9 | Azcapotzalco * | 44 | Nopaltepec |
| 10 | Benito Juarez * | 45 | Otumba |
| 11 | Chalco | 46 | Ozumba |
| 12 | Chiautla | 47 | Papalotla |
| 13 | Chicoloapan | 48 | Paz, La |
| 14 | Chiconcuac | 49 | San Martin de las Piramides |
| 15 | Chimalhuacan | 50 | Tecamac |
| 16 | Coacalco | 51 | Temamatla |
| 17 | Cocotitlan | 52 | Temascalapa |
| 18 | Coyoacan * | 53 | Tenango del Aire |
| 19 | Coyotepec | 54 | Teoloyucan |
| 20 | Cuajimalpa * | 55 | Teotihuacan |
| 21 | Cuauhtemoc * | 56 | Tepetlaoxtoc |
| 22 | Cuautitlan | 57 | Tepetlixpa |
| 23 | Cuautitlan Izcalli | 58 | Tepotzotlan |
| 24 | Ecatepec | 59 | Texcoco |
| 25 | Ecatzingo | 60 | Tezoyuca |
| 26 | Gustavo A. Madero * | 61 | Tlahuac * |
| 27 | Huehuetoca | 62 | Tlalmanalco |
| 28 | Huixquilucan | 63 | Tlalnepantla |
| 29 | Isidro Fabela | 64 | Tlalpan * |
| 30 | Ixtapaluca | 65 | Tultepec |
| 31 | Iztacalco * | 66 | Tultitlan |
| 32 | Iztapalapa * | 67 | Venustiano Carranza * |
| 33 | Jaltenco | 68 | Xochimilco * |
| 34 | Jilotzingo | 69 | Zumpango |
| 35 | Juchitepec | | |

Note: *Federal District Delegations.

## Conclusions

This chapter presented data and information necessary to understand the remainder of this volume. Subsequent chapters further elucidate information sources and analytical techniques. Each chapter touches on a variety of topics, any one of which could be explored in further detail. The GIS work in this volume illustrates the utility of such approach in exploring and understanding the globalization of the Mexican economy. Much remains to be accomplished. This chapter demonstrates the methodology we utilized in producing this volume. The methodology we have developed could be used to explore globalization of an economy in other countries. We fervently hope that this will be done and that this methodology will be further utilized by others to continue exploration of the globalization of the world economy.

## Case Studies

Included in this book are a number of case studies of Mexican and international corporations with major presence in Mexico. Nearly all of these case studies are based upon interviews that were supplemented by other documents, reports, and data provided by the corporations. However, also accessed were data from a variety of other sources external to these organizations. For some of these case studies we utilized GIS techniques to illustrate relationships of these corporations in the globalization process and networks within Mexico. A case study presents a great deal of information about the corporation being examined and then illustrates its international relationships and strategies as well as relationships internally within Mexico.

**Figure 2.1 Conceptual Diagram of Mexican GIS**

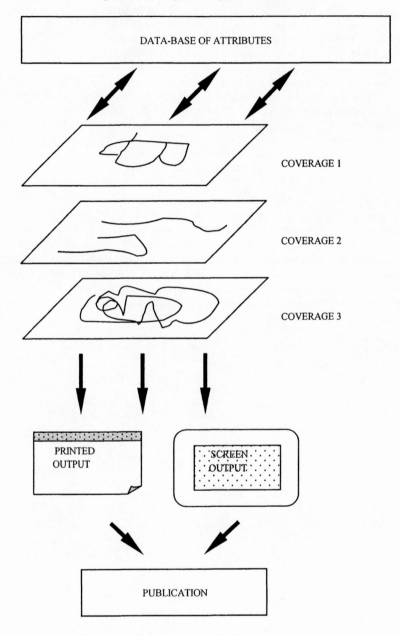

DATA-BASE OF ATTRIBUTES

COVERAGE 1

COVERAGE 2

COVERAGE 3

PRINTED OUTPUT

SCREEN OUTPUT

PUBLICATION

**Figure 2.2 System Diagram of Mexican GIS**

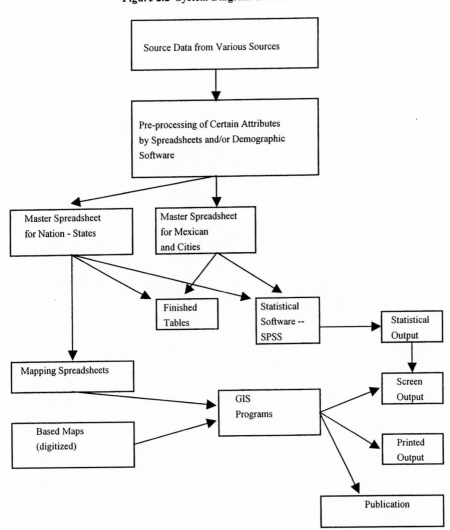

**Map 2.1**
**World Nation - States, 1995**

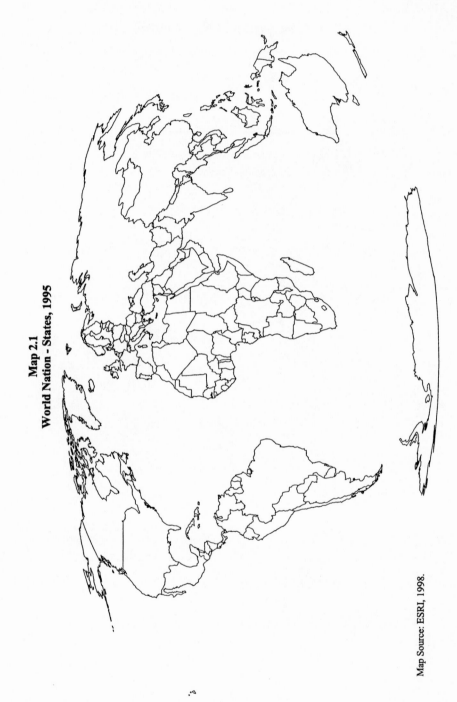

Map Source: ESRI, 1998.

## Map 2.2
## States of Mexico

| | | | |
|---|---|---|---|
| 1 | Aguascalientes | 17 | Morelos |
| 2 | Baja California | 18 | Nayarit |
| 3 | Baja California Sur | 19 | Nuevo Leon |
| 4 | Campeche | 20 | Oaxaca |
| 5 | Coahuila | 21 | Puebla |
| 6 | Colima | 22 | Queretaro |
| 7 | Chipas | 23 | Quintana Roo |
| 8 | Chihuahua | 24 | San Luis Potosi |
| 9 | Distrito Federal | 25 | Sinaloa |
| 10 | Durango | 26 | Sonora |
| 11 | Guanajuato | 27 | Tabasco |
| 12 | Guerrero | 28 | Tamaulipas |
| 13 | Hidalgo | 29 | Tlaxcala |
| 14 | Jalisco | 30 | Veracruz |
| 15 | Mexico | 31 | Yucatan |
| 16 | Michoacan | 32 | Zacatecas |

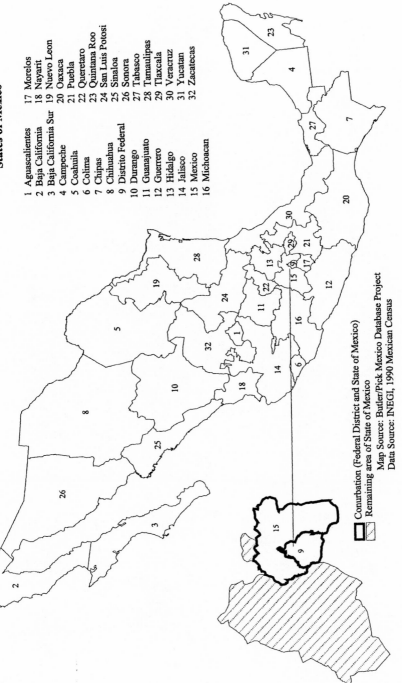

■ Conurbation (Federal District and State of Mexico)
░ Remaining area of State of Mexico

Map Source: Butler/Pick Mexico Database Project
Data Source: INEGI, 1990 Mexican Census

**Map 2.3**
**Mexico Megacity Base Map**

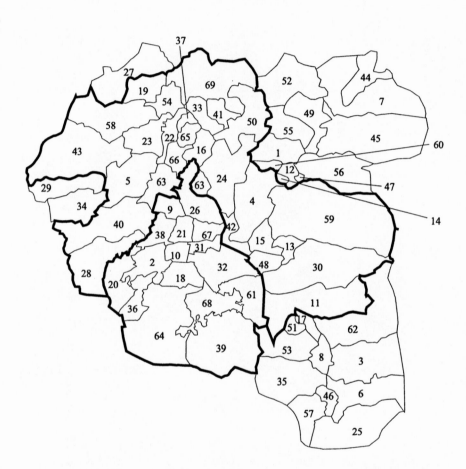

Map Source: Butler/Pick Mexico Database Project

**Map 2.4**
**Federal District**

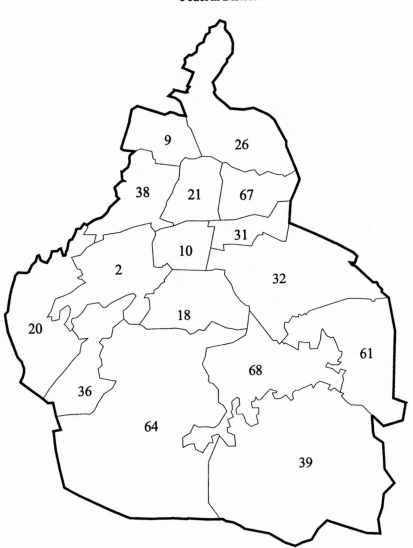

Map Source: Butler/Pick Mexico Database Project

**Map 2.5**
**Features of Mexico Megacity**

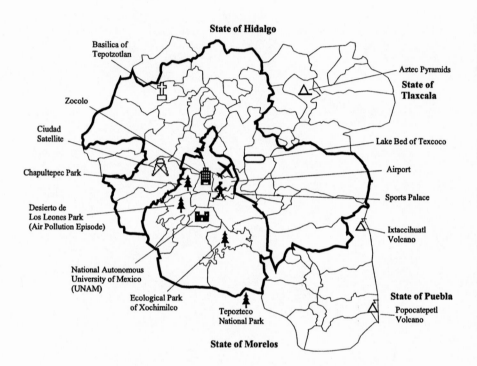

Map Source: Butler/Pick Mexico Database Project

## Map 2.6
## Monterrey

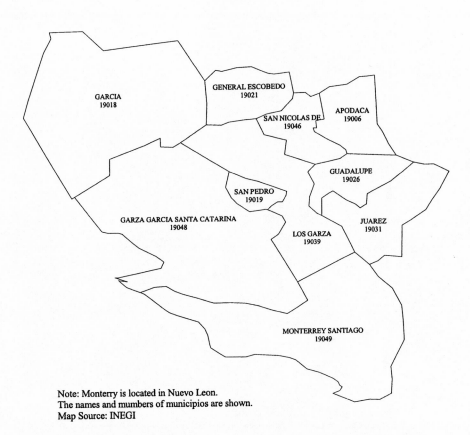

GARCIA
19018

GENERAL ESCOBEDO
19021

SAN NICOLAS DE
19046

APODACA
19006

GUADALUPE
19026

SAN PEDRO
19019

GARZA GARCIA SANTA CATARINA
19048

LOS GARZA
19039

JUAREZ
19031

MONTERREY SANTIAGO
19049

Note: Monterry is located in Nuevo Leon.
The names and mumbers of municipios are shown.
Map Source: INEGI

**Map 2.7**
**Guadalajara**

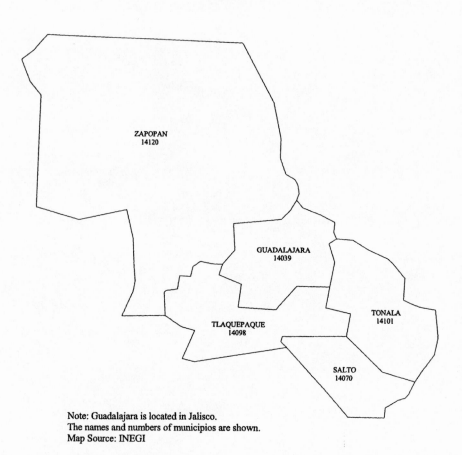

Note: Guadalajara is located in Jalisco.
The names and numbers of municipios are shown.
Map Source: INEGI

# 3

## Mexico and Mexico City
## In the Larger Global Context

- **Introduction**
  - Nation-State Development Level Cluster Analysis
- **Nation-State Developmental Levels: Cluster Analysis**
  - Upper Level Development
  - Middle Level Development
  - Lower Level Development
- **Mexico States Developmental Cluster Analysis**
- **Major Mexican Cities**
  - Mexico's Large Cities
  - Mexico City Cluster Analysis
  - Other Mexican Cities
- **Mexico's World System Relationships**
  - Transnational Corporate Penetration
  - Foreign Direct Investment (FDI)
  - Exports and Imports
  - In-Bond Industry (Maquiladoras)
  - Oil
  - Tourism
  - Other Flows and Exchanges
- **Conclusions**

## Introduction

This chapter first presents the results of cluster analyses we carried out examining developmental levels of the world's nation-states. We then introduce cluster analyses for the States of Mexico and for the Mexico City metropolitan area, which we sometimes refer to as Mexico Megacity. While the present book is a case study of Mexico, the utility of case studies in world system analysis has been illustrated by Smith (1996) for several different nations. Our examination involves expanded analysis beyond that ordinarily conducted in the globalization process. We argue that our perspective applies at all levels and can be generalized to other nations and areas within nations.

### Nation-State Development Level Cluster Analysis

Variables selected for the nation-state cluster analysis were derived from the *World Bank* (1995, 1997) and *CIA* (1996). We have other nation-state variables in the database, some of which will be incorporated in subsequent analyses. Dimensions selected for this analysis were based on past development and world systems research.

(1) Population in 1994, log
(2) GNP/capita, 1994 (Peacock et al. 1988; Jackman 1982; Kirman and Tomasini 1969; Chase-Dunn 1998).
(3) Life expectancy, 1994.
(4) Illiteracy, 1995 (Snyder and Kick 1979 use secondary school enrollment ratio; Boli and Thomas 1997 use both primary and tertiary school enrollment).
(5) Population growth, 1990-1994 (Korzeniewicz and Moran 1997).
(6) Infant mortality, 1994.

Our results are consistent with other research operating from somewhat different perspectives illustrating that stopping points in clustering are sensitive enough given the distribution of data. There are such large differences among categories that they are substantially internally consistent; that is, variation is between clusters rather than within them. However, it still may be problematic as to what to label a category (see Snyder and Kick 1979: 1110).

## Nation-State Developmental Levels: Cluster Analysis

As a result of our analysis, we labeled a large number of countries as being at the economic *lower level;* among these nations, there was virtually no change in position regardless of the number of clusters examined – five to ten in this analysis. Substantially similar results also were noted for nations classified in the *middle-level* of development. However, *upper-level* developed nations broke into several important clusters when different cluster steps were utilized, with a few nations clustering differently. For presentation here, the six-cluster output appeared to be the best fit. Because of space limitations, only a few results are presented here. Table 3.1 illustrates categorization results of the six-step cluster analysis for each nation, while Map 3.1 shows world development levels for nation-states using six clusters.

### Upper Level Development

Two nations always formed one upper-level development cluster, Japan, which may not be surprising while the other one may be -- Switzerland. Two other clusters formed what appeared to be upper-level developed nations. One cluster of upper-level nations included a number of European nations, along with Hong Kong, Singapore, and the United

States. The other cluster included Australia, Canada, Finland, Italy, and perhaps again surprising -- Kuwait and the United Arab Emirates. In world systems analysis, these countries would be labeled as core nations.

### Table 3.1

#### World Systems Nation-State Cluster Analysis, 1995

**Core A**
Japan
Switzerland

| Core B | Core C | Semi-Periphery A | Semi-Periphery B | | Periphery |
|---|---|---|---|---|---|
| | | | | | All other nations, including |
| Austria | Australia | Argentina | Belarus | Botswana | China |
| Belgium | Canada | Greece | Brazil | Bulgaria | Columbia |
| Denmark | Finland | Ireland | Chile | Czech Republic | India |
| France | Italy | Israel | Kazakastan | Latvia | Indonesia |
| Germany | Kuwait | Korea, Republic | Lithunia | Malaysia | |
| Hong Kong | United Arab Emirates | Saudi Republic | Mauritus | Mexico | |
| Netherlands | United Kingdom | Slovenia | Panama | Poland | |
| Norway | | Spain | Romania | Russian, Fed. | |
| Singapore | | | South Africa | Thailand | |
| Sweden | | | Trinidad/Tobago | Turkey | |
| United States | | | Turkmenistan | Ukraine | |
| | | | Uruguay | Uzbekistan | |
| | | | Venezuela | | |

Note: The cluster placement remains consistent with only slight shifts whether 5, 6, or 7 clusters are examined.

### Middle Level Development

Our cluster analysis identified what we consider as two middle levels of middle-level developed nations – the semi-periphery. One cluster consists of Argentina, Greece, Ireland, Israel, Republic of Korea, Saudi Arabia, Slovenia, and Spain. A second cluster at a somewhat lower of middle-level of development includes Belarus, Botswana, Brazil, Bulgaria, Chile, Costa Rica, Czech Republic, Kazakastan, Latvia, Lithuania, and Malaysia.

### Lower Level Development

All other nations were classified as being at a lower level of development, or periphery nations.

It should be noted here that China and Brazil are often included as examples in world system analysis as core nations. Our developmental level analysis places Brazil in the middle level development category – semi-periphery and China in the lower level development classification -- periphery. With these two exceptions, and a few others, there is substantial overlap between our developmental clusters and other world systems research. However, we argue that developmental level dissection should be the first step and the second stage of resolution then should be developing network analyses focusing on specific relationships among nations, in this instance, our case study of Mexico. We also believe that similar analyses should be carried out *within* nations – in this case study instance, for the States of Mexico and *within* cities of that nation.

Of particular interest in subsequent longitudinal analyses will be nation-states that have made some upward or downward movement. As an example, Botswana undoubtedly will have shown remarkable upward movement in developmental level as will some East Asian

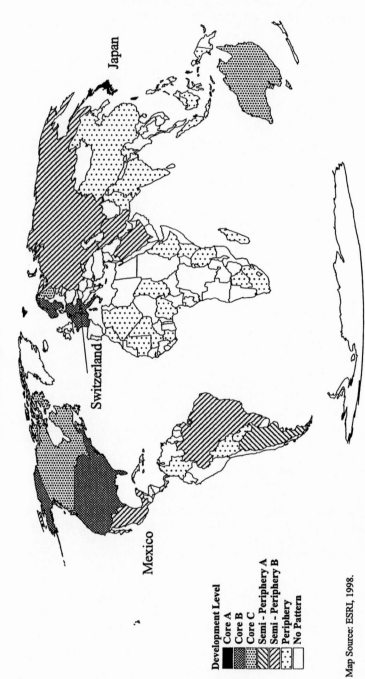

**Map 3.1**
**State Development Level Cluster Analysis**
**of the World's Nations, 1995**

Japan

Switzerland

Mexico

Development Level
Core A
Core B
Core C
Semi - Periphery A
Semi - Periphery B
Periphery
No Pattern

Map Source: ESRI, 1998.

countries (see Korzeniewicz and Moran 1997) and Mexico. Others may have had some downward mobility.

## Mexico States Developmental Cluster Analysis

Variables used in the *States* of Mexico developmental level cluster analysis were derived from various sources in Mexico that are included in our Mexico Database. The methodological procedure was the same as for the nation-state cluster analysis. Inasmuch as possible variables were the same ones used for the nation-states developmental analysis. For Mexico, several surrogate variables were used because in Mexico data-gathering focuses on production rather than consumption.

Variables used in the analysis were;
(1)  Population size, 1990, log;
(2)  Gross state revenues, 1988;
(3)  Standardized mortality rates, 1990;
(4)  Illiteracy, 1990;
(5)  Annual population growth, 1990-1995; and
(6)  Autos per capita, 1995.

These dimensions were deemed closest to those used in the nation-state cluster analysis.

Analytic results shown on Table 3.2 and Map 3.2 are not surprising since the Federal District and Baja California form a separate, highest level development cluster—the core. Three middle-level clusters are clearly demarcated for the States of Mexico – the semi-periphery. Two lower level development clusters reinforced our belief that this cluster analysis reflects contemporary developmental levels in Mexico. The lowest development cluster includes the states of Chiapas, Guerrero, and Oaxaca that are well known to be less developed and largely impoverished.

**Table 3.2**
**States of Mexico Cluster Analysis, 1990**

**Core States**
Federal District
Baja California

| Semi-Periphery A | Semi-Periphery B | Semi-Periphery C | Periphery A | Periphery B |
|---|---|---|---|---|
| Coahuila | Aguascalientes | Campeche | Guanajuato | Chiapas |
| Chihuahua | Jalisco | Durango | Hidalgo | Guerrero |
| Colima | Mexico | Puebla | Michoacan | Oaxaca |
| Morelos | Sonora | Queretaro | Nayarit | |
| Nuevo Leon | Yucatan | Quintana Roo | San Luis Potosi | |
| Tamaulapis | | Sinaloa | Tabasco | |
| Baja California Sur | | | Tlaxcala | |
| | | | Veracruz | |
| | | | Zacatecas | |

## Major Mexican Cities

### Mexico's Large Cities

Mexico in 1990 had a city population totaling 38.6 million or 48 percent of the nation. Of this by far the biggest part was Mexico City at 15.0 million. The very high population concentration in Mexico City is one reason that we emphasize the primate city in this book. Mexico City is important as an economic and business center of the nation, as well as being the political and cultural Capital (Pick and Butler 1997). As seen in Table 3.3 and Map 3.3, there were many other cities that are concentrated in the central flank of the nation but also some located at the U.S. border as well as other areas. The numbers on Map 3.3 represent the population rank order of cities in 1990. The second and third largest cities are Guadalajara at 2.9 million and Monterrey at 2.6 million.

### Mexico City[1] Cluster Analysis

We have already carried out a series of cluster analyses for Mexico Megacity using 30 variables and selected other cluster analyses focusing on specific concerns such as the economy, labor force, and environmental degradation (Pick and Butler 1997). Subsequent analyses for this project will utilize variables similar to those for the nation-state and states of Mexico analyses. Map 3.4 presents the 30 variable cluster analysis for Mexico City (see Table 3.4 for delegation and municipio classifications).

Our cluster analysis shows quite clearly that Mexico City has a "traditional urban development core" consisting of a few delegations in the Federal District. Other aspects of the cluster analysis demonstrate that Mexico City does not fit the traditional development of cities in the U.S. That is, various areas identified by cluster analysis showed varying developmental levels with the poorest areas being located on the outer perimeters of the city. Zones identified by cluster analysis clearly have substantially different developmental levels. One is tempted to utilize world system theory terminology and label the traditional center as a 'core' area. This core contains most of the major multinational and "Mexican 500" corporations located in Mexico Megacity (see Pick and Butler 1997 and Chapter 13). Also inviting is to label the outer areas of the metropolitan region as peripheral areas in the context of world systems theory. Of course, that leaves a number of areas that could be catalogued as semi-periphery, most of which form a half-circle in the north, west and east of the city.

Of special interest also is that an earlier factor analysis using a somewhat different definition of Mexico City and 1980 data identified substantially similar areas demonstrating that while some change has taken place, the major types of areas remained substantially the same (Rubalcava and Schteingart 1987).

### Other Mexican Cities

At the unit of analysis level of municipios, other Mexican cities do not have enough municipios to carry out a cluster analysis. However, some dimensions of Monterrey and Guadalajara are discussed in subsequent sections of this book.

---

[1]  Note that our definition of Mexico City includes all of the delegations (N=16) of the Federal District and 53 surrounding municipios in the State of Mexico.

## Table 3.3 Large Cities of Mexico, 1990

| No. | City | State | 1990 Pop. | 1990 No. Households | 1990 Sex Ratio | 1980 Pop. | %Change 1980-1990 |
|---|---|---|---|---|---|---|---|
| 1 | Mexico City AM | D.F./Mexico * | 15,047,685 | 3,133,834 | 94.17 | 13,354,271 | 12.68 |
| 2 | Guadalajara AM | Jalisco * | 2,870,417 | 557,378 | 93.80 | 2,192,557 | 30.92 |
| 3 | Monterrey AM | Nuevo Leon * | 2,558,494 | 529,242 | 98.41 | 1,913,075 | 33.74 |
| 4 | Puebla MU | Puebla * | 1,157,386 | 238,388 | 92.31 | 772,908 | 49.74 |
| 5 | Juarez | Chihuahua | 789,522 | 176,902 | 98.02 | 544,496 | 45.00 |
| 6 | Leon | Guanajuato * | 758,279 | 128,951 | 94.93 | 593,002 | 27.87 |
| 7 | Tijuana | Baja California | 698,752 | 155,710 | 100.40 | 429,500 | 62.69 |
| 8 | Torreon/G.P. MU | Coahuila/Durange | 689,212 | 141,370 | 94.37 | 445,053 | 54.86 |
| 9 | San Luis Potosi MU | San Luis Potosi * | 613,181 | 122,928 | 92.31 | 471,047 | 30.17 |
| 10 | Merida MU | Yucatan * | 532,964 | 118,328 | 91.94 | 400,142 | 33.19 |
| 11 | Toluca MU | Mexico * | 517,150 | 103,102 | 93.05 | 199,778 | 158.86 |
| 12 | Chihuahua | Chihuahua * | 516,153 | 116,669 | 94.17 | 385,603 | 33.86 |
| 13 | Acapulco de Juarez | Guerrero | 515,374 | 109,144 | 93.05 | 301,902 | 70.71 |
| 14 | Tampico/C. M. MU | Tamaulipas | 490,003 | 112,556 | 92.68 | 400,401 | 22.38 |
| 15 | Aguascalientes MU | Aguascalientes * | 455,234 | 86,000 | 93.05 | 293,152 | 55.29 |
| 16 | Veracruz MU | Veracruz | 447,202 | 105,594 | 89.39 | 367,339 | 21.74 |
| 17 | Cuernavaca MU | Morelos * | 446,739 | 97,223 | 93.42 | 192,770 | 131.75 |
| 18 | Saltillo MU | Coahuila * | 441,739 | 89,842 | 97.63 | 284,937 | 55.03 |
| 19 | Mexicali | Baja California * | 438,377 | 99,140 | 98.02 | 341,559 | 28.35 |
| 20 | Queretaro MU | Queretaro * | 431,905 | 82,356 | 93.42 | 215,976 | 99.98 |
| 21 | Morelia | Michoacan * | 428,486 | 86,912 | 91.94 | 297,544 | 44.01 |
| 22 | Culiacan | Sinaloa * | 415,046 | 82,333 | 94.93 | 304,826 | 36.16 |
| 23 | Hermosillo | Sonora * | 406,417 | 86,769 | 98.41 | 297,175 | 36.76 |
| 24 | Durango | Durango * | 348,036 | 70,988 | 92.68 | 321,148 | 8.37 |
| 25 | Oaxaca MU | Oaxaca * | 295,658 | 49,761 | 89.04 | 154,223 | 91.71 |
| 26 | Jalapa MU | Veracruz * | 291,038 | 66,050 | 87.27 | 204,594 | 42.25 |
| 27 | Tuxtla | Chiapas * | 289,626 | 60,982 | 93.05 | 131,096 | 120.93 |
| 28 | Matamoros | Tamaulipas | 266,055 | 59,089 | 94.17 | 188,745 | 40.96 |
| 29 | Reynosa | Tamaulipas | 265,663 | 59,085 | 97.24 | 194,693 | 36.45 |
| 30 | Irapuato | Guanajuato | 265,042 | 49,549 | 92.68 | 170,138 | 55.78 |
| 31 | Mazatlan | Sinaloa | 262,705 | 56,331 | 95.31 | 199,830 | 31.46 |
| 32 | Villahermosa/Centro | Tabasco * | 261,231 | 57,531 | 93.42 | 158,216 | 65.11 |
| 33 | Monclova MU | Coahuila | 254,376 | 54,479 | 100.00 | 115,786 | 119.69 |
| 34 | Cajeme/C.O. | Sonora | 219,980 | 46,664 | 95.69 | 165,572 | 32.86 |
| 35 | Nuevo Laredo | Tamaulipas | 218,413 | 47,546 | 95.31 | 201,731 | 8.27 |
| 36 | Celeya | Guanajuato | 214,856 | 41,048 | 92.68 | 141,675 | 51.65 |
| 37 | Tepic | Nayarit * | 206,967 | 43,705 | 91.94 | 145,741 | 42.01 |

AM = Area Metropolitana

MU = Mancha Urbana

G.P. = Gomez Palacio

C.M. = Ciudad Madero

C.O. = Ciudad Obregon

* City is capital of state.

** Large city pipulation data not avaliable for 1980.

Source: INEGI, 1993; Estadisticas Historicas de Mexico, 1985.

Map 3.2
Mexico States Development Cluster Analysis

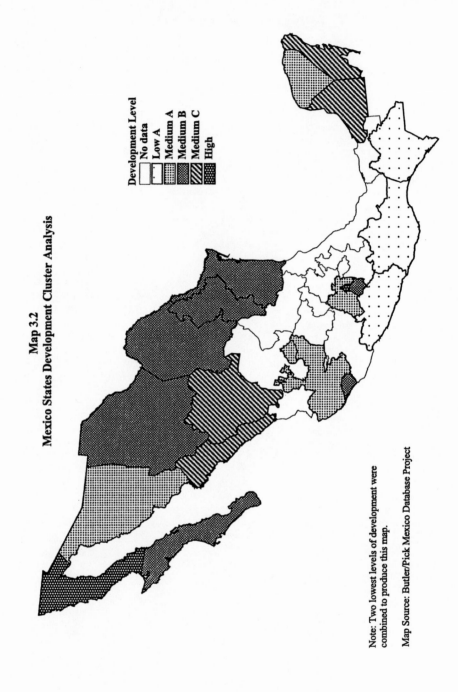

Development Level
No data
Low A
Medium A
Medium B
Medium C
High

Note: Two lowest levels of development were combined to produce this map.

Map Source: Butler/Pick Mexico Database Project

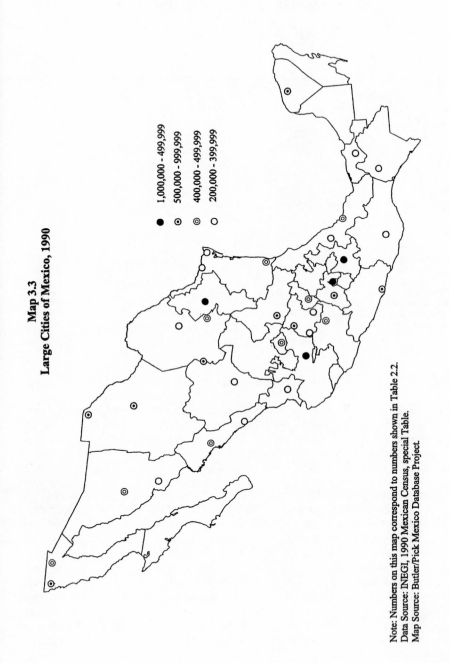

**Map 3.3**
**Large Cities of Mexico, 1990**

● 1,000,000 - 499,999
◉ 500,000 - 999,999
◎ 400,000 - 499,999
○ 200,000 - 399,999

Note: Numbers on this map correspond to numbers shown in Table 2.2.
Data Source: INEGI, 1990 Mexican Census, special Table.
Map Source: Butler/Pick Mexico Database Project.

**Map 3.4**
**Mexico City Cluster Analysis, 1990**

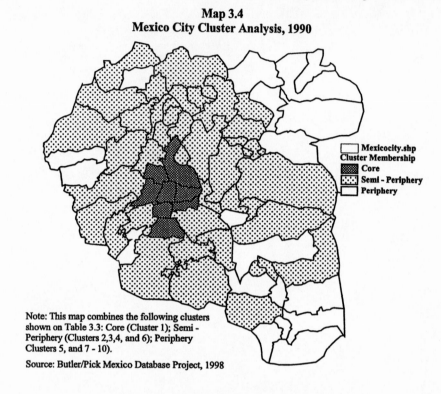

Note: This map combines the following clusters
shown on Table 3.3: Core (Cluster 1); Semi -
Periphery (Clusters 2,3,4, and 6); Periphery
Clusters 5, and 7 - 10).

Source: Butler/Pick Mexico Database Project, 1998

## Mexico's World System Relationships

Our cluster analysis, carried out separately from the *World Bank* (1995) but reinforcing their presentation, has quite firmly established that contemporary Mexico is in a middle-level of development – a semi-periphery country. A longitudinal analysis of Mexico's developmental level also undoubtedly would have shown Mexico in a lower level of development at earlier dates. Thus, developmental level is not seen as being immutable but subject to change, both upward and downward (see Shannon 1996 for a long-term historical view). Thus, we do not envisage development as occurring in an ordered sequence as modernization theory posits. In contrast, we make two assumptions: (1) the most likely happenstance is that there is stability in a nation's world system position and (2) that while upward and downward mobility takes place, these movements are atypical.

One such upward movement apparently is Mexico since earlier world system research placed Mexico in the periphery (Snyder and Kick 1979: 1110 ff.). However, more recent world systems research, in concert with our finding, has placed Mexico in the semi-periphery category (Rossem 1996). So, some change in Mexico's position has been reported. An important question is whether or not changes in the world system using relationships or our analysis using social and economic level took place simultaneously or at different times. Only by separating out developmental level from network changes can this be determined.

In this research we demonstrate that Mexico's network associations are heightened with the U.S. since that relationship is substantially stronger than with any other nation. This is true in the contemporary world as well as historically during the last 150 years but not prior to that time. Historically, Mexico's level of development has changed but its relationship with the U.S. has included dimensions used by world system researchers, including arms sales, diplomatic relations, armed interventions, trade, large labor force flows, and economic penetration. However, the time period analyzed becomes an important element in Mexico's development and its relationship with the U.S. As an example, during the middle 1800s, the U.S. essentially annexed over half of Mexican territory. Similarly, the U.S. in the 1940s through the 1960s actively encouraged Mexican workers to come to the U.S. via the Bracero Program. However, migration, which formally was encouraged by the U.S., is now considered as a major social problem by many in the U.S., while it is ignored or discouraged in official policy (Massey 1998). Currently, simultaneously as extensive migration from Mexico to the U.S. is taking place, there has been extensive U.S. corporate penetration into Mexico. Thus, any analysis must not ignore such monumental bi-national shifts. The flows and exchanges are two ways, albeit fluctuating *over time*.

**Table 3.4 Mexico City Cluster Analysis Groupings\*, 1990**

| Cluster 1 (C) | Cluster 2 (SP) | Cluster 3 (SP) | Cluster 4 (SP) | Cluster 5 (P) |
|---|---|---|---|---|
| Azcapotzalco | Acolman | Atenco | Coacalco | Chalco |
| Benito Juarez | Alvaro Obregon | Atizapan De Zaragoza | Cuautitlan Izcalli | |
| Coyoacan | Chicoloapan | Chiautla | | |
| Cuauhtemoc | Chiconcuac | Chimalhuacan | | |
| Gustavo A. Madero | Cuajimalpa | Cocotitlan | | |
| Iztacalco | Cuautitlan | Ecatepec | | |
| Miguel Hidalgo | Huehuetoca | Huixquilucan | | |
| Venustiano Carranza | Iztapalapa | Nicolas Romero | | |
| | Jaltenco | Papalotla | | |
| | Magdalena Contreras | Paz, La | | |
| | Melchor Ocampo | Tecamac | | |
| | Naucalpan | Teoloyucan | | |
| | Nextlalpan | Teotihuacan | | |
| | Nezahualcoyotl | Tepotzotlan | | |
| | Temamatla | Tezoyuca | | |
| | Texcoco | Tlalmanalco | | |
| | Tlahuac | Tlalpan | | |
| | Tlalnepantla | Tultitlan | | |
| | Tultepec | Xochimilco | | |
| | Zumpango | | | |

| Cluster 6 (SP) | Cluster 7 (P) | Cluster 8 (P) | Cluster 9 (P) | Cluster 10 (P) |
|---|---|---|---|---|
| Ixtapaluca | Amecameca | Axapusco | Atlautla | Ecatzingo |
| Juchitepec | Ayapango | Jilotzingo | Isidro Fabela | |
| Milpa Alta | Coyotepec | Nopaltepec | | |
| | San Martin De - Las Piramides | Otumba | | |
| | Temascalapa | Ozumba | | |
| | Tenango Del Aire | Tepetlixpa | | |
| | Tepetlaoxtoc | | | |

Source: Pick and Butler, *Mexico Megacity*, Westview Press, 1997.
\* This table shows the cluster groupings for the delegations and municipios in
Mexico City in 1990.
C = Core, SP = Semi periphery, P = periphery

    Our procedure, then, was to first classify contemporary Mexico into a developmental level. This process placed Mexico into an upper-middle developmental level or semi-periphery. Independently from our analysis, the World Bank (1995, 1997) carried out a somewhat similar analysis with the same results. Next we determined Mexico's relationship with other countries of the world using dimensions suggested by world systems research *and* other variables that have not been examined previously, but not using these variables to classify Mexico as a core, semi-periphery, or periphery nation. Among contemporary variables examined are corporate penetrations by U.S. and other international companies, foreign direct investment, export and imports by specific nations, in-bond maquiladora industry, oil, and tourism. Other favorite dimensions of world system researchers, such as diplomatic relations, arms trade, military intervention, etc., are only minimally explored in our analysis of contemporary Mexico, as they are appropriate in our coetaneous analysis and for historical reference.

## Transnational Corporate Penetration

This section presents only minimal historical information from that available illustrating transnational corporate penetration into Mexico; this penetration by individual corporations is explored in more detail in subsequent chapters, especially Chapter 13. Mexico's major 500 corporations are located primarily in Mexico City (the Federal District and municipios in the State of Mexico surrounding the Federal District). This concentration increased between 1986 and 1993.

The vast majority of foreign corporations in Mexico in 1986 and 1993 were of U.S. origin. As foreign origin of capital in Mexico increased between 1986 and 1993, over half was from the U.S. In 1986, 96 of the major Mexican "500" corporations were U.S. corporations; of these, 29 percent were prominent in the U.S. "Fortune 500". The concentration of "500" corporations in Mexico increased in the Federal District from 149 in 1986 to 206 in 1993.

There was a concentration of both foreign and Mexican corporations in the Federal District (Mexico City). Concentration was enhanced in Mexico City during the same time period into two adjoining areas – Miguel Hidalgo and Cuauhtemoc and in two adjacent areas in greater Mexico City in the State of Mexico – Ecatepec and Tlalnepantla.

Thus, in Mexico, there was geographic concentration of major corporations by state, by city, and by area within city (Pick and Butler 1997). Subsequent economic penetration and exchange analyses, as reflected here by multinationals, will take into account nations, magnitude, and directionality.

## Foreign Direct Investment (FDI)

Mexico's acceptance of foreign direct investment has varied substantially over the years – 488 million 1985 dollars in the 1955–1961 period to 3,189 million 1985 dollars in the 1989–1993 period (Calderone, Mortimore, and Peres 1996). Currently there are more substantial FDI inflows to Mexico than in the past (Bleakley 1995; United Nations 1992; Calderson, Mortimore, and Peres 1996). Any account of Mexico's international relationships must take note of the debt crisis in 1982. Probably as a result of the 1982 crisis, in 1983 Mexico substantially changed its FDI rules and regulations with broad liberalization (UN 1992: 83; also see Pick and Butler 1997); the result was extensive FDI increases in 1987 and following years. A United Nations report implies that Mexico then moved from a 'restrictive high growth' nation into a 'liberal, low growth' nation (UN 1992: 68). The impact of FDI, of course, may be viewed as positive or negative depending upon host country or countries from which FDI originates (see Chase-Dunn 1975: 726) and its impact upon the host country.

Generally, FDI changes have resulted in an industrial restructuring in Mexico, but only in specific sectors. In any case, these changes have not been static either by states within Mexico, by city in Mexico, or by areas within cities. The changes have been drastic and international, and domestic networks have dramatically changed over the past few years. Some of these changes are examined in substantial detail in subsequent chapters.

*Exports and Imports*

As illustrated on Figures 3.1 and 4.1 in the next chapter, the magnitude of exports from and imports to Mexico has changed considerably over the years. In addition, the balance of imports and exports has been at equilibrium at times and at other years there has been an imbalance in either exports or imports. While countries exported to and imported from have also varied over time (IMF 1979, 1991, 1998; Pick and Butler 1997), its primary trading partner has been the United States. While these changes in magnitude have been substantial, the U.S. has dwarfed the trade of all other countries put together. Thus, any networked relationship needs to take into account the historical context. In any case, a one-way binary relationship misses the direction and magnitude of the relationship. The following chapters examine in more detail exports and imports by sectors and countries involved in transactions.

**Figure 3.1 Import of Goods, Export of Goods, and Balance of Trade,
Mexico, 1979-1998**

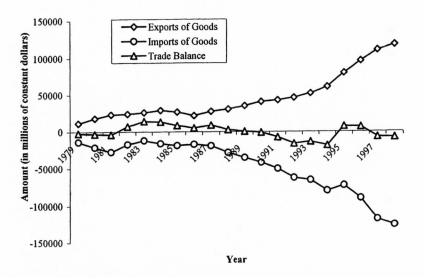

**Year**

Source: International Financial Statistics Yearbook, 1998;
Estadisticas Historicas de Mexico, 1999.

*In-Bond Industry (Maquiladoras)*

In 1980, there were almost 120,000 employees in the in-bond or maquiladora industry, mostly along the U.S. – Mexico border. As shown in Table 3.5, by 1998 the number of maquiladora workers had increased to 975,380. Extensive data for 1989 and 1998 illustrate variation in maquiladoras concentration among border states and cities, salaries, gender differences and foreign and domestic components used in the industry. Overwhelmingly, foreign components were used as opposed to domestic components – 23.2 billion pesos versus 0.37 billion pesos for example in 1989 (see Pick and Butler 1994).

### Table 3.5 Mexican Maquiladora Employment, 1998

| State | Maquiladora Employment | Percent of Total |
|-------|------------------------|------------------|
| Chihuahua | 256,930 | 26.3 |
| Baja California | 207,801 | 21.3 |
| Tamaulipas | 149,689 | 15.3 |
| Coahuila | 88,296 | 9.1 |
| Sonora | 87,438 | 9.0 |
| Nuevo Leon | 43,448 | 4.5 |
| | | |
| Durango | 23,207 | 2.4 |
| Jalisco | 20,646 | 2.1 |
| Aguascalientes | 18,305 | 1.9 |
| Puebla | 17,413 | 1.8 |
| Yucatan | 13,187 | 1.4 |
| State of Mexico/D.F. | 10,832 | 1.1 |
| | | |
| Others | 38,188 | 3.9 |
| | | |
| Border States | 833,602 | 85.5 |
| Total | 975,380 | 100.0 |

Source: Secretaria de Comercio, 1998.

Growth of the in-bond industry increased substantially between 1990 and 1998, with almost half in the two border states of Chihuahua and Baja California (INEGI 1995; Secretaria de Comercio 1998). Growth of the maquiladora industry thus accelerated during 1996 to 1998, perhaps a result of the passage of NAFTA. Maquiladoras are almost exclusively foreign controlled entities with the U.S. dominating the overall industry. However, other countries are involved in the process especially Asian. Any analysis of contemporary Mexico must consider how the maquiladora industry is related to exports and imports in the Mexican context and especially to the origin of component parts and the final destination of completed products. In addition, as with other exchanges in the world system, there is great variation in magnitude, direction, and in product sectors. The labor force in maquiladoras is mostly young women at lower level jobs working for minimal wages. However, in some locations and product lines, for example Tijuana television maquiladoras, the labor force is more highly skilled. In Mexico, transnational corporations are dominated by enterprises concerned with autos, computers and electronics, auto parts, chemicals, fabricated metals, and transportation equipment. However, maquiladoras are dominated by electronic, auto supply, and textile corporations. A subsequent chapter is devoted to the development of maquiladoras and their current status.

### Oil

During the past few years in Mexico, many nationalized enterprises have been privatized and many of them are now subsidized by the government. The upstream oil industry in Mexico, however, has remained nationalized. Mexico is one of the world's largest crude oil producers and is invited to attend meetings of Organization of Petroleum Exporting Countries (OPEC). As with most other relationships of Mexico with other world-states, the oil industry's major crude oil export partner is the U.S., exceeding all other countries (see Table 3.6). The U.S. is the refiner of most of the oil, some of which is sold back to Mexico. There also is extensive variation in Mexico of PEMEX with the other states and cities since oil production and refining are dominated by two states (Tabasco and

Veracruz) and in a limited number of other states. On the other hand, distribution is nation-wide while consumption takes place primarily in Mexico Megacity. More in-depth dissection of petroleum, chemicals, and petro-chemicals is reported in Chapter 8.

**Table 3.6 Oil Exports**

| Nation | Volume | Percent |
|---|---|---|
| United States | 771.7 | 56.4 |
| Spain | 247.1 | 18.0 |
| Japan | 144.6 | 10.6 |
| Nation of San Jose Agreement | 44.2 | 3.2 |
| Others | 161.0 | 11.8 |
| Total | 1368.6 | 100.0 |

Note: Figures are in thousands of barrels daily.

Source: PEMEX, 1992.

*Tourism*

As with most other economic aspects in Mexico, the flow of tourists entering Mexico by place of origin is dominated by the U.S. – 94 percent (see Table 3.7). Similarly, 90 percent of tourists from Mexico have the U.S. as their destination (see Table 3.7). Thus, again any analysis that only is concerned with a one-way relationship is misleading. In addition, while tourism in both directions is growing with the U.S., Latin American tourists increasingly are not visiting Mexico (Pick and Butler 1994; World Tourism Organization 1999).

**Table 3.7 Tourists Entering and Leaving Mexico**

**by Place of Origin and Destination**

| | Tourists Entering Mexico by Place of Origin | | | | | |
|---|---|---|---|---|---|---|
| Year | 1985 | 1986 | 1987 | 1988 | 1989 | 1990 |
| United States | 3,541 | 3,895 | 4,620 | 5,016 | 6,385 | 5,598 |
| Canada | 193 | 247 | 336 | 313 | 361 | 294 |
| Europe | 146 | 149 | 219 | 112 | 157 | 189 |
| Latin America | 301 | 318 | 205 | 225 | 261 | 276 |
| Other | 26 | 16 | 27 | 26 | 22 | 36 |
| Total | 4,207 | 4,625 | 5,407 | 5,692 | 6,186 | 6,393 |

| | Tourists Leaving Mexico by Place of Destinaiton | | | | | |
|---|---|---|---|---|---|---|
| Year | 1985 | 1986 | 1987 | 1988 | 1989 | 1990 |
| United States | 2,542 | 2,303 | 2,687 | 3,116 | 3,587 | 4,005 |
| Canada | 10 | 9 | 11 | 12 | 14 | 17 |
| Central America | 41 | 34 | 39 | 45 | 51 | 59 |
| South America | 16 | 14 | 16 | 21 | 25 | 28 |
| Europe | 102 | 91 | 106 | 130 | 154 | 176 |
| Asia | 7 | 6 | 8 | 8 | 10 | 11 |
| Other | 13 | 13 | 15 | 19 | 22 | 25 |
| Total | 2,731 | 2,470 | 2,882 | 3,351 | 3,863 | 4,321 |

Definition: Tourists Entering Mexico are classified by their place of origin and place

of destination in thousands of persons.

Source: Secretaria de Turismo, Banco de Mexico, 1992.

Within Mexico there are substantial regional differences in the ratios of national to foreign visitors. In 1990, this variation occurred whether planned, traditional, grand city, interior city, or border cities tourist centers are the focus of analysis (Secretaría de Turismo 1998). As examples, the planned tourist centers of Cancún and Los Cabos, Baja California Sur attracted substantially more foreign visitors than domestic while the planned tourist centers of Ixtapa and Bahias de Huatulco in Oaxaca and La Paz, Baja California were more attractive to Mexican tourists. The overall conclusion is that tourism is associated with other nation-states and internally in substantially different manners. Like maquiladoras, the lower level workers are domestic, low paid, and in menial jobs. Tourism is delved into in more detail in Chapter 10.

*Other Flows and Exchanges*

Substantial information on other types of flows and exchanges of Mexico with other world nations, including telephone calls, personnel, technology transfer, airline passengers to and from, etc. is presented in other chapters of this book. Other aspects that need to be investigated include cartel arrangements, patent license exchanges, subsidiaries, alliances etc. Substantial data also are presented on domestic flows and exchanges (see CONAPO 1991; Pick and Butler 1997).

## Conclusions

We assume that there is a relationship between the level of development of a nation, in this instance Mexico, and its exchanges with other nations. Exchanges between countries, in our opinion, are not binary nor always in the same dominant direction. Further, some exchanges are more consequential than others and their significance changes over time.

We believe that eventually development and world systems research will have to come to grips with the problem of causality. That is, how do development levels and world systems interact with each other at different times? Does developmental level cause a nation's relationship in the world system or does position in the world system cause developmental level? Or, is there an interactive system with various iterations impacting the relationship?

The little longitudinal research that has been accomplished suggests that nations, both in developmental and world systems position, remain relatively stable across time. Mexico illustrates that some upward mobility may be occurring; Botswana in our analysis shows another country ascending. One study postulated that there might be other changes, in the long run (Hartman 1998). There is research demonstrating that ascendancy and downward mobility do in fact occur over longer periods of historical epochs (see Shannon 1996) and may be occurring in the contemporary world (see Korzeniewicz and Moran 1997: 1025 ff.). If so, the proposition that strength begets strength in economic systems needs to be examined more thoroughly. What are the conditions under which a country ascends or descends in developmental level and the world system?

Even in the long run we expect substantial stability, both at the world systems level, but also within a country, and area within regions and cities. The most interesting aspect of all, of course, is the question of what leads to the fall and rise of countries and as to some units within them. There is some indication from our analysis that most weak countries are getting weaker; similar results appear within Mexico by state and region. Another implication of our research is that there are subcategories among the core, semi-periphery, and periphery, whether at the country, state, or smaller units of analysis (also suggested by Snyder and Kick 1979 using different analytic techniques).

Finally, we want to emphasize that our analysis is time-bound and that it will be necessary to carry out longer term analysis to ascertain changes in development level and world systems position.

# 4

# Industry

## Introduction

Manufacturing is a major part of the economy of Mexico, and one undergoing the processes of globalization. This chapter examines changes that have taken place in Mexico over the past thirty years that have positioned Mexico as a more important worldwide industrial player. These changes have stemmed from government policy shifts, from economic changes, from business decisions by private sector companies, and from trade agreements such as North American Free Trade Agreement (NAFTA). In North America, NAFTA has encouraged companies and their subsidiaries to work together in collaborative arrangements. Foreign companies have emerged with stronger Mexican divisions over time. Certain companies in Mexico have graduated to the world manufacturing arena. These tend to be large firms with global brand names, such as General Motors, IBM, HP, Cemex, or Tamsa. It is remarkable that some Mexican firms, such as Cemex, Desc, and Tamsa, have emerged as worldwide leaders.

The stimulus for this change away from import substitution towards global business has been foreign direct investment, that is capital investment in plant and equipment in Mexico made by foreign owned companies. Another stimulus has been the need perceived by the Mexican government to open up the economy to foreign investors and capital and to privatize. This reflects the inability of Mexico to support its companies through domestic financing. Mexico has had a large national debt and a currency that has weakened over time versus the dollar. Hence, the government faced the dilemma of an inward orientation leading to stagnation and lack of competitiveness versus the opportunity of outside capital investment to strengthen its competitive stance. It was decided during the Salinas administration to strongly support opening up of the economy and manufacturing to outside investment.

The manufacturing sector in Mexico may be divided into the non-maquiladora and maquiladora sub-sectors. The non-maquiladora sector comprises about 90 percent of manufacturing production and about three quarters of manufacturing employment. This sector varies greatly from small enterprises in traditional industries such as textiles to large, sophisticated multi-national manufacturing plants such as IBM's ThinkPad plant in Guadalajara. The maquiladora sector of manufacturing involves co-production consisting of close collaboration between a Mexican and foreign counterpart firm. The Mexican counterpart firm is responsible for assembly of products and takes advantage of inexpensive Mexican labor, while the foreign firm provides components, legal advice, technical expertise, marketing and distribution to foreign markets. The foreign firm is commonly a U.S. one. This arrangement stems from legal structures first established in the late 60s. Today, many major foreign companies are partners in the maquila industry, and the industry employs about one million workers. Maquiladoras are covered in detail in Chapter 9.

This chapter examines the comparative productivity of different sectors and, based on studies of Banamex, concludes that the most productive parts of manufacturing are the large, export-oriented firms, followed by small manufacturing firms. Maquiladoras have the lowest productivity. This may be surprising giving the publicity of certain high profile and high-tech maquilas. But overall, the maquila sector has low-skilled labor and adequate but not world class equipment and technology. Over the past 30 years, the maquiladora sector has nevertheless grown rapidly, but that has been due to sharply increasing volume rather than productivity.

Not surprisingly, the location of manufacturing in Mexico is predominantly in the advanced developmental parts of Mexico, in particular in the Federal District, Baja

California, the State of Mexico, Jalisco, and most northern border states. In this chapter, industry and manufacturing are examined at the municipio (i.e., county) level throughout the nation. There is a high degree of concentration of manufacturing in a relatively small number of municipios. Large sections of the nation, especially those in the south, southeast, and center north, have little manufacturing. The largest concentration of manufacturing is in Mexico City (Pick and Butler 1997). There are also major concentrations in Monterrey, Guadalajara, Ciudad Juarez, Tijuana, and Puebla. Some national manufacturing corridors are evident. Largest is the corridor extending over several hundred miles from Mexico City northwest to Aguascalientes. Another corridor is evident to the west of Monterrey. By sub-industry, other patterns emerge. For instance, the textile industry is concentrated in four or five central states, as well as in border cities adjoining Texas, while the steel industry and related manufacturing are predominantly in Monterrey, Mexico City, and certain border cities.

The chapter examines Mexico's largest manufacturing industry that of autos and auto parts. This industry has grown in exports over time, shipped predominately to the U.S. At the same time, a significant domestic market has been maintained. Other manufacturing industries of computers and telecommunications, steel tubing, and soft drink bottling are examined briefly. Each of them has international aspects, although in different ways that will be discussed.

In the transition of Mexico's manufacturing from domestic to global levels of quality and competition, improvements in technology transfer and employee skill levels have been crucial and are discussed.

The chapter shows that a major shift has taken place in Mexico to more open and often globally based manufacturing. The chapter also points out how some of the problems and issues can be better understood from the perspective of world systems theory. The chapter concludes by examining two case studies of strong companies, Cemex and Vitro, from the northern city of Monterrey. Cemex has been truly remarkable in moving into second place worldwide in the cement industry. Vitro, a Mexican "grupo" i.e. a family controlled conglomerate, demonstrates successes and failures in forays into global markets.

## History of Manufacturing in Mexico: Import Substitution to World Competition and Export

In 1950s and 1960s, the Mexican government sought to protect its domestic industry through a policy of import substitution. In other words, instead of importing goods from overseas, domestic companies were protected by subsidies and tariffs from foreign competition. This allowed domestic firms to prosper, but the cost was decreasing competitiveness. More of the economy was nationalized than today and the manufacturing sector was protected from foreign competition. However, the shock of the debt crisis of the 1980s shifted the Mexican government to consider modernization of the industrial sector and a more outward looking policy that favored foreign investments and exports.

In the late 80s, and during the Salinas administration of 1988-1994, Mexican government policy shifted sharply in favor of exports, foreign investment, and privatization (see Figure 3.1). Manufacturing firms that bridged this transformation realized the advantages of investing in technology, increasing quality standards, and, for many, regarding Mexico as a key location for global manufacturing, especially to serve the U.S. market. There were different ways this took place. One was the maquiladora approach that favored legally bound investment by Mexican partner companies in Mexican facilities, coupled with foreign component supply and low cost assembly in Mexico. This led to finished good export by binational maquiladora enterprises, mostly into the U.S. market. A quite different approach was present in Mexican technology sectors. This type of export was based on highly efficient and technology-driven facilities, with a mixture of low- and high-skilled workers. There is an emphasis on excellent quality control in order to market products competitively in the U.S. and other advanced countries. These different pathways to much higher export were pursued simultaneously, with the Mexican government providing different types of incentives and encouragement.

There has been a range of labor intensiveness in Mexican industry. For instance, the textile industry, maquila or not, is labor intensive, while the chemical industry, which has a strong foreign presence, is capital intensive. Mexico does not just need to depend on inexpensive labor, since, for many industries, it has very large domestic markets, and for other industries, it produces world class products sold at market prices in North America and beyond.

Manufacturing production has grown substantially over the past three decades. As seen in Figure 4.1, manufacturing production tripled between 1968 and 1996. Production has moved steadily upwards with two exceptions, in the years of the debt crisis in the early to mid 80s and following the peso devaluation of December of 1994. In both of those periods, a weakened economy lessened production.

The importance of manufacturing to Gross Domestic Product (Producto Interno Bruto or PIB) is shown in Figure 4.2. The major importance of auto production is also evident.

During the past two decades, as manufacturing in Mexico increased in production volume, quality and competitiveness, it has become much more prominent as a component of exports. For instance, if exports are measured by those from Mexico to the OECD nations, which include the U.S., most European nations, and some other advanced nations, the proportion of exports that are natural resources declined between 1980 and 1992 from 67 percent to 29 percent (Data from OECD; cited in Calderón, Mortimore, and Peres 1996). This decrease mostly involved lowering the proportion of petroleum from 50 to 18 percent, while agriculture decreased little from 13 to 9 percent. On the other hand, manufacturing as a proportion of OECD exports increased 1980-1992 from 31 to 67 percent (Data from OECD; cited in Calderón, Mortimore, and Peres 1996).

Out of manufacturing's 31 percent of exports, the most important components in 1992 were: passenger vehicles (7.7 percent), vehicle parts and accessories (5.4 percent), equipment for electricity distribution (4.8 percent), telecommunications equipment and parts (3.1 percent), internal combustion motors and parts (3.0 percent) and television receivers (2.9 percent), with the remaining manufacturing of 4.1 percent. (OECD data; cited in Calderón, Mortimore, and Peres 1996). These manufacturing areas grew rapidly over the 12 year period. For instance, passenger vehicles only comprised 0.3 percent of exports in 1980 and vehicle parts 1.3 percent. Clearly Mexican manufacturing is dominated by the auto and auto accessory subsectors.

Foreign and domestic firms shared in this transformation. Although foreign ownership of firms in the manufacturing sector remained fairly stable at about one third, foreign firms were of greater importance in export. Foreign firms recognized the advantages of Mexico as a key location for export to the huge U.S. market. They also sensed the lowering of government restrictions and opening up of opportunities to combine technology with a low cost and productive labor force. One example is automobile manufacturing, where foreign firms especially the U.S. big three, as well as Nissan, and Volkswagen dominate. In 1997, General Motors, Chrysler de Mexico, and Ford were third, fourth and fifth most important corporations in Mexico; Volkswagen was number 10. Nissan has a large presence in Mexico but did not respond to inquire regarding economic data (Expansión 1998). Auto

**Figure 4.1 Index of Manufacturing Production, 1968-1997**

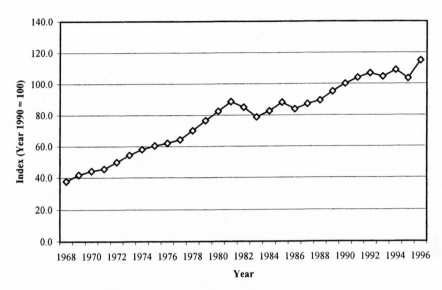

Source: International Financial Statistics Yearbook, 1998.

**Figure 4.2 PIB, Manufacturing Industry Production, and Auto
Industry Production, 1988-1994 (in millions of 1993 pesos)**

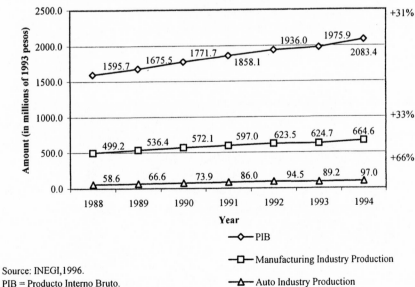

Source: INEGI,1996.
PIB = Producto Interno Bruto.
Note: the percentages are percent increase, 1988 - 1994.

part exporting firms comprise a mixture of U.S. firms such as Delphi and Mexican ones such as Desc. In these auto subsectors, foreign firms stimulated the growth through substantial foreign direct investment in the 1980s and 1990s. Overall, foreign firms in 1992 accounted for $9.9 billion dollars in the private sector, compared to domestic firms' $8.9 billion, or 47 percent (Calderón, Mortimore, and Peres 1996). Foreign firms were 36 percent of total public and private exports that also includes the nationalized petroleum industry. The influence of foreign firms applies also to imports. Foreign firms accounted for 39 percent of imports in the private sector and 36 percent of total imports in 1992. The import and export flows are mostly from and to the U.S. In the case of imports, maquiladora components were important but also electronics and technology components outside of the maquiladora.

The impact of manufacturing and particularly of foreign firms on exports and imports has been rapidly increasing since 1986. As seen in Figure 3.1, exports, in dollars, increased from $21.8 billion in 1986 to $96.0 billion in 1996 (IMF 1998). Concomitantly, imports grew from $18.8 billion in 1986 to $89.5 billion in 1996 (IMF 1998). In the early to mid-90s, a stronger peso led to higher pricing and contributed to a negative balance of trade for four years, but the peso crisis in late 1994 restored a positive balance of trade, since exports became more affordable. However, regardless of fluctuations in the balance of trade, from the mid 80s the volume of both exports and imports has grown substantially.

## Productivity and Competitiveness of Manufacturing Sectors

An outcome of transformation from import substitution manufacturing to outward looking, competitive manufacturing has been growing productivity. This section looks at the productivity of Mexican manufacturing during the past two decades including several major sectors. It compares this productivity to other Mexican and U.S. economic and manufacturing benchmarks. Increasing productivity combined with attention to quality standards has contributed to enhanced competitiveness.

The annual gain in Mexican manufacturing productivity from 1988 to 1995 was substantial at 1.7 percent yearly. It was much higher than the 0.2 percent annual increases for the Mexican economy as a whole (Banamex 1998). On the other hand, it is lower than the average annual U.S. manufacturing productivity gain of 3.1 percent from 1988 to 1995. The higher manufacturing productivity in the U.S. is also mirrored in the higher annual growth rates in constant dollar GDP, which was 1.4 percent for 1981-1995, compared to 0.5 percent for constant peso PIB in Mexico (Banamex 1998 based on INEGI data).

Manufacturing productivity was much higher for large non-maquila companies (referred to here as "large firms") and less for middle and small non-maquila firms ("middle/small firms") and maquilas. Large firms increased in productivity from 1988 to 1993 by 7 percent, while middle and small companies had 0 productivity gain and maquiladoras increased by 0.8 percent (INEGI's Monthly Industrial Survey, cited in Banamex 1998). This result reflects the greater technological and export-oriented focus of larger firms. In addition, foreign ownership associated with export orientation is more present in larger firms (see Chapter 13). Greater productivity gains in large firms versus maquiladoras are not surprising if one considers the emphasis on low cost in most maquilas (see Chapter 9). On the whole, maquiladoras are oriented towards a strategy of low cost and efficient assembly, utilizing minimally paid workers. This strategy is successful but not because of breaking records for worker productivity. Another reflection of this is that some highly productive maquiladoras, which have shifted to higher cost labor, have eventually "graduated" to the regular manufacturing sector. As seen in Figure 4.3, maquila firms had higher manufacturing PIB and employment gain than non-maquilas from 1988 to 1993, but maquilas had lower manufacturing productivity gain. As will be seen in Chapter 9, the huge growth in the maquila sector over the past three decades has been driven by volume in firm size and output rather than by employee productivity. Maquiladoras have outperformed the rest of manufacturing in PIB and employment, while trailing in productivity.

**Figure 4.3 Percent Annual Growth in Manufacturing PIB, Employment, and Productivity, 1988-1993**

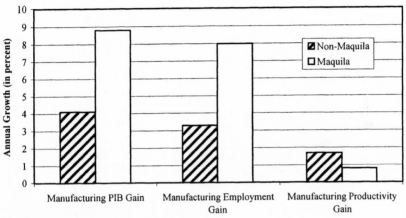

PIB = Producto Interno Bruto.
Source: Economic Research Department, Banamex, 1998.

## Sources of Investment in Industry

The expansion of Mexican manufacturing has been due largely to foreign direct investment. Foreign direct investment (FDI) is direct investment by firms in business operations in a foreign nation (Hill 1993). FDI may be a good mechanism to stimulate overseas business if there are restrictions on financial investment and/or tariff barriers to trading. Earlier in the twentieth century, FDI in Mexico was directed towards natural resource businesses. For instance, as seen in Chapter 8, the Mexican petroleum industry was built in the first third of the twentieth century through a combination of foreign direct investment and financial investment. These investments were later nationalized. In the era of import substitution in the 50s and 60s, there was little FDI, because manufacturers utilized domestic materials and did not need sophisticated or expensive facilities to perform reasonably well in the protected domestic market. During most of the 80s, FDI increased, although it declined during the debt crisis of 1983-85 (see Table 4.1). The general growth in the 80s had to do with the many shifts taking place in the economy at that time and the motivation of some larger enterprises to export since the domestic economy was weak. FDI increased further in the 1990s, even though there was some setback following the peso crisis in 1994.

**Table 4.1 Foreign Direct Investment Flows, to and from Mexico,**
**1955-1993, in Millions of 1985 Dollars**

| Period | FDI Total to Mexico Inflows | FDI Outflow from Mexico to the United States* |
|--------|------------------------------|-----------------------------------------------|
| 1955-1961 | 488 | NA |
| 1962-1973 | 731 | NA |
| 1974-1977 | 1,271 | NA |
| 1978-1982 | 2,347 | NA |
| 1983-1985 | 467 | 176 |
| 1986-1988 | 2,495 | 140 |
| 1989-1993 | 3,189 | 235 |

\* The Mexican government does not tabulate total outflows.

The FDI outflow from Mexico to the U.S. constitutes the predominant outflow.

Source: Calderon, Mortimore, and Peres, 1996.

During the past 25 years of increasing FDI, the areas of FDI investment have shifted in a manner paralleling production discussed earlier i.e. from FDI to exploit natural resources to FDI for high technology and export oriented sectors such as automobiles and electronics. An important change in law took place in 1993, at the end of the Salinas Administration. The old law on foreign direct investment from the era of import substitution was replaced by a modernized law encouraging foreign direct investment and making it easier. At the same time, foreign financial investment was encouraged by a different law (Calderón, Mortimore, and Peres 1996). NAFTA went into effect in January of 1994 and encouraged FDI, especially from North American firms and firms utilizing North American components.

The overseas sources of FDI have been principally from the United States and secondarily from Europe, as shown by Table 4.2.

**Table 4.2 World Wide Source of Foreign Direct Investment in Mexico, 1993**

| Country | Percentage of FDI |
|---------|-------------------|
| United States | 63.8 |
| United Kingdom | 6.0 |
| France | 4.6 |
| Switzerland | 4.6 |
| Germany | 4.5 |
| Netherlands | 3.6 |
| Japan | 2.5 |
| Canada | 2.0 |
| Spain | 1.8 |
| Others | 1.1 |

Source: SECOPI, 1993, cited in Calderon, Mortimore, and Peres, 1996.          11.0

From a world systems theory perspective, this list represents advanced nations to obtain labor and locational advantages, rather than natural resource ones investing in the semi-periphery. European nations account for a quarter of FDI. European enterprises can make efficient investments that directly access the growing Mexican market as well as indirectly accessing the U.S. markets.

An important new aspect of foreign direct investment is outward FDI, in other words direct investment by a Mexican corporation in business operations of an overseas nation. This implies foreign operations by Mexican firms, a relatively recent development. As seen in Table 4.1, this started in the mid 80s and in the early 90s and was at a level of 7 percent of inward FDI. There are remarkable corporate examples of this, including the cement company Cemex and the conglomerate Vitro, which are case studies at the end of this chapter. As the larger and more efficient and more globally competitive Mexican firms look for expansion and new markets, outward FDI can be expected to rise relative to inward FDI.

Besides FDI, there have been other forms of investment in Mexican manufacturing over the past two decades including private financial investment and investment in times of duress by international bodies such as the IMF. These, however, have not been as important as FDI in stimulating the expansion and competitiveness of manufacturing.

## Regional Location of Manufacturing in Mexico

This section examines the regional distribution of manufacturing sector in Mexico and some implications of this regional distribution based on world systems theory. The data are drawn from the 1994 Mexican Economic Census at the municipio level (INEGI 1997). The municipio level reveals many spatial details that are not evident at the state level. This section considers the distribution of overall manufacturing levels before examining two manufacturing subsectors of steel and textiles. The subsectors reflect a contrast between a more modern and technological industry and a more traditional one.

The distribution of total remuneration in manufacturing is shown in Maps 4.1 and 4.2. Map 4.1 displays the central section of the nation and emphasizes the manufacturing "belt" that stretches from Guadalajara in the west to Puebla in the east, and slightly south. This central "belt" is important historically in the industrialization of the nation (Garza 1985) and today constitutes the major industrial production zone of Mexico. It is referred to in this chapter as the Central Zone. This belt contains three out of the four largest Mexican cities (Mexico City, Guadalajara, and Puebla) and nine medium sized ones. The large and medium sized cities had a combined 1990 metropolitan population of 23.2 million, comprising 60 percent of the national metropolitan population (Pick and Butler 1994). The cities are interconnected by transportation, communications, and trade in many respects form a system of cities (CONAPO 1991).

Total manufacturing remuneration is concentrated in particular border locations (Map 4.2) and in the central zone (see Map 4.1). The most important border city for manufacturing remuneration is Ciudad Juarez, the sister city of El Paso, Texas, followed by Tijuana, opposite San Diego. In Chapter 9, we demonstrate that these are the two dominant cities for maquiladoras. Tijuana has electronics manufacturing while Ciudad Juarez emphasizes autos and machinery. In the 1990s, the two cities accounted for approximately 40 percent of maquila employment and plants. Maquiladora manufacturing in these and other border cities grew rapidly since the early 1970s and continues to increase. In manufacturing remuneration, the other important border cities adjacent to the border are Mexicali, Nogales, Ciudad Acuña, Piedras Negras, Reynosa, and Matamoros. Deeper in the border states are the important cities of Hermosillo and Chihuahua, both of which have major auto industry manufacturing, and the sister cities of Torreon/Gomez Palacio located on the Durango/Coahuila border, and Monclova in central Coahuila (see Map 3.3).

The nation's second largest manufacturing complex is located in the Monterrey metropolitan area and stretches into the Coahuila municipios of Ramos Arizpe and Saltillo (see Map 4.2). Saltillo had a 1990 population 441,739. The largest manufacturing remuneration for any municipio is the municipio of Los Garza, which had 1994 manufacturing remuneration of 2.8 billion pesos. This is also reflected in its 1998 PIB of 4.8 billion pesos (INEGI 1990). Neighboring San Nicolas is also very high at manufacturing remuneration of 1.38 billion pesos. The geographically concentrated manufacturing complex in Monterrey parallels the concentrated manufacturing zone in the center belt of Mexico.

The central manufacturing "belt" has the very large manufacturing center of Guadalajara in the west. Within Guadalajara, the central municipio of Guadalajara has high manufacturing remuneration of 2.41 billion pesos, followed by the adjacent municipio to the northwest with remuneration of 876,574 pesos. There are many important manufacturing centers located in a "strip" between the city of Aguascalientes and Mexico City, including Leon, Irapuato, Celeya, and Queretaro.

Mexico City is evident as the largest manufacturing complex in Mexico. Its manufacturing is concentrated in delegations to the northwest and north of the Federal District and in adjoining areas in the State of Mexico. The largest municipios for manufacturing remuneration are Tlalanepantla and Naucalpan in the State of Mexico, along the northwestern border of the Federal District with totals of 2.65 and 2.18 billion pesos respectively, and Azcapotzalco and Miguel Hidalgo in the northern Federal District with total of 2.62 and 2.06 billion pesos. Together, these four adjoining municipios had a total manufacturing remuneration of 9.51 billion pesos. They are surrounded by seven other municipios in the 1-2 billion peso(s) range. The Mexico City manufacturing complex is the largest in Mexico, and depending on the measure, accounts for 30-50 percent of the nation's manufacturing.

There also is a growing manufacturing corridor extending from Naucalpan to the west; it goes through Lerma; and ends at Toluca, a fast growing city and manufacturing center having total manufacturing remuneration of 1.31 billion pesos.

The central "belt" ends at the city of Puebla, consisting mostly of the municipio of Puebla with total manufacturing remuneration of 1.51 billion pesos. Puebla was important historically in textile manufacturing, and today has significant auto and auto parts production.

Manufacturing subsectors are distinctive in their spatial patterns. Two examined in more detail are steel and related products and textile/clothing/leather. Maps 4.3 and 4.4 show the average number of employees per enterprise for steel and related products. Larger sized steel enterprises are located mostly in the border region and Monterrey, with some concentration in the state of Mexico to the north of the Federal District. Overall, for steel, the north dominates, rather than Mexico City. There are especially large complexes of steel firms in Tijuana/Tecate/Mexicali and northern Chihuahua running from Ciudad Juarez south to Chihuahua City. This region consists of 10 municipios. A lot of the steel and steel-related industry in Chihuahua supports the large auto and auto parts industry of that state, which is spread out from the border down to Chihuahua City.

There are substantial although not huge concentrations of steel and related industries along the border in northern Baja California, northeastern Sonora, Ciudad Acuña, Nuevo Laredo, Reynosa, and Tamaulipas. In these areas, the steel industry supplies auto and auto parts manufacturing and as well as various types of maquiladora industry.

Monterrey and surrounding area constitutes a very large complex for steel and steel-related products. The neighboring municipio in Coahuila of Ramos Arizpe has large steel firms, with an average size of 254 employees. General Zuazua to the northeast has large average firm size of 188 and a number of other neighboring municipios are substantial in

**Map 4.1**
**Total Remuneration in Manufacturing,**
**Central Region, 1994 (in 1000s of pesos)**

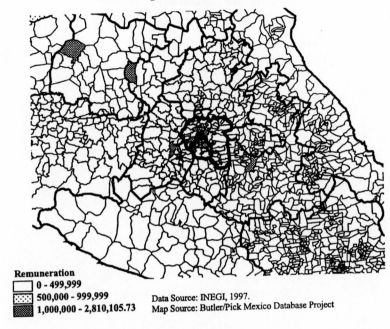

**Remuneration**
☐ 0 - 499,999
▨ 500,000 - 999,999
▨ 1,000,000 - 2,810,105.73

Data Source: INEGI, 1997.
Map Source: Butler/Pick Mexico Database Project

**Map 4.2**
**Total Remuneration in Manufacturing,**
**Border Region, 1994 (in 1000s of pesos)**

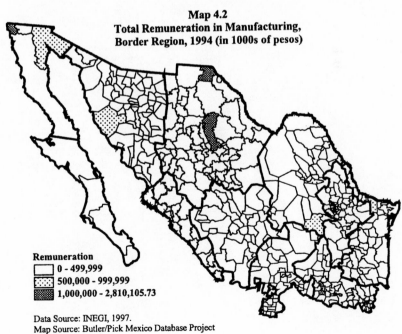

**Remuneration**
☐ 0 - 499,999
▨ 500,000 - 999,999
▨ 1,000,000 - 2,810,105.73

Data Source: INEGI, 1997.
Map Source: Butler/Pick Mexico Database Project

**Map 4.3**
**Average Number of Employees for Enterprises**
**in Steel and Related Products,**
**including Machinery and Equipment, Border Regions, 1994**

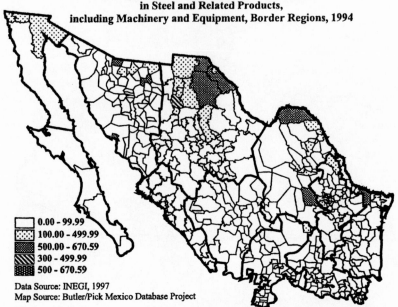

| | |
|---|---|
| ☐ | 0.00 - 99.99 |
| ▦ | 100.00 - 499.99 |
| ▦ | 500.00 - 670.59 |
| ▨ | 300 - 499.99 |
| ▦ | 500 - 670.59 |

Data Source: INEGI, 1997
Map Source: Butler/Pick Mexico Database Project

**Map 4.4**
**Average Number of Employees for Enterprises in**
**Steel and Related Products,**
**including Machinery and Equipment,**
**Central Region, 1994**

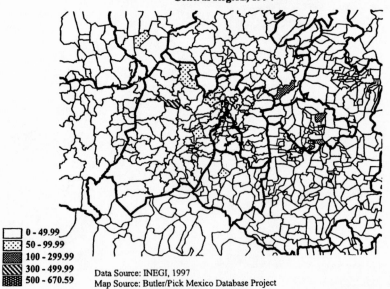

| | |
|---|---|
| ☐ | 0 - 49.99 |
| ▦ | 50 - 99.99 |
| ▦ | 100 - 299.99 |
| ▨ | 300 - 499.99 |
| ▦ | 500 - 670.59 |

Data Source: INEGI, 1997
Map Source: Butler/Pick Mexico Database Project

steel. In steel and steel-related industries, Guadalajara is by contrast moderate in average company size.

Texile/clothing/leather industries are concentrated in the northern border next to Texas and in Mexico City as well as the group of four central states that surround Mexico City to the northwest, north, and northeast, in particular the states of Mexico, Queretaro, Hidalgo, and Tlaxcala. This is mostly in the old and fairly impoverished central zone known as the Bajio. This location for these industries is due to the historical factors of growth of textile/clothing industries in Puebla, Mexico City, and the Bajio in the nineteenth century (Garza 1985).

Textiles/clothing/leather contrasts with steel and related products by: (1) the northern concentration is mostly along the Texas - Mexico border rather than in the west, and (2) the concentration of larger companies is in traditional areas in the central and Bajio regions.

## Automobiles and Auto Parts

Mexico produces over one million motor vehicles per year, most destined for export and especially to the U.S. In addition Mexico exported in the late 1990s well over $5 billion in auto parts annually. The magnitude of this production is seen in the Mexican auto industry production revenue in 1992 accounting for about a sixth of total manufacturing and about a twentieth of PIB (INEGI 1997). The auto industry has grown steadily as reflected in 66 percent increase over the 1988-94 period, about double that of PIB. The growth has continued in the mid to late 1990s.

Together motor vehicles and parts account for a major portion of exports, approximately one fifth in 1996. Only petroleum production is more important as an export item, and that segment benefits from a rich natural resource. There is a strong foreign presence in the automotive sector, and especially for auto production, which requires advanced technologies and economies of scale coming from multinationals. Auto parts companies are much more domestic, although one major Mexican auto parts firm recently moved to the U.S.

Paralleling trends in manufacturing as a whole, the auto industry over the past twenty years has become much more oriented towards the export market. In fact, as seen in Table 4.3, under one percent of passenger car sales in 1978-82 were exported, but ten years later this increased to 34.4 percent (Mexican Automobile Manufacturer's Association, cited in Calderón, Mortimore, and Peres 1997). It is a higher percentage today. During the same ten year period, percent of sales into the domestic market dropped by 49.7 percent to 12.3 percent.

The growth in auto export was driven by easing of government regulations and by FDI investment discussed earlier. In 1994, $2.5 billion of FDI was invested by auto industry companies in Mexico. This investment was made by all major manufacturers in Mexico during the 1990s. The U.S. Big Three (GM, Ford, Chrysler) made huge FDI including for the domestic market, since restrictions on auto imports into Mexico apply for the first ten years of the trade agreement. The NAFTA rules of origin dictate that Volkswagen and Nissan have to invest and locate in Mexico, which they have done.

In 1992, Mexico was ranked twelfth in the global auto industry and produced 1,096,000 motor vehicles. World leaders were Japan in first place producing 12.5 million vehicles and the U.S. second with 9.4 million vehicles (INEGI 1997). The world's production was dominated by the advanced nations. Besides Mexico, only Russia and Brazil were developing nations in the top twelve. Those nations are much more populous than Mexico and have huge potential domestic markets. A factor that must be mentioned in this comparison is the much lower wages paid to autoworkers in Mexico. Table 4.4 contrasts the hourly wages for five nations in the top twelve.

### Table 4.3 Mexican Sales of Passenger Cars, by Domestic versus Export Markets, 1978-1992

|                          | 1978-82 | 1983-87 | 1988-92 |
|--------------------------|---------|---------|---------|
| *Number of Vehicle Units*|         |         |         |
| Domestic Market*         | 147.1   | 78.3    | 70.8    |
| Dual Market**            | 138.6   | 116.9   | 307.5   |
| Export Market***         | 10.5    | 54.5    | 199.0   |
| Total                    | 296.1   | 249.7   | 577.4   |
|                          |         |         |         |
| *Percentages*            |         |         |         |
| Domestic Market*         | 49.7    | 31.4    | 12.3    |
| Dual Market**            | 46.8    | 46.8    | 53.3    |
| Export Market***         | 0.4     | 21.8    | 34.4    |
| Total                    | 100.0   | 100.0   | 100.0   |

\* vehicle lines sold entirely in domestic market
\*\* vehicle lines sold more than 50 percent in domestic market
and less than 50 percent in export markets
\*\*\* vehicle models sold more than 50 percent in export markets
Source: Calderon, Mortimore, and Peres, 1997. Their data were from
Mexican Automobile Manufacturers Association.

### Table 4.4 Automobile Wage Rates for 5 Nations in the Top Twelve Auto Producing Nations, 1992

| Nation        | Hourly Compensation (in 1992 dollars) | Rank in Top Twelve Nations for Motor Vehicles |
|---------------|---------------------------------------|-----------------------------------------------|
| Japan         | 19.97                                 | 1                                             |
| United States | 25.12                                 | 2                                             |
| Canada        | 20.92                                 | 5                                             |
| South Korea   | 7.05                                  | 7                                             |
| Mexico        | 4.35                                  | 12                                            |

Source: INEGI, 1997; data from World's Automotive Yearbook, 1994.

Mexico's very low wages have helped it build a more competitive stance in spite of major threats from the world's most advanced nations.

Automotive production gains of the past ten years have been mostly in foreign exports. This is seen in Table 4.5, which reveals that from 1990 to 1994, motor vehicle exports increased by 296,000 cars and trucks, while the domestic market decreased by a few thousand. What had been mostly a domestic market in 1990 shifted by 1994 to a half foreign market. The percentage shifts 1990 to 1994 show strong increase in the foreign market sector especially for trucks, but slight percentage reductions in the domestic market (see Figure 4.4). This export is predominantly to the U.S (INEGI 1997). In 1994, 77 percent of exports went to the U.S. versus eleven percent to Canada and about seven percent to Latin America (see Table 4.6). This pattern underscores the North American linkages of markets and supply for the auto industry.

The Mexican auto industry has high productivity standards and they have been growing at a more rapid rate than the economy as a whole and about equal rate to the manufacturing sector (INEGI 1997). In recent years, the U.S. Big Three tended to maintain productivity standards in Mexican production that equal or exceed those in the U.S. For instance, the Ford assembly plant in Hermosillo, Sonora, has been cited as one of the most productive manufacturing plants in North America (Calderón, Mortimore, and Peres 1996). Another exemplary Ford site is its engine plant in the state of Chihuahua..

The average annual productivity gain for the auto industry from 1988 to 1997 was 2.65 percent, which is much higher than for the economy as a whole (1.2 percent) and a little lower than for manufacturing as a whole (3.05 percent). This high rate of productivity gain is not surprising since the Mexican auto industry is increasingly competitive and export-driven.

**Table 4.5 Domestic Versus Foreign Production of Autos and Trucks in Mexico, 1990-1994**

| | Unit Volume of Auto Production | | | Unit Volume Change 1990-1994 |
|---|---|---|---|---|
| | 1990 | 1994 | Change 1990-1994 | |
| Production of Trucks for Domestic Market | 179,582 | 169,375 | -6 | -10,207 |
| Production of Autos for Domestic Market | 345,551 | 352,975 | 2 | 7,424 |
| Production of Trucks for Foreign Market | 26,016 | 71,443 | 175 | 45,427 |
| Production of Autos for Foreign Market | 252,542 | 503,588 | 99 | 251,046 |
| Subtotal | 803,691 | 1,097,381 | 37 | 293,690 |
| Other types of vehicles | 26,488 | 38,243 | 44 | 11,755 |
| Total | 830,179 | 1,135,624 | 37 | 305,445 |

Source: INEGI, 1997.

**Figure 4.4 Change in Domestic Versus Foreign Production of Autos and Trucks in Mexico, 1990-1994**

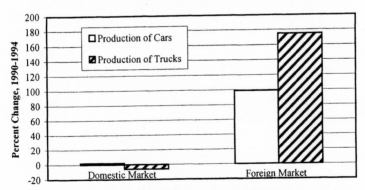

**Change in Unit Production, 1990-1994**

Source: INEGI, 1997.

The location of auto manufacturing is predominantly in Mexico City. This reflects the megacity's dominance in most major economic spheres, including manufacturing, PIB, and corporate headquarters (see Pick et al. 1997). As shown in Table 4.7, nearly half of auto production was in Mexico City. The topic of centralization is discussed in Chapter 14 and elsewhere in this book. The centralization of auto production highlights this concern, since not only are the financial benefits of the auto industry not spread around the nation, but the adverse aspects of this massive industry including air pollution and water consumption disproportionately impact a small geographical area (Pick and Butler 1997).

#### Table 4.6 Destination of Export from Mexico of Automobiles, 1990 and 1994

| Country | 1990 | Percent 1990 | 1994 | Percent 1994 | Change in percent of export market, 1990-1994 |
|---|---|---|---|---|---|
| Canada | 13,079 | 4.7 | 60,284 | 10.6 | 5.9 |
| Brazil | 0 | 0.0 | 6,243 | 1.1 | 1.1 |
| Columbia | 0 | 0.0 | 7,005 | 1.2 | 1.2 |
| Chile | 9,664 | 3.5 | 12,734 | 2.2 | -1.2 |
| United States | 238,271 | 86.1 | 437,170 | 77.1 | -9.0 |
| Japan | 5 | 0.0 | 13,481 | 2.4 | 2.4 |
| Other | 15,840 | 5.7 | 30,190 | 5.3 | -0.4 |
| TOTAL | 276,859 | 100.0 | 567,107 | 100.0 | |

Source: INEGI, 1997.

Auto production is also high in Morelos and Puebla, located near Mexico City. Those may also be considered part of the central production region. The other major states of Coahuila, Sonora, and Chihuahua, with about ten percent of production are border states. From a world systems theory perspective, all these are seen to be from the high or medium development levels (see Map 3.2). The low development areas (periphery) have very low auto industry PIB. The industry appears to confirm the theoretical tenets of the penetration of foreign firms into a developing nation. What is interesting is that, within Mexico, penetration is into the advanced and semi-peripheral regions and not the periphery.

#### Table 4.7 Major Manufacturing States for Auto Industry,
#### 1993 (in thousands of 1993 pesos)

| State | PIB for Auto Industry, 1993 | Percent of Total |
|---|---|---|
| Distrito Federal | 5,794,462 | 25.3 |
| Mexico (State of) | 5,404,284 | 23.6 |
| Coahuila | 1,913,354 | 8.3 |
| Puebla | 1,765,989 | 7.7 |
| Morelos | 1,437,900 | 6.3 |
| Sonora | 1,276,202 | 5.6 |
| Chihuahua | 1,011,714 | 4.4 |
| Total for seven largest states | 18,603,905 | 81.2 |
| Others | 4,315,001 | 18.8 |
| Total | 22,918,906 | 100.0 |

Source: INEGI, 1996.

One example of a foreign auto manufacturer is Ford. In 1994, Ford/Mexico produced 26,804 cars and 35,534 trucks, which comprised eight percent of Mexican car production and a fifth of trucks. This is increasingly production for export. In 1998, Ford's motor vehicle production was 82 percent for the export market, while it imported 38,915 vehicles, equal to about a third of its exports. The latter trend reflects the increasing integration of Ford's worldwide production. Ford's imports will likely grow substantially after NAFTA's auto import restrictions are lifted in 2004.

Today, Ford cooperates in production between the U.S. and Mexico. For instance, Ford's Cuautitlán plant in Mexico Megacity is cooperating with the plant in Kansas for production of Mystique and Contour models, as well as Series F trucks. The ability to cooperate globally has improved Ford's bottom line (Tamayo 1998).

Ford is attempting to stave off criticism of its environmental impacts by acting as a good corporate citizen and sponsoring some environmental activities such as clean-up initiatives. It is exemplary in the modernity of its plants and in some of its community interactions. It appears to be an auto firm of global influence that is also doing things the right way locally.

Auto parts is another huge subsector of the auto industry. In 1996, auto parts amounted to $5 billion (Expansión 1997). Since NAFTA was passed, the protective aspects of import substitution on parts manufacture disappeared so that presently Mexican parts firms line up directly against North American competitors. This is leading to some consolidation in the auto parts subsector. In many cases, the auto parts firm has become a close collaborator with a large parent firm.

There are a large number of auto parts firms -- some indicate as many as 50, in contrast to only five major Mexican auto makers. This makes the structure of the auto industry more complex, since "parts companies" vary a lot in their actual business mix.

Recently, some prominent auto parts companies are seeking U.S. involvement or U.S. exposure. For instance, the leading Mexican auto parts firm, Desc, purchased a U.S. office firm Unik for about $700 million. Another example is the Mexican manufacturer Easton's purchase of the auto parts division of the American firm Dana. Many other such alliances are taking place.

## Telecommunications and Personal Computer Industry

The telecommunications and computer industries have been growing segments in Mexican manufacturing for the past thirty years. Mexico's personal computer industry originated in the 1980s by IBM's leadership in working through the regulatory hurdles to establish a viable early industry. Later in the 80s, IBM was key in convincing the state of Jalisco about the importance of technology manufacturing companies locating there. Following the lead of IBM, HP, Motorola, and other prominent U.S. brand names established production plants. They were followed in turn by many Mexican supplier firms. Today, the manufacturing complex in Guadalajara is referred to as "Silicon Valley of Mexico." Some of its plants are patently world class, such as the IBM ThinkPad laptop plant and HP's printer plants.

There is also a segment of electronics manufacturing that tends to locate as maquiladoras just south of the border. Tijuana is important for maquila electronics manufacturing, especially in televisions, computer printers, and personal computers. It has one of the largest TV assembly plants in the world from SONY and many other large plants in TV and related areas.

The growth and development in these industries are discussed in Chapters 6 and 7. Suffice it to point out that these industries epitomize the foreign firms' leading the way in the productivity growth, innovation, and export orientation. With the opening of the Mexican industry to free trade, foreign ownership, and privatization, many of these communications and computer companies have developed into world leaders in manufacturing.

## Workforce and Skill Levels

Historically, the focus for maquiladora manufacturing was on import substitution. Products did not need to meet worldwide standards, but only satisfy the Mexican domestic consumer. With the opening up of the economy, many manufactured products have entered the world competitive markets, and there is much more demand for high quality products.

The original motivations of low cost manufacturing have given way to a mixture of approaches. These include the following:

- Traditional maquiladora firms having an emphasis on cost-cutting and repetitive assembly. Here the labor force has low education and moderate training. However, the workers are often compelled to meet certain factory quality goals that are closely monitored.
- Maqiladora firms with high tech manufacturing. These, located in Tijuana and to a lesser extent in Ciudad Juarez and other cities, have invested more in advanced manufacturing capability that tends to require fewer but more skilled and educated workers. Here, there are greater needs for greater skills to operate and control more sophisticated production.
- Traditional manufacturing in older industries such as textiles and clothing. This industry tends to be located in the center and south of Mexico. The skill levels are lower, and the size of firms smaller.
- World class manufacturing with greater foreign investment and management participation. The electronics industry that has grown and prospered in Monterrey and Guadalajara typifies this category. This type of facility draws design engineers and production supervisors, many of whom are college graduates. Many of the firms have close ties with universities.

This typology points to a diversity of workforce and skills in different manufacturing subsectors. The variety corresponds to diverse levels of technology, sophistication of manufacturing, pay levels, and quality standards, i.e. domestic versus worldwide.

A recent example of these differences is the Delphi R&D Center in Ciudad Juárez. Delphi is the major auto parts subsidiary of General Motors. As Mexico emphasized higher quality products, Delphi moved into Mexico, mostly into Ciudad Juárez. Initially, it emphasized high quality assembly line production of auto parts. There was comparative advantage achieved, since high quality goods could be produced at low labor cost. The success of this approach is reflected by Delphi; today it has grown to 72,000 workers in 53 plants in Mexico, mostly in Juárez and surrounding areas.

A significant change was the move in 1995 of the Delphi Technical Center from Texas to Ciudad Juárez. This center employs engineers and designers for specific auto parts that include antilock braking systems, emission products, air conditioning compressors, and components for steering (Catán 1998). The workforce is the world leader in designing these products.

There is substantial pay saving from hiring Mexican engineers and product designers, versus comparable workers in the U.S. Mexican designers in Mexico have the advantage that there are many Delphi assembly lines nearby. Assembly line managers and workers can be consulted in product engineering and design. It is even possible to simulate a real assembly line for a new product idea. Delphi has positioned this Center as its most advanced for R&D worldwide (Catán 1998). It is planned to expand to a size of 2,000 workers in the next two years.

This short case highlights the wide variation in manufacturing workforce and skill levels. The original Delphi concept was to utilize low skilled assembly workers to meet high level manufacturing quality standards. Because of market and regulatory changes, this concept has evolved to a mixture of the original low skilled profile plus a new personnel profile that emphasizes very educated and skilled labor force engaged in creative design and having worldwide responsibilities. The strong educational advances in Mexico over the past 50 years (see Pick and Butler 1994) have enabled this "mixed" approach, which may be a better fit to the rising education of workers, especially in the advanced parts of the country (see Chapter 6).

## Conclusions

This chapter emphasized growth in manufacturing in Mexico over the past forty years. What had been a protected import substitution economy with moderate manufacturing quality has been transformed into an export-based manufacturing economy with higher and in some cases world-class standards. Mexican manufacturing labor force remains lower cost than in advanced nations, but segments of the manufacturing workforce have moved to higher skill and educational levels. This is especially evident in higher technology sectors such as certain electronics and automotive manufacturing.

The old maquiladora concept of value added assembly that minimized cost is also shifting. The Tijuana electronics industry is aspiring to higher quality standards in order to face world competition. At the same time, most of the maquila sector remains in the mode of very low wages and other cost cutting.

Manufacturing is a fundamental cornerstone of the Mexican economy representing about a third of PIB. However, it is predominantly located in the border states, i.e. maquiladora and automotive manufacturing, and in the largest cities of Mexico City, Monterrey, and Guadalajara. From a world systems perspective, these regions are mostly advanced areas of Mexico and some are semi-periphery of Mexico. The components and raw materials for these products vary a lot, with some shipped in from advanced nations and others coming from the periphery and semi-periphery areas of Mexico. The workforce for these industries varies in its origin. For the maquiladoras, much of the workforce has migrated from semi-peripheral or peripheral areas to the border region. For the more advanced manufacturing such as in the "Silicon Valley" of Guadalajara, the workforce has come from the advanced areas and is sometimes even college educated. The consumers of the manufacturing product are either in advanced nations, mostly the U.S., or in the advanced areas of Mexico i.e. the border and Mexico City. Decision making regarding manufacturing is based mostly in Mexico City or in advanced countries, especially the United States. The general picture is that of manufacturing located in the advanced parts of Mexico and producing for advanced level markets, but utilizing labor that often originates from the semi-periphery or periphery. Raw materials utilized depend on the strategy of manufacturing.

There are exceptions to this trend of dependency, which form an interesting countertrend. For instance, Cemex represents a company at world-class level from Mexico that is acquiring and re-designing companies located in advanced and semi-peripheral nations. Cemex's labor force is higher level. Its entrepreneurial and management innovations originate in Mexico. This counter-trend needs to be watched and observed carefully, since it points to a balancing and re-adjustment of the world systems theory relationships and flows.

## Case Study: Cemex

Cemex is the world's third largest cement company, with 1998 sales of 4.32 billion dollars. It is highly successful and had profits in 1998 of $803 million. In 1997 it had 486 plants and shipped 42 million metric tons of cement. It is a global firm operating currently in 21 overseas markets. Cemex is entirely Mexican owned and is headquartered in Monterrey. Its business strategy is to have highly efficient production based on sophisticated management information systems and networking. It has also pursued a strategy of acquisitions worldwide of dominant national cement companies, which Cemex has transformed into more efficient and technologically able units. It has a coordinated system of worldwide distribution centers, a large fleet of ships, and can coordinate shipping and deliveries exactly through a satellite network.

Cemex was founded in the city of Hidalgo, Nuevo Leon, in 1906 by Lorenzo Zambrano, the grandfather of the present CEO, who has the same name. It has always had family ownership and even today is 30 percent owned by the Zambrano family. In the first half of the century, it moved to Monterrey and expanded throughout Mexico. It purchased two large Mexican cement firms between 1987 and 1989 and verged on becoming Mexico's leading cement producer, but found that it was being threatened by the practice of dumping, i.e. competing firms selling cement at below cost in order to exert strong competitive pressure.

As a response to dumping practices, in 1992, it started a long string of foreign acquisitions by purchasing Spain's two largest cement companies, Valenciana and Sanson. It has continued to make many foreign acquisitions, often at times of financial duress either in Mexico or in the country of acquisition. For instance, in 1995, just after the peso had been sharply devalued in Mexico, Cemex purchased Corp. Venezolana de Cementos SA, that nation's leading producer. That purchase happened just before major currency devaluation in Venezuela. These economic downturns did not deter Cemex from overhauling Corp. Venezolana including modernizing its information technology, integrating production, cutting the workforce, and streamlining administration.

Cemex in 1994 also acquired the Balcones Plant in Braunfels, Texas, which is the largest provider of white cement in the U.S. Again, it overhauled the plant and turned into an award winning factory.

The string of acquisitions has continued to the present. Cementos Nacionales of the Dominican Republic was purchased in 1996. In 1996, Cemex acquired two cement firms in Columbia. In 1997, Cemex moved into Asia buying 30 percent of the $1 billion Rizal Cement Co. in the Philippines, and in 1998, it acquired PT Semen Gresik a formerly nationalized Indonesian company. In 1999, it acquired facilities in Chile, Costa Rica, and Egypt.

Cemex today is present throughout the world (see Map 4.5). It is especially strong in Mexico, northern South America, and Spain. In 1994, Cemex held 8th place in the Mexican 500 (Expansión 1998).

During its foreign acquisitions, it has continued to develop its Mexican operations, which today still comprises about 45 percent of corporate sales. Because of its growing population and its need to modernize infrastructure, Mexico forms a strong domestic platform for the now global company. Mexico began a huge process of privatization in the later 1980s that continues today. Among other things, Mexico is privatizing airports, maritime ports, gas distribution, and railroads. This trend is leading to upgrading infrastructure throughout the nation, all of which enhances Cemex's domestic opportunities.

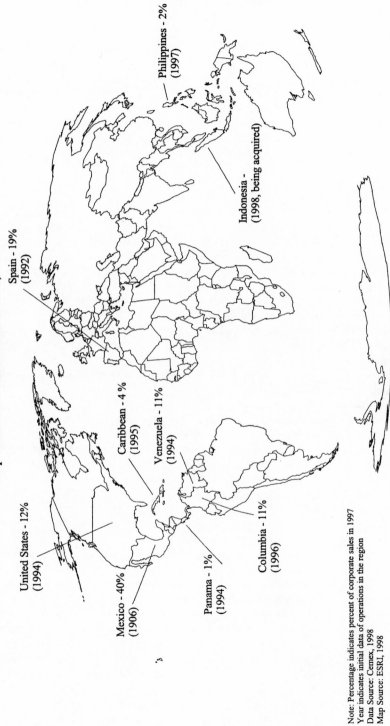

**Map 4.5 Cemex's Worldwide Locations, 1998**

Spain - 19%
(1992)

Philippines - 2%
(1997)

Indonesia -
(1998, being acquired)

United States - 12%
(1994)

Caribbean - 4 %
(1995)

Venezuela - 11%
(1994)

Mexico - 40%
(1906)

Panama - 1%
(1994)

Columbia - 11%
(1996)

Note: Percentage indicates percent of corporate sales in 1997
Year indicates initial data of operations in the region
Data Source: Cemex, 1998
Map Source: ESRI, 1998

A number of key overseas countries that Cemex moved into also parallels this profile of Mexico, for instance Venezuela and the Philippines. Cemex has taken advantage of worldwide trends in the developing world to upgrade national infrastructures.

In technology, Cemex is a worldwide industry leader. This includes its own satellite network in Mexico, GPS (Global Positioning Systems) and GIS (Geographic Information Systems) to guide delivery trucks, elaborate MRP (Materials Resource Planning) and quality control systems, advanced factory production systems, video conferencing for decision making and employee training, and executive management systems. The commitment of Cemex to MIS (Management Information Systems) is reflected in its investment in IT of $150 million over the past 12 years (Industry Week 1997). The company has developed several especially noteworthy information systems that give it a competitive advantage. It has a satellite based delivery dispatching system that is patterned after that of Federal Express and the City of Houston's 911 system. Among other things, the system allows a loaded ship enroute to be re-directed to a different delivery destination. The GPS/GIS in its delivery trucks allow central dispatching to continually modify and optimally adjust deliveries as customers make changes and there are delays and other unforeseen events. The deliveries are so precisely controlled that Cemex is able to give customers discounts proportional to the time delay of a late delivery.

In the area of employee training, each plant in Mexico has a training center connected to a private satellite network. The plants can provide training and workshops, with various units participating through videoconferencing. This also allows employees and managers throughout the country to exchange ideas with co-workers.

All these systems are interconnected, and support a style of management that expects exacting follow-through, meeting of schedules, and precise control of production processes. Managers are encouraged to delegate responsibilities for goals, but assume that the subordinate will reach the goals. The delegation process is possible through the information technology.

Most of these systems are world class commercial products that are used by top manufacturers in advanced nations. However, Cemex has often gone further by modifying and integrating these systems together to a greater competitive advantage.

Financially, Cemex seeks to achieve better margins by increasing pricing and revenues and lowering costs. This is the major indicator of competitive strength in the cement industry, and the company has among the highest margins in the industry. Another financial strategy that is opposite to much of Mexican manufacturing is outward FDI, in other words investment by Cemex in plant and equipment overseas. Through carefully planned outward FDI, it is able to transform the often mediocre efficiency of acquired national companies into state-of-the-art efficient and productive units.

In summary, Cemex illustrates a contrary trend to much of Mexican manufacturing. Instead of depending on foreign technology leadership and financing, Cemex provides those features in Mexico. It exports and utilizes its highly efficient management and systems to achieve worldwide technological leadership. It invests in improving acquired operations overseas, the opposite of say the maquiladora or the Mexican electronics industry. Besides the entrepreneurial spark of the Zambrano family and great management, Cemex has been helped by having a product that is well suited to the growing infrastructure needs of its domestic base. It learned to excel in serving these infrastructure needs in Mexico and yet can and expertly implement them in other developing nations with similar needs. The success of Cemex is echoed in smaller ways in some other counter-trends discussed in the chapter, for instance in the success of largely domestic engineering talent at Delphi R&D. The counter-trend represented so well by Cemex may point towards future areas of growth and change in Mexican manufacturing.

## Case Study: Vitro

Vitro is a prominent Grupo in Mexico. It is one of the two companies worldwide that produce a complete line of glass products, the other company being the French firm Saint Gobain. Vitro produces clear glass, plastics, automotive glass, glass containers, household goods including appliances, chemicals and packing materials, and glass crystal. Vitro has benefited by its ability to sell glass to the huge Mexican auto industry. The original company was founded by Federico Sada and Isaac Garza in 1909 in Monterrey, and like Cemex, the founding family has continued to manage the firm. Currently, the CEO is Federico Sada, the great grandson of one of the founders.

The company today is a Grupo that has six divisions and owns more than 50 firms worldwide (U.S./Mexico Business 1997). It 1996, it had sales of $2.3 billion and assets of $3.4 billion. It has suffered losses in recent years having to do with a disastrous foreign acquisition of Anchor Glass and also problems with its investments in the now troubled bank Grupo Serfin Financiero. In 1996, the company had losses of $598 million, coupled with a large debt problem.

Although the firm had operated profitably and had been respected for good management for many decades, in 1989 it undertook the first hostile takeover of a U.S. firm, Anchor Glass, by a Mexican one. Anchor was one of the largest U.S. glass makers, with 25 percent of the U.S. market and 22 plants. Anchor had a major market in glass for the soft drink industry. The acquisition was accomplished at a cost of $900 million. Originally, this acquisition was touted, and it appeared as if Vitro was following some of Cemex's outward directed strategy of foreign acquisition and investment.

However, the Anchor purchase turned out to be a disaster and Vitro eventually sold the unit at a large loss. The mistake that Vitro made was to fail to see a shift made by leading U.S. soft drink companies in the early 90s from principally glass to less expensive plastic containers. The switch caused severe losses to Vitro and it accumulated a debt of $550 million by the end of 1995 (U.S./Mexico Business 1997). It was at this point that Federico Sada took over as CEO. Although he initially was determined to turn Anchor around, he soon decided to sell the unit and in late 1996 sold it to a consortium of Consumer Packaging in the U.S. and Owens Brockway Containers in Canada for $392 million. Around the same time, Vitro also sold domestic stakes in Cydsa, a domestic chemical and textile firm and stopped investing further in the troubled bank Grupo Serfin Financiero. The problems with Serfin stem from deep and widespread mismanagement problems in the Mexican banking industry that are covered in Chapter 6. Since the sale and the other divestitures, Vitro has developed a five year strategic plan to recuperate from these disasters that involves emphasizing its domestic businesses. The ambitious a five year plan focuses on consolidating its long time businesses and growing and improving them financially. Part of the challenge that Vitro faces is that major traditional markets of clear glass and glass containers are not growing very rapidly.

# 5

## Finance and Commerce

- **Introduction**
- **Commerce Sector**
  - History of Commerce in Mexico
  - Commerce Sector: Sectoral Growth and Development
- **Regional Location of Commerce in Mexico**
- **Banking Sector**
- **Geography of Banking**
- **Cifra/Walmart: a Global Counter Example**
- **Case Study: El Puerto de Liverpool**
- **Case Study: Bancomext**
- **Case Study: Bancomer**

## Introduction

This chapter examines the commerce and banking sectors in Mexico and how they relate to globalization and regional/local tendencies. The chapter presents the history of commerce in Mexico, from pre-colonial to colonial and modern times. Mexico has always had commerce and has had opportunities and constraints on commerce throughout its history. Some forms of commerce have developed historically in unique ways to Mexico such as the tianguis[1], while other developments are common to many nations and societies. In the latter half of the 20th century, the relative economic size of the commerce sector has been dropping, while the per capita workforce and numbers of commerce firms have been increasing. The trends favoring commerce as well as adverse to commerce and favoring other sectors will be discussed.

The chapter considers major commerce firms and their characteristics. Commerce enterprises tend to be Mexican owned and to be located in the large cities and the central part of the nation. A major exception is Cifra/Walmart, which is part of a U.S. multinational and is expanding away from the traditional central zone.

Another chapter section analyzes the regional location of the commerce sector in Mexico. The populous states with large cities and the border states have a relatively larger commerce sector, while the less populous and central and southern states lacking major cities have less commerce. Based on municipio data, national commerce is concentrated in the central populous flank especially Mexico City and some northern cities. A major overall finding is that commerce is associated with large cities and with the advanced parts of the nation and is weak in peripheral regions. This is not surprising since most of the valuable goods and services being exchanged are produced and consumed in or near major cities.

Commerce is related to the banking sector, since it fosters and supports commercial exchange, as one of its functions. The second half of the chapter examines the banking sector in Mexico. This sector has undergone major changes over the past thirty years, from a private and somewhat corrupt banking system through a period of nationalization to re-privatization in the early 1990s and resulting disastrous outcomes for the system. The banking sector today has not recovered. After tottering on insolvency, the government helped to "bail out" the system, but many banks have been taken over by foreign banks and the Fobaproa agency mishandled further the "bailout," necessitating the movement of the bailout apparatus to IPAB, which may do somewhat better. The underlying result of all of this turmoil has been restrictions on availability of credit. Credit tightening has had less impact on large export-oriented firms, which can obtain capital overseas, and greater impact on middle and small size firms including commercial firms. The reasons for the banking crisis are examined and prospects for the future are considered.

Another aspect of banking is regional distribution. The three major cities, and particularly Mexico City, dominate bank deposits and encompass the headquarters of nearly all of the nation's major banks. The seventeen lowest states have only 8.2 percent of bank deposits. These states include the southern peripheral states, the Yucatan peninsula, and most of the Bajio region, all traditionally poorer areas. On the other hand, bank offices and branches are spread more evenly including the less prosperous states. The chapter examines the geography of Mexican banking in the context of world systems theory. The banking sector is emphasized in this chapter, rather than other financial sectors, which are covered briefly in the Chapter 6 section, "Financial and Insurance Service." We have chosen to emphasize banking in depth because it is more well developed that the other financial sectors. For instance, although the Mexican securities market is becoming more important, fewer than 200 corporations are part of this market, and it is weak in the area of commerce

---

[1] Tianguis is discussed in Chapter 12.

and manufacturing (Cabello, 1999). Another factor lending importance to banks is that Mexican law allows the construct of "universal banking." This means that Mexico has the legal entity of "grupo financiero." This entity can be headed according to law either by a bank or a brokerage house and can include a mixture or financial entities including banks, brokerage houses, insurance companies, etc. An example is the case study of Bancomer, which is a "grupo financiero." Although primarily a bank, Bancomer also jointly owns the Mexican insurance company Valores Monterrey Aetna.

Several case studies are explored in greater detail in an era of globalization, *El Puerto de Liverpool* represents continuing Mexican ownership, and in the nation's commerce sector. It reinforces the importance of the central flank and largest cities of Mexico for commerce. Liverpool's financial strength after 150 years demonstrates that a Mexican firm can compete strongly in this sector. The company has been successful in modern technology in its distribution and warehousing.

*Bancomext* is a special bank with a principal mission to bolster the national theme of exports underscored in the last chapter. It has had the force of the federal government behind it, and has had some successes. However, lowering federal government subsidies lead Bancomext to compete in semi-commercial markets, and its success record has only been mixed there.

*Bancomer* is one of Mexico's two largest commercial banks. It has the largest banking network. Although its financial status remains shaky due to the 1990s banking industry crisis and Bancomer's mistakes in lending, it has forged a number of global partnerships that have helped it weather the banking industry storm. So far, its majority of ownership is Mexican and it remains one of two "flagship" banks. Bancomer is in merger discussions with Spain's Banco Bilbao Vizcaya Argentaria (BBVA), which may give BBVA up to 40 percent control. Bancomer has moderate technology to support its strong geographical presence throughout the nation.

### Commerce Sector

*History of Commerce in Mexico*

Commerce has a long history including pre-Colonial Mexico. The Aztecs were well known for their central market located in the center of cities and involving the barter trading of local as well as external goods.

During the Spanish colonial era, systems were in place for trade and commerce. Commerce was important in this era in providing sources of capital to agriculture, the dominant sector. Commercial markets for corn and wheat were better developed and made use of European mechanisms to control the markets (INEGI 1994). Commerce was constrained by poor infrastructure of roads and transport. There were unique customs for commerce. The custom of tianguis stemmed from pre-Colonial times. It involves informal markets with a group of vendors setting up at several specific times and places each week. The institution has carried all the way to the present day, and is discussed further in its present context in Chapter 12. Another commerce custom developed during colonial times was the annual trade fair. These were especially famous in Xalapa, Veracruz, and in Acapulco (INEGI 1994).

In the early 19th century, commerce continued to grow and contribute as a source of capital. However, it was constrained by lack of paper currency, so barter was dominant. This was altered in the Benito Juárez Administration when federal paper currency was first issued in 1862 in the amount of 500,000 pesos (INEGI 1994). In that same year, the nationwide value of commerce was about 400 million pesos (INEGI 1994). Commerce in mid 19th century took several forms: (1) small shops, (2) central markets, a hold over from pre-colonial times, (3) tianguis, i.e. continuation of the custom, and (4) fairs. The fair ("feria") increased in importance. There were many annual trading fairs, often lasting several days and drawing both national and foreign merchants. They stimulated national exchange as well as import and export.

The central market grew in importance and involved exchange of numerous products. Small shops became prevalent throughout the country and reflected greater amounts of retail trade including foreign goods. Some larger stores began to develop in the large cities and often involved foreign owners or merchants or foreign origin of capital. An example is El Puerto de Liverpool, which was founded by a French immigrant in 1847 in Mexico City.

During the late 19$^{th}$ and early 20$^{th}$ century Porfirio Diaz Administration (Porfiriate), commerce continued to develop but also had certain constraints. Among constraints were restrictions in communications and transportation, and the presence of an inhibiting sales tax. Advances in the late 19$^{th}$ century in communications, such as the telephone, and transportation helped to lift the constraints. The national railroad system was built during the Porfiriate (see Pick, Butler, and Lanzer 1989) and helped in the movement of goods nationally. The sales tax had been present in the reform period. Although it was formally abolished by the Constitution of 1857, the turbulent years that followed led to its reappearance. It wasn't until 1895 in the Porfiriate that the sales tax was again abolished, stimulating commerce and trade.

Another positive factor for commerce was the rising urbanization of Mexico. This was a long-term trend continuing during the entire 20$^{th}$ century (Pick and Butler 1994). The growth in cities stimulated most forms of commerce, including the central market, smaller stores and department stores, more elaborate tianguis, and annual fairs.

*Commerce Sector: Sectoral Growth and Development*

As seen in Table 5.1 and Map 5.1, the commerce sector has grown substantially in the mid to late 20$^{th}$ century. This growth has surpassed that of the rapidly growing population. The enhanced growth of commerce relates to the increasing urbanization of Mexico. For instance Mexico increased from 35.0 percent urban in 1940 to 71.3 percent urban in 1990 (Pick and Butler 1994). As seen in Figure 5.1, the per capita prevalence of commercial establishments grew from 2.1 in 1940 to 9.3 in 1988, an over four-fold increase. As will be seen in the next section, the establishments were disproportionately located in the highly urban states and especially in Mexico City (Pick and Butler 1997). Likewise, the per capita number of commerce workers increased by three times during these five decades, from 8.7 to 26.7 commerce workers per 1,000 persons (see Figure 5.1).

Economic trends are better understood by recognizing the large shifts in exchange rate that have taken place versus the dollar. As seen in Table 5.2 and Figure 5.2, the peso has increased in value versus the dollar by over 700 fold between 1975 and 1998! It is positive that the rate of change in the peso seems to have moderated over the past 12 years except for the shock of 1994. This lends more stability to the Mexican economy and its international trade. Corresponding to the devaluation of the peso, the consumer price index has advanced rapidly in Mexico since 1980, reflecting inflationary trends.

Even though commerce became more prevalent, the proportion of commerce overall in the national economy has declined somewhat. The reason for this is that other economic sectors are growing even more rapidly. As seen in Table 5.3, the commerce sector decreased from 28.0 percent of PIB in 1980 to 19.7 percent of PIB in 1996, continuing a trend of several decades. The reason for the decline was the more rapid growth in other sectors, in particular FIRE, i.e. finance, insurance, real estate, and business services, and in other, which includes growth in petroleum exports (see Figure 5.3). The commerce sector increased in absolute dollar terms. For example, the Commerce PIB in 1990 was 26.3 billion dollars, but was 65.0 billion dollars in 1996 (IMF 1996). However, while the whole

**Map 5.1**
**Commerce Workforce, 1990**

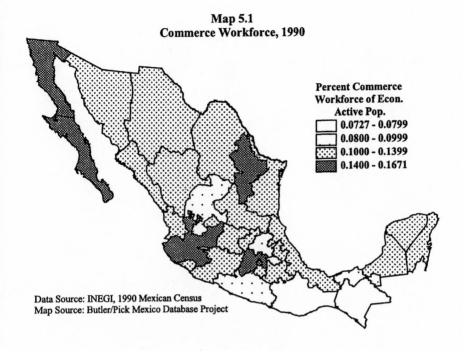

Percent Commerce
Workforce of Econ.
Active Pop.
☐ 0.0727 - 0.0799
☐ 0.0800 - 0.0999
▨ 0.1000 - 0.1399
▨ 0.1400 - 0.1671

Data Source: INEGI, 1990 Mexican Census
Map Source: Butler/Pick Mexico Database Project

**Figure 5.1  Growth in Commerce Per Capita, 1940-1988**

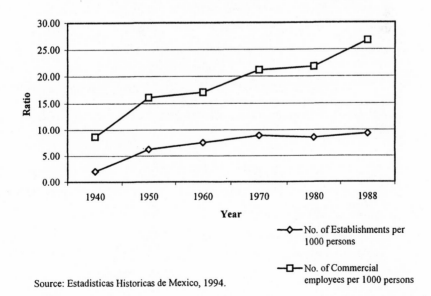

Source: Estadisticas Historicas de Mexico, 1994.

Table 5.1 Growth in the Commercial Sector, 1940-1988

| Year | Number of Commercial Establishments | No. of Establishments per 1000 Persons | Commercial Workers (in thousands) | No. of Commercial Employees per 1000 Persons | No. of Commercial Workers per Establishment | Population (in thousands) |
|---|---|---|---|---|---|---|
| 1940 | 40,533 | 2.06 | 170.3 | 8.67 | 4.20 | 19,652.6 |
| 1950 | 161,137 | 6.25 | 415.8 | 16.12 | 2.58 | 25,791.0 |
| 1960 | 262,806 | 7.53 | 596.2 | 17.07 | 2.27 | 34,923.1 |
| 1970 | 429,480 | 8.91 | 1,020.10 | 21.15 | 2.38 | 48,225.2 |
| 1980 | 568,830 | 8.51 | 1,457.30 | 21.80 | 2.56 | 66,846.8 |
| 1988 | 754,848 | 9.29 | 2,169.30 | 26.70 | 2.87 | 81,249.6 |

Source: Estadisticas Historicas de Mexico, 1994.

**Figure 5.2 Value of Peso in Dollars and Consumer Price Index for Last Quarter of 20th Century**

Value of Peso in Dollars

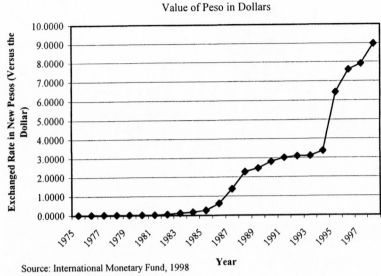

Source: International Monetary Fund, 1998 and Oanda Classic 164 Currency Converter, 1999.

Consumer Price Index

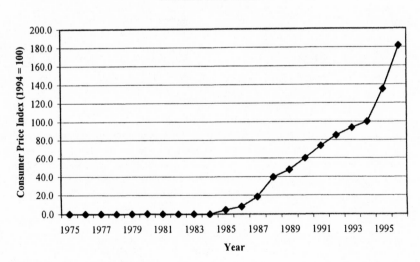

Source: International Financial Statistics Yearbook, 1998.

Figure 5.3 Components of PIB, Mexico, 1980 and 1996

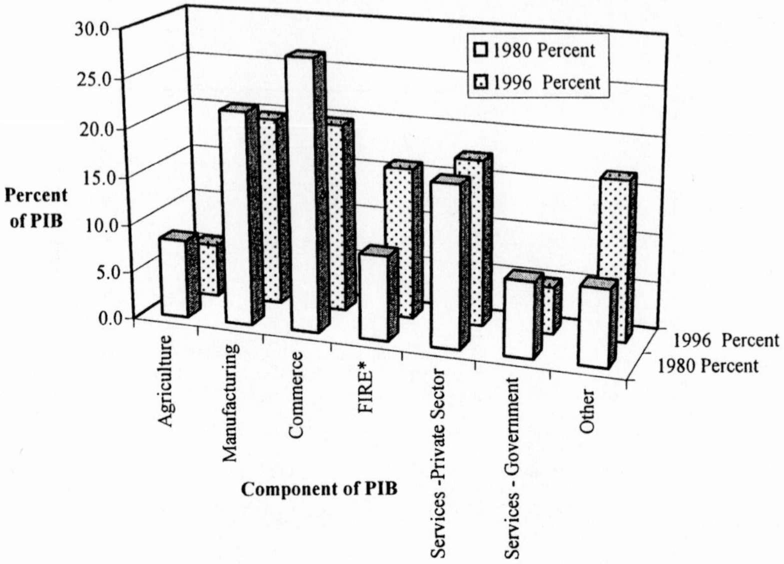

*FIRE = Finance, Insurance, Real Estate, and Business Services.
Source: UN: Statistical Yearbook for Latin America and the Caribbean, 1997.

Mexican economy has been growing over the past two decades in absolute terms, commerce did not do comparatively as well as a sector.

By contrast, the proportion of commerce in the U.S. economy is somewhat higher. In 1997, the GAF (general merchandise, apparel and furniture) part of U.S. GNP was $2.7 trillion, which was about one third of GNP (Hoovers On-line 1999). Thus, the U.S. economy has a higher extent of commerce, both domestic and international than Mexico.

The Mexican commerce sector consists partly of large firms, predominantly domestic in ownership. The largest fifteen Mexican commerce companies in 1997 are shown in Table 5.4. The top 15 account for 17.2 billion dollars in sales. This is one quarter of 1997 Commerce PIB. The companies are predominantly headquartered in Mexico City. This corresponds to Mexico City's dominance in general as a headquarters location for large companies (see Chapter 13). However, the capital's dominance in commerce is even more extreme. For instance, on a revenue basis for the commerce 15, 83 percent of corporate revenues come from firms headquartered in Mexico City. This dominance stems from Mexico City's central role in commercial enterprises and exchange as well as from Mexico's dependence on it as a primate city (Pick and Butler 1997).

The commerce 15 are also predominantly Mexican owned. The Commerce 15 contrasts with the largest Mexican companies in general, about one third of which are foreign owned for example in autos (see Chapter 13 and Pick and Butler 1997, Table 11.6). The most visible counter example of foreign ownership of a commercial firm is Cifra, which was purchased by Walmart. Cifra is discussed in the next section. *Controladora Comercial México* is the nation's second largest retail chain, operating under the names of Bodegas Comercial Mexicana, Price Club México and Sumesa, and owns the chain of California Restaurants. Its retail stores combine supermarkets, general merchandise, and over-the-counter drugs. Although spread out in 31 cities, it is mostly in the central flank, i.e. Mexico City (56 percent) and the Bajio region (14 percent). Several other commerce firms are important to mention. *Gigante*, the third largest firm, is predominantly in supermarkets and is spread out in the central and northern parts of the nation. *Liverpool* is a financially-strong Mexican department store chain that appears as a case study.

**Table 5.2 Peso Exchange Rate (versus the Dollar), 1975-1997,**
**and Consumer Price Index, 1980-1996**

| Year | Exchange Rate (new pesos versus dollar) Period Average | Consumer Price Index |
|---|---|---|
| 1975 | 0.0125 | NA |
| 1976 | 0.0154 | NA |
| 1977 | 0.0226 | NA |
| 1978 | 0.0228 | NA |
| 1979 | 0.0228 | NA |
| 1980 | 0.0230 | 0.4 |
| 1981 | 0.0245 | NA |
| 1982 | 0.0560 | NA |
| 1983 | 0.1201 | NA |
| 1984 | 0.1678 | NA |
| 1985 | 0.2569 | 4.3 |
| 1986 | 0.6118 | 8.0 |
| 1987 | 1.3782 | 18.5 |
| 1988 | 2.2731 | 39.6 |
| 1989 | 2.4615 | 47.5 |
| 1990 | 2.8126 | 60.1 |
| 1991 | 3.0184 | 73.7 |
| 1992 | 3.0949 | 85.2 |
| 1993 | 3.1156 | 93.5 |
| 1994 | 3.3751 | 100.0 |
| 1995 | 6.4194 | 135.0 |
| 1996 | 7.5994 | 181.4 |
| 1997 | 7.9141 | NA |
| 1998* | 8.9850 | NA |

NA = not available
* Rate for June 30, 1998
Source: International Financial Statistics Yearbook, 1998 and SeMaTech Foreign Exchange Rates, 1999.

**Table 5.3 Components of Producto Interno Bruto (PIB), 1980-1996**
**(millions of pesos)**

| | 1980 | Percent | 1990 | Percent | 1996 | Percent |
|---|---|---|---|---|---|---|
| Agriculture | 368 | 8.2 | 53,057 | 7.2 | 139,753 | 5.6 |
| Manufacturing | 991 | 22.2 | 140,608 | 19.0 | 494,671 | 19.8 |
| Commerce | 1,250 | 28.0 | 167,202 | 22.6 | 494,272 | 19.7 |
| FIRE* | 396 | 8.9 | 98,120 | 13.3 | 397,284 | 15.9 |
| Services - Private Sector | 754 | 16.9 | 111,861 | 15.1 | 435,693 | 17.4 |
| Services - Government | 353 | 7.9 | 30,394 | 4.1 | 124,017 | 5.0 |
| Other | 358 | 8.0 | 137,656 | 18.6 | 418,124 | 16.7 |
| PIB | 4,470 | 100.0 | 738,898 | 100.0 | 2,503,814 | 100.0 |

*FIRE = Finance, Insurance, Real Estate, and Business Services.
Source: Statistical Yearbook for Latin America and the Caribbean, 1997.

Finally, *Grupo Elektra* is a retailer of brand recognized consumer electronics, as well as large appliances and home furniture. It has grown very rapidly and has numerous mostly smaller stores throughout the nation. In fact it operates in 145 cities and nearly every state. Its rapid growth has been stimulated by foreign borrowing and aggressive entrepreneurial leadership of Ricardo Salinas Pliego. In fact, he has been so successful that he is one of Mexico's wealthiest persons and purchased TV Azteca, Mexico's second largest network in 1994 (Muñoz Valencia 1998). In many respects, Elektra represents a company like Cemex demonstrating world class standards of management and technology. Unlike Cemex, Elektra's business is domestic. The other major commercial firm is Sears Roebuck of Mexico. It has recently become part of the conglomerate, *Grupo Carsa*, which is controlled by the entrepreneur, Carlos Slim. Sears has been in Mexico since 1945 and serves middle to high-end customers. Unlike Cifra/Walmart, it has had mixed success and has been impacted by large-scale theft and security-related losses.

In summary, the commerce sector is about a fifth of the economy and is mostly Mexican owned. It is concentrated in Mexico City and the central flank of the nation. The two chapter cases present polar business approaches. Cifra/Walmart is an exception in its foreign ownership, while El Puerto de Liverpool demonstrates how a Mexican-owned traditional firm can be modernized and improved to be very competitive.

## Regional Location of Commerce in Mexico

The regional distribution of commerce reflects the historical and urban patterns of the nation, as well as the location of commerce exchanges and consumers. The present geographical patterns reflect the historical overconcentration in the advanced, major cities and central flank and lack of commerce in peripheral states (see Map 5.1). Within cities, commerce is most prevalent in Mexico City and especially in the traditional "business center" of the city. While manufacturing was located closer to major cities, transport, and border access, commerce is more concentrated in the largest cities where the largest commercial exchanges and most important consumers are located.

About 25 to 30 percent of the commerce workforce has been located in either Mexico City or the State of Mexico. Table 5.5 shows that the proportion of commerce workers in the Federal District and State of Mexico declined from 36 to 29 percent from 1955 to 1988. The Mexico City part declined from 34 to 26 percent. This reduction in Mexico City reflects the extension of commerce to other parts of the nation. The gain has been spread out among the other regions and states. Although Mexico City is an overly primate city (Pick and Butler 1997), it was even more primate in the mid century, especially in commerce. Also helping to encourage the spread of commerce is the continuing process of urbanization during the entire 20th century. The other major and regional cities have grown substantially in the second half of the century, encouraging more commerce. The national distribution of commerce workers in 1990 is seen in Map 5.1. This map reinforces the weakness of commerce in the south and in parts of the economically deprived Bajio region.

In Table 5.5, the right column shows the differential between the distribution of commerce workers and the distribution of population. Specifically, the differential is equal to: proportion of commerce workers - proportion of population. A positive value for this differential reflects states or regions where the concentration of commerce workers is greater than the population, and a negative value indicates a deficit of commerce workers relative to population. The state with the largest surplus of commerce workers is the Federal District; in fact there is a surplus of ten percent. The border states have a surplus of about 5 percent, reflecting strong commerce in the north. On the other hand, there is a slight deficit in the State of Mexico. This may be surprising but may be explained by Mexico City's

Table 5.4 Mexico's Fifteen Largest Commerce Companies, 1997

| Position* | Name | Location | Category | Ownership** | Sales (in dollars) | Debt (in dollars) | Ratio Debt to Equity | Percent Foreign Debt | No. of Employees | Year of Founding |
|---|---|---|---|---|---|---|---|---|---|---|
| 6 | Cifra/Wal-Mart | Mexico, DF | Self-service | domestic | 4,158,216 | 993,411 | 26 | 16 | 57,649 | 1958 |
| 15 | Controladora Comercial Mex. | Mexico, DF | Self-service | domestic | 2,272,024 | 746,807 | 45 | 36 | 30,177 | 1930 |
| 16 | Gigante | Mexico, DF | Self-service | domestic | 2,121,527 | 537,102 | 37 | 3 | 30,665 | 1983 |
| 27 | Organizacion Soriana | Torreon, Coah | Self-service | domestic | 1,479,863 | 868,324 | 87 | 5 | 19,621 | 1968 |
| 37 | Grupo Casa Autrey | Mexico, DF | Distribution | domestic | 1,105,169 | 264,897 | 54 | 0 | 7,114 | 1892 |
| 42 | Nadro | Mexico, DF | Distribution | domestic | 1,013,887 | 147,094 | 45 | 0 | 3,524 | 1943 |
| 50 | Liverpool | Mexico, DF | Dept. store | domestic | 835,010 | 286,210 | 27 | 22 | 12,243 | 1944 |
| 52 | Grupo Elektra | Mexico, DF | Self-service | domestic | 806,083 | 517,687 | 53 | 43 | 10,119 | 1950 |
| 56 | Grupo Corvi | Mexico, DF | Distribution | domestic | 723,859 | 120,080 | 48 | 6 | 4,377 | 1979 |
| 57 | Grupo Comercial Chedraui | Xalapa, Veracruz | Self-service | domestic | 683,598 | 184,392 | 32 | 1 | 9,669 | 1987 |
| 78 | Grupo Sanborn's | Mexico, DF | Dept. store | domestic | 469,979 | 273,102 | 43 | 14 | 18,131 | 1919 |
| 84 | Sears Roebuck of Mexico | Mexico, DF | Dept. store | foreign-U.S. | 421,383 | 361,051 | 48 | 62 | 6,652 | 1945 |
| 88 | Far-Ben | Monterrey, N.L. | Self-service | domestic | 411,342 | 119,004 | 52 | 3 | 7,509 | 1917 |
| 90 | Femsa Comercio | Monterrey, N.L. | Self-service | domestic | 375,684 | 95,244 | 69 | 32 | 1,943 | 1979 |
| 98 | Grupo Palacio de Hierro | Mexico, DF | Dept. store | domestic | 302,453 | 213,543 | 33 | 0 | 6,564 | 1989 |
| Average | | | | | 1,145,338 | 381,863 | 47 | 16 | 15,064 | 1952 |

* Position in Expansión 500, 1997.
** Majority ownership domestic or foreign. All domestic firms listed are private sector.
Source: Expansión 500, 1999.

**Table 5.5 Commerce Workforce by Selected States, 1955 and 1988**

| | 1955 | | 1988 | | 1990 | | Commerce Worker-Population Differential. |
| --- | --- | --- | --- | --- | --- | --- | --- |
| | Commerce Workers | Percent of Nation | Commerce Workers (1) | Percent of Nation | Population (2) | Percent of Nation | Difference of (1) and (2). |
| Distrito Federal | 168,146 | 33.9 | 434,862 | 20.0 | 8,213,843 | 10.1 | 9.9 |
| Mexico | 9,975 | 2.0 | 189,539 | 8.7 | 8,285,207 | 10.2 | -1.5 |
| Jalisco | 25,629 | 5.2 | 162,406 | 7.5 | 4,340,432 | 5.3 | 2.1 |
| Veracruz | 25,041 | 5.1 | 126,876 | 5.8 | 3,501,726 | 4.3 | 1.5 |
| Nuevo Leon | 21,863 | 4.4 | 117,142 | 5.4 | 2,850,657 | 3.5 | 1.9 |
| Border States* | 87,978 | 17.8 | 336,485 | 15.5 | 8,363,652 | 10.3 | 5.2 |
| South Region | 22,625 | 4.6 | 139,001 | 6.4 | 3,857,581 | 4.7 | 1.7 |
| Guerrero | 5,730 | 1.2 | 44,978 | 2.1 | 1,369,536 | 1.7 | 0.4 |
| Oaxaca | 9,442 | 1.9 | 47,244 | 2.2 | 1,191,303 | 1.5 | 0.7 |
| Chiapas | 7,453 | 1.5 | 46,779 | 2.2 | 1,296,742 | 1.6 | 0.6 |
| Other Regions | 155,938 | 31.5 | 780,181 | 36.0 | 44,687,204 | 55.0 | -19.0 |
| Total | 495,332 | 100.0 | 2,169,350 | 100.0 | 81,249,645 | 100.0 | |

*Five Border States of Baja California, Sonora, Chihuhua, Coahuila, and Tamaulipas.
Source: Estadisticas Historicas de Mexico, 1994.

commerce sector being concentrated in the center of the Federal District. Surprisingly, the differential for the South is somewhat positive. The rest of the deficit is located in 18 moderately prosperous states (semi-periphery). Those states have fewer cities; tend to be moderate economically; and are less urbanized. Commerce has not extended to those areas. However, its spread may be helped in the future, if national chains such as Cifra/Wal-Mart become more powerful.

The number of commercial enterprises is likewise concentrated in the cities and more so in Mexico City and the central flank. This is seen in Maps 5.2 and 5.3, which show the number of commercial enterprises by municipio for the border region (Map 5.2) and the rest of nation (Map 5.3). In the border region, the largest concentrations are in the city of Monterrey and the major border cities of Tijuana, Mexicali, Ciudad Juaréz, and Nuevo Laredo, as well as Hermosillo and Cajeme/Ciudad Obregon in Sonora, Chihuahua city in Chihuahua, and Torreon and Saltillo in southern Coahuila. For the central region in Map5.2, the commerce corresponds to the large cities (compare Maps 5.2 and 3.3). As expected, the major populations centers of Mexico City, Guadalajara, Leon, Puebla and all the major central cities have especially strong commerce. On a municipio basis, there are no surprises regarding commerce enterprises; it corresponds to the major northern and central cities, but is more weighted towards the center.

**Map 5.2**
**Number of Commercial Enterprises,**
**Border Region, Mexico, 1994**

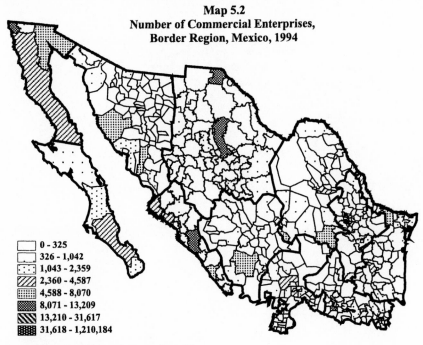

| | |
|---|---|
| ☐ | 0 - 325 |
| ☐ | 326 - 1,042 |
| ☐ | 1,043 - 2,359 |
| ▨ | 2,360 - 4,587 |
| ▦ | 4,588 - 8,070 |
| ▨ | 8,071 - 13,209 |
| ▨ | 13,210 - 31,617 |
| ▨ | 31,618 - 1,210,184 |

Map Source: INEGI, Censos Economicos, 1994
Note: The Map 5.3 depicts the Number of
Commercial Enterprises, Central Region, 1994

**Map 5.3**
**Number of Commercial**
**Enterprises, Central Region,**
**1994**

0 – 326
326 - 1043
1043 - 2360
2360 - 4588
4588 - 8071
8071 - 13210
13210 - 31618
31618 - 1210184

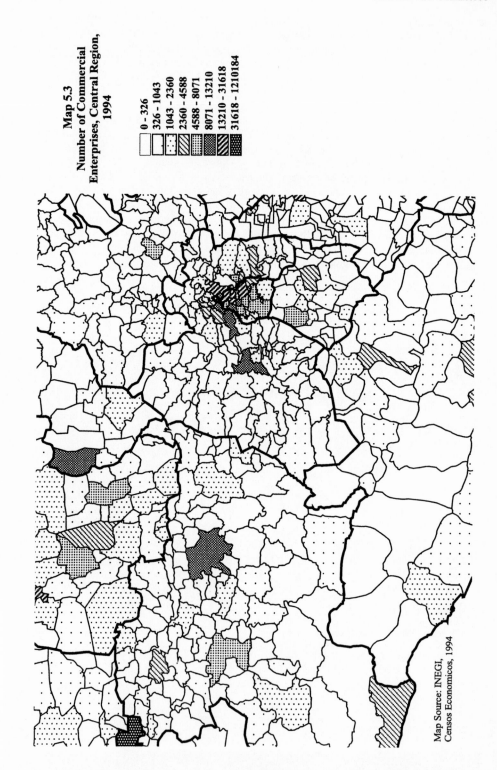

Map Source: INEGI,
Censos Economicos, 1994

As seen in Map 5.4, commerce sector revenues are highly concentrated in the northern Federal District. In fact, it is hyper-concentrated in a few central delegations. The central delegations of Cuauhtemoc, Miguel Hidalgo, Benito Juarez, and Iztapalapa account for about a fifth of commerce revenues for the nation. This core area of Mexico City in a sense constitutes the commerce business center of the nation. This business center has more wholesale emphasis than retail. For instance, when commerce revenues are divided into wholesale and retail for Mexico City, they appear more concentrated in wholesale in the northern Federal District and northwestern parts of Mexico City, while retail is somewhat more prevalent in other areas (see Map 5.5).

Nationally, the size of commercial enterprises has influenced its geographical patterning. There is not space in this book to discuss the geography of the many finer differences between large and small enterprises and subsectors within commerce. One example of such fine distinction is the distribution of workforce per small enterprise, in particular the ratio of number of small enterprise workers to small enterprises. These small enterprises are ones reporting to the economic census of INEGI, so most of the informal sector is missed. The commerce distribution by municipio is shown for the border states in Map 5.6 and for the central region in Map 5.7. There is a loose correspondence to major cities (compare with Map 3.3), but many broad areas that are not major cities now have higher workforce proportions. In Chihuahua, there is a corridor of high small area worker intensities that runs from the border to south of Chihuahua City. The central flank areas with high small enterprise work intensities are northeastern Jalisco, northwestern Sate of Mexico and large parts of Guanajuato and Queretaro. The state of Michoacan and the south also have high proportions. This characteristic reflects patterns of small enterprises that are much more spread out in the semi-periphery and periphery of the nation than for larger enterprises. The spreading out of small enterprise patterns is not surprising, since such small commerce enterprises are sustainable in markets anywhere in the nation.

**Map 5.4**
**Commerce Sector Revenues, Mexico City, 1993**
**(in thousands of pesos)**

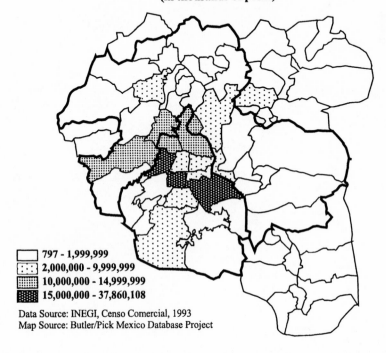

- ☐ 797 - 1,999,999
- ⠿ 2,000,000 - 9,999,999
- ▦ 10,000,000 - 14,999,999
- ▓ 15,000,000 - 37,860,108

Data Source: INEGI, Censo Comercial, 1993
Map Source: Butler/Pick Mexico Database Project

**Map 5.5**
**Proportion Wholesale of**
**Commerce Revenues, Mexico City, 1993**

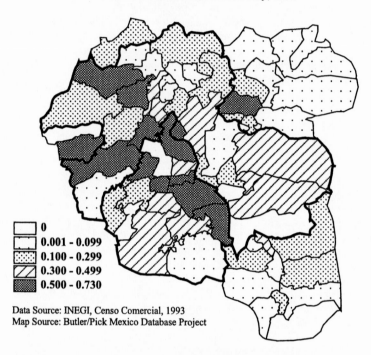

- ☐ 0
- ☐ 0.001 - 0.099
- ☐ 0.100 - 0.299
- ▨ 0.300 - 0.499
- ▨ 0.500 - 0.730

Data Source: INEGI, Censo Comercial, 1993
Map Source: Butler/Pick Mexico Database Project

**Map 5.6**
**Average Number of Workers Per**
**Small Enterprise in Commerce, Mexico, 1994**

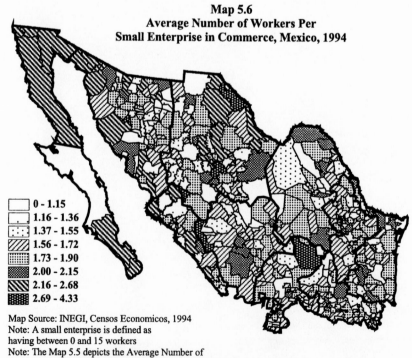

- ☐ 0 - 1.15
- ☐ 1.16 - 1.36
- ☐ 1.37 - 1.55
- ▨ 1.56 - 1.72
- ▦ 1.73 - 1.90
- ▨ 2.00 - 2.15
- ▨ 2.16 - 2.68
- ▨ 2.69 - 4.33

Map Source: INEGI, Censos Economicos, 1994
Note: A small enterprise is defined as
having between 0 and 15 workers
Note: The Map 5.5 depicts the Average Number of
Workers Per Small Enterprise in Commerce, Mexico, 1994

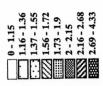

Map 5.7
Average Number of
Workers Per Small
Enterprise in Commerce,
Central Region, 1994

0 - 1.15
1.16 - 1.36
1.37 - 1.55
1.56 - 1.72
1.73 - 1.9
2 - 2.15
2.16 - 2.68
2.69 - 4.33

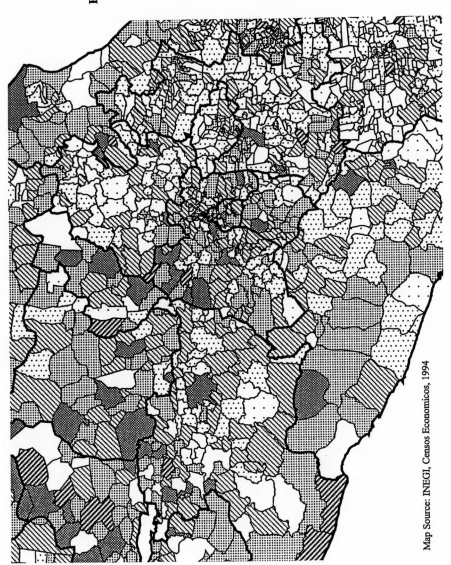

Map Source: INEGI, Censos Economicos, 1994

In summary, the commerce sector is geographically concentrated in the northern and central cities, especially the latter, and even more so in Mexico City. Within Mexico City, commerce is concentrated in the traditional business city center and has a stronger wholesale aspect. There are other patterns evident for small business, which extends out more broadly across the semi-peripheral and peripheral areas.

### Banking Sector

The Mexican banking sector is crucial to the success of the economy. The banking sector also is important to the manufacturing sector covered in Chapter 4 and to the commerce sector. The Mexican banking industry is even more important to the commerce sector versus manufacturing, since commerce has a smaller proportion of foreign ownership and, for Mexican owned firms, less foreign debt (see Table 5.4). The commerce sector suffered in the 1990s due to the credit crunch, resulting from the nation's banking crisis. This section delineates history of the Mexican banking industry in the past several decades leading up to its present crisis status. It discusses how, after a decade of nationalization, foreign interests have reentered into the picture and in some sense are rescuing the faltering industry.

In the period of the Mexican debt crisis in the early 1980s, there was pressure to rid the then privatized banks of inefficiencies and even "mismanagement" (Febre Pruneda 1999). In 1982, all of the banking industry was nationalized. The banks were run by the government for nearly a decade. In the late 1980s, the government began to realize many of its protective policies were failing, and in the late years of the De La Madrid Administration, winds of change began to circulate pointing to greater privatization and opening up of the economy. One of the consequences was the re-privatization of the banks in the early Salinas Administration in 1991-92. However, the privatization was not well thought out in the sense of preparation and management abilities of the buyers to run the banks. Rich tycoons bought the banks and in some cases did not have the necessary experience in banking. This was most extreme in the case of the new manager Jorge Lankenau of Grupo Financiero Abaco-Confía. He was later jailed for taking 170 million dollars from the Confía group (U.S. Mexico Business 1998). Two other notorious cases of mis-management were the owner of Crim-Unión, Carlos Cabal Peniche, who was ousted by regulators on corruption charges and Angel Rodrígues Sáez, owner of Asemix-Banpaís, who was later arrested for mismanagement. Even some owners with extensive business experience did not fare well in banking. For instance, the experienced Sada family of Monterrey controlled Serfín, but it did not perform well in the 1990s, leading eventually to government-imposed sale of the bank.

The situation of faltering management was exacerbated by the peso crisis of 1994. The financial losses were enormous for middle class Mexicans, who were unable to pay their mortgages, loans, and credit card bills. The results were huge amounts of non-performing loans. The amount of these non-performing loans led to the formation of Fobaproa, a government entity to bail out the banking industry, and roughly equivalent to the role of the Resolution Trust Corporation in the Savings and Loan crisis in the U.S. in the 1980s.

The magnitude of the loan losses is staggering. As seen in Table 5.6, the total loan losses and the ratio of bank bailout cost to PIB have increased since the peso crisis. By March, 1999, Fobaproa had non-performing loan portfolios of 686 billion pesos, equivalent to 75 billion dollars (INEGI 1999; Krueger and Tornell 1999). This is equal to about one sixth of PIB!

The non-performing loans were weighted in certain economy sectors. As seen in Table 5.7, the worst ratios of non-performing loans were for durable consumer goods and non-bank intermediaries, where about a half of loans were non-performing. Corporations have done a little better than households; yet have a quarter of non-performing loans. This chart underscores that whole segments of the economy defaulted en masse.

#### Table 5.6 Gross Domestic Product (PIB) and Mexican Government Estimated Cost of the Banking Bailout Package

| Year | PIB* | Cost of Bank Bailout -Year End* | Ratio of Bailout Cost to PIB |
|------|------|--------------------------------|------------------------------|
| 1995 | 394,983 | 21,724 | 5.5 |
| 1996 | 415,378 | 34,892 | 8.4 |
| 1997 | 444,481 | NA | NA |
| 1998 | 464,127 | 75,189 | 16.2 |

*in millions of U.S. dollars.

Sources: INEGI, 1999; Krueger and Tornell, 1999.

#### Table 5.7 Ratio of Nonperforming Loans to Total Loans, Mexican Banks, 1995-1997

| Category of Loan | 1995 | 1996 | 1997 |
|------------------|------|------|------|
| Corporate | 18.5 | 21.9 | 27.0 |
| Households | 12.0 | 18.3 | 38.0 |
| -Consumption | 25.2 | 34.2 | 28.3 |
| -credit cards | 19.5 | 23.0 | 19.1 |
| -durable consumer goods | 44.2 | 67.1 | 55.6 |
| -Housing | 7.9 | 12.2 | 42.0 |
| Non-bank intermediaries | 10.7 | 28.9 | 49.4 |
| Average | 10.7 | 28.9 | 49.4 |

Source: Informes Anuales del Banco de Mexico, 1995-1997.

Fobaproa and the government tried to deal with the crisis in a number of ways. Fobaproa has sold off a number of banks to domestic and foreign entities, and others have been purchased by foreign banks. Of the 18 banks that the government sold to Mexican buyers in 1991/1992, only three have survived in the original form and remain independent in 1999. These are Bancomer, Banamex, and Banorte. However, Bancomer is in Process of merger with Spain's Banco Bilboa Vizcaya. Among the foreign acquisitions were Banco Confía by Citibank, and Banco Inverlat by Bank of Nova Scotia. It is important to recognize that Fobaproa could have dealt more sternly with this crisis, including letting some of the banks go bankrupt, nationalizing some of the problematic banks, and/or getting rid of poor management. Fobaproa was not able to take these stronger steps.

Although the banking industry in 1998 was still mostly under Mexican ownership, about a third of the top 15 banks are foreign (U.S. or Spain), and Serfin and Bancomer are likely to fall to foreign hands (see Table 5.8). Of the remaining largest banks, others will likely be taken over by foreigners over the next five years.

The federal government has taken steps to counter the adverse effects of the devaluation. One was to continue to liberalize following the crisis, in order the reassure businesses and investors about the adverse effects. Among the steps taken were the continuing effort to privatize ports, airports, highways, and railroads (Krueger and Tornell 1999). Telecomm services have continued to be opened and more foreign ownership restrictions have been lifted (Krueger and Tornell 1999).

**Table 5.8 Mexico's Top 15 Banks, 1998**

**(in millions of pesos)**

| Rank | Bank | Assets | Percent of Industry | Capital | Percent of Industry | Country of Ownership |
|---|---|---|---|---|---|---|
| 1 | Bancomer* | 252,750 | 20.8 | 19,665 | 19.2 | Mexico* |
| 2 | Banamex | 251,829 | 20.7 | 26,410 | 25.8 | Mexico |
| 3 | Serfin** | 165,109 | 13.6 | 9,186 | 9.0 | Mexico* |
| 4 | Bital | 102,842 | 8.4 | 6,200 | 6.1 | Mexico |
| 5 | Santander Mexicano | 77,602 | 6.4 | 5,017 | 4.9 | Spain |
| 6 | Banco Bilbao Viscaya | 69,182 | 5.7 | 4,695 | 4.6 | Spain |
| 7 | Banorte | 39,203 | 3.2 | 4,046 | 4.0 | Mexico |
| 8 | Banpais | 35,419 | 2.9 | 10,578 | 10.3 | Mexico |
| 9 | Centro | 28,446 | 2.3 | 1,296 | 1.3 | Mexico |
| 10 | Citibank | 27,698 | 2.3 | 1,904 | 1.9 | U.S. |
| 11 | Inbursa | 22,327 | 1.8 | 1,212 | 1.2 | Mexico |
| 12 | Interaccions | 11,483 | 0.9 | 381 | 0.4 | Mexico |
| 13 | Afirme | 5,944 | 0.5 | 439 | 0.4 | Mexico |
| 14 | J.P. Morgan | 4,236 | 0.3 | 1,392 | 1.4 | U.S. |
| 15 | Invex | 3,767 | 0.3 | 441 | 0.4 | Mexico |
| | Industry Total | 1,217,486 | 100.0 | 102,421 | 100.0 | |

* In process of being merged with Spain's Banco Bilboa Vizcaya.
** In process of being sold off by federal government agency, IPAB.

Source: Mexican National Banking and Securities Commission, 1999.

Another set of procedures have been Fobaproa measures to provide relief to banks and debtors. Among the steps have been (1) to absorb a significant proportion of the bad loans i.e. through Fobaproa; (2) to give certain types of relief to debtors, and (3) to assist the banks with dollar liquidity (Krueger and Tornell 1999). However, the effects of both the open economy and "bank bailout" program have been mixed. Many critics have been concerned about the favoritism shown by Fobaproa to certain large individual creditors.

For the successor banks that remain under foreign or domestic ownership, there are challenges. One of the factors is that there are too many banks for a nation of Mexico's size. With too many banks, the average deposit size has been reduced. Non-performing loans remain very high; one estimate is 18 percent (U.S./Mexico Business 1998). This operating problem is exacerbated by the need to market and advertise aggressively which drives up costs. At the same time, there are too few bank branches.

In spite of its intentions, Fobaproa has opened up conflict of interest and other problems. The Mexican federal legislature debated these problems and in spring of 1999 decided to replace Fobaproa with IFAB. IFAB's charge is to clean up the mess created by Fobaproa and to address the pressing needs of banks' operating problems.

What are the overall lessons to be learned from two decades of disruption, shocks, and deficiencies in the Mexican banking system? First of all, the crisis was provoked originally by trying to peg the peso to the dollar. A lesson for a developing nation such as Mexico is to let the currency float, so a large "hiccup" of adjustment will not be necessary. Another lesson is that just removing non-performing assets from bank portfolios is not enough. It is also necessary to set standards to assure that non-performance will not recur (Krueger and Tornell 1999).

The very bad credit crunch created by this crisis has particularly adversely impacted certain segments, not the larger export-oriented firms but rather small firms that are dependent on national lending. In spite of the ups and downs of the past two decades in banking, the nation's economy has survived and is fairly robust at the end of the century. A surprising lesson is that a viable banking system is not necessary for a developing nation.

One of the reasons is growing globalization, so many larger firms are either already multinationals, not dependent on local capital, or able to obtain loans overseas to sustain growth.

The case studies of Bancomext and Bancomer that follow highlight two aspects of the somber banking and credit picture. Bancomext exemplifies a nationalized bank that is supposed to place export ahead of everything else, but is finding itself pinched economically. Bancomer is a leader in Mexican banking that has been able to weather the storms of the past ten years partly through its foreign partnerships.

## Geography of Banking

It is important to consider the geographical distribution of banking. In 1998, there were 6,110 bank offices and branches in Mexico. This network is not adequate to serve a population of nearly 100 million and a land area of more than two million kilometers. Other nations have higher ratios of bank locations to population. For instance, the ratio for Korea is 2.2 times higher; the U.S is 6.2 times higher, and Canada and Spain are 16 times higher. Mexico also has substantially lower ratio of bank accounts per person compared to most other nations.

The regional differences in banking are seen in Table 5.9 and Map 5.8. It is clear that bank deposits are hyper-concentrated in the Federal District and sparse in the more remote areas in the Bajio, south, and southeast. Fifty eight percent of bank deposits is in the Federal District, and another fifteen percent in Jalisco, Nuevo Leon, and State of Mexico. A similar pattern is evident for bank locations; however, bank locations for the three major metropolitan states of Federal District, Jalisco, and Nuevo Leon and the northern border states are more favorable, compared to the rest of the nation. These inequalities are similar to inequalities in PIB, but are even more exaggerated.

A result of the deficit of banking, especially in the rural and remote areas, is inability to serve the banking needs of the people. Hence, those areas have a harder time funding appropriate infrastructure, and may not be able to diversify their economic base. This may contribute to discontent, outmigration, and social problems.

It is also important to point out that the banking deposits, bank locations, and bank assets are concentrated in relatively few large banks located in the Federal District (see Table 5.8). As seen in Figure 5.4, on a variety of parameters, the Federal District is disproportionate in its banking role. This adds to the challenge of providing widespread banking throughout Mexico.

## Cifra/Wal-Mart: a Global Counter Example

Cifra was founded in 1938 by Jerónimo Arango. He had studied discount retailing in the U.S. and in 1958 started the first Aurrerá discount department store. In 1966, the Chicago-based retailer Jewel purchased 49 percent of Cifra, an association that lasted until 1984, when Jewel sold its interest back to the Arango family (Poole 1998). Cifra grew beyond Aurrerá to encompass stores under the names of Bodega, Suburbia, Superama, as well as the VIP restaurant chain. Stores include combinations of discount and self service department stores, supermarkets, hypermarkets, and clothing stores. The VIP restaurant chain is the largest in Mexico in seating capacity, with 33,500 customers. Cifra has historically and up to present been located mostly in Mexico City and the central region of Mexico.

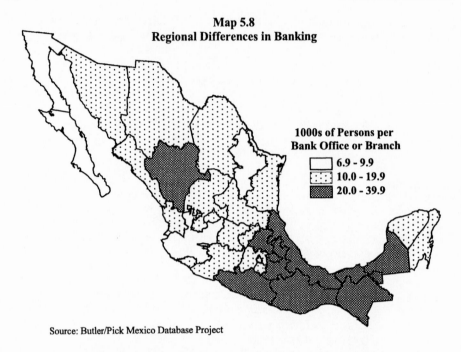

**Map 5.8**
**Regional Differences in Banking**

**1000s of Persons per**
**Bank Office or Branch**
  6.9 - 9.9
  10.0 - 19.9
  20.0 - 39.9

Source: Butler/Pick Mexico Database Project

**Figure 5.4 Banking Imbalances: Federal District's Share Versus**
**the Rest of Mexico**

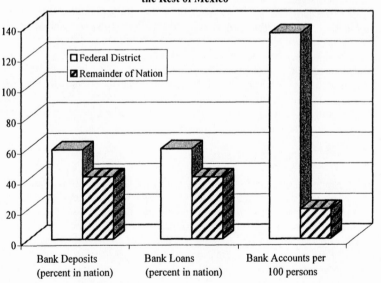

Source: Febre Pruneda, 1999.

In 1991, Cifra restored an association with a U.S. company, in this case by a joint venture with the retailer giant Wal-Mart. The joint venture opened 145 new stores including 18 Wal-Mart Supercenters, 28 Sam's Clubs, and 99 Cifra units. The number of stores nearly doubled the number Cifra had before the joint venture. Among the mistakes by the joint venture was stocking the stores with Mexican goods, whereas Mexican customers were expecting U.S.-made goods (Poole 1998).

The shock of the peso crisis of 1994 reinforced this strategy since an outcome of the crisis was that U.S. goods became too pricy for Mexican consumers, so the joint venture had to emphasize Mexican goods to a greater extent. Because this threw off Wal-Mart's strategy's, Wal-Mart cut back on its expansion plans in Mexico. Cifra's market share dropped after the peso crisis by about ten percent.

**Table 5.9 Regional Differences in Banking**

| State | Percent of Bank Deposits | 1000s of Persons per Bank Office or Branch |
|---|---|---|
| Distrito Federal | 58.80 | 6.9 |
| Jalisco | 7.00 | 9.6 |
| Nuevo Leon | 4.86 | 8.5 |
| State of Mexico | 3.55 | 15.8 |
| Guanajuato | 2.43 | 16.3 |
| Michoacan | 2.09 | 15.7 |
| San Luis Potosi | 1.97 | 17.7 |
| Veracruz | 1.82 | 26.4 |
| B. California Norte | 1.51 | 9.4 |
| Tamaulipas | 1.48 | 11.2 |
| Purbla | 1.48 | 24.2 |
| Chihuahua | 1.34 | 12.5 |
| Sinaloa | 1.30 | 16.2 |
| Sonora | 1.15 | 10.8 |
| Coahuila | 1.05 | 11.7 |
| Chiapas | 0.83 | 38.0 |
| Guerrero | 0.77 | 25.3 |
| Hidalgo | 0.69 | 28.2 |
| Oaxaca | 0.68 | 39.3 |
| Morelos | 0.63 | 18.3 |
| Zacatecas | 0.59 | 16.9 |
| Queretaro | 0.57 | 12.7 |
| Aguascalientes | 0.54 | 12.5 |
| Yucatan | 0.53 | 19.7 |
| Durango | 0.44 | 24.7 |
| Tabasco | 0.40 | 22.7 |
| Nayarit | 0.35 | 18.7 |
| Colima | 0.28 | 11.3 |
| Quintana Roo | 0.28 | 14.1 |
| Tlaxcala | 0.22 | 23.2 |
| B. California Sur | 0.21 | 9.9 |
| Campeche | 0.19 | 22.9 |
| Total Bank Deposits | 893,605.00 | |
| Average | 3.13 | 17.9 |

Source: Febre Pruneda, 1998.

The Wal-Mart purchase represents globalization. Wal-Mart is the number three firm in the U.S. Fortune 500, with 1999 estimated sales at $138 billion and estimated income of $4.4 billion. It has nearly one million employees. From Wal-Mart's perspective the Cifra acquisition solidified its largest overseas expansion. In fact, the 416 Cifra/Wal-Mart stores constitute 12 percent of Wal-Mart's 3,599 stores. Mexico is by far its largest foreign presence, constituting about three fifths of its foreign units.

In 1997, Wal-Mart Stores purchased control of Cifra for $1.2 billion. With the Mexican economy improving, Wal-Mart/Cifra started a large expansion, mostly of Bodegas, Aurrerás and Wal-Marts (Poole 1998).

Among the fundamental questions raised are the extent of standard format Wal-Mart wishes to maintain overseas, and the extent of U.S. versus Mexican goods that the Mexican customer seeks. Wal-Mart's famous warehousing and inventory technology will help Cifra/Wal-Mart expand and compete strongly on costs. Nevertheless, there is a period of transition, in which the Cifra technology and systems need to be merged with the advanced Wal-Mart systems. It will probably be several years before there is unified Cifra/Wal-Mart corporate technology and systems. At that point, the company may move rapidly to parts of Mexico away from its traditional central region. The competitive capability that will emerge will put pressure on the largely Mexican owned sector and on traditional companies even ones as strong as Liverpool. More foreign takeovers may be in the making as a consequence of this strategic threat.

### Case Study: El Puerto de Liverpool

El Puerto de Liverpool is a 150 year old company with ties to Europe that has not only survived but prospered in the contemporary competitive, global environment. The company represents many of the trends in commerce discussed in this chapter, but also demonstrates cutting edge strength to compete nationally, but not internationally.

Liverpool was founded by a French immigrant, Juan Bautista Ebrard, in 1847 in Mexico City. The original small store, called El Cajón de Ropa, emphasized clothing imports from France and Europe. The company grew and prospered in the 19th century; it even served customers during the brief French rule of Maximilian. In 1875, the first Puerto de Liverpool department store was opened in an elegant building in downtown Mexico City. "Liverpool" was chosen as a name because of its fame as a port of embarkation of goods for North America. This store set a tone of high quality goods, prestigious imports, association with French and European designers, and attention to customers that has carried through to today.

In the post World War II period, the company grew and changed. In the 1960s, a second store, Liverpool Insurgentes, was opened. The company went public and was listed on the Mexican stock exchange, although descendents of the founding family including the present chairman M. Michel remain involved. In the 70s, the firm opened a distribution center in Mexico City. A new business idea for Liverpool in the 80s was to develop and manage shopping centers; naturally a Liverpool store served as one of the anchors. The first such shopping center was Perisur in 1980. The new Liverpool anchor store was surrounded by 150 smaller stores and shops, with the entire space managed by Liverpool. Two years later, the firm opened a store outside Mexico City for the first time, in Villahermosa, Tabasco.

In 1985, Liverpool purchased Fábricas de Francia, a 120 year old Guadalajara company that had smaller and less expensive stores mostly in the western States. In the early 90s other Liverpool locations were started in Mexico City, including the firm-managed shopping centers of Centro Comercial Galerías Coapa in the south and Centro

Comercial Galerías Insurgentes, as well as in the new shopping center of Santa Fe. The new Polanco department store included an advanced computer center.

A new distribution center was initiated in 1993 in Tultitlán in northern Mexico City. This distribution center is highly automated and one of the most advanced in North America. The world class facility was built by Allan Bradley based on U.S. and European technology. With only 200 workers, it handles 288,000 pieces of merchandise daily. It is connected by a wide area network to the company's 28 stores and distribution centers.

The center is container-based, so small and medium sized merchandise is put in containers and moved automatically through the center and onto trucks for transport. Bar code labels are put on the containers and on large merchandise items. The labels are scanned throughout the distribution process. A small percent of arriving items are pre-bar coded. EDI (Electronic Data Interchange) is commonly utilized for exchanges with larger companies.

Recently Liverpool added other technological enhancements. It started in 1998 an automated Center of Telecom Customer Support that provides telephone sales, promotions, customer service, and a suggestion line. It has opened an e-commerce site that initially offered books, CDs, perfumes, and cosmetics. The firm's ConSENTIDO was opened, which is a point-based system in partnership with prestigious travel, vacation, and car rental offerings.

Most goods are from international sources. About one third are purchased overseas mostly in the U.S., Canada, Germany, and Hong Kong. However, the company also owns a clothing "maquila" that imports raw materials and design from the U.S., but unlike most "maquilas," sells domestically i.e. mostly to Liverpool. The "maquila" is a way to average costs for overseas products. About one third of the supply comes from Mexico. The firm serves domestic markets, in particular only ten percent of goods are exported.

Geographically, Liverpool stores are concentrated in Mexico City, which has seven stores, and in the central region (See Map 5.9). Recently some stores have opened in the southeast. Fábricas de Francia, on the other hand, is mostly in the western part of Mexico, including three stores in metropolitan Guadalajara.

Liverpool is highly successful and financially powerful. Its sales in 1998 were 1.1 billion dollars, with a profit of 102 million dollars. It has large amounts of cash and property, and owns real estate including shopping centers and land holdings in many cities for future development. The geographical reach of the firm parallels that of commerce in general, with hyper-concentration in Mexico City and emphasis on the central region and largest cities. The company's financial strength, appeal to customers, and world-class technology demonstrate that the traditional commercial firm can be modernized to be competitive. Currently, it has mainly domestic competition since Confía/Wal-Mart mostly serves a lower sector. However, if global commerce enters Mexico, El Puerto de Liverpool should be well positioned to compete.

### Case Study: Bancomext

Bancomext is the Mexican government's import/export bank, with an emphasis on export. It is 60 years old and has emphasized financing of Mexican exports. There is not an analogy in the U.S. of a comprehensive bank promoting exports. Instead, the functions are spread around to commercial banks, non-profits, and government agencies. Bancomext has helped stimulate the large growth in exports of the past 20 years discussed in Chapter 3. In order to sustain itself, the bank has also moved somewhat into regular commercial loans. In recent years, it has had a large proportion of non-performing loans and has had to cut back on riskier lending.

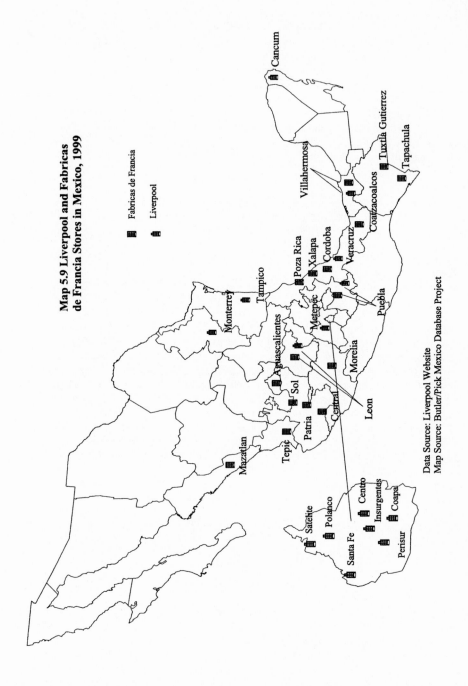

**Map 5.9 Liverpool and Fabricas de Francia Stores in Mexico, 1999**

Fabricas de Francia
Liverpool

Cancum

Tuxtla Gutierrez

Tapachula

Villahermosa

Coatzacoalcos

Poza Rica
Xalapa
Cordoba
Veracruz

Tampico

Metepec

Puebla

Monterrey

Aguascalientes

Morelia

Sol

Central

Leon

Patria

Tepic

Mazatlan

Satelite

Polanco

Centro
Insurgentes
Coapa

Santa Fe

Perisur

Data Source: Liverpool Website
Map Source: Butler/Pick Mexico Database Project

Bancomext is part of the export office of the federal government, SECOFI and its Chairman is the Minister of Finance. At the same time, Bancomext has its own offices and an experienced management staff. Its principal goal is to provide Mexican export firms with a full package of support including loans, consulting on the market, computer systems, technical assistance, and advice. Its goal is to stimulate over 100 billion dollars in annual Mexican exports. The target company for Bancomext is a smaller firm that is planning on starting an export thrust. When a client has matured and is self-sufficient in export, Bancomext ceases its help and refers the company to other banks. Bancomext success stories of support to clients include Cemex, Vitro, and Bimbo. Today those firms are self sufficient and have substantial offices and exports overseas.

Bancomext has shifted to medium and smaller sized companies as clients for several reasons. One is that it perceives that globalization is moving to the level of smaller businesses. Secondly, the banking crisis has caused a credit shortage to smaller firms. Because of this, Bancomext may also provide direct credit not just for foreign export but also for domestic operations of smaller firms.

Bancomext provides workshops for foreign firms and a large number for domestic ones. It also supports fairs and export-related events. It has personnel located in 36 offices in dozens of foreign nations. These personnel carry diplomatic passports and are attached to Mexican embassies and consulates.

Bancomext is serving a client base of around 10,000 small and medium sized export businesses. There is a large base of 50,000 customers of the full services of the bank, which include credit, consulting, information, and training. Most loans Bancomext has provided are to commercial banks, which in turn loan funds to small and medium sized firms allowing them to develop as exporting entities.

A more recent area of banking activity is direct loans to companies and lending to private banks such as Bancomer, Serfin, etc. The yearly amounts of direct loans in the mid 1990s averaged $5 billion and have lowered due to loan losses. However, this reduction would be in line with a general industry-wide reduction in direct loans. In 1996, Bancomext provided $13 billion in loans, with half in direct credit granted to commercial banks and half direct loans. However, direct loan amounts and total credit grants have decreased in recent years (Gutiérrez and Gatsiopoulos 1999). This is because bad loans increased and in 1998 were over 700 million dollars, causing Bancomext to cut off many direct loans to its export clients.

One of Bancomext's goals is to increase the Mexican content of exported products. It is attempting to help develop the quality and productivity of suppliers to large exporting corporations. For example, if a Mexican supplier gains the approval of General Motors, it immediately becomes a worldwide supplier; Bancomext aims to help the supplier firm obtain the approval. For suppliers directly exporting, Bancomext helps them link to the global chain of buyers and sellers and to increase product quality in order to compete. Most emphasis is on the U.S. market, since it is nearby, but Bancomext also focuses on Latin America, which has market similarities and, to a lesser extent, Europe.

In summary, Bancomext represents an unusual federal bank extending beyond normal banking roles to "nurture" firms for the global export market, especially the U.S. It provides information, consulting, workshops, and training, as well as contacts. It has had mixed success, with major contributions to export including some notable firms nurtured into world producers, but had problems of over-extension of direct loans and loan losses. It is still sorting out its true role vis a vis the government and private sector.

## Case Study: Bancomer

Bancomer is one of the two largest commercial banks in Mexico (see Table 5.8 and Figure 5.5). It remains in Mexican control and yet has formed important overseas alliances that have helped it to get through the banking crisis period. It is currently in process of merging with Spain's Banco Bilbao Vizcaya Argenaria, creating Mexico's largest bank, BBVA-Bancomer. BBVA will have a 40 percent stake.

Bancomer serves the national domestic market. It has the largest branches and ATM networks in Mexico, with over 1,200 branches and 2,000 ATMs. It has done little intside of the U.S., due to regulations and other constraints, but has entered a small amount of NAFTA-related "niche banking."

Bancomer was founded in 1932 as Banco de Comercio. It grew by purchase and consolidation. When Bancomer was privatized in 1991, a group of well known Mexican businessmen gained control. Today, the government owns 10 percent of shares and Banco de Montreal owns 16 percent.

Bancomer's principal focus is on providing a full range of banking services to customers throughout its broad geographic network, the largest of any bank in Mexico. To support the domestic network, it has a medium level of technology, which is average or somewhat below average by U.S. standards. At the same time it has entered into strategic alliances with ventures and companies in the U.S. and Canada. In 1996, it established a strategic alliance with Bank of Montreal. Thus, Bancomer received the support of one of the ten strongest banks in North America. This also provided some U.S. banking ties, since the Harris Bank of Chicago is a subsidiary of the Montreal bank. Although this tie has limited benefit today, it can lead to more activity internally in the future.

There are several other international alliances:

- Joint venture with Aetna. Bancomer and Aetna have a joint venture in owning a large Mexican insurance company, Valores Monterrey Aetna (VAMSA). VAMSA is a national insurance leader and provides Bancomer with counter-cyclical diversification, and participation in growth of the dynamic insurance sector.
- Alliance with Aetna to Administer Retirement Funds. In 1996, Bancomer and Aetna formed a strategic alliance to administer federal retirement funds known as AFORE. To this administration, Bancomer contributes its large computer network and prior experience in retirement funds. Contribution of this alliance is to lower the operating costs of the Bancomer branch and computer network infrastructure.
- Alliance with Commercial Credit Corporation. In 1996, Bancomer and Commercial Credit Corporation, subsidiary of Travelers Group, formed a strategic alliance to develop consumer credit in Mexico targeting low income customers.
- Partnership with the U.S. Postal Service for Electronic Mail Transfer. This partnership was formed so that money could be transferred electronically and securely from selected U.S. postal offices to Bancomer. This particular service covers the U.S. southwest.
- Alliance with Alestra. Bancomer controls 26 percent of Alestra, a national phone company that provides AT&T phone products, based on a modern network in Mexico. This alliance is discussed in the Alestra case study in Chapter 7.
- Proposed merger with Spain's BBVA. The merged entity BBVA-Bancomer will be 40 percent controlled by BBVA.

**Figure 5.5 Bancomer\* Transnational Relationships**

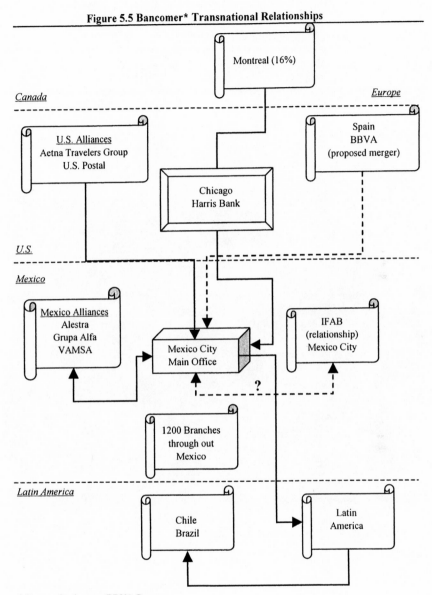

\* Proposed to become BBVA-Bancomer

In conclusion, Bancomer is a banking leader with the most extensive geographic presence in Mexico. In the mid and late 1990s, it has had very difficult times because of large loan defaults and some implications of money laundering. It has, however, diversified itself through a series of international partnerships and alliances with very high quality U.S. and Canadian organizations. Its global thrust is not in marketing its products overseas, but participating in various alliances, mostly U.S. and Canadian, that assist in participating in the Mexican market. Through the proposed merger with BBVA it would solidify its number one position, but have two-fifths foreign control.

# 6

# Services

- **Introduction**
- **Educational Services**
- **Health Services**
- **Social Services and Poverty**
- **Financial and Insurance Services**
- **Business, Accounting, Legal, and Information Services**
- **Personal Services**
- **Conclusions**
- **Case Study: Seguros Comercial America**
- **Case Study: IBM/Mexico**

## Introduction

Services form a crucially important element in Mexico. As the nation aspires to be more advanced, services expand in importance. For instance, in proportion, the U.S. workforce in service related occupations grew from one third in 1920 to two thirds in 1980 (Ott 1987). Similar increases may be expected in the 21st century in Mexico as its economy advances further and globalizes.

This chapter discusses services overall and specific service sectors. Some service sectors are included as parts of other chapters, such as automotive repair (Chapter 4), banking (Chapter 5), communications and transport (Chapter 7), tourism (Chapter 10), and the informal sector (Chapter 12). This chapter focuses on education, health and social services, non-bank financial services, information and business services, and personal services. In this and other chapters, the book covers all the tertiary sector categories from the NACE rev. 1 list from the European Union (see Illeris 1996), with the exception of public administration and diplomacy/international organizations. However, some of the global policy aspects of those items are discussed as parts of Chapters 14 and 15. All of this service-related discussion meets the defining characteristics of services: (1) users participate in its production, (2) labor intensive activities, depending on the skill of the personnel, (3) no well-defined product that can be measured, and (4) services are unique each time (Illeris 1996).

An important element of services in Mexico is the extent of government versus private involvement. Some nations over the past half century have reduced the role of government in services. Through privatization or outsourcing, they have transferred large amounts of services to the private sector. For instance, in Latin America, there has been a trend over the past fifteen years to privatize health care services (Economist 1999). Although there are advantages, this creates several problems. One is the reluctance in certain cases for the government and citizenry to agree to privatize. A second problem is that private groups taking over the management of former government entities after privatization may not be capable of managing. An example of this problem was discussed in the last chapter for the Mexican banking industry in the early to mid 1990s.

Another issue discussed in this chapter is the concentration of services in Mexico City. For instance, 29 percent of service workers in 1990 were located in Mexico City, seven percent higher than the economically active population (Pick and Butler 1997). This becomes a hyperconcentration in certain sectors such as in higher education and non-bank financial services. This geographical concentration needs to be examined relative to the overall differences of advanced and peripheral parts of Mexico and how it relates to globalization trends.

The chapter concludes with two case studies. The Seguros Comercial America case illustrates a traditional company in the Mexican service industry of insurance that is preparing itself for greater foreign competition. The second case of IBM illustrates both services and manufacturing. On the service side, IBM has been largely a success story and a leading company in providing information processing services, even under the cloud of a botched consulting job for the Mexico City government. The manufacturing side of this case study relates to Chapter 4 and other sections of the book.

The overall concentration of services is seen in service and support occupations in 1990. There were 7,524,060 workers in service and support occupations, out of an economically active population of 24,063,283, or 31.3 percent (Pick and Butler 1994). This compares to service sector as a proportion of total employment of 71.1 percent for the U.S. in 1991, 58.2 percent for Japan in 1992, and 63.5 percent for Germany in 1991 (ILO 1993). As a semi-peripheral nation, Mexico's service sector is smaller and less elaborate than in advanced countries. Geographically within Mexico, the service sector is concentrated most heavily in Mexico City, Baja California, and Nuevo Leon (Monterrey), while it has low levels in the Bajio, eastern states, and the south region (see Map 6.1). There is a striking resemblance to the map of Mexico states by development level (see Map 3.2), although the border states of Nuevo Leon, Baja California, and Baja Sur are especially high in services.

**Map 6.1**
**Service and Support**
**Occupations, 1990**

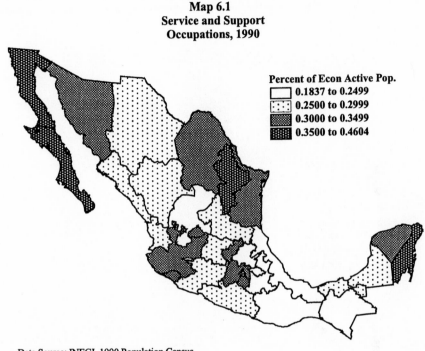

**Percent of Econ Active Pop.**
☐ 0.1837 to 0.2499
▦ 0.2500 to 0.2999
▩ 0.3000 to 0.3499
▨ 0.3500 to 0.4604

Data Source: INEGI, 1990 Population Census
Map Source: Butler/Pick Mexico Database Project

Another indicator of service are sector revenues, which are summarized for the nation in Table 6.1 (INEGI 1994 Censos Economicos). The largest categories are for professional/technical, real estate and finance, and restaurants/hotels and leisure. The "third sector," consisting of government and nonprofits, is also very substantial.

Mexico City is again much higher for such service sector revenues. As seen in Table 6.1 and Map 6.2, 43 percent of service revenues are located in the Federal District, i.e. the central, core section of Mexico City. In fact, on the average a third of the nation's service revenues are located in one to four city delegations (i.e. wards) located in the northern part of the Federal District (INEGI 1994 Censos Economicos).

In summary, Mexico has a large service sector, although it is about half the proportion of that of advanced nations. The service sector is disproportionately concentrated in Mexico City and especially in the northern part of the Federal District. This concentration relates to the location of the seat of the federal government and the business center of the nation in this very small area. The statewide distribution of services resembles that for development zones of the nation. Aside from tourism services, the most important service sub-categories of professional, governmental, non-bank financial and real estate are discussed in this chapter.

**Map 6.2**
**Service Sector Revenues, Mexico City, 1993**
**(in thousands of pesos)**

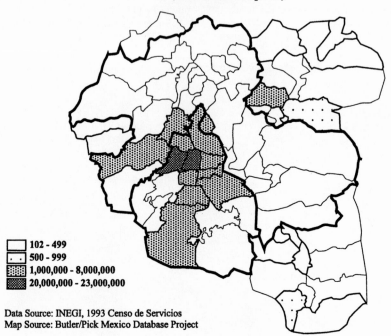

102 - 499
500 - 999
1,000,000 - 8,000,000
20,000,000 - 23,000,000

Data Source: INEGI, 1993 Censo de Servicios
Map Source: Butler/Pick Mexico Database Project

### Educational Services

Mexican educational services are predominantly provided by the federal government. The advances in educational services over the past forty years have been remarkable. For instance the average number of school years completed for people 15 and older increased from 2.6 in 1960 to 3.4 in 1970, 4.6 in 1980, 6.5 in 1990, and 7.2 in 1995. In other words, during one third of a century, average education has increased from low primary to completion of primary. The impact of this can be better seen by examining the educational levels for population 15 and older in 1970 and 1995 (see Figure 6.1). At the low end, persons without schooling are becoming rare, while secondary and higher education have moved from ten percent to nearly half. Among the impacts of this change are: (1) there is a much larger educated middle class and (2) there is a larger educated workforce available for more demanding jobs required by world-class or global standards.

This amazing educational change within Mexico is little noted in discussions in the U.S., which often focus on the lower educated in-migrant population. However, U.S. companies, whether maquiladora or not, are aware and often taking advantage of the opportunities. Several examples are the highly educated assembly and factory workers that IBM/Mexico sought for its plants and the more highly skilled and educated workforce that SONY and other firms have sought in Tijuana electronics factories.

Advances are revealed in the present international context for Mexico. Compared to the U.S. and Brazil, Mexico is roughly equivalent to Brazil and trails the U.S., but not by a

**Table 6.1 Service Revenues: Comparison of Federal District with Rest of Nation on Service Indicators, 1993**

| Services Sector | Service Revenues | National Percent in Federal District | Federal District | Rest of Nation | Dominating Zones in Federal District | National Percent in Dominant Zones |
|---|---|---|---|---|---|---|
| Services - Total | 164,877 | 43 | 71,465 | 93,412 | Cuauhtemoc, Miguel Hidalgo | 26 |
| Third Sector | 20,978 | 36 | 7,454 | 20,978 | Cuauhtemoc, Miguel Hidalgo Benito Juarez Alvaro Obregon | 24 |
| Real Estate | 10,670 | 44 | 4,729 | 5,941 | Miguel Hidalgo | 20 |
| Finance / Insurance | 1,403 | 71 | 998 | 405 | Cuauhtemoc, Miguel Hidalgo Alvaro Obregon | 58 |
| Leisure | 14,427 | 61 | 8,804 | 5,623 | Cuauhtemoc, | 31 |
| Restaurants, Hotels | 33,423 | 27 | 9,013 | 24,410 | Cuauhtemoc, Miguel Hidalgo Benito Juarez | 17 |
| Professional / Teacher | 48,575 | 60 | 28,921 | 19,654 | Cuauhtemoc, Miguel Hidalgo | 42 |
| Scientific Research in Private Sector | 196 | 45 | 88 | 108 | Benito Juarez Iztacalco, Alvaro Obregon Miguel Hidalgo | 33 |
| Average | | 48 | | | | 31 |

Note: all Figures are in millions of new pesos.
Source: INEGI: 1994 *Censos Economicos*.

Figure 6.1 Change in the Educational Levels of the Population,
1970-1995

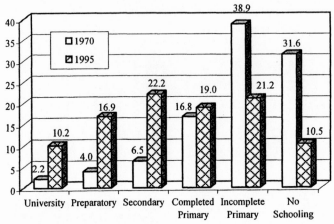

Note: Population 15 or older.
Source: Banamex, 1997.

Table 6.2 Educational Indicators for Mexico, Brazil, and U.S., 1997

| Educational Indicator | Mexico | Brazil | United States |
|---|---|---|---|
| School-Age Population (in 1000s) | 12,462.0 | 10,012.0 | 21,372.0 |
| Adult Illiteracy | 10.4 | 16.7 | NA |
| Compulsory Education | 6.0 | 8.0 | 10.0 |
| School Life Expectancy | 10.9 | 9.4 | 14.7 |
| School-Teacher Ratio | 29.0 | 23.0 | 16.0 |
| No. Students per 10,000 persons | 1,586.0 | 1,094.0 | 5,395.0 |
| Percent Educ. Expenditure at Tertiary Level | 19.3 | 23.3 | NA |

Source: UNESCO, 1998.

huge gap (see Table 6.2). Compared to Mexico, the U.S. average school years completed in 1997 was higher by about 4 years and its student teacher ratios were about half that of Mexico. It is important also to note that the U.S. minimal school requirements exceeded those of Mexico by four years. There was over three times the prevalence of students in the U.S.; a large part of that difference may be due to the much greater opportunities for adult education in the U.S.

Geographically, the advanced parts of the nation are in Mexico City and the border states, especially Nuevo Leon. These areas in 1997 had average number of school years completed of 8 or 9. On the other hand, the south region has low levels of education, averaging only 5 years of school completed. The Bajio region consisting of a number of states surrounding Mexico City has a low level also at 6 years. This region corresponds fairly well to the peripheral development level groups in Table 3.2.

An important stimulus to educational growth has been a rapid increase in the numbers and prevalence of teachers at all levels. For instance, as seen in Table 6.3, the number of secondary level teachers increased from 39,139 in 1960 to 1,430,600 in 1996, a 36-fold increase! On a per capita basis, this increase was from 1.03 per 1,000 population in 1960 to 15.4 per 1,000 in 1996 (UN 1990, 1997). The growth in teacher numbers has been supported by greatly enlarged teacher training programs in universities (Lorey 1993).

As seen in Figure 6.2, there are six major parts to the educational system. Basic education consists of pre-school, primary, and secondary education accounting for 82.1 percent of the 27.9 million students enrolled in 1997-98 (Banamex 1998). Middle level education ("educación media superior") comes after secondary and prepares the student for higher levels. It constitutes 9.9 percent of the enrolled students. One of the sub-tracks at the middle level, middle professional ("profesional media") is a terminal track that produces technicians and low level professionals. Higher education (licenciatura), equivalent to a college degree in the U.S., constitutes 5 percent, while graduate education, i.e., masters and doctorates, accounts for only 0.4 percent. At the licenciatura level, there is a new element in Mexican education, which is "Licenciatura Normal." This is a two-year program that has a practical thrust to it and is growing rapidly. It resembles in some respects community colleges in the U.S.

Two parts of this system that are less familiar in the U.S. are technical training schools ("capacitación"), accounting for 1.9 percent of enrollees, and technological universities ("Universidad Tecnológica"), focusing on preparing teachers of technology. The Mexican educational system resembles in many aspects the U.S., but it has more tracks to produce skilled and practically oriented, technical, workers at different levels.

One of the most important developing areas of Mexican educational services is higher education. It is also the dimension that has the most potential to interact with global forces and which can influence the capacity of the nation to become more globalized.

The rapid growth in higher education is reflected in the number of "egresados" from licentiatura programs from 1970 to 1989. An "egresado" is a student who has completed all of his or her coursework but not yet finished a required thesis. The number of egresados grew by six-fold from 22,595 in 1970 to 140,440 in 1989 (Lorey 1993). At the same time, the proportions changed from domination by the national universities to a broader representation of higher education. The national universities consist of the huge UNAM (Universidad Nacional Autónoma de México) and Instituto Politécnico. In 1970, the proportion of egresados in UNAM/Politécnico, other public universities, and private universities were 45.8, 43.0, and 11.2 respectively. By 1989, the distribution had shifted to 19.6 percent, 60.8 percent, and 19.6 percent (Lorey 1993). National universities no longer dominate in numbers, although they may still be the leaders. Other public universities throughout the nation have become more important. The largest growth with a near doubling over two decades, has been in private universities. These include such prominent institutions as ITESM, Universidad Iberoamericana, Universidad Anáhuac, and over 150 others.

Public and private university sectors differ in contributions they are making to global and international changes. Public universities have produced graduates in a wide variety of fields. They are more keyed to the public sector. For instance, there is a large influence of Marxist thought at the public universities. They have been slower to move towards technological advances in undergraduate education.

Private universities, on the other hand, are focused on producing professional graduates for specific fields in the private sector (Lorey 1993). Private industry has hired not only the private university graduates, but also the egresados who don't graduate, at a lower level.

**Table 6.3 School Attainment in Mexico, 1960-1996**

| Year | Population | School Enrollment Secondary | Secondary School Enrollment Per 1000 Persons | Teachers Secondary | Teachers Secondary Per 1000 Persons | School Enrollment Tertiary | School Enrollment Tertiary Per 1000 Persons |
|------|-----------|------------------------------|-----------------------------------------------|--------------------|--------------------------------------|-----------------------------|----------------------------------------------|
| 1960 | 38,020,000 | 512,216   | 13.47 | 39,169    | 1.03  | 78,599    | 2.07  |
| 1970 | 52,771,000 | 1,584,342 | 30.02 | 109,470   | 2.07  | 247,637   | 4.69  |
| 1980 | 70,416,000 | 4,791,262 | 68.04 | 897,726   | 12.75 | 897,726   | 12.75 |
| 1990 | 88,598,000 | 6,813,284 | 76.90 | 1,143,040 | 12.90 | 1,143,040 | 12.90 |
| 1996 | 92,712,000 | 8,107,200 | 87.45 | 1,430,600 | 15.43 | 1,430,600 | 15.43 |

Source: UN, 1990, 1997.

**Figure 6.2 Structure of the National Education System**

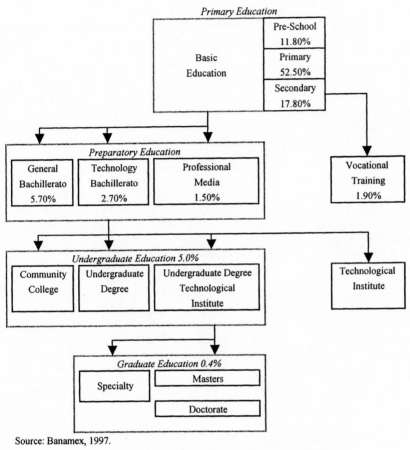

Source: Banamex, 1997.

Note: the percentages represent the percent of matriculated students in 1997-1998.

For instance, Instituto Technológico de Estudios Superiores de Monterrey (ITESM) was founded with the goal of producing graduates to fill business jobs in Monterrey. It is based on a model of MIT, with a focus on engineering and other professions. It has expanded this educational model on a nationwide basis through numerous regional campuses and through its very large national program in distance learning and virtual university.

These educational trends relate to the global economy in a number of ways. First, Mexico's increasingly open and export-driven economy has need for more professionals, including some key recruits at a world-class level in order to compete. Many of the case studies in this book point to the need for high skill levels and often for higher level key technologists or lead professionals in order to compete at a world-class level (e.g., case studies of IBM, Alestra, Hoteles Presidente). This swelling demand has led to a growth in private sector universities. At the same time, the key technologists are often either brought in from overseas e.g. Alestra, or they remain located overseas, e.g. in the maquiladora industry in the U.S. One challenge for private universities is to move their quality levels even higher to produce some graduates at this level.

Public universities also play an important role in supporting the more open and global economy. They are complementing private universities to some extent in producing graduates for this new economy. At the same time, they are dominant in R&D, in doctoral programs, and in national research systems and provide graduates for the efforts in R&D in Mexico, such as in the Delphi mini-case. Further, they have the potential to form alliances globally that can benefit the process of globalization. This has not yet been significantly realized. Among the reasons are bureaucratic obstacles that remain. For instance, the Mexican Education Ministry is rather old fashioned in putting up obstacles to accepting credits from foreign universities (Rymer-Zavala and Benavides 1999). There are curricular and pedagogical differences inhibiting foreign interchanges. Also, some Mexican universities, public and private, lack the necessary academic infrastructure to support foreign interchanges and joint programs.

A final point on educational services is that they provide a channel for social mobility at a variety of levels. The great expansion in education of the past 40 years has enabled many working class students to advance in their careers and climb the social ladder to the middle class. Generally, private universities already serve students in the middle class. They are able to preserve or advance their socioeconomic status further. At the highest levels of education, going outside Mexico to the U.S. or Europe for postgraduate degrees has often led to high career attainments, some of which have stimulated the globalization process from a leadership level.

One example of the latter point is the trend towards foreign graduate education among Mexico's top leaders. As seen in Table 6.4, the top leaders of Mexico have increasingly had postgraduate education and that education has been predominantly overseas. In the Salinas de Gotari administration, for instance, seventy percent of the top leaders had a postgraduate degree, and of them, five sixths were educated in the U.S. or Europe (Camp 1997). National leaders of the 1990s, often called "technocrats," received their "technocrat" graduate education mostly in U.S. universities. This tends to ground them with U.S. business and technology, and other global aspects.

**Table 6.4 Graduate Education of Top Administration Leaders in Mexico, 1950-1994,**
**by Location of Graduate Education (percent)**

| Mexican Presidential Administration | Years | No Postgraduate Study (percent) | Location of Graduate Study | | | | |
|---|---|---|---|---|---|---|---|
| | | | Mexico | United States | Europe | Both U.S. and Europe | Total |
| Ruiz Cortines | 1952-1958 | 89 | 3 | 4 | 3 | 1 | 100 |
| Lopez Mateos | 1958-1964 | 82 | 10 | 5 | 2 | 1 | 100 |
| Diaz Ordaz | 1964-1970 | 82 | 3 | 8 | 6 | 1 | 100 |
| Echeverria | 1970-1976 | 68 | 6 | 14 | 10 | 2 | 100 |
| Lopez Portillo | 1976-1982 | 71 | 9 | 9 | 9 | 2 | 100 |
| De La Madrid | 1982-1988 | 56 | 10 | 18 | 13 | 3 | 100 |
| Salinas | 1988-1994 | 30 | 11 | 38 | 19 | 2 | 100 |
| Average | | 68 | 7 | 14 | 9 | 2 | 100 |

Source: Camp, 1997.

## Health Services

Health care services in Mexico are provided by a combination of public versus private means. Lower levels of Mexican society are predominantly served by several federal systems, while higher social levels are served by a combination of private and public services. The present government approach has been in place for over twenty years, with only mixed success. It is beginning to see some signs of international influences, but realizing that potential will depend on implementing changes in government policies. This section describes the health care system, assesses its level of quality, compares it to the U.S., and discusses advances that are beginning to occur in private health care, including the roles of foreign providers.

The right of every Mexican to health care is constitutional. This was amplified by the General Law of Health in Mexico, approved by Congress in 1984. That law made the Secretary of Health the governing authority of the "national system of health," including executive authority for all health activities in the nation. In 1996, Mexico decentralized its health care system and also introduced a program of health services for its extreme poor.

Public health care is delivered by two systems, IMSS (Instituto Mexicano del Seguro Social) and ISSSTE (Instituto de Seguridad Social para los Trabajadores al Servicio del Estado). The larger IMSS system serves 35 million people and has an annual budget of $5.5 billion U.S. dollars (U.S./Mexico Business 1998). IMSS is regarded as having insufficient funding to support its large burden (Mexican Foundation of Health Survey, 1995).

The public part of health spending is 57 percent. In 1993, Mexico had 423 social security hospitals with 39,181 beds and 410 public welfare hospitals with 32,309 beds, compared to 472 private hospitals with 17,707 beds. In addition, there were 15,472 small clinics and health centers, public and private, of under 15 beds. The persistence of this huge public system is due in part to the attitude among the Mexican public that health care is part of the national patrimony (Mexican Foundation of Health Survey 1995). This is similar to the public perception regarding Pemex as, patrimony subsequently discussed in Chapter 8.

At first glance, level of health care does not seem so different for Mexico, compared to the U.S. and Canada. As seen in Table 6.5, the three countries have life expectancies that are not too different. This may be partly explained by the offsetting risk factors of lower quality disease prevention and health care, with an often healthier nutritional and environmental quality for some disease modalities (Pick and Butler 1998). The prevalence of doctors is similar, although there are substantially fewer nurses in Mexico.

#### Table 6.5 Health Care Indicators in Mexico, the U.S. and Canada

| Health Care Indicators | Mexico | United States | Canada |
|---|---|---|---|
| Life expectancy, 1990 | 70.0 | 76.0 | 77.0 |
| Infant mortality rate 1990-91 | 36.0 | 7.0 | 6.0 |
| Infant emaciation rate, 1980-90 | 6.0 | 2.0 | 1.0 |
| Health care employees | 633,000 | 10,000,000 | 900,000 |
| Percentage of econ. active population | 7.3 | 7.5 | 2.7 |
| Number of active doctors | 143,496 | 600,000 | 60,559 |
| Doctors per 1,000 population | 1.8 | 2.4 | 2.2 |
| Number of licensed nurses | 176,927 | 2,000,000 | 262,288 |
| Nurses per 1,000 population | 2.1 | 8.0 | 9.6 |

Source: Flores Escárzaga, 1997.

The overall trend in health care from the past 36 years shows steady hospital bed capacity, but increasing prevalence ratios of physicians (see Table 6.6). The per capita decline in hospital beds has become a deficiency that is impacting the quality of care. It is due mostly to the expense of adding sufficient hospital beds in the public systems. This is somewhat offset by ambulatory care and some growth in small clinics and centers.

**Table 6.6 Health Care Indicators in Mexico, 1960-1996**

| Year | Population | Hospital Beds | Hospital Beds Per 1000 Persons | Physicians | Physicians Per 1000 Persons |
|------|-----------|--------------|-------------------------------|-----------|----------------------------|
| 1960 | 38,020 | 62,964 | 1.6561 | 20,227 | 0.5320 |
| 1970 | 52,771 | 71,381 | 1.3527 | 33,981 | 0.6439 |
| 1980 | 70,416 | 56,426 | 0.8013 | 62,009 | 0.8806 |
| 1990 | 88,598 | 63,122 | 0.7125 | 89,842 | 1.0140 |
| 1996 | 92,712 | 69,547 | 0.7501 | 113,876 | 1.2283 |

Source: UN, 1990, 1997.

Mexico's health care system expenditures can be compared to those of the U.S. and Canada. The raw amount of health care spending is much lower in Mexico. The average Mexican spends only $89 per year on health care, versus $2,763 in the U.S. and $1,945 in Canada (Flores Escárzaga 1997). As seen in Table 6.7, Mexico spends a relatively low proportion of GDP, only 2.1 percent on health care, much lower than for the U.S. and Canada (Flores Escárzaga 1997). This in part reflects spending priorities for a limited federal budget and also cultural traditions that do not call for the sometimes excessive amount of services in the U.S. and Canada. The Mexican government's key role is reflected in the recognized legal right of health care and in the dominance of federal health care insurance. In many respects especially in the government's role, the Mexican system is closer to that of Canada than the U.S.

**Table 6.7 Comparison of Health Care Systems of Mexico, the U.S. and Canada**

| Health System Characteristic | Mexico | United States | Canada |
|------------------------------|--------|--------------|--------|
| Recognized legal right for health services | yes | no | no |
| Universal coverage | no | no | yes |
| Dominant government-funded insurance | yes | no | yes |
| Public/private proportions of health spending | 57/43 | 43/57 | 72/28 |
| Percent of GDP spent on health | 2.1 | 12.2 | 9.4 |
| Ability of patient to elect services | rare | high | medium |
| Cases of civil and criminal malpractice | rare | excessive | rare |
| Scientific and technological advances | rare | very high | high |

Source: Flores Escrzaga, 1997.

Mexico has a potential to offer privatized health care to a much greater extent. However, barriers need to be overcome. Currently, companies need permission to opt for private health care. Some exceptions exist. For instance, the banking sector has always been allowed to have private health care, since the founding of IMSS in 1943. Although the Zedillo administration proposed to have this option widely available, action on the request is being held up until after the 2000 election. Currently, only 70 firms have been permitted to opt out of the IMSS system. These include some very prominent firms such as Alfa, Vitro, and Cervecería Cuauhtémoc (U.S./Mexico Business 1998). Companies providing private health care include Valores Monterrey Aetna, which offers health care services to corporate workers at companies such as Bancomer, and Pulsar International, the parent firm of the chapter case company Seguros Commercial America. Pulsar recently purchased a leading private hospital in Mexico City to offer these services. This is only a start, since Pulsar has plans to construct 20 outpatient surgery centers in Mexico City.

In the small private sector, there are successes and failures. For instance the private El Hospital ABS has been operating in Mexico for over 100 years. It has continued to modernize, surviving such traumatic periods as the peso crisis of 1994 (Expansión 1998). On the other hand, the few U.S. owned private hospitals have had mixed success. The well known Scripps Health from San Diego started to implement an 80 bed private hospital in Aguascalientes in 1993. Scripps would manage the facility, but the funding would be Mexican. The effort was halted due to lack of funding from the 1994 peso devaluation crisis (Expansión 1994).

A number of other companies are readying themselves to enter this market, including prominent Mexican companies and several hospital chains and HMOs from the U.S.

Among the potentials of expanding private health care are growing interdependencies of Mexican health care with other systems internationally and especially in NAFTA countries. For instance, some huge foreign insurance and health care firms are assessing rather than entering the market in Mexico including CIGNA, Aetna, and Metropolitan Life (Expansión 1999). Among factors that may induce them to enter are the approval of opting out for public recipients and indications that the broad Mexican public will accept private and even foreign options. This would especially apply to poorer and more rural clientele. There is also the opposing factor of Mexican labor unions.

The NAFTA agreement offers longer term potential for major changes for Mexico. There is a potential to improve the quality, efficiency, accessibility, and technology of health care, increase employment, and reduce the capital flight of patients who go outside of the country for care (Gómez-Dántes et al. 1997). In addition, Mexican health care firms have large potential markets of Hispanic population in the U.S., while U.S. firms evaluating Mexico have the potential market of the large contingent of ex-patriots residing in Mexico, estimated at 400,000.

Among challenges in this process for Mexico are quality and equity. Mexico needs to put in place better government quality standards of health care. This has been helped already by a 57 million dollar loan from the World Bank in 1998, focusing on strategies and ideas to streamline the operations of IMSS. The challenge of equity is to narrow the huge gaps existing between health care for the poor rural Mexican and care for the upper middle class and wealthy. The role that globalization plays in the process will depend on the level of acceptance by the Mexican public and government leaders of options beyond the traditional "patrimony" of the federal programs.

## Social Services and Poverty

Each Mexican federal administration has provided programs of social services including those to combat poverty. These programs have varied considerably from administration to administration. Many of these programs have provided large amounts of benefits for a needy population, but at the same time they have been criticized for weaknesses, including inefficiencies and claims of using programs for political influence. These criticisms should not be too unfamiliar to observers of U.S. social service programs.

The leading federal social service programs of the Zedillo Administration emphasize poverty, health, and education, rural infrastructure, employment for rural women, the indigenous, water, and sanitation (see Table 6.8). Funds are dispersed at the federal, state, and municipio levels. The Zedillo Administration has decentralized some programs to a greater extent than prior governments. Geographically, emphasis is on the south and central regions extending east to Veracruz. These are the less prosperous states, many of which have high indigenous populations. For instance, social development funds dispersed in 1997 at the municipio level are shown in Map 6.3. These funds totaled $1.04 billion equivalent U.S. dollars (Banamex 1998). It is noteworthy that 18.7 percent of the funds were destined for the south region, which is classified as peripheral in development in Table 3.2. The Zedillo Administration is actually providing funds to the deprived areas. The question is the quality and effectiveness of programs.

#### Table 6.8. Mexican Government Poverty Programs
#### in the Period 1995-2000

**Programs to Support the Growth of Human Capital**
Progresa
Nutrition programs: school lunches, supply of milk and tortillas
Health Programs: IMSS-Solidaridad
Education Programs

**Programs to Support Employment Opportunities**
Program of temporary employment
Program for rural infrastructure for farmers of low income
Support for arid zones
Support for the National Indigenous Institute
National Fund to Support Social Businesses
"Mujeres en Solidaridad" (Women in Solidarity)
"Jornaleros Agrcolas" (Agricultural Workers)
Mujeres Campesinas (Rural Women)
Program for Development of Forests

**Programs to Support Growth of Physical Capital**
Growth of basic social infrastructure in marginal regions
Potable water and sanitation in marginal urban zones and in rural zones
Pilot Program in Housing
Telephones and rural roads
Program of National Water Commission

Source: Sedesol. 1996, modified from Banamex, 1998.

Perhaps the most prominent of the Zedillo Administration programs is the poverty program Progresa. This program addresses a key national problem that in spite of globalization and export-orientation that some see in Mexico today, poverty has risen sharply. There are an estimated 30 million individuals in extreme poverty in 1999, or about 30 percent of the population (Centro de Estudios Economics y Sociales, UNAM, as quoted in Philpott 1999). This is up from 14 percent of the population in 1984. It is also noteworthy that 15 percent of the population in 1999 spent less than one dollar per day (Philpott 1999). There are an estimated 4.6 million households in extreme poverty. There are a number of reasons for this extent of poverty. First, the Mexican labor force is increasing rapidly and has been going so for the past ten years, at a rate of approximately one million net new workers per year (Pick, Butler, and Gonzalez 1993). There are a limited number of jobs being created, so many workers even skilled ones cannot find jobs. One estimate is that two thirds of persons seeking new positions are high school graduates and one fifth have attended undergraduate programs (cited in Philpott 1999). Thus, in spite of higher educational levels for the nation, poverty is on the increase.

The Progresa poverty program was started in 1997. It does not focus on all 30 million persons in extreme poverty, but rather on 2 million impoverished families in rural areas throughout the nation. The program provides health, education, and nutritional assistance. Education money is provided for every child in school, with girls receiving a somewhat larger amount. It includes a nutritional supplement and is provided to pregnant or lactating mothers and to children two years of age or under (Ruiz 1999). In 1998 the program budget was equivalent to 631 million dollars. It was offered in 28 states, 1,530 municipios, 45,873 localities and to 2 million families. Forty percent of Progresa funds went to the urgent need states of Chiapas, Oaxaca, Guerrero, Veracruz, Puebla, and Mexico.

The program has been praised and criticized. Supporters point to its benefits to millions of impoverished families. The program does seem to be more efficient than the mostly failed Pronasol and Procampo poverty programs of earlier administrations. On the other hand, it has been criticized in the Mexican legislature on several counts. Some have claimed that it has involved local conflicts of interest. For instance, the mayor of a small town can make dispersal of the funds dependent on recipients' repairing a school. Another past criticism is that it was being used as an electoral arm. Currently, this is undergoing positive changes with new agency leadership.

**Map 6.3**
**Percentage Distribution of Municipio-Based**
**Social Development Funds, by State, 1997**

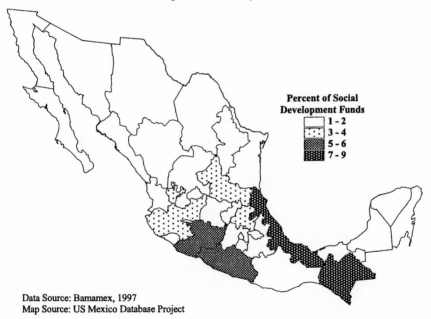

Data Source: Bamamex, 1997
Map Source: US Mexico Database Project

**Table 6.9 Indicators for Financial Sector Companies, 1993**
**(in thousands of 1993 dollars)**

| | No. of Employees | Salaries | Income | Expenses | Income Minus Expenses | Interest Payments Received | Interest Payments Paid | Net Interest Payments |
|---|---|---|---|---|---|---|---|---|
| Banco de Mexico | 21,691 | 755,627 | 805,387 | 1,273,911 | (468,524) | 5,436,182 | 4,145,536 | 1,290,646 |
| Commercial Banks | 163,129 | 4,264,210 | 6,514,881 | 6,528,382 | (13,501) | 28,266,669 | 18,685,240 | 9,581,428 |
| Brokerage Firms | 8,923 | 527,055 | 5,196,184 | 1,723,541 | 3,472,644 | 140,819 | 57,260 | 83,559 |
| Insurance Institutions | 21,914 | 537,477 | 5,668,350 | 4,806,040 | 862,310 | 463,639 | 31,093 | 432,546 |
| Money Exchange Houses | 4,904 | 49,669 | 347,108 | 191,435 | 155,672 | - | - | - |
| Other | 43,490 | 836,558 | 3,973,736 | 2,264,407 | 1,709,330 | 8,954,206 | 5,513,405 | 3,440,801 |
| National Total | 264,051 | 6,970,596 | 22,505,647 | 16,787,716 | 5,717,931 | 63,261,515 | 28,432,534 | 14,828,980 |

Source: INEGI, 1995.

## Financial and Insurance Services

The major area of financial, insurance, and real estate services accounted in 1993 for $5.7 billion U.S. dollars in net income (INEGI, Censos Economicos 1994). As shown in Table 6.9, this sector includes the national Banco de México, commercial banks, brokerage firms, insurance companies, foreign exchange ("casas de cambio"), and other entities including real estate. They differ in a number of ways, for instance, on whether they are deposit and lending institutions, such as banks and savings institutions, or whether they transfer and exchange funds such as brokerage and money exchange houses. It is clear from Table 6.9 that in 1993 there were considerable differences in profitability, with the national bank and commercial banks showing losses, while other institutions were profitable.

Commercial banks were discussed in the last chapter. We pointed out that banking is the most developed of the financial sectors. Even with the severely downtrodden condition of the banking industry, they play major roles in providing a wide array of personal and corporate services. There is potential to expand services stemming from prospective financial recovery of impacted banks as well as from foreign takeovers of formerly Mexican banks such as by Citibank, Santander, and Banco Bilbao Viscaya.

The Mexican insurance industry plays a major role in certain products. For instance, it is strong in auto and life insurance, but weak as already mentioned in health insurance. The positive example of Seguros Comercial America is discussed as a case study. The industry has potential stemming from possible de-regulation of health and other forms of insurance.

Brokerage houses were an important part of this service sector and grew in the 1990s along with stock market activity. The Mexican stock market is currently limited in size (Cabillo 1999). The money exchange subsector is relatively small in size, but it relates to the international business and global economy through commerce, sales and purchases, or tourist exchanges. Money exchange houses are constrained in growth as modern technology offers alternative ways to make payments in foreign currencies.

Regional distributions of financial sectors (banking and non-banking) reveal unevenness, with a disproportionate amount of services located in the Federal District and relatively little in the poor south region. Some other regions with high concentrations are Nuevo Leon, the State of Mexico including parts of Mexico City, and for some sectors, Baja California. The distribution corresponds to Mexico's most highly developed areas.

Both Banco de Mexico and commercial banks have 30-45 percent of workforce and net interest payments located in the Federal District (see Table 6.10). The south region (Periphery B from Table 3.2) has only 2 to 5 percent of banking workforce and net interest. However, Periphery A including the Bajio Region accounts for 9 to 15 percent of banking workforce and net interest. This larger amount stems from significant banking activities in the large although rather poor to middling states of Guanajuato and Veracruz.

Brokerage firms are highly concentrated in the Federal District, while insurance companies follow the banking pattern of being about half in Mexico City. Again for insurance, the south region is very low at 2 to 4 percent, while the Periphery A accounts for 13 to 14 percent. Nuevo Leon, mostly from Monterrey, has significant proportion brokerage and insurance, about 6 to 9 percent. Money exchange firms are highest in Federal District, followed by Nuevo Leon, a level matched by Baja California. This is the only subsector for which Baja California has a substantial contribution. The reason may be the elevated levels of money exchange in the commerce and maquiladora, as well as border tourism.

Overall, there is a hyperconcentration of financial firms in the Federal District. Very careful spatial analysis indicates that within the Federal District, financial services are further concentrated in the central to north central delegations. This reflects the headquarter

**Table 6.10 Bank Sectors by Major Development Regions, 1993**
**(in 1993 dollars)**

| | Banco de Mexico | | | | Commercial Banks | | | |
| --- | --- | --- | --- | --- | --- | --- | --- | --- |
| | No. of Employees | Percent | Net Interest Payments | Percent | No. of Employees | Percent | Net Interset Payments | Percent |
| Distrito Federal | 9,482 | 44 | 524,255 | 41 | 65,298 | 40 | 2,732,782 | 29 |
| State of Mexico | 338 | 2 | 48,071 | 4 | 3,085 | 2 | 168,268 | 2 |
| Nuevo Leon | 301 | 1 | 24,005 | 2 | 11,725 | 7 | 1,526,227 | 16 |
| Jalisco | 806 | 4 | 34,466 | 3 | 14,549 | 9 | 830,289 | 9 |
| Baja California | 317 | 1 | 31,005 | 2 | 4,263 | 3 | 259,405 | 3 |
| South Region - Periphery | 1,186 | 5 | 46,913 | 4 | 4,245 | 3 | 162,637 | 2 |
| Periphery A (includes Bajio Region) | 3,275 | 15 | 198,566 | 15 | 16,365 | 10 | 839,708 | 9 |
| Other | 5,986 | 28 | 383,365 | 30 | 43,619 | 27 | 3,065,112 | 32 |
| National Total | 21,691 | 100 | 1,290,646 | 100 | 163,129 | 100 | 9,581,428 | 100 |

Source: INEGI, 1995.

locations of these companies either in the modern business areas along the major balance of Reforma and in Las Lomas, or in a zone in the south of the city. It is amazing that so much of the nation's financial power and decision-making are concentrated in central Mexico City zones that are within ten miles of each other. However, financial regulatory ministries, the Mexican stock exchange, and most of the nation's major corporate headquarters and decision makers are also within this small area.

From the standpoint of world systems theory, this concentration is not unexpected. That theory has focused mostly on the hyperconcentration of financial power in advanced nations (Sassen 1991); however, the same concentration is evident here within a nation and corresponds to Mexico's major development zones.

## Business, Accounting, Legal, and Information Services

The service sector has already been seen to be smaller in Mexico than in advanced nations. Nevertheless it still has substantial parts encompassing business, accounting and consulting, legal, and information services. Some of these services are provided by large multinational firms for which service is only part of their product line. An example is IBM, which is not classified in the Expansión 500 as a service firm, but nevertheless has among the largest service revenues for private firms in the economy. IBM is discussed as a chapter case study.

The fifteen largest business service companies, shown in Table 6.11, are based on the service designation in the Expansión 500 for 1997. It is important to note that this list excludes financial, hotel and restaurant, and transport and communication services. Business service companies are much smaller than commercial companies from the Expansión 500 list presented in Table 5.4. The smaller size of private sector services reflects both deficits in the sectors versus advanced nations and the high government participation in some realms. Like commercial firms, nearly all business service companies are located in the Federal District and are Mexican owned. In extent of foreign debt, they vary between extremes, with half under 10 percent and three others approaching 100 percent (Expansión 1998).

By contrast, major accounting and consulting firms in Mexico are dominated by U.S. companies (Jamar and Salaman 1998). As seen in Table 6.12, these firms are headquartered in Mexico City and perform a variety of accounting, consulting, and Information Systems (IS) consulting services. Accounting majority of firms are formerly Mexican ones that have become associated with a Big 6 accounting firm or major consulting firms. Several U.S. consulting firms are present. The opportunities for these firms appear to be present in both good and bad times. For instance, they did very well during the peso crisis period in the mid 90s, since many teetering companies came to them for economic consulting and restructuring or merger advice. In better times, they offer ideas and services for companies to improve their technologies and value added. U.S.-based firms offer advantages for Mexican consulting or auditing teams to interchange ideas and information with experts in the U.S. and elsewhere.

The major law firms in Mexico are a mixture of Mexican and mostly U.S. foreign ownership. These firms have grown and benefited by the large amount of privatization that has taken place over the past 12 years (Jamar and Salaman 1998). They also benefit by NAFTA-related business agreements as well as export issues. Firms maintain competitive edge by emphasizing bilingualism (Jamar and Salaman 1998). In some cases, there are overlaps between law firms and accounting firms, which are also able to employ lawyers and to offer legal advice.

Information services are quite varied. Consulting and advice are provided by diverse parties ranging from IBM consulting services, to accounting firms, to specialized Mexican-owned firms.   An example of a rapidly growing Mexican-owned firm with a strong service

**Table 6.11 Non-Bank Financial Sectors by Major Development Regions**
**(in 1993 dollars)**

| | Brokerage Firms | | | |
| | No. of Employees | Percent | Income Minus Expenses | Percent |
|---|---|---|---|---|
| Distrito Federal | 7,031 | 79 | 2,983,627 | 86 |
| State of Mexico | 309 | 3 | 236,408 | 7 |
| Nuevo Leon | 775 | 9 | 206,112 | 6 |
| Jalisco | 321 | 4 | 30,128 | 1 |
| Baja California | 69 | 1 | 2,305 | 0 |
| South Region - Periphery | 27 | 0 | 16 | 0 |
| Periphery A (includes Bajio Region) | 115 | 1 | 3,167 | 0 |
| Other | 276 | 3 | 10,880 | 0 |
| National Total | 8,923 | 100 | 3,472,644 | 100 |

| | Insurance Institutions | | | |
| | No. of Employees | Percent | Income Minus Expenses | Percent |
|---|---|---|---|---|
| Distrito Federal | 8,352 | 38 | 387,808 | 44 |
| State of Mexico | 1,566 | 7 | 60,050 | 7 |
| Nuevo Leon | 1,676 | 8 | 64,779 | 7 |
| Jalisco | 1,507 | 7 | 55,874 | 7 |
| Baja California | 340 | 2 | 12,245 | 2 |
| South Region - Periphery | 922 | 4 | 88,154 | 2 |
| Periphery A (includes Bajio Region) | 3,094 | 14 | 112,591 | 13 |
| Other | 4,457 | 20 | 80,809 | 19 |
| National Total | 21,914 | 100 | 862,310 | 100 |

| | Money Exchange Firms | | | |
| | No. of Employees | Percent | Income Minus Expenses | Percent |
|---|---|---|---|---|
| Distrito Federal | 1,380 | 28 | 92,585 | 59 |
| State of Mexico | 58 | 1 | 1,823 | 1 |
| Nuevo Leon | 281 | 6 | 15,334 | 10 |
| Jalisco | 376 | 8 | 6,373 | 4 |
| Baja California | 519 | 11 | 7,234 | 5 |
| South Region - Periphery | 153 | 3 | 2,241 | 1 |
| Periphery A (includes Bajio Region) | 629 | 13 | 10,452 | 7 |
| Other | 1,508 | 31 | 19,630 | 13 |
| National Total | 4,904 | 100 | 155,672 | 100 |

Source: INEGI, 1995.

Table 6.12 Large Accounting and Consulting Firms in Mexico, 1998

| Accounting-Consulting Firm | Country of Origin | No. of Employees | Services | Other Offices Besides Mexico City |
|---|---|---|---|---|
| Deloitte&Touche Consulting/ Galaz, Gomez Morfin, Chavero, Yamzaki | U.S. | 1,680 | accounting and consulting | 17 |
| Price Waterhouse | U.S. | 1,550 | business advice | 10 |
| Mancera Ernst and Young | U.S. | 1,500 | accounting,consulting, and legal | 16 |
| Despacho Roberto Casas Altriste - Coopers and Lybrand | U.S. | 1,500 | accounting and consulting | 11 |
| Arthur Anderson/Ruiz, Urquiza y Cia | U.S. | 1,400 | accounting and consulting | 8 |
| KPMG Cardenas Dosal | U.S. | over 1,300 | accounting and consulting | 13 |
| A.T. Kearney | U.S. | 1,301 | information technology and management consulting, executive search | NA |
| Anderson Consulting | U.S. | 500 | consulting | 1 (Monterrey) |
| McKinsey and Co. | U.S. | 250 | consulting | 1 (Monterrey) |

Source: Jamar and Salaman, 1998.

side is Dataflux. This firm had 1998 revenues of 298 million U.S. dollars. It has purchased a variety of distributors of computing and communications equipment, including Genetec, Vertex del Norte, and MacWarehouse of Mexico. Through an arrangement with Cisco Systems, Dataflux's Interax division distributes Cisco products in Mexico. Most divisions have service units providing advice on acquiring, configuring, managing and utilizing smaller computers and networks. Dataflux also offers computer training, including to teenagers, through El Colegio Nacional de Computo e Ingles (CNCI). This branch is growing very rapidly, and should have over 150 locations by 1999, each accommodating up to 2,000 persons. Dataflux services are meeting the potential of transitioning the small and obsolete base of computing in Mexico to an up-to-date base (Expansión 1997).

**Map 6.4**
**Personal Services**
**Work Force, 1990**

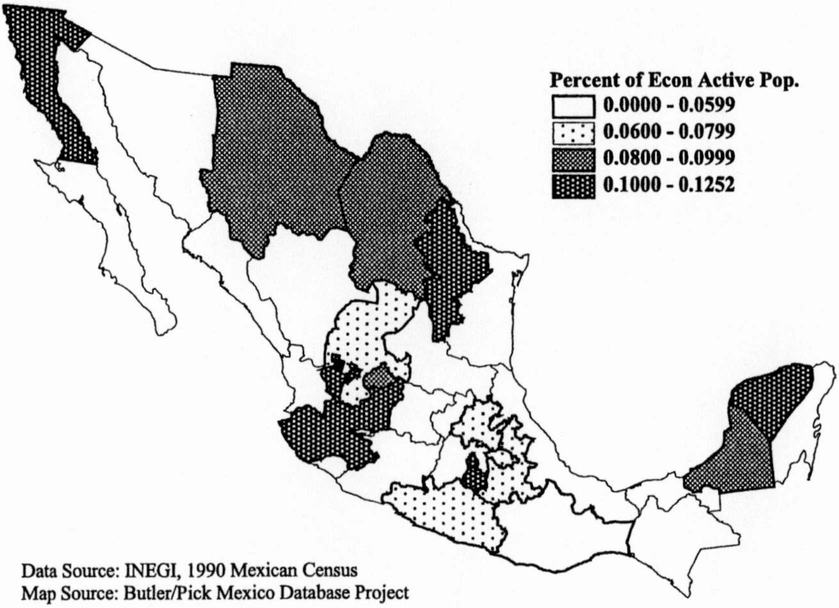

Percent of Econ Active Pop.

- 0.0000 - 0.0599
- 0.0600 - 0.0799
- 0.0800 - 0.0999
- 0.1000 - 0.1252

Data Source: INEGI, 1990 Mexican Census
Map Source: Butler/Pick Mexico Database Project

## Personal Services

There are a variety of personal services prevalent in Mexico including domestic services, language instruction, etc. In 1990, there were 2.1 million workers in personal services, accounting for 8.9 percent of the economically active workforce (Pick and Butler, 1994). As seen in Map 6.4, this workforce is concentrated in the Federal District and surrounding states, Baja California and northwest Mexico, and Nuevo Leon and Tamaulipas. Unsurprisingly, it is very low in the south region and in certain central and Bajio states. In fact, this geographic distribution also corresponds to Mexican development regions in Map 3.2 and confirms that personal services follow the trends discussed up to now for other types of services including education, health, and business.

## Conclusions

This chapter presented an overview of the service sector in Mexico. It avoided repeating types of services discussed in other chapters including banking, communications/transportation, and tourism.

The service sector is smaller and less elaborate than in advanced nations such as the U.S. and in Western Europe. This reflects economic constraints and in some cases government regulations restraining the private sector from offering service products.

The nation has had remarkable educational advances, which have lifted the schooling level of the whole nation and opened up untold labor force potential. Some of that potential has been constrained by economic lapses of the 1990s. The educational advance has been based on a succession of national policies that have invested heavily in education as a priority. One of the stimuli for this growth has been rapid increase in educating a large number of teachers.

The sector of higher education was historically constrained and was dominated by several national universities. In the second half of the twentieth century, this has changed with private universities growing rapidly as well as public universities in the regions. Private universities have been keyed to the open, growing, and world competitive export economy. Public universities have also been successful but in a different way, emphasizing a balance of disciplines and harboring the nation's R&D capability. Universities have provided a great mechanism for social mobility. The weakness has related to equity of education especially in poor, rural areas.

The Mexican public health care systems account for most health services. However, government subsidized private health care is also very important. The government has been restrictive in allowing private health care plans. However, in the next administration, this may open up. Meanwhile, U.S. health care giants are waiting and readying themselves for opportunities.

The Mexican health care system has much lower funding than for the U.S. and Canada. On some indicators, however, it is not too different including life expectancy and number of physicians per capita. The chapter discusses prospective advantages and disadvantages stemming from greater NAFTA-related openness, although heretofore this openness has been limited by the government.

Social services including the high profile poverty program Progresa have had many successes under the Zedillo Administration. At the same time, extreme poverty is growing and is now a major national problem. Although the Progresa program had been criticized by some for local corruption and political conflicts of interest, much benefit is now being derived from a modernized poverty initiative.

The private sector dominates financial, business, accounting, and legal services. These sectors are highly concentrated in Mexico City and have very reduced presence in the south region. Geographically, they conform to the expected world development regions. The border region and in particular Baja is mostly moderate in these services, in spite of its advanced development level. This may be partly because of the large presence of the maquiladora in Tijuana, which often obtains these services in the U.S. side of the border.

Of the major parts of the economy in this book, the service sector has among the greatest potential to expand in the long term. It also has large potential for foreign participation, provided that old-fashioned regulations are removed. Global corporations are, par excellence, a trader in services (Sauvant and Mallampally 1993). They create demands for intermediate products across national boundaries. Events of the past several decades have influenced the role of services in international production, transportation, and consumption. The demand for international related-services has increased and the modes of service provision have undergone profound change.

### Case Study: Seguros Comercial America

Seguros Comercial America is the largest insurance firm in Mexico. It provides a full range of insurance products including life, casualty, liability, automobile, and health insurance. It is a private company owned by Alfonso Romo, the second richest person in Mexico whose fortune is estimated at $2 billion. Seguros Comerical America was formed in 1993 by the merger of Seguros La Comercial, which Romo purchased in 1989, and Seguros America. Both of the firms were old and leading Mexican insurance firms founded in the 1930s.

The firm has growth very rapidly over the past six years with increases often of 10 fold. The company in 1997 had total income of 97.2 million U.S. dollars and net income of 28.3 million U.S. dollars. Seguros had 25.2 percent of the total Mexican insurance market, including 15 percent of life insurance, 28 percent of auto insurance, and 42 percent of property and casualty insurance. It is playing an expanding role in the nascent health insurance business. It offers a full line of health insurance products. These are sold nearly entirely to companies rather than to individuals, since the businesses have more clout and are more willing to sign up. One year ago, Pulsar purchased Medica Sur, a major surgical center in the south of Mexico City. This company was still listed on the 1997 Expansión list as number 335 (see Table 6.13) and had 3.2 million U.S. dollars in revenue at the time of purchase. The strategy in acquiring Medica Sur positions Seguros to gain experience and be ready to take advantage of the possible opening up after 2000 of the private health care sector.

Besides insurance, Seguros Comercial America has the following parts:
- ASEMEX Division. Specializes in risk management for the public sector.
- Fianzas Comercial América. Financing.
- Arrendadora Comercial América. Leasing.
- Hipotecaría Comercial América. Mortgages.
- Amacenadora Comercial América. Storage.
- Factoring Comercial América. Sale of currency.
- Autofinanciamiento Comercial América. Personal finance.

All these products provide diversification that balances out the ups and downs in the insurance markets.

Seguros benefits also by its vertically upward diversification. It is one of the holdings of Grupo Pulsar, which is also 100 percent owned by Alfonso Romo. A family or

**Table 6.13 Mexico's Fifteen Largest Service Companies, 1997**

| Position* | Name | Location | Type of Services | Ownership** | Sales (in dollars) | Sales-Pesos | Debt (in dollars) |
|---|---|---|---|---|---|---|---|
| 101 | SanLuis Corporacion | Mexico, DF | Professional | domestic | 291,534 | 2,307,232 | 488,961 |
| 110 | Servicio Panameriano de Proteccion y Subs | Mexico, DF | Professional | U.S. | 259,106 | 2,050,593 | 55,622 |
| 171 | Manpower | Mexico, DF | Human Resource | domestic | 128,928 | 1,020,348 | 8,434 |
| 193 | Grupo Videovisa | Mexico, DF | Sports, Entertainment | domestic | 99,629 | 788,473 | 61,151 |
| 202 | Corporacion Interamericana de Entretenimiento | Mexico, DF | Sports, Entertainment | domestic | 93,483 | 739,834 | 72,714 |
| 258 | Hospital ABC IAP | Mexico, DF | Health Care | domestic | 54,051 | 427,767 | 25,143 |
| 286 | Servicios Empresarilaes Soran | Mexico, DF | Storage | domestic | 38,366 | 303,631 | 12,189 |
| 305 | Bufete Industrial Disenos y Pryectos | Mexico, DF | Business Advisory | domestic | 31,867 | 252,201 | 1,317 |
| 309 | G Accion | Mexico, DF | Real Estate | domestic | 30,788 | 243,662 | 138,724 |
| 335 | Medica Sur | Mexico, DF | Health Care | domestic | 25,551 | 202,213 | 7,496 |
| 337 | Sociedad Industrial | Tampico, Tamaulipas | Business Advisory | domestic | 25,409 | 201,087 | 4,945 |
| 362 | Q Tel | Mexico, DF | Professional | domestic | 21,085 | 166,869 | 16,030 |
| 366 | Grinnell Sistemas de Proteccion Contra Incendio | Mexico, DF | Professional | U.S. | 20,458 | 161,909 | 6,839 |
| 373 | Impactos Exteriores y Espectaculares | Mexico, DF | Business Advisory | domestic | 19,888 | 157,396 | 8,240 |
| 390 | Vivienda y Desarrollo Urbano y Subs | Monterrey, NL | Real Estate | domestic | 17,073 | 135,121 | 4,306 |
| Average | | | | | 77,148 | 610,556 | 60,807 |

Note: Excludes Hotel and Restauarant, Transport, and Communication Services.

* Position in Sales in Expansión 500.

** Majority ownership domestic or foreign. Domestic firms are privately owned.

Source: Expansión 500, 1999.

Table 6.13 Mexico's Fifteen Largest Service Companies, 1997 (Continued)

| Position* | Name | Ratio Debt to Equity | Percent Foreign Debt | No. of Employees | Year of Founding |
|---|---|---|---|---|---|
| 101 | SanLuis Corporacion | 70 | 94 | 6,251 | 1984 |
| 110 | Servicio Panameriano de Proteccion y Subs | 21 | 0 | 11,217 | 1965 |
| 171 | Manpower | 32 | 0 | 566 | 1967 |
| 193 | Grupo Videovisa | 52 | 59 | 2,543 | 1993 |
| 202 | Corporacion Interamericana de Entretenimiento | 44 | 9 | 2,011 | 1995 |
| 258 | Hospital ABC IAP | 104 | 54 | 1,088 | 1941 |
| 286 | Servicios Empresarilaes Soran | 39 | 0 | 1,361 | 1989 |
| 305 | Bufete Industrial Disenos y Pryectos | 3 | 51 | 5,690 | 1962 |
| 309 | G Accion | 49 | 68 | 92 | NA |
| 335 | Medica Sur | 11 | 18 | 653 | 1966 |
| 337 | Sociedad Industrial | 39 | 0 | 94 | 1972 |
| 362 | Q Tel | 104 | 86 | 760 | 1979 |
| 366 | Grinnell Sistemas de Proteccion Contra Incendio | 58 | 87 | 530 | 1972 |
| 373 | Impactos Exteriores y Espectaculares | 82 | 0 | 406 | 1986 |
| 390 | Vivienda y Desarrollo Urbano y Subs | 14 | 0 | 1,307 | 1974 |
| | Average | 48 | 35 | 2,305 | 1975 |

individually controlled conglomerate is referred to as "grupo." Besides the Seguros Comercial America, the major parts of Pulsar are: (1) Seminis, a world leader in producing seeds for fruits and vegetables, (2) Packaging Division, consisting of leading packaging firms of Aluprint and Empaques Ponderosa, (3) Contex Mexicana, providing new technology to the Latin American construction business, in alliance with a German firm. Seminis is particularly notable in its world leadership. It almost ranks with Cemex as an example of a wholly owned Mexican firm that is world competitive.

Seguros is clearly a part of a conglomerate, but one that is highly efficiently managed with very clear goals and mission. In technology, Seguros is using up-to-date systems imported from outside. This includes PEGASO, an information system allowing regional offices to produce policies digitally, company-wide intranet, voice recognition technology for insurance agents, and mobile trucks that can go to a crash location and authorize instant payments. This level of technology is similar to standards for large sized firms in the U.S.

Employee motivation and training are emphasized. For instance, in 1997, there were more than one million hours of training sessions including general courses, diploma courses, seminars, and masters programs. Outside of Seguros, Alfonso Romo has created his own graduate business school called Duxx in Monterrey (Poole 1998). He was frustrated with the current inadequate business education. Duxx has very few students and is a blend of an MBA and a training course for executives. The school exemplifies the entrepreneurial and bold spirit in Alfonso Romo.

This case study demonstrates several important trends in services and business. The first is that the Mexican insurance industry is doing well and is able to innovate with new products as has happened with Seguros' line of health insurance products and its purchase of Medica Sur. Second, the insurance industry in Mexico up to now has been largely protected from foreign entrants. Third, a conglomerate approach can work well in Mexico. Grupo Pulsar illustrates the power of this approach by balancing the ups and downs through a number of business lines including its world class seed business. Seguros Comercial America and its parent Pulsar represent a strong and even partially world class company in some respects like a Cemex. The difference is that, unlike cement, insurance products are at present largely protected from foreign competition.

### Case Study: IBM/Mexico

IBM/Mexico is a large division of IBM. The manufacturing output from Guadalajara was about $2.7 billion in 1997 and the total revenues are much higher perhaps around $4 billion. Since IBM/Mexico does not release official figures and is not listed in the Mexico 500, its established sales would place it in the top 15 firms of the 500. The company employs 9,500 workers, 6,500 in the Guadalajara manufacturing complex. The firm was founded in 1927. It provides products and services. IBM Mexican manufacturing started in the 1950s and moved to Guadalajara in 1974. Now the Guadalajara plan is the largest site for manufacture of laptops in the world. Guadalajara and a plant in Scotland produce two thirds of IBM's laptops worldwide. In addition, Guadalajara produces 30-40 percent of the motherboards for the worldwide pc industry.

The manufacturing operation differs substantially from maquiladoras. Forty percent of the content comes from local content. The suppliers are reputable local and international firms, rather than maquila suppliers. The workforce is young and highly educated for Mexico. Excluding the assembly line, 80 percent of the workforces have a licenciatura or higher, and 35-40 percent have masters or other graduate degrees or diplomas. Women are very well represented in the workforce and at much higher than the Mexican average. The manufacturing philosophy is one of *value added*, rather than *low cost* that is prevalent in maquila production.

Besides manufacturing, IBM provides sales and distribution of products in Mexico. However, for IBM/Mexico, the largest growth has been in services. It has had a 35-40 percent annual growth rate for services over the past nine years; this compares to 20-26 percent annual growth overall. This follows a trend worldwide in IBM of movement to more services. IBM/Mexico's services are 95 percent to local companies and organizations. Five percent are provided to global firms, for example to the G.E. Turbine division.

Although the firm has mostly been successful in Mexico, there was one widely publicized failure. In 1996 IBM obtained a 27 million dollar contract to design a new network computer system and data-base for the criminal investigations division of the Federal District Prosecutor's Office. However, when the system was installed in 1997, it failed. Since it didn't work well and was unable to be corrected, the Prosecutor's Office disconnected it, and it hasn't been used. Three directors of IBM/Mexico were charged with prison-bearing civil offenses. IBM has contested the charges including pointing out that the system met the contract requirements and was used before being disconnected.

This incident reflects problems that both service companies and users of services face in Mexico. It may even occur for companies of world renown. One problem was that standards were not made clear enough. Another problem related to how to judge failures in services. This problem is being worked out, and is an exception in respect to IBM's overall record. However, it underscores the challenges of providing computer services in Mexico. IBM/Mexico expects services will continue to increase more rapidly than the business as a whole. It is being forced to adopt competitive standards in services, an area differing greatly from its traditional manufacturing base.

# 7

## Transport and Communication

## Introduction

This chapter focuses on transportation and communication. The globalization process has influenced both in Mexico. However, the true extent of its impact remains to be seen. Clearly, communication in Mexico is in the process of being drastically altered. Transportation modifications in Mexico are a result primarily of the privatization process that has taken place over the past decade or so. Communication modalities in Mexico have been influenced by privatization but also likewise extensively by emerging electronic technology and globalization. The utilization of esoteric communication technology in Mexico is in a neophyte stage. The 1993 economic census reported 22,011 communication and transportation enterprises, or 0.8 percent of the Mexican total. The number of employees in this sector numbered 511,443, or 3.6 percent of the Mexican total (INEGI 1994).

Historically, cargo transportation in Mexico relied mainly upon road transportation with rail, air, and marine services lagging. Long-haul cargo is primarily road. There has been a lack of investment in transportation modalities other than roads and especially neglected have been the air and maritime infrastructure. Figure 7.1 shows the relative investment in transport sector from 1991 through 1996. There was growth in 1992 and 1993 but there has been a serious investment decline after 1994. During the entire period well over half of the total investment was in roads followed by rail.

One of the more recent events in Mexico has been the privatization of many state owned enterprises, among them communication and transportation entities. Of these, privatization of the railroads has been slow but generally with positive outcomes. Seaports are still federally owned, with one exception, but are run independently of the government by concessionaires and thus are quasi-governmental. Airports and airlines are in process of being privatized with slow and mixed results. Tollroads have clearly been a disaster and remain so to this day.

Overall, "Mexico's impressive rise to the world trade big leagues has occurred despite, rather than because of its transport infrastructure" (Fineren 1999). Rail and maritime have been declining significantly over the past several decades, though still ample, but to expand them will be costly. Truck robberies are a major problem with 750 in 1998 and up 15 percent in 1999 (Fineren 1999). Finally, mordida, bribery still exists in the transport industry.

## Major Transportation and Communication Enterprises

Table 7.1 shows that in the Mexican 500 in 1997, 10 entities were transportation, two in services to transportation, two with a storage orientation, and 11 that were listed as communication enterprises, for a total of 25. Note that the vast majority of these corporations were Mexican owned, with some U.S. and Phillipines influence. One of these enterprises was federally owned - number 453, transportation of salt. This federally owned corporation is related to another one focused on the production of salt - number 218. These two related enterprises are described in more detail in a mini case study at the end of this chapter.

Telmex is the number 2 corporation in Mexico and controls local telephone calls throughout the country. It is the second telephone company in sales in Latin America. It has half the sales of Telebras, the Brazilian telephone company, but has twice the sales of the third ranked telephone enterprise, Telesp, also of Brazil (Thomson and Bowen 1997). In Mexico, the next three major entities in sales were Grupo Televisa with over 14 billion pesos of sales and two aviation firms with 8-9 billion pesos each of sales.

### Table 7.1 Leading Transport, Storage, and Communications Firms, 1997

| Company | Position in 500 | Sales* | Profits | Position in 500 | Net Profit margin (%) |
|---|---|---|---|---|---|
| **Transport** | | | | | |
| Cintra | 13 | 18,606,570 | 1,879,264 | 5 | 10.10 |
| Aerovias de Mexico | 36 | 8,903,404 | 755,009 | 8 | 8.50 |
| Corporacion Mexicana de Aviacion | 40 | 8,258,716 | 941,494 | 7 | 11.40 |
| Transportacion Maritima Mexicana y Subs | 46 | 7,350,972 | (84,536) | SP | (1.20) |
| Transportacion Maritima Mexicana | 81 | 3,558,530 | (85,049) | SP | (2.40) |
| Grupo Aeromar | 260 | 418,901 | 96,934 | 6 | 23.10 |
| Enfriadora y Transportadora Agropecuaria | 378 | 154,689 | 31,665 | 3 | 20.50 |
| Transportes Pitic | 402 | 118,689 | 8,003 | 1 | 6.80 |
| Transportadora de Sal | 453 | 75,628 | 5,370 | 4 | 7.10 |
| Cargo Master's Internacional | 463 | 69,308 | 4,678 | 2 | 6.70 |
| Subtotal | | | 1,943,371 | | 10.40 |
| | | | | | |
| **Transport Services** | | | | | |
| Aeroservicios Especializados | 254 | 442,232 | 114,140 | SP | 25.80 |
| Internacional de Contenedores Asociad de Ver | 284 | 324,498 | 52,504 | 1 | 16.20 |
| Subtotal | | 766,730 | 166,644 | | 21.00 |
| | | | | | |
| **Storage** | | | | | |
| Servios Empresariales Soran | 286 | 303,631 | 66,799 | 1 | 22.00 |
| Almacenadora Accel | 396 | 130,391 | 12,387 | SP | 9.50 |
| Subtotal | | 454,520 | 81,133 | | 15.80 |
| | | | | | |
| **Communication** | | | | | |
| Telefonos de Mexico | 2 | 60,723,871 | 47,874,700 | 7 | 78.80 |
| Grupo Televisa | 20 | 14,164,129 | 6,247,797 | SP | 44.10 |
| TV Azteca y Subs | 79 | 3,637,754 | 1,152,441 | 3 | 31.70 |
| Telefonos del Noroeste | 100 | 2,336,768 | 538,859 | 5 | 23.10 |
| Iusacell | 117 | 1,860,486 | (72,559) | 9 | (3.90) |
| Grupo Radio Centro | 209 | 662,009 | 146,966 | 2 | 22.20 |
| Fomento Radio Beep | 310 | 239,193 | 9,544 | 4 | 4.00 |
| Carso Global Telecom | 360 | 168,748 | 734,054 | 8 | 435.00 |
| Biper | 367 | 161,797 | 30,758 | 1 | 19.00 |
| Marcatel | 380 | 148,601 | 0 | SP | NS |
| Radio Beep | 434 | 90,593 | 9,558 | 6 | 10.60 |
| Subtotal | | 81,708,580 | 56,133,257 | | 64.20 |

Source: Expansión, 1997.

* indicates 1000s of pesos.

Table 7.1 Leading Transport, Storage, and Communications Firms, 1997 (Continued)

| Company | Return on Investment | Total Assets Miles de $ | Position | Miles de $ |
|---|---|---|---|---|
| **Transport** | | | | |
| Cintra | 34.95 | 14,401,004 | 6 | 8,046,011 |
| Aerovias de Mexico | 34.02 | 5,565,127 | 9 | 1,858,105 |
| Corporacion Mexicana de Aviacion | 33.35 | 7,841,839 | 7 | 5,443,575 |
| Transportacion Maritima Mexicana y Subs | (2.73) | 10,554,652 | 4 | 4,283,938 |
| Transportacion Maritima Mexicana | (3.37) | 8,572,075 | 10 | 1,779,478 |
| Grupo Aeromar | 37.13 | 895,796 | 8 | 765,541 |
| Enfriadora y Transportadora Agropecuaria | 16.15 | 209,683 | 3 | 199,094 |
| Transportes Pitic | 19.88 | 72,126 | 2 | 50,944 |
| Transportadora de Sal | 1.65 | 373,697 | 5 | 363,495 |
| Cargo Master's Internacional | 46.91 | 27,377 | 1 | 631 |
| Subtotal | 20.88 | 26,549,977 | | 13,717,761 |
| | | | | |
| **Transport Services** | | | | |
| Aeroservicios Especializados | 75.23 | 1,047,359 | 2 | 735,556 |
| Internacional de Contenedores Asociad de Ver | 16.46 | 380,051 | 1 | 253,204 |
| Subtotal | 35.40 | 1,427,410 | | 988,760 |
| | | | | |
| **Storage** | | | | |
| Servios Empresariales Soran | 43.48 | 250,105 | 1 | 146,645 |
| Almacenadora Accel | 3.28 | 499,489 | 2 | 441,089 |
| Subtotal | 13.73 | 828,113 | | 657,073 |
| | | | | |
| **Communication** | | | | |
| Telefonos de Mexico | 54.23 | 127,802,002 | 10 | 91,672,661 |
| Grupo Televisa | 37.87 | 34,163,578 | 9 | 9,850,897 |
| TV Azteca y Subs | 42.03 | 10,668,850 | 4 | 2,080,571 |
| Telefonos del Noroeste | 60.60 | 3,064,597 | 11 | 2,624,694 |
| Iusacell | (2.18) | 6,675,195 | 7 | 3,014,660 |
| Grupo Radio Centro | 12.14 | 1,337,980 | 6 | 395,036 |
| Fomento Radio Beep | 3.73 | 871,443 | 2 | 654,131 |
| Carso Global Telecom | 4.66 | 21,193,037 | 5 | 15,793,650 |
| Biper | 11.11 | 344,802 | 3 | 165,677 |
| Marcatel | nc | 729,582 | 1 | 633,355 |
| | | | | |
| Radio Beep | 10.31 | 141,861 | 8 | 20,777 |
| Subtotal | 43.69 | 203,928,331 | | 124,281,415 |

It is expected that a number of electronic, high technology firms will be emerging over the next several years with accompanying alterations in respective ranking of transport and especially of communication enterprises.

## Roads and Vehicles

One of the first aspects of transport and communication in Mexico that must be recognized is that Mexico City since first recorded times has been the principal point of distribution and consumption of products, both within Mexico and to and from other countries (INEGI 1994: 661). The major roads map and railroads maps in Mexico are shown on Map 7.1 – Map 7.6.

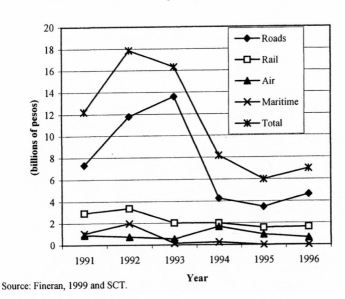

**Figure 7.1**
**Total Investment in Transport by Subsector in Mexico**

Source: Fineran, 1999 and SCT.

The early main roads were from Mexico City to Veracruz, the north of the country, the Bajio, and to Oaxaca. The way to Veracruz passed through Jalapa or Orizaba. This route during the colonial era was the passageway to Europe. It was not until around 1821 that routes were opened to the northeast and to the Pacific that tied the central region and the Bajio to these other districts. Roads were the cardinal means of moving people and cargo from one region to another.

By 1835 there was a beginning of a more elaborate road system necessary for movement of goods and people. This expanded road network was accompanied by the development of hotels, paradors, and passable roads. The most important roads continued to be from Mexico City to Veracruz. However, other roads to Tepic via Queretaro, Lagos, and Guadalajara, to Morelia passing through Toluca, to Cuautla via Cuernavaca, and to Tulancingo via Pachuca emerged as important byways.

Historical data show very few registered autos and trucks in Mexico prior to 1950. After that time there was a slow increase until 1975 and 1980 when growth accelerated for both trucks and automobiles. In 1990, there were 6.47 million registered automobiles in Mexico, of which 6.4 million were personally registered. In addition, there were over 200,000 personally owned motorcycles, over 4,700,000 trucks, and almost 13,000 buses (see Table 7.2).

In 1990, Mexico had more registered vehicles than telephones. Of the over six million automobiles, 2.6 million of them were registered in the Federal District and State of Mexico (Mexico City); thus, a relatively small region of Mexico accounted for over one third of automobiles in Mexico. The region along the U.S. border accounted for 1.6 million more; thus, Mexico City and the border region accounted for 4.0 million of the total 6.47 million autos in Mexico. A corollary of automobiles, trucks and buses in Mexico City is that for the most part they do not have emission controls resulting in the devastating smog that covers Mexico City during parts of the year (Mumme 1991). In 1993, there were 12,972 corporations hauling cargo; however, the three federal entities of the Federal District, State of Mexico, and nearby Hidalgo had 29 percent of them (INEGI 1994).

**Table 7.2 Motor Vehicle Ownership, 1990**

|  | Pers. Owned | Rental | Official | Total |
|---|---|---|---|---|
| Automobiles | 6,439,620 | 282,263 | 32,213 | 6,754,096 |
| Motorcycles | 229,860 | 667 | 976 | 231,503 |
| Buses | 12,690 | 78,633 | 2,681 | 94,004 |
| Trucks | 4,759,189 | 117,182 | 16,477 | 4,892,848 |
| Total | 11,441,359 | 478,745 | 52,347 | 11,972,451 |

Source: INEGI, 1991 Anuario Estadistico, Table 2.2.2.

Table 7.3 illustrates the number of registered personally owned automobiles by state for 1988 and 1990, ratio per capita for both years, and ratio change between 1988 and 1990; Map 7.2 illustrates this information for 1990.

Overall the national road network increased from 224,225 km in 1985 to 332,301 km in 1996. This increase was limited to toll roads that were built at great expense. Toll roads increased from 1985 to 1996 by 594 percent while free road kilometers actually decreased by 2.8 percent. Toll roads have not paid for themselves and a number of bungled projects have had to be bailed out by the government to the tune of 60 billion pesos in 1997 (Diaussart 1999). Also, rural roads in particular have suffered from maintenance deficits. Subsequently, the Zedillo administration claims to have build 6,000 km of new roads.

The emergence of globalization has influenced transportation in Mexico, especially to and along the U.S. border. Over 90 percent of trade between Mexico and the U.S. moves by truck. A 1993 agreement developed special border zones in which Mexican trucks could travel unimpeded for up to 14 miles across the border into the U.S. This was done so that they could reach the major cities in the U.S. border region. Currently, it is estimated that every 12 seconds a truck from Mexico is entering the U.S.

NAFTA rules and regulations state that international cargo transportation in U.S.-Mexico border states was to be opened to competition in December, 1995. However, the U.S. has refused to validate this provision, and will likely not do so in January, 2000, unless the commitment is once again not honored (Lota 1999). The argument against accepting the NAFTA agreement is that Mexican trucks do not meet U.S. safety standards since they do not have front brakes or undergo regular roadside inspections. Further, there are no restrictions on how long Mexican truck drivers can keep driving in contrast to U.S. drivers who are limited to 10 hour stretches. In addition, U.S. limits weights to 80,000 pounds while Mexican trucks are limited to 97,000 pounds but often haul up to 130,000 pounds! Truck driver licenses in Mexico are to be had with virtually no restrictions (Adelson 1999).

Currently, regulations covering cargo crossing the border to the U.S. from Mexico mandates three truck cab changes, with a U.S. driver on the U.S. side of the border. A further complication is that Mexican drivers make one-third of the pay of U.S. drivers thus U.S. unions want a U.S. driver in the U.S. or require that Mexican companies pay the same scale as U.S. companies.

## Transportation in Mexico City

While there is little railroad passenger traffic in Mexico, thousands of long-distance buses traverse the countryside to even the smallest towns. In addition, the three largest Mexican cities - Mexico City, Guadalajara, and Monterrey - have subway and/or light rail systems. In greater Mexico City, over 134,000 paratransit vehicles transport passengers all over the city (see Table 7.4). In addition, there is the metro (see Map 7.3), taxis, and private automobile transportation. As shown on Table 7.5, the metro system totals almost 4 ½ million trips per day. Surface diesel buses and other modes almost equal that number for 9 million trips per day. The paratransit system accounts for almost 13 million trips and there are an estimated 1.7 million taxi trips. Finally, well over ten million private automobile trips are made on a daily basis. All of these trips total almost 37 million trips per day.

## Railroads

In 1873 Mexico had 539,000 meters of railroad lines. Map 7.4 shows the 1880 rail lines; this was the year that the railroad from Mexico City to Veracruz was completed. During that era, for every ton of freight hauled, there were approximately five passengers. There was slow growth in railroad length in meters up to 1880 and then relatively larger increases in 1881 and 1882 to over five million meters. In 1884 the first Mexican rail line to the U.S. border was completed (see Map 7.5). After 1884, growth in railroad lineage was slow until the early 1900s. However, in the late 1800s the first railroads were being developed to Yucatan was completed (see Map 7.6). In the 1900s slow growth took place until 1910 when the civil wars in Mexico commenced. From 1910 until very recently only small increases in length have taken place.

As the years passed, freight became more important as the number of passengers gradually decreased. A substantial decline in passengers took place between 1970 and 1975. This decline in passengers was accompanied by a dramatic increase in the movement of cargo during the same years (INEGI 1994). By 1990, the railroad network in Mexico was completed and little construction has taken place since that time (see Map 7.7). Rail passenger transportation in Mexico is now almost extinct except for a few foreign tourists taking the Copper Canyon train.

The influence of globalization on the rail network so far appears to be minimal although there may be additional reasons for growth in the future with connecting lines in the U.S. One such effort to increase rail cargo to and from Mexico is the planned multi-billion dollar Alameda Corridor. It has the potential through future extensions to connect Los Angeles and Long Beach Harbors to Mexicali, Baja California.

## Air and Maritime

The first commercial airport opened in Mexico City in 1929. In 1965 Mexico had a total of 34 commercial airports and the Airports and Auxiliary Services (ASA) was created to administer and oversee modernization of the system. In 1993 there were 249 airline related corporations with over 20,000 employees. Thirty-nine of the 249 were foreign companies with approximately 2,000 employees (INEGI 1994).

**Table 7.3 Registered Personally Owned Automobiles, 1988 and 1990**

| No. | State | Automobiles 1988 | Ratio | Automobiles 1990 | Ratio | Ratio % Change 1988-1990 |
|---|---|---|---|---|---|---|
| 1 | Aguascalientes | 40,388 | 0.0561 | 44,240 | 0.0005 | 9.5 |
| 2 | Baja California | 365,388 | 0.2200 | 395,087 | 0.0049 | 8.1 |
| 3 | Baja California Sur | 34,796 | 0.1095 | 37,668 | 0.0005 | 8.3 |
| 4 | Campeche | 23,729 | 0.0443 | 30,507 | 0.0004 | 28.6 |
| 5 | Coahuila | 160,376 | 0.0813 | 204,353 | 0.0025 | 27.4 |
| 6 | Colima | 49,257 | 0.1149 | 48,343 | 0.0006 | (1.9) |
| 7 | Chiapas | 48,238 | 0.0150 | 62,435 | 0.0008 | 29.4 |
| 8 | Chihuahua | 309,721 | 0.1268 | 321,590 | 0.0040 | 3.8 |
| 9 | Distrito Federal | 1,619,541 | 0.1966 | 1,944,479 | 0.0239 | 20.1 |
| 10 | Durango | 53,159 | 0.0394 | 57,295 | 0.0007 | 7.8 |
| 11 | Guanajuato | 128,495 | 0.0323 | 147,301 | 0.0018 | 14.6 |
| 12 | Guerrero | 58,806 | 0.0224 | 64,910 | 0.0008 | 10.4 |
| 13 | Hidalgo | 56,598 | 0.0300 | 74,109 | 0.0009 | 30.9 |
| 14 | Jalisco | 363,407 | 0.0685 | 409,047 | 0.0050 | 12.6 |
| 15 | Mexico | 557,565 | 0.0568 | 671,551 | 0.0083 | 20.4 |
| 16 | Michoacan | 113,416 | 0.0320 | 130,834 | 0.0016 | 15.4 |
| 17 | Morelos | 119,384 | 0.0999 | 120,750 | 0.0015 | 1.1 |
| 18 | Nayarit | 25,431 | 0.0308 | 26,464 | 0.0003 | 4.1 |
| 19 | Nuevoleon | 271,383 | 0.0876 | 303,085 | 0.0037 | 11.7 |
| 20 | Oaxaca | 38,194 | 0.0126 | 46,053 | 0.0006 | 20.6 |
| 21 | Puebla | 191,450 | 0.0464 | 218,640 | 0.0027 | 14.2 |
| 22 | Queretaro | 40,348 | 0.0384 | 54,530 | 0.0007 | 35.1 |
| 23 | Quintana Roo | 16,722 | 0.0339 | 22,381 | 0.0003 | 33.8 |
| 24 | San Luis Potosi | 63,380 | 0.0316 | 73,422 | 0.0009 | 15.8 |
| 25 | Sinaloa | 95,668 | 0.0434 | 105,511 | 0.0013 | 10.3 |
| 26 | Sonora | 123,792 | 0.0679 | 149,932 | 0.0018 | 21.1 |
| 27 | Tabasco | 47,840 | 0.0319 | 56,493 | 0.0007 | 18.1 |
| 28 | Tamaulipas | 223,771 | 0.0995 | 239,634 | 0.0029 | 7.1 |
| 29 | Tlaxcala | 23,483 | 0.0308 | 28,813 | 0.0004 | 22.7 |
| 30 | Veracruz | 196,516 | 0.0316 | 223,272 | 0.0027 | 13.6 |
| 31 | Yucatan | 77,316 | 0.0567 | 86,768 | 0.0011 | 12.2 |
| 32 | Zacatecas | 31,564 | 0.0247 | 40,123 | 0.0005 | 27.1 |
| National Total | | 5,569,122 | 0.0685 | 6,439,620 | 0.0793 | 15.6 |
| Mean | | 174,035 | 0.0629 | 201,238 | 0.0025 | 16.1 |
| Median | | 70,348 | 0.0439 | 80,439 | 0.0010 | 14.4 |
| S.D. | | 292,618 | 0.0489 | 349,516 | 0.0043 | 9.7 |
| C.V. | | 168.14 | 77.76 | 174 | 173.68 | 60.1 |
| Minimum | | 16,722 | 0.0126 | 22,381 | 0.0003 | (1.9) |
| Maximum | | 1,619,541 | 0.2200 | 1,944,479 | 0.0239 | 35.1 |

Definition: Ratio is the number of registered privately owned vehicles 1988 or 1990 to the total population 1990. Ratio percent change was calculated by subtracting the 1990 ratio from the 1988 ratio, multiplying by 100, and dividing by the 1988 ratio.

Source: INEGI, 1988-89 Anuario Estadistico, Table 2.1.18, and 1991 Anuario Estadistico, Table 2.2.2.

### Table 7.4 Mexico City's Hierarchy of Smaller Commercial Transport Services, 1994

|  | Seating Capacities (No. of Passengers) | Typical Route Operating Ranges (One-Way Kilometers) | Vehicle Inventory Federal District | State of Mexico | Total |
|---|---|---|---|---|---|
| Taxis | 2 - 3 | 3 - 6 | 56,059 | 8,456 | 64,515 |
| Peseros: Sedans | 5 - 6 | 2 - 4 | 763 | 2,626 | 3,389 |
| Peseros: VW Vans | 10 - 14 | 5 - 10 | 22,690 | 13,860 | 36,550 |
| Minibuses | 22 - 25 | 10 - 20 | 20,493 | 9,527 | 30,020 |
| Total |  |  | 100,005 | 34,469 | 134,474 |

Source: La Coordinacion General de Transportate del DDF, data files; field surveys, November 1994.

### Table 7.5 Daily Motorized Trips in Greater Mexico City, 1994

|  | Federal District Total | Percent | State of Mexico Total | Percent | Metropolitan Area Total | Percent |
|---|---|---|---|---|---|---|
| Public Transportation |  |  |  |  |  |  |
| Metro | 4,488,000 | 17.6 | 0 | 0.0 | 4,488,000 | 12.2 |
| Light rail | 15,000 | 0.1 | 0 | 0.0 | 15,000 | 0.1 |
| Ruta Cien (surface diesel bus) | 3,208,000 | 12.6 | 0 | 0.0 | 3,208,000 | 8.7 |
| Electric trolley bus | 330,000 | 1.3 | 0 | 0.0 | 330,000 | 0.8 |
| Other bus (autobus) | 0 | 0.0 | 4,385,000 | 38.2 | 4,385,000 | 11.9 |
| Paratransit |  |  |  |  |  |  |
| Minibuses | 5,738,000 | 22.5 | 2,287,000 | 19.9 | 8,025,000 | 21.7 |
| Peseros (combis and sedans) | 2,772,000 | 10.9 | 1,831,000 | 16.0 | 4,603,000 | 12.5 |
| Taxis | 1,615,000 | 6.3 | 102,000 | 0.9 | 1,717,000 | 4.6 |
| Private Automobile | 7,316,000 | 28.7 | 2,864,000 | 25.0 | 10,180,000 | 27.5 |
| Total | 25,482,000 | 100.0 | 11,469,000 | 100.0 | 36,951,000 | 100.0 |

Source: Instituto Nacional de Estadistica Geografia e Informatica (INEGI), Encuesta de Origen y
Destino de los Viajes de los Residentes del Area Metropolitana de la Ciudad de México
(Mexico City: INEGI, 1994). Cervero, 1998.

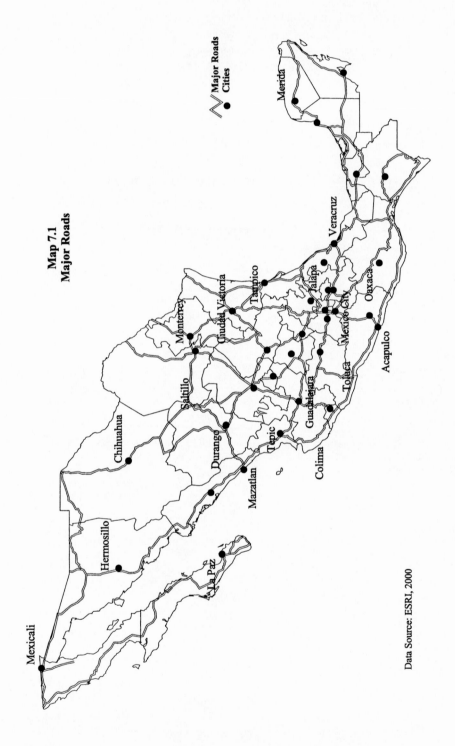

Map 7.1
Major Roads

Major Roads
● Cities

Mexicali

Hermosillo

Chihuahua

La Paz

Durango

Mazatlan

Saltillo

Monterrey

Ciudad Victoria

Tepic

Tampico

Guadalajara

Colima

Toluca

Mexico City

Jalapa

Veracruz

Oaxaca

Acapulco

Merida

Data Source: ESRI, 2000

**Map 7.2**
**Registered Personally Owned**
**Automobiles, 1990**

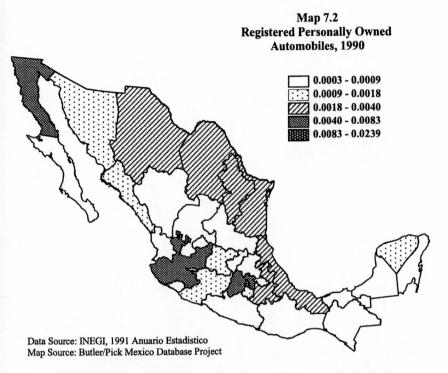

0.0003 - 0.0009
0.0009 - 0.0018
0.0018 - 0.0040
0.0040 - 0.0083
0.0083 - 0.0239

Data Source: INEGI, 1991 Anuario Estadistico
Map Source: Butler/Pick Mexico Database Project

Of the current 70 commercial airports, Map 7.8 shows the major ones. Privatization of the airlines has resulted in Cintra becoming the holding company for formerly state owned airlines, Aeromexico, Mexicana, and Aeromexpress. Cintra is joining with five international airlines to share flight codes throughout the world. Included in the alliance are Delta and Air France (Guenette 1999). Currently underway are efforts seeking expanded private investment to take over the airports.

In air traffic there are distinctive regional patterns. The west and southeast have quite high levels of commercial air flights. This is due partly to tourism-related traffic, especially in the southeast. The central region is a contrast with a large number of air flights to the Federal District, but few flights elsewhere. The border region has a moderate number of commercial flights (see Pick and Butler 1994).

Also shown on Map 7.8 are the major Mexican seaports. Many of them are undergoing a construction boom attempting to keep pace with the demand. Modernization of ports began in 1993 (Gellner 1999), although note that investment for maritime efforts was not very great that year or in subsequent years (see Figure 7.1). In 1993, there were 516 maritime corporations listed in the economic census with 9,756 employees (INEGI 1994). Of these 516, 148 of them were in Baja California Sur, undoubtedly related to the fishing and tourist industries. A substantial number of the other entities were in Quintana Roo and Jalisco also most likely associated with tourism.

While still in government hands, all ports, except Acapulco, are responsible for their own operation and attending to service demands. Acapulco is special because of its tourist-based traffic. Each port appears to have a distinguishing emphasis -- Lazaro Cardenas is an industrial exporter; Veracruz is the port for domestic manufacturers and exporters; Progreso is a grain-export facility; Manzanillo is a growing port with exporting automobiles; while

## Map 7.3 Mexico City's Metro Network, 1997

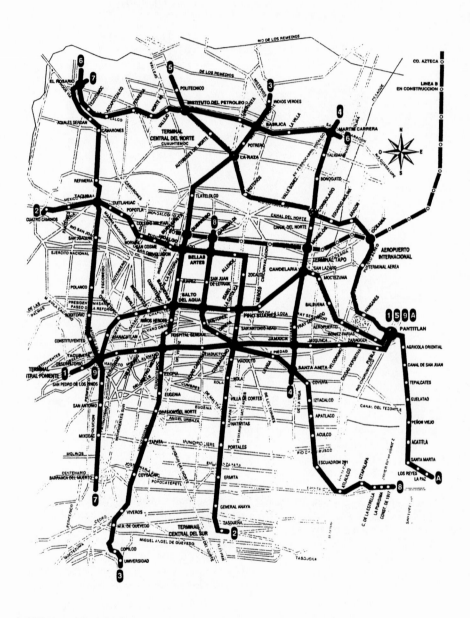

**Map 7.4
Railroad, 1880**

Railroads,1880

Source: Butler/Pick Mexico Database Project.
University of California, Riverside. Florenscano, 1983.

**Map 7.5
Railroads, 1884**

Railroads, 1884

Source: Butler/Pick Mexico Database Project.
University of California, Riverside. Florenscano, 1983.

**Map 7.6**
**Railroads, 1898**

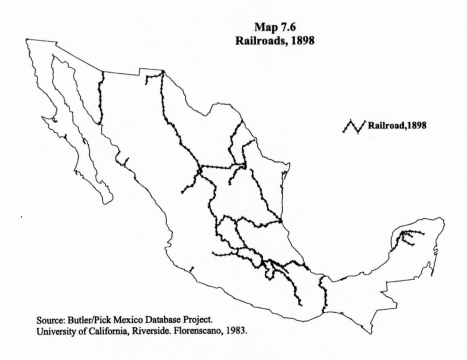

Railroad,1898

Source: Butler/Pick Mexico Database Project.
University of California, Riverside. Florenscano, 1983.

**Map 7.7**
**Railroads, 1990**

Railroads, 1990

Source: Butler/Pick Mexico Database Project.
University of California, Riverside. Florenscano, 1983.

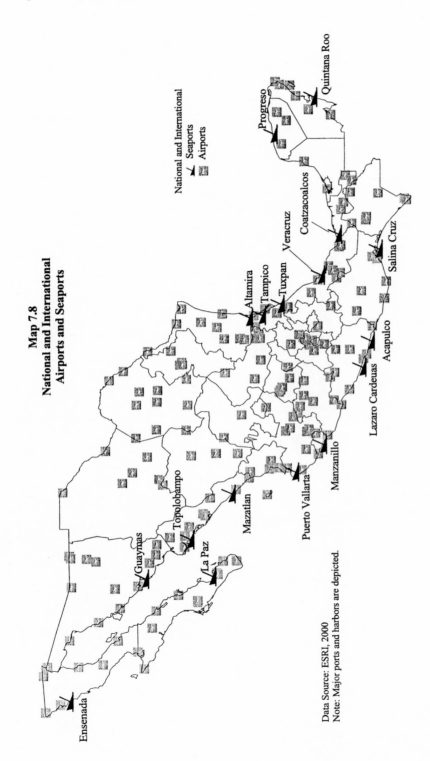

Map 7.8
National and International
Airports and Seaports

National and International
Seaports
Airports

Ensenada
Guaymas
Topolobampo
La Paz
Mazatlan
Puerto Vallarta
Manzanillo
Lazaro Cardeuas
Acapulco
Salina Cruz
Coatzacoalcos
Veracruz
Tuxpan
Tampico
Altamira
Progreso
Quintana Roo

Data Source: ESRI, 2000
Note: Major ports and harbors are depicted.

Coatzacoalcos and Pajarito, the major ports in terms of bulk, each move about 32 million tons a year of crude oil.

So far it is difficult to determine the impact that globalization and maquiladoras have had upon the air and maritime traffic. Given recent events regarding the potential of tariff reduction on Mexican products in Europe, it might be anticipated that the east coast ports may have an increase in exports, especially automobiles.

## Electronic Media

This section is divided into three major parts. The first division discusses radio and television stations. The second component describes some of the major changes taking place in the Mexican telephone industry, especially the emergence of long distance companies. The final part of this section accentuates the emerging electronic media in Mexico.

### Radio and Television

Radio and television stations do not follow the same pattern in their distribution in Mexico among the states. Radio station concessions, permits, and per capita are shown on Table 7.6 and their distribution on Map 7.9. Radio station permits in 1988 had high rates per capita in the northern border states, in Guanajuato, Veracruz, and the Federal District. Some states had very few radio stations and Baja California Sur, Morelos, and Nayarit had no permits. In addition, the state of Puebla had no radio permits even though it contains the fourth largest city in Mexico. Undoubtedly, the higher number in the border states was because radio waves from these stations carry into the United States (see Pick, Butler, and Lanzer 1994: 277-278, 282-283).

Television stations on a per capita basis in 1988 were concentrated in states such as Baja California Sur, Quintana Roo, and Sonora, states with a relatively low density but also with tourism (see Pick, Butler, and Lanzer 1994: 278, 282-283). Their distribution was not significantly associated with radio stations (see Table 7.6 and Map 7.10). During that year, Sonora, Chihuahua, and Durango had the most stations; however, on a per capita basis they were concentrated in Baja California Sur, Quintana Roo, as well as in Durango and Sonora.

What impact globalization and free trade will have on radio and television stations remains unknown at this time.

### Telephones

Nationally, in 1989 there was one phone for about every eight Mexicans, an increase from one phone for every 13 Mexicans in 1980; every state except Tlaxcala had an increase in phones (Pick, Butler, and Lanzer 1987: 352). As with many other dimensions, the north and the central region that makes up Mexico City had a high per capita of telephones, which was in contrast to the south with few telephones (see Table 7.7 and Map 7.11). In an earlier work, our statistical analysis found that telephones per capita were associated with a variety of urbanization, modernization, and educational measures (Pick and Butler 1994: 277).

The Mexican economic census of 1993 reported 4,941 corporations devoted to communications with 114,625 employees. About half of these enterprises were local telephone companies spread out among the various states. According to the census, 99 percent of these entities were privately owned. Unrelated to these communication enterprises was population size. In 1993, there was substantial deficit coverage of telephones in rural areas.

In spite of the lack of rural coverage in Mexico, Telmex and others have looked outside of Mexico to expand their market (EFI Staff 1998). This may be because of the high cost

**Map 7.9**
**Radio Stations**
**Per 10,000 Population**
**1988**

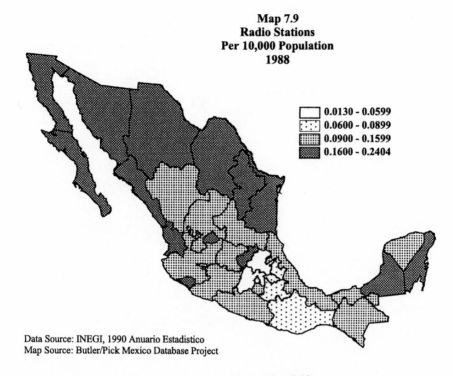

| | |
|---|---|
| | 0.0130 - 0.0599 |
| | 0.0600 - 0.0899 |
| | 0.0900 - 0.1599 |
| | 0.1600 - 0.2404 |

Data Source: INEGI, 1990 Anuario Estadistico
Map Source: Butler/Pick Mexico Database Project

**Map 7.10**
**Television Stations**
**Per 10,000 Population**
**1988**

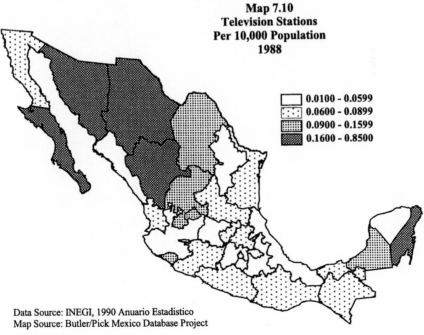

| | |
|---|---|
| | 0.0100 - 0.0599 |
| | 0.0600 - 0.0899 |
| | 0.0900 - 0.1599 |
| | 0.1600 - 0.8500 |

Data Source: INEGI, 1990 Anuario Estadistico
Map Source: Butler/Pick Mexico Database Project

## Table 7.6 Radio and Television Stations, 1988

| No. | State | Radio Stations | | | | TV Stations | | | |
|---|---|---|---|---|---|---|---|---|---|
| | | Concessions | Permits | Per Capita | Perc. Of Nation | Concession | Permits | Per Capita | Perc. Of Nation |
| 1 | Aguascalientes | 10 | 3 | 0.1810 | 1.30 | 2 | 5 | 0.0970 | 1.26 |
| 2 | Baja California Sur | 48 | 2 | 0.3010 | 5.00 | 8 | 3 | 0.0660 | 1.99 |
| 3 | Baja California | 6 | 0 | 0.1890 | 0.60 | 5 | 22 | 0.8500 | 4.87 |
| 4 | Campeche | 10 | 3 | 0.2430 | 1.30 | 4 | 3 | 0.1310 | 1.26 |
| 5 | Coahuila | 49 | 1 | 0.2540 | 5.00 | 12 | 15 | 0.1370 | 4.87 |
| 6 | Colima | 7 | 1 | 0.1870 | 0.80 | 2 | 4 | 0.1400 | 1.08 |
| 7 | Chiapas | 28 | 2 | 0.0900 | 2.90 | 12 | 15 | 0.0840 | 4.87 |
| 8 | Chihuahua | 56 | 2 | 0.2380 | 5.80 | 18 | 22 | 0.1640 | 7.22 |
| 9 | Distrito Federal | 63 | 10 | 0.0890 | 7.30 | 6 | 2 | 0.0100 | 1.44 |
| 10 | Durango | 14 | 1 | 0.1110 | 1.50 | 4 | 71 | 0.5560 | 13.54 |
| 11 | Guanajuato | 47 | 5 | 0.1310 | 5.20 | 3 | 8 | 0.0280 | 1.99 |
| 12 | Guerrero | 24 | 4 | 0.1070 | 2.80 | 10 | 9 | 0.0730 | 3.43 |
| 13 | Hidalgo | 6 | 4 | 0.0530 | 1.00 | 1 | 11 | 0.0640 | 2.17 |
| 14 | Jalisco | 61 | 4 | 0.1230 | 6.50 | 10 | 9 | 0.0360 | 3.43 |
| 15 | Mexico | 10 | 3 | 0.0130 | 1.30 | 3 | 9 | 0.0120 | 2.17 |
| 16 | Michoacan | 35 | 2 | 0.1040 | 3.70 | 10 | 13 | 0.0650 | 4.15 |
| 17 | Morelos | 13 | 0 | 0.1090 | 1.30 | 1 | 1 | 0.0170 | 0.36 |
| 18 | Nayarit | 14 | 0 | 0.1700 | 1.40 | 3 | 3 | 0.0730 | 1.08 |
| 19 | Nuevoleon | 43 | 7 | 0.1610 | 5.00 | 6 | 3 | 0.0290 | 1.62 |
| 20 | Oaxaca | 20 | 3 | 0.0760 | 2.30 | 10 | 13 | 0.0760 | 4.15 |
| 21 | Puebla | 28 | 0 | 0.0680 | 2.80 | 3 | 5 | 0.0190 | 1.44 |
| 22 | Queretaro | 14 | 3 | 0.1620 | 1.70 | 3 | 4 | 0.0670 | 1.26 |
| 23 | Quintana Roo | 7 | 2 | 0.1820 | 0.90 | 4 | 21 | 0.5070 | 4.51 |
| 24 | San Luis Potosi | 26 | 2 | 0.1400 | 2.80 | 6 | 7 | 0.0650 | 2.35 |
| 25 | Sinaloa | 38 | 1 | 0.1770 | 3.90 | 8 | 2 | 0.0450 | 1.81 |
| 26 | Sonora | 53 | 8 | 0.6650 | 6.10 | 17 | 32 | 0.2690 | 8.84 |
| 27 | Tabasco | 15 | 2 | 0.1130 | 1.70 | 3 | 8 | 0.0730 | 1.99 |
| 28 | Tamaulipas | 62 | 1 | 0.2800 | 6.30 | 16 | 3 | 0.0840 | 3.43 |
| 29 | Tlaxcala | 4 | 1 | 0.0660 | 0.50 | 0 | 4 | 0.0530 | 0.72 |
| 30 | Veracruz | 77 | 3 | 0.1280 | 8.00 | 9 | 7 | 0.0260 | 2.89 |
| 31 | Yucatan | 18 | 2 | 0.1470 | 2.00 | 5 | 2 | 0.0510 | 1.26 |

## Table 7.6 Radio and Television Stations, 1988 (Continued)

| | | | | | | | | |
|---|---|---|---|---|---|---|---|---|
| 32  Zacatecas | 12 | 1 | 0.1020 | 1.30 | 7 | 7 | 0.1100 | 2.53 |
| National Total | 918 | 82 | 0.4830 | | 211 | 343 | 0.4077 | |
| Mean | 28.6875 | 2.5625 | 0.1510 | 3.1250 | 6.5938 | 10.7188 | 0.1270 | 3.1244 |
| Median | 22.0000 | 2.0000 | 0.1360 | 2.5500 | 5.5000 | 7.0000 | 0.0700 | 2.1700 |
| S.D. | 20.9922 | 2.3132 | 0.0750 | 2.2088 | 4.7305 | 13.1744 | 0.1810 | 2.6846 |
| C.V. | 73.18 | 90.27 | 496.69 | 70.68 | 71.74 | 122.91 | 1,425.20 | 85.92 |
| Minimum | 4.0000 | 0.0000 | 0.0130 | 0.5000 | 0.0000 | 1.0000 | 0.0100 | 0.3600 |
| Maximum | 77.0000 | 10.0000 | 0.3350 | 8.0000 | 18.0000 | 71.0000 | 0.8500 | 13.5400 |

Definition: Per capita values are the number of radio and television stations to the total population of the year 1998.

Source: INEGI, 1988-89 Anuario Estadistico.

of putting in telephone lines in rural areas (Gonzales 1998). The cost for rural areas is up to five times what it costs to install lines in urban areas. When Telmex was privatized in 1990, only 10,221 rural Mexican towns had phones; now at least 12,000 additional towns have phones. In addition, the Communications and Transportation Ministry (SCT) is connecting towns with cellular technology. Midite, using satellite technology, obtains a signal and then distributes it along wires to each house; the company needs at least 80 customers in a town to make a profit (Gonzales 1998).

Telmex (Telefonos de Mexico) for many years held a monopoly on the local telephone market. Even though now privatized, Telmex still controls the local market but also covets the long-distance trade. However, beginning in January 1997, other telephone companies were allowed to compete for the long-distance market. As long-distance companies began competing for customers with Telmex, some of them had insulting ads and begin "slamming," and there were regulatory fights (Smith 1998). This put such giants as MCI and AT&T in conflict with Telmex. "Slamming" refers to a practice in the telecommunications industry of aggressively seeking competitors' customers through strong purereductions and "marketing assaults" on competitors' customer lists. Telmex, as of 1997, remained the second major corporation in Mexico, superceded only by Pemex.

After one year of competition, Telmex's market share had dropped by more than 25 percent but it still maintained a 73 percent share of the market. Its main competitors were Alestra and its U.S. partner AT&T having 24 percent (see case study at the end of this chapter), Avantel and its U.S. partner MCI with 12 percent, and others with one percent (Smith 1998). Telmex uses its "Mexican-ness' to influence investors and customers. When Mexicans had the opportunity to select a long-distance carrier, most customers did not select one and thus remained with Telmex by default. Telmex's international partners are Southwestern Bell of St. Louis and France Telecom. Long-distance companies and their main foreign partners are shown on Table 7.8.

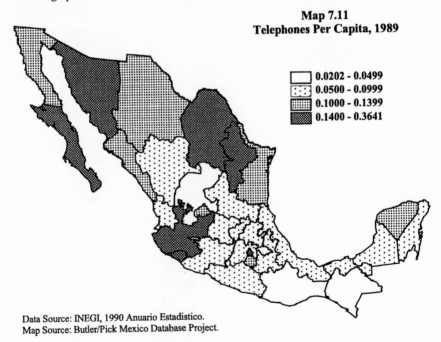

**Map 7.11**
**Telephones Per Capita, 1989**

| | |
|---|---|
| ☐ | 0.0202 - 0.0499 |
| ▦ | 0.0500 - 0.0999 |
| ▦ | 0.1000 - 0.1399 |
| ▓ | 0.1400 - 0.3641 |

Data Source: INEGI, 1990 Anuario Estadistico.
Map Source: Butler/Pick Mexico Database Project.

The confrontation over the market is not yet resolved and should continue well into the next decade.

### Table 7.7 Telephones, 1988-1989

| | | 1988 | | 1989 | | Per Capita |
|---|---|---|---|---|---|---|
| | | Total | Telephones | Total | Telephones | % Change |
| No. | State | Telephones | Per Capita | Telephones | Per Capita | 1988-89 |
| 1 | Aguascalientes | 71,476 | 0.0993 | 80,929 | 0.1125 | 13.23 |
| 2 | Baja California | 179,683 | 0.1082 | 207,433 | 0.1249 | 15.44 |
| 3 | Baja California Sur | 59,200 | 0.1863 | 62,657 | 0.1977 | 5.84 |
| 4 | Campeche | 28,238 | 0.0528 | 30,880 | 0.0577 | 9.36 |
| 5 | Coahuila | 257,493 | 0.1306 | 277,208 | 0.1405 | 7.66 |
| 6 | Colima | 55,216 | 0.1289 | 61,582 | 0.1437 | 11.53 |
| 7 | Chiapas | 96,108 | 0.0299 | 100,023 | 0.0312 | 4.07 |
| 8 | Chihuahua | 302,585 | 0.1239 | 336,107 | 0.1376 | 11.08 |
| 9 | Distrito Federal | 2,643,869 | 0.3210 | 2,998,951 | 0.3641 | 13.43 |
| 10 | Durango | 92,531 | 0.0686 | 101,740 | 0.0754 | 9.95 |
| 11 | Guanajuato | 265,230 | 0.0666 | 286,368 | 0.0719 | 7.97 |
| 12 | Guerrero | 141,151 | 0..0539 | 155,192 | 0.0592 | 9.95 |
| 13 | Hidalgo | 90,585 | 0.0480 | 95,177 | 0.0504 | 5.07 |
| 14 | Jalisco | 708,326 | 0.1336 | 784,645 | 0.1480 | 10.77 |
| 15 | Mexico | 692,312 | 0.0705 | 721,169 | 0.0735 | 4.17 |
| 16 | Michoacan | 214,609 | 0.0605 | 239,990 | 0.0676 | 11.83 |
| 17 | Morelos | 128,570 | 0.1076 | 142,339 | 0.1191 | 10.71 |
| 18 | Nayarit | 52,871 | 0.0641 | 57,791 | 0.0701 | 9.31 |
| 19 | Nuevoleon | 554,587 | 0.1790 | 601,171 | 0.1940 | 8.40 |
| 20 | Oaxaca | 83,117 | 0.0275 | 90,426 | 0.0299 | 8.79 |
| 21 | Puebla | 281,554 | 0.0682 | 320,752 | 0.0777 | 13.92 |
| 22 | Queretaro | 70,370 | 0.0669 | 77,708 | 0.0739 | 10.43 |
| 23 | Quintana Roo | 31,472 | 0.0638 | 35,154 | 0.0713 | 11.70 |
| 24 | San Luis Potosi | 128,862 | 0.0643 | 152,036 | 0.0759 | 17.98 |
| 25 | Sinaloa | 207,419 | 0.0941 | 230,919 | 0.1048 | 11.33 |
| 26 | Sonora | 242,806 | 0.1331 | 265,349 | 0.1455 | 9.28 |
| 27 | Tabasco | 80,567 | 0.0536 | 90,071 | 0.0600 | 11.80 |
| 28 | Tamaulipas | 260,271 | 0.1157 | 283,681 | 0.1261 | 8.99 |
| 29 | Tlaxcala | 26,701 | 0.0351 | 15,361 | 0.0202 | (42.47) |
| 30 | Veracruz | 438,508 | 0.0704 | 479,580 | 0.0770 | 9.37 |
| 31 | Yucatan | 130,869 | 0.0960 | 141,280 | 0.1037 | 7.96 |
| 32 | Zacatecas | 48,156 | 0.0377 | 52,081 | 0.0408 | 8.15 |
| | National Total | 8,665,312 | 0.1066 | 9,575,750 | 0.1179 | 10.60 |
| | | | | | | |
| | Mean | 270,791 | 0.0925 | 299,242 | 0.1014 | 8.34 |
| | Median | 129,866 | 0.0695 | 147,188 | 0.0764 | 9.66 |
| | S.D. | 468,828 | 0.0581 | 529,663 | 0.0656 | 9.75 |
| | C.V. | 173.13 | 62.79 | 177.00 | 64.68 | 116.86 |
| | Minimum | 26,701 | 0.0275 | 15,361 | 0.0202 | (42.47) |
| | Maximum | 2,643,869 | 0.3210 | 2,998,951 | 0.3641 | 17.98 |

Definition: Per capita values are the number of telephones to the total population of the year shown. Per Capita Percent Change was calculated by subtracting the 1988 Per Capita rate from the 1989 Per Capita rate and dividing by the 1988 Per Capita rate multiplied by 100.
Source: INEGI, 1988-1989 Anuario Estadistico, Table 2.1.11, 1990 Anuario Estadistico, Table 2.1.9.

*Emerging Electronic Media*

Satellite communication services are offered by Iridium and Globalstar. Iridium, an 18 nation multination company, began trials in Mexico in 1998. These new companies also will allow the use of handheld satellite phones that are useful in remote sections of Mexico such as farms, mining, and construction sites (EFI 1998a). Iridium had 66 satellites on six axes that cover the globe and began offering telephone and pager services in September 1998. Globalstar, along with government controlled Satmex, was to have 46 satellites in orbit by late 1998. First services were to be direct to home television.

Emerging is a vast struggle with a potential large payoff; that is the securing of a share of the burgeoning Spanish-speaking market on the Internet, telecoms, and PCs. In Mexico, as of October 1999, one percent of Mexicans used the Internet. Illustrating part of the globalization of the welling up the electronic media market are the main long-distance companies and their main partners shown on Table 7.8. Among the major players are Carso Global Telecom, who owns a 49 percent share in U.S. ISP and 26.5 percent share in Telmex. Telmex, in turn, has a 19 percent share in Prodigy. Prodigy, successively controls Telmex's Internet service Internet-Directo. This firm has joined Acer to market goods and services.

Thus, as shown on Figure 7.2, what is emerging in Mexico is a puzzling relationship among Mexican companies and foreign enterprises all in an effort to control the plethora of potential customers. Turbulence and shakeouts, as well as great opportunities, are expected in the early 21$^{st}$ century, as the global technology and internet revolutions import Mexico.

## Conclusions

Historically, cargo and passenger transportation in Mexico relied mainly upon road transportation modalities and undoubtedly will continue to do so well into the future. There has been a lack of relative investment in other transportation forms such as air, maritime, and railroads. Overall, the impression is that the impact of globalization on Mexico so far has not substantially changed transportation.

Mexico City remains the hub of transportation in Mexico but with an increasing emphasis on the U.S. border region as a result of the globalization process, notably as it has been influenced by the growth of the maquiladora industry. So far the globalization process along the border has continued to highlight roads and truck transportation modalities. There are some indications that rail transit in the future may inspire upgrading and expansion of rail routes. So far it appears that the globalization process has not influenced very greatly maritime and air traffic. Even so, recent changes in tariffs between Mexico and Europe may alter this conclusion.

What impact globalization will have upon the radio and television industry remains problematic at this time. What is more certain is that the telephone industry in Mexico is undergoing drastic transformation and what firms will emerge as the winners has not yet been determined. What is settled is that foreign companies are forming extensive alliances with Mexican companies. There is a spectacular market awaiting investors in emerging electronic media in Mexico. Who will control this market is not yet determined. However, foreign companies are well aware of this huge potential market and are jockeying for position. This vast struggle so far has resulted in a puzzling relationship among Mexican firms and those from foreign countries.

**Table 7.8 Long-Distance Companies and their Main Partners.**

| Company | Partner | Partner | Partner | Partner |
|---|---|---|---|---|
| Telmex | Grupo Carso (23.7%) | Southwestern Bell (10.8%) | France Telecom (5.4%) | Stock holders (59.9%) |
| Alestra | AT&T (49%) | Grupo Alfa (25.6%) | Bancomer-VISA (25.4%) | |
| Marcatel | Radio Beep (51%) | IXC Communications (24.5%) | Westel (24.5%) | |
| Iusatel | Iusacel (40%) | Bell Atlantic (60%) | | |
| Investcom | Compania San Luis (51%) | Nextel (16.3%) | LCC (16.3%) | Carlyle (16.3%) |
| Miditel | Antonio Canavati (100%) | | | |
| Cableados y Sistemas | Grupo Varo (100%) | | | |

Source: Different Articles from Expansion, Alto Nivel (both 1996).

**Figure 7.2 Globalization of Telmex**

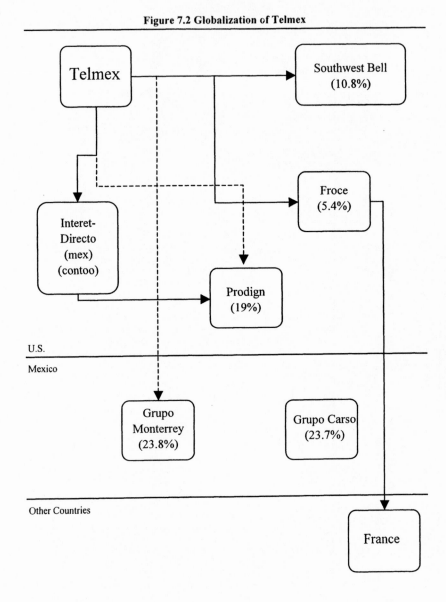

## Case Study: Alestra/AT&T

Alestra is a relative newcomer to the telephone market in Mexico. In 1997, Alestra employed ten persons and had not installed one meter of fiber optic cable. Its office space was rented from AT&T and Alfa. One year later, on December 1, 1998, Alestra employed 3,000 persons and was competing directly with Telmex. In one year, the company went from zero to one million customers.

Alestra has to be somewhat cooperative with Telmex since Telmex provides the local connections to Alestra's long distance lines. In Mexico, there are 9 million lines for a population of 95 million.

Physically the Alestra network utilizes the latest technology including fiber optics, ultrafast switches, etc. The hardware adheres to international standards of AT&T, not with local standards that are less stringent. The network design and materials originated in the U.S., in particular with Lucent, the AT&T spinoff. The company now has over 3,000 employees who are being trained to emphasize customer satisfaction and service. The market is 100 percent Mexican; however, for every call from Mexico to the U.S. there are 2.5 calls from the U.S. to Mexico. Incoming calls to Mexico must be carried by a Mexican company. The ratio is 60 percent Telmex, 20 percent each for Alestra and Avantel. Alestra delivers all of its U.S. calls to AT&T. Its calls are about equally split between business and residential calls. A substantial part of its business is along the border.

Alestra's headquarters is in Mexico City but its offices there are relatively small. Monterrey has larger offices for technical systems, service centers, and a customer care center. Also located in Monterrey is the main switch that controls the network. Guadalajara has a sales office and in other important cities there are sales offices.

In the beginning of Alestra, experts from AT&T around the world were utilized to start operations. AT&T was the founder of the alliance known as Alestra/AT&T and it belongs to AT&T's world partners providing "seamless" telecom services. Alfa provided administrative personnel. An important Mexican partner is Bancomer which has nearly 1,000 branches all over Mexico. In most branches there is a small booth with documents available from Alestra. The ownership distribution is AT&T 49 percent; Bancomer with 25.4 percent; and Grupo Alfa 25.6 percent (after reducing its original 51 percent).

Spanish language is the language of the corporation and meetings are conducted in Spanish. Experts generally visit for a one year period. Their mission is to train and leave behind newly skilled Mexican personnel. Nevertheless, the salary scale is higher for bilingual employees. Over half of the operators speak English and all have rudimentary English capability to transfer calls. The operator workforce is unionized.

Current call volume is approximately 750,000 per month with a capability of one million per month. There are two major switches, one in Monterry and one in Guadalajara. The fiber network consists of three rings, north, central, and south.

### Mini Case Study: Exportadora de Sal (ESSA)

Exportadora de Sal (ESSA) is located at Guerrero Negro, Baja California Sur and heavily transport based. Originally it was a completely owned by federal government. It began production of salt in 1954 and shipped its first salt in 1957. The salt is produced by a solar manufacturing process from sea water. In 1976, ESSA became a joint venture with the Mitsubishi Corporation with the government owning 51 percent and Mitsubishi 49 percent. Another federal state owned company in the Mexican 500 transports the salt. Currently, ESSA produces seven million tons of salt annually. Most of the salt is sent to Japan, the United States, Canada, Korea, Taiwan, and New Zealand. Over 1,000 people are employed in the production of the salt, with most personnel living in Guerrero Negro. The company argues that it has played a significant role in the improvement of the quality of life of the region and has made positive socioeconomic effects in Guerrero Negro. On the other hand, the area is the spawning area of whales and a controversy has emerged over whether or not the plant should be allowed to expand its operations and for the piers and docks to jut into the marine area. Currently, the government and Mitsubishi have put expansion on hold.

# 8

# Petroleum and the Energy Sector

## Introduction:  History of Energy Sector and Petroleum in Mexico

This chapter focuses on petroleum in Mexico and to a lesser extent other important forms of energy, including natural gas and electricity. The emphasis on energy is due to Mexico's status as a large petroleum-producing nation with important petroleum-related trade with other nations. The chapter looks at the origin and present status of the petroleum resource. It has been regarded by the government and public in general as part of the national patrimony since the late-1930s. At the same time, Mexican petroleum sector is dependent on technology, processing, and refining capacities of the United States, as well as its huge and nearby consumer markets. The tension between autonomy and dependence of petroleum in Mexico is an important issue also explored in this chapter. This chapter also compares Mexico's situation as a world producer from Latin America with that of its producing counterpart Venezuela. The areas of natural gas, liquid gases, and petrochemicals are examined. In petrochemicals, the national proscription on oil industry privatization has been broken the past ten years, and private and foreign interests are taking over parts of this subsector. The final part of the chapter analyzes Mexico's petroleum situation in the context of world systems theory including its regional elements.

The first petroleum well in Mexico was drilled in 1862 in the Federal District. More exploration took place in subsequent decades. The first refinery opened in Veracruz in 1886. A boom soon took place based on the participation of foreign giants of the time, including Standard Oil of New Jersey, which had opened large refineries in the late century. There was rapid growth of national petroleum output to 10,000 barrels per day by 1910. Even in the revolutionary period of 1910 - 1917, petroleum production increased. In 1921, Mexico was second only to the U.S. in the world's ranks of oil producers at 530,000 barrels per day (U.S. Energy Information Administration 1998).

In the 1930s oil production fell substantially due to the depression and increasing inefficiencies including over-production of the oil deposits. In 1938, the government of President Laszlo Cardenas expropriated and nationalized the oil industry taking over all assets of seventeen oil firms, including prominent foreign ones. Several months later, the government created Petróleos Mexicanos or Pemex as the national oil entity. It was responsible for the management and production for the entire oil sector of the nation.

In subsequent decades, Pemex increased its size and importance both in Mexico and the world. As a result of heightened production, the nation's electrical system was able to be expanded greatly in the mid century period. Exploration of petroleum proved successful and vast oil deposits were discovered and production started in the Gulf of Mexico. Proven petroleum reserves increased to 66.5 billion barrels by 1990 (U.S. Energy Information Administration 1998). In the 1990s the hydrocarbon sector, consisting of petroleum, natural gas, and their derivatives, contributed 1–2 percent of PIB. As seen in Figure 8.1, this percent was five to ten times as great in the 1980s, when oil prices soared.

There were several exceptions to the dominance of the nationalized sector. In 1971, the Mexican constitution was modified to allow private companies to participate in the secondary petrochemical industry. There have been additional changes allowing greater privatization of downstream aspects of the petroleum sector; for instance in 1991, a law was passed allowing transport, storage, and distribution of natural gas to be conducted as a partnership of Pemex with private firms. However, today the nation and its government remain united in the belief that the primary production of oil should remain a part of the government. This is in spite of a wave of privatization over the past decade that has altered most formerly nationalized industries in Mexico including telephone, steel, banks, and hotels.

**Figure 8.1 National PIB and PIB of Hydrocarbon Subsector**
**(Millions of current pesos)**

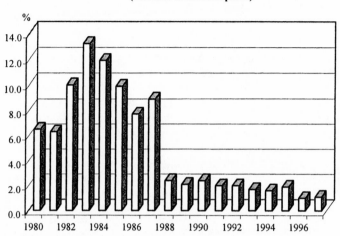

Note: The hydrocarbon subsector includes crude petroleum and natural gas extraction, as
well as petroleum and its derivatives.
Source: Mexican Secretary of Energy, with data from INEGI.

## Mexico's Energy Situation in the 1990s

Currently, Mexico is one of the world's largest producers of petroleum and a
significant exporting nation. It has today conservatively 48 billion barrels in proven oil
reserves and 64 trillion cubic feet (tcf) of gas reserves (World Oil 1999). Mexico produces
3.4 million barrels per day (mb/d) of oil, of which 3.0 million mb/d are crude oil. Much of
this production is heavy oil that is environmentally polluting and difficult to refine into
consumer products. Oil consumption is 1.9 mb/d. Net exports are 1.5 mb/d while gross
exports are 1.9 mb/d. Of this 1.3 mb/d or two thirds is exported to the U.S. The large U.S.
consumption is in synchrony with late 20th century U.S. energy policy, which favors supply
of petroleum from non-middle eastern nations.

Natural gas is also present in abundance in Mexico. Annual production of one trillion
cubic feet however is small compared to total deposits. Natural gas is over 95 percent
consumed domestically. The amount of imports and exports is quite small. For instance in
1997, the U.S. exported only 38.3 billion cubic feet (bcf) of natural gas to Mexico while the
U.S. imported a mere 16.3 bcf from Mexico (U.S. Energy Information Administration
1998). The total traded resource between the two nations (imports plus exports) was only
5.5 percent of Mexico's production, substantially below the comparable figure for oil of
approximately 45 percent. Reasons for relatively low natural gas production volume
include the location of natural gas deposits in the south away from the major population
centers; the type of natural gas i.e. primarily associated with oil; and the lack, until recently,
of modern gas transport and distribution systems.

Of the other forms of energy in Mexico, coal is minor accounting in 1997 for only four percent of Mexican energy consumption (U.S. Energy Information Administration 1998). Mexico, on the other hand, has very large hydroelectric energy production located mostly in the south and especially in the periphery state of Chiapas. Its hydroelectric production is substantial; amounting to around 25 percent of final energy consumed (U.S. Energy Information Administration 1998).

The most important energy source for Mexico is thermal i.e. petroleum, gas, and coal, accounting for about two thirds of energy consumption (see Figure 8.2). Hydroelectric energy is high, accounting for about a quarter of energy consumption. Nuclear and renewable energy i.e. geothermal and solar are minor. This pattern contrasts with the U.S. The U.S. has slightly higher proportion of thermal energy than Mexico but it has very small hydroelectric. The low hydro is due to the huge energy needs in the U.S. and the inability of even large water resources in the U.S. to meet the huge demand. On the other hand nuclear and renewable energy sources are much higher, in the range of 10 to 15 percent each. These energy forms mostly require a high level of technology that is available in the U.S.

Final consumption of energy in Mexico is dominated by petroleum and natural gas, as shown in Table 8.1. Electricity as a form of final consumption amounts to 10 percent, while combustibles mostly coal and firewood equal about 12 percent. It is not surprising that petroleum and electricity increased 1985-92, while natural gas and combustibles decreased. The lack of a natural gas delivery infrastructure has constrained it, while combustibles have natural limits.

**Figure 8.2 Distribution of Energy Types in Mexico and the U.S., 1997**

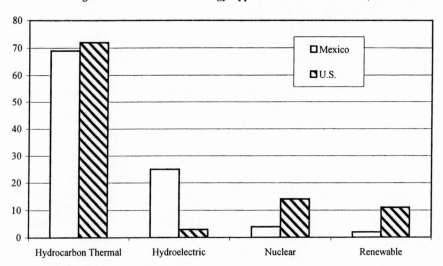

Source: U.S. Energy Information Administration, 1998.

Table 8.1 Final Energy Consumption by Source, 1985-1992*

| Year | Petroleum Products | | | | | | Natural Gas | Electricity | Combustible Solids | Total |
|---|---|---|---|---|---|---|---|---|---|---|
| | Gasoline | Diesel Fuel | Liquid Gas | Combustibles | Kerosine | Total | | | | |
| 1985 | 152.4 | 105.5 | 69.5 | 77.0 | 25.8 | 430.2 | 145.3 | 60.5 | 113.5 | 749.5 |
| 1986 | 156.4 | 98.7 | 68.4 | 73.0 | 24.8 | 421.3 | 124.2 | 62.6 | 112.0 | 720.1 |
| 1987 | 163.8 | 98.5 | 68.0 | 83.9 | 26.1 | 440.3 | 130.9 | 66.9 | 115.6 | 753.7 |
| 1988 | 170.6 | 97.4 | 69.4 | 77.1 | 23.8 | 438.3 | 125.9 | 70.4 | 111.0 | 745.6 |
| 1989 | 191.1 | 101.2 | 72.5 | 85.0 | 24.0 | 473.8 | 133.6 | 76.0 | 115.5 | 798.9 |
| 1990 | 211.1 | 108.0 | 76.6 | 87.9 | 22.8 | 506.4 | 131.9 | 79.2 | 104.4 | 821.9 |
| 1991 | 227.4 | 115.3 | 80.8 | 80.1 | 22.4 | 526.0 | 143.9 | 81.5 | 104.2 | 855.6 |
| 1992 | 230.0 | 123.1 | 88.1 | 73.3 | 24.5 | 539.0 | 139.7 | 83.9 | 102.6 | 865.2 |
| % Change 1985-1992 | 51 | 17 | 27 | -5 | -5 | 25 | -4 | 39 | -10 | 15 |
| Percent of Total | | | | | | 62 | 16 | 10 | 12 | 100 |

* In Billions of kilocalories.

Source: INEGI, 1996.

The location of Mexico's crude oil and natural gas production is predominantly in the two gulf states of Campeche and Tabasco (see Figure 8.3). These states have major offshore and onshore fields.

**Figure 8.3 Crude Oil and Natural Gas Production, 1988**

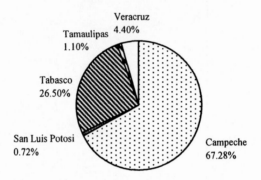

Note: The percentages are for value of production volume of crude oil and natural gas.
Source: 1989 Censos Economicos.

| No | State | Workers | Total Assets | Value of production Volume | Percent of Nation |
|---|---|---|---|---|---|
| 4 | Campeche | 7,726 | 20,203,655 | 15,057,692 | 67.2732 |
| 5 | Coahuila | 278 | 485,231 | 14,361 | 0.0642 |
| 24 | San Luis Potosi | 4,147 | 1,560,245 | 160,667 | 0.7178 |
| 27 | Tabasco | 15,594 | 15,739,717 | 5,935,836 | 26.5195 |
| 28 | Tamaulipas | 4,106 | 4,831,332 | 240,651 | 1.0752 |
| 30 | Veracruz | 25,371 | 17,744,764 | 973,677 | 4.3501 |
| National Total | | 57,222 | 60,564,944 | 22,382,884 | 100.0000 |
| Mean | | 9,537 | 10,094,157 | 3,730,481 | 16.6667 |
| Median | | 5,937 | 10,285,525 | 607,164 | 2.7126 |
| S.D. | | 9,327 | 8,780,234 | 5,991,683 | 26.7690 |
| C.V. | | 97.80 | 86.98 | 160.61 | 160.61 |
| Minimum | | 278 | 485,231 | 14,361 | 0.0642 |
| Maximum | | 25,371 | 20,203,655 | 15,057,692 | 67.2732 |

Definition: The production figures are shown in millions of pesos.
Source: INEGI, 1989 Censos Economicos.

    Mexico is an energy-exporting nation and this has greatly helped the nation financially. In 1997, Mexico had net oil export revenues of $10.3 billion. Of that amount, 87 percent was to the U.S and nine percent to Europe (see Table 8.2). The export of petroleum is an important factor in achieving a rough trade balance with the U.S. That balance from a Mexican standpoint was somewhat negative in 1993 and 1994, sharply positive in 1995-1997 and in 1998 significantly reduced. In 1998, a year of declining oil prices, petroleum production served to offset the negative U.S.-Mexico trade balance from the maquiladora industry and from Mexican consumption of U.S. goods. However, petroleum prices rose sharply in 1999.

**Table 8.2 Destination of Crude Oil Production from Mexico, 1997-1998**

| Year | Total Value of Production of Crude Oil Exported (in $millions) | Total Value of Crude Oil Exported by Export Destination (in $millions) | | |
|---|---|---|---|---|
| | | United States | Europe | Other |
| 1997 (Jan.-June) | 10,341 | 8,958 | 887 | 496 |
| 1998 (Jan.-June) | 3,450 | 3,010 | 298 | 141 |
| 1997 percentage | 100 | 87 | 8 | 5 |
| 1998 percentage | 100 | 87 | 9 | 4 |

Source: Pemex home page, 1998.

There is trade juxtaposition between an advanced nation producing refined and processed goods that are sought in the semi-peripheral nation of Mexico, while the semi-peripheral nation produces and exports largely natural resources. The world systems theory implications of this juxtaposition will be discussed later in the chapter. Suffice it to say that this exchange supports the classical dependency of a developing nation on an advanced one, including elements of capital penetration and exploitation. Another factor examined later is how exchanges of natural resources affect the advanced, semi-peripheral, and peripheral regions within Mexico.

## Mexico's Oil, Pemex, and Cantarell

Mexico's most important energy source is petroleum, and its entire national petroleum production is located in the national oil company of Pemex. This section examines the structure, production fields, geography, and foreign dependencies of Pemex. In 1997 Pemex had total sales of $32 billion. It is one of the world's largest petroleum companies and in Latin America is in third place, after Venezuela's two giant national firms of Petrobras and Petróleos de Venezuela. It is a giant world company, as shown in Table 8.3. Its unique role is seen by being one of only three companies from the semi-periphery, out of the world's 150 largest companies according to the Fortune Global 150 (*Fortune Magazine* 1998). Pemex is by far the largest corporation in Mexico (Expansión 1998)

Pemex had a productive workforce of 75,000 in 1998, much less than the 280,000 workers it had in 1982 (Expansión 1998). The reduction in workforce is due to technology gains that increased worker productivity.

Pemex is highly profitable, as seen in Table 8.4, contributing over fifty percent of its gross revenue to the federal government. This enormous donation is due to the extent of its natural resource and low labor costs. An adverse factor for Pemex is the very high proportion of the profit that is absorbed by federal government taxes. In 1995, these taxes amounted to ninety percent of gross profit. Later in the chapter, the role of this large contribution to the Mexican federal government is examined, as well as the resultant dependency.

**Table 8.3 World's 20 Largest Petroleum Companies, 1997**

| Firm | Nation | Rank in World's Petroleum Industry | Rank in World's 500 Largest Industrial Firms | Revenues (billions of dollars) | Assets (in billions of dollars) | Profit | Profit Percentage of Revenues |
|---|---|---|---|---|---|---|---|
| Royal Dutch Shell | Britain/Netherlands | 1 | 5 | 128.1 | 113.8 | 7.76 | 6.1 |
| Exxon | U.S. | 2 | 7 | 122.4 | 96.1 | 8.46 | 6.9 |
| British Petroleum | Britain | 3 | 20 | 71.2 | 54.1 | 4.05 | 5.7 |
| Mobil | U.S. | 4 | 26 | 60.0 | 60.0 | 3.27 | 5.5 |
| Texaco | U.S. | 5 | 40 | 45.2 | 29.6 | 2.66 | 5.9 |
| ELF Aquitaine | France | 6 | 44 | 43.6 | 42.0 | 0.96 | 2.2 |
| ENI | Italy | 7 | 61 | 37.0 | 49.3 | 3.00 | 8.1 |
| Chevron | U.S. | 8 | 63 | 36.4 | 35.5 | 3.26 | 9.0 |
| PDVSA | Venezuela | 9 | 66 | 34.8 | 47.1 | 4.77 | 13.7 |
| SK | South Africa | 10 | 71 | 33.8 | 17.9 | 0.13 | 0.4 |
| AMOCO | U.S. | 11 | 72 | 32.8 | 32.5 | 2.72 | 8.3 |
| TOTAL | France | 12 | 74 | 32.7 | 25.2 | 1.30 | 4.0 |
| **Pemex** | **Mexico** | **13** | **102** | **28.6** | **42.7** | **1.00** | **3.5** |
| USX | U.S. | 14 | 171 | 21.1 | 17.3 | 0.99 | 4.7 |
| Atlantic Richfield | U.S. | 15 | 192 | 19.3 | 25.3 | 1.77 | 9.2 |
| Petrobras | Brazil | 16 | 211 | 18.1 | 34.2 | 1.40 | 7.7 |
| Statoil | Norway | 17 | 217 | 17.6 | 17.7 | 0.61 | 3.5 |
| Nippon Oil | Japan | 18 | 223 | 17.1 | 21.4 | 0.09 | 0.5 |
| REPSOL | Spain | 19 | 224 | 17.1 | 17.5 | 0.86 | 5.0 |
| Phillips Petroleum | U.S. | 20 | 251 | 15.4 | 13.8 | 0.96 | 6.2 |
| Average | | | | 41.6 | 39.7 | 2.5 | 5.8 |

Source: Kahn, 1998.

**Table 8.4 Pemex Gross Revenue and Federal Tax Contribution of Pemex, 1980-1996**
**(Millions of pesos)**

| Year | Gross Revenue (1) | Federal Tax Contribution of Pemex (2) | Proportion in percent (2/1) |
|---|---|---|---|
| 1980 | 352.6 | 162.0 | 45.9 |
| 1981 | 499.2 | 238.0 | 47.7 |
| 1982 | 968.6 | 327.0 | 33.8 |
| 1983 | 2,787.5 | 1,496.0 | 53.7 |
| 1984 | 4,661.8 | 2,376.0 | 51.0 |
| 1985 | 6,457.0 | 3,734.0 | 57.8 |
| 1986 | 9,164.7 | 5,107.0 | 55.7 |
| 1987 | 23,714.8 | 14,702.0 | 62.0 |
| 1988 | 41,340.4 | 24,327.0 | 58.8 |
| 1989 | 46,549.4 | 29,435.0 | 63.2 |
| 1990 | 61,236.5 | 35,736.0 | 58.4 |
| 1991 | 68,952.2 | 43,889.0 | 63.7 |
| 1992 | 77,932.9 | 52,335.0 | 67.2 |
| 1993 | 83,339.1 | 55,409.0 | 66.5 |
| 1994 | 91,071.4 | 58,662.0 | 64.4 |
| 1995 | 163,360.0 | 102,999.0 | 63.1 |
| 1996 | 240,458.0 | 154,339.0 | 64.2 |

Source: Secretary of Energy of Mexico, with information provided by Pemex
from the Anuario Estadístico of Pemex.

Pemex has been criticized for seeking immediate profit at the expense of long term development of technology and world competitive facilities. As mentioned earlier, a high proportion of its crude oil production is transported to U.S. refineries, rather than being input to petrochemical industry within Mexico. Often the refined product is purchased back in Mexico at a much higher price. This creates a pattern of high profit margin, with the dividends flowing primarily to the Mexican federal government (Expansión 1998).

This process is further complicated by a tendency for Mexican federal agencies to over control and in some cases be corrupt in their oversight roles (Expansión 1998). There have been reports of widespread corruption in such areas as awarding of contracts.

There are several adverse business factors impinging on the long-term success of Pemex. The company has been forced to invest in extractive facilities and processes in order to keep production flowing; this has increased its debt substantially. Pemex's 1998 debt was about $8 billion.

One sign of the need in Mexico for additional petroleum production is the history and future plans for Pemex's Cantarell oil production field. Cantarell is a giant oil field located offshore in the Gulf of Mexico 45 miles northeast of the city of Ciudad del Carmen in the state of Campeche. Wells are drilled platforms to 1,000 to 3,200 meter depths below sea level. The field's production in 1996 was 1.06 million barrels of crude oil per day (El Financiero International 1998), equivalent to 38 percent of national crude oil production.

The dependence on Cantarell is substantial. The field has produced for the past 18 years at levels of 0.90 to 1.2 million barrels daily. The field also has natural gas production of around 450 million cubic feet daily. In terms of total hydrocarbon reserves, Cantarell accounts for 7.6 percent of Mexico's 17.1 billion barrels of hydrocarbon reserves.

The challenge to produce more oil largely for export is leading to plans to intensify drilling and bolster production at Cantarell. It plans to drill several hundred new wells in the field and add 23 new oil-drilling platforms over a two-year period. These changes would bolster the field's production to 1.7 billion barrels of crude oil per day in 2000 (Shields 1998).

However, there is a growing problem in exploitation of the Cantarell field. The field pressure has been dropping for years and continues to decline. This in turn has caused rising water levels in the field, which in turn reduce production. The upshot is that the mean production per well has dropped from 35,000 barrels per day in 1990 to only 1,400 barrels per day in 1998 (El Financiero International 1998).

In response to Cantarell's production depletion, Pemex has decided to implement a huge nitrogen injection plant. Pemex is basing this huge investment on an unproven theory that field pressure will be maintained and will not drop further through injection of nitrogen into the field. Then through increased drilling, production can be increased. However, potential problems include that the injected nitrogen may not sustain the field pressure and that the nitrogen may mix into the oil flow of pipelines and reduce the effectiveness of flow (El Financiero 1998).

Pemex awarded a contract of over $1 billion for construction of the nitrogen plant to a group of foreign contractors, with building expected to be completed in 2000 or 2001. The plant is privately owned by the contractors and represents an exception to historical policy of oil nationalization. The international consortium is shown in Table 8.5.

**Table 8.5 Participation in Construction of Nitrogen Plant for Pemex - Cantarell Field**

| Company | Country | Percent of consortium | Role |
|---------|---------|------------------------|------|
| Marubeni Corporation | Japan | 30 | Project management. Financing. |
| BOC Gases * | Britain | 30 | Plant operation. |
| Westcoast Energy Inc. | Canada | 20 | Underwater pipelines, power plants |
| Linde AG | Germany | 10 | Design of the air separation plant |
| ICA-Fluor Daniel | U.S.-Mexico | 10 | Industrial Construction |

Source: McKinlay, 1998.

The foreign participating companies are from Asia, Europe, and the U.S. This reinforces the fact that the technology is unproven and sophisticated international companies from advanced nations are needed to support this plant design and construction.

Another set of potential problems involves threats from the pipeline that will be constructed offshore and onshore between Cantarell and the nitrogen plant site at Atasta in the state of Campeche. There is a risk of possible pipeline leakage or rupture that could create major degradation to the oceanic or terrestrial environment.

Pemex may be viewed as a legacy of national pride, accounting for a large proportion of the export value of the nation. At the same time, the quality of petroleum production has been compromised. Oil, which is exported predominantly to the U.S., is mostly of such low quality that even after refining it has limited uses. From a world systems standpoint, dependency of a semiperipheral nation on an advanced nation is maintained. Another strategic problem is that in the effort to produce more and more, the quality of Pemex's major production fields and of associated land areas may be depleted.

## Global Impact of Mexico's Petroleum Sector

Mexico is a significant major world player in the petroleum sector. As one of the major developing nations today, it is a substantial producer and consumer of petroleum and has among the largest petroleum reserves worldwide, as well as very large natural gas reserves. The size of its petroleum sector creates global influence for Mexico.

In terms of production, Mexico produced in 1998 3.4 million barrels of oil per day. As seen in Table 8.6, this production increased in the ten years from 1987-1996 by about 1.2 percent per year, a rate nearly the same as world oil production increased. Its production places it fifth worldwide, around the production levels for Iran, Norway, Venezuela, and China. In export status, Mexico has even more regional importance, since the U.S. consumes almost all of its crude production (Energy Information Administration 1999).

**Table 8.6 World's Largest Petroleum Producing Nations, 1996**

| Nation | Petroleum Production (in millions barrels/day) | | Change | Percent of World Production |
|---|---|---|---|---|
| | 1996 | 1987 | 1987-1996 | 1996 |
| United States | 9,445 | 10,648 | -11 | 13.2 |
| Saudi Arabia | 8,930 | 4,698 | 90 | 12.4 |
| Russia | 6,035 | 10,986 | -45 | 8.4 |
| Iran | 3,758 | 2,330 | 61 | 5.2 |
| **Mexico** | **3,306** | **2,914** | **13** | **4.6** |
| Norway | 3,245 | 1,080 | 200 | 4.5 |
| Venezuela | 3,220 | 1,863 | 73 | 4.5 |
| China | 3,131 | 2,690 | 16 | 4.4 |
| United Kingdom | 2,872 | 2,611 | 10 | 4.0 |
| Canada | 2,494 | 1,950 | 28 | 3.5 |
| Nigeria | 2,193 | 1,346 | 63 | 3.1 |
| Kuwait | 2,151 | 1,689 | 27 | 3.0 |
| Indonesia | 1,624 | 1,372 | 18 | 2.3 |
| Libya | 1,450 | 1,002 | 45 | 2.0 |
| Algeria | 1,393 | 1,189 | 17 | 1.9 |
| Total Top 15 nations | 55,247 | 48,368 | 14 | 77.0 |
| World Total | 71,764 | 62,427 | 15 | |

Note: production includes crude oil, NGPL, other liquids, and refinery processing gain.

Source: U.S. Energy Information Administration, 1999.

Mexico also is a very important petroleum consumer, accounting for 2.6 percent of world oil consumption (see Table 8.7). This huge consumption reflects in large part the petrochemical and other industrial uses of petroleum within Mexico. Mexico's petroleum consumption on a per capita basis is at about half the level of advanced nations, such as France, the UK, and Canada. This is an exceptional consumption situation for a developing nation and one that stems largely from its petroleum wealth.

Although it produces and exports high levels of crude petroleum, Mexico depends on other nations for its refined petroleum products. Its total refined exports in 1995 were only 140 thousand barrels per day, which is much lower than peer crude producing nations of Norway (it exported 258 thousand barrels per day or bpd), Venezuela (661 thousand bpd), the UK (578 thousand bpd), and Canada (595 thousand bpd). On the other hand, peer producing nation Iran was lower in refined exports (96 thousand bpd) and so was China

(113 thousand bpd). These nations may be very low due to political-economic conditions in Iran and peripheral nation status for China.

### Table 8.7 World's Largest Petroleum Consuming Nations, 1996

| Nation | Petroleum Consumption (in millions barrels/day) | | Change 1987-1996 | Percent of World Consumption 1996 |
|---|---|---|---|---|
| | 1996 | 1987 | | |
| United States | 18,309 | 16,665 | 10 | 25.6 |
| Japan | 5,867 | 4,484 | 31 | 8.2 |
| Russia | 5,840 | 7,762 | -25 | 8.2 |
| China | 3,548 | 2,120 | 67 | 5.0 |
| South Korea | 2,159 | 639 | 238 | 3.0 |
| Italy | 2,058 | 1,855 | 11 | 2.9 |
| France | 1,935 | 1,789 | 8 | 2.7 |
| **Mexico** | **1,895** | **1,520** | **25** | **2.6** |
| United Kingdom | 1,845 | 1,603 | 15 | 2.6 |
| Canada | 1,799 | 1,548 | 16 | 2.5 |
| India | 1,661 | 988 | 68 | 2.3 |
| Brazil | 1,530 | 1,263 | 21 | 2.1 |
| Saudi Arabia | 1,195 | 975 | 23 | 1.7 |
| Spain | 1,175 | 898 | 31 | 1.6 |
| Iran | 1,175 | 865 | 36 | 1.6 |
| Total Top 14 nations | 51,991 | 44,974 | 16 | 72.7 |
| World Total | 71,524 | 62,999 | 14 | |

Source: U.S. Energy Information Administration, 1999.

In 1995, Mexico struck a balance between refined petroleum product imports and exports, with 138 thousand barrels per day i.e. almost exactly equivalent to exports. This is especially remarkable, since it is such a world leader in petroleum resources. It reflects an unusual amount of dependency on technology of advanced nations, mainly the U.S.

Mexico's global impact is not just a temporary or declining phenomenon, as reflected in its vast petroleum reserves. It was seventh in the world in 1997 in petroleum reserves, with 48.5 billion barrels (World Oil 1999), accounting for four percent of world reserves. This is of huge importance for Mexico's future and points to its long-term status among the world's leading producers (see Table 8.8). A problem is that large proportions of its reserves are offshore, so extraction may be more expensive relative to terrestrial resources. By contrast, U.S. petroleum reserves were only 22.0 billion barrels, but its annual production was nearly threefold that of Mexico.

In natural gas reserves, Mexico was fifteenth globally in 1997 and only accounted for 1.23 percent of world reserves. Unlike petroleum, the U.S. has much larger natural gas reserves with 3.22 percent of the world total. This contrast underscores Mexico's situation as a net importer of natural gas from the U.S. However, Mexico still remains as a major future player in natural gas. It is likely in the future that natural gas reserves will be consumed predominantly domestically, reflecting the more modern natural gas distribution systems that are being developed in Mexico.

The key position of Mexico, as well as its dependency status, is seen in the worldwide corporate structure of petroleum companies. From a national perspective, Pemex is by far the largest firm in Mexico with the most assets and employees. Put in a global view as seen in Table 8.3, Pemex is 13th among the world's largest oil companies. It is smaller than would be expected due to its lack of refining capacity. In fact, it is unique among the 20 largest firms in lacking refining capacity (Kahn 1998). Among semi-peripheral nations, only Venezuela's PDVSA and South Africa's SK are larger firms, and they have significant refining capacity. This lack of Pemex refining capability further demonstrates Mexico's dependency on advanced nations principally the U.S. As seen in Figure 8.4, the commercial balance of trade for hydrocarbons has varied, but mostly been positive.  As oil prices dropped in the early 1990s, this commercial balance turned negative for several years. During the two decades portrayed, Pemex has maintained a positive contribution.

In summary, Mexico is among the top petroleum nations worldwide. Its reserves are very large, although somewhat constrained by their offshore nature. Its global impact is strongest in crude products especially oil. It has not yet entered the world arena as a major factor in refined products.

### Table 8.8 World Petroleum Reserves, 1997

| Nation | Reserves (billions of barrels) | Percent of World total |
|---|---|---|
| Saudi Arabia | 261.8 | 22.57 |
| Former USSR | 183.8 | 15.84 |
| Iraq | 112.0 | 9.65 |
| Iran | 90.5 | 7.80 |
| Venezuela | 72.6 | 6.26 |
| United Arab Emirates | 63.5 | 5.47 |
| **Mexico** | **48.5** | **4.18** |
| China | 34.1 | 2.94 |
| Libya | 29.5 | 2.54 |
| Norway | 26.9 | 2.32 |
| United States | 22.0 | 1.90 |
| Nigeria | 20.8 | 1.79 |
| Total Top 12 nations | 966.0 | 83.27 |
| World Total | 1160.1 | |

Source: World Oil, 1999.

### Economic Impact of Pemex on the Mexican Federal Government

For the past 60 years, Mexico has built a dominant entity Pemex, the national petroleum company. Since Pemex is nationalized, the federal government has been able to divert a large and perhaps excessive proportion of its profits to support the federal government budget. This different type of "dependency" is central to Mexico's national strategy. It is due in part to the lack of strength to collect taxes and enforce ordinary means of government financing.

The extent of governmental dependence on Pemex is revealed in Figure 8.5. Thirty seven percent of the Federal budget in 1997 came from petroleum. Taxes only accounted for 35 percent, which is low versus many semi-peripheral nations. Payments other than taxes from businesses amounted to about one fifth of the income. However, Pemex's proportion of the federal budget varied between 20 and 50 percent over the past two decades (see Table 8.9). Its contribution was stronger in times of domestic economic crisis such as in the 1995-97 period or in the mid 80s. This is because oil revenues depend to a large extent on foreign markets, while other sources of federal funding tend to be lower during hard times in the economy.

**Figure 8.4 Commercial Balance of Hydrocarbon Sales with
Contribution of Pemex**

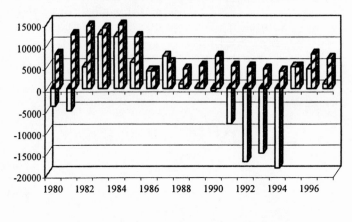

☐ Commercial Balance of Hydrocarbon Sales          ▨ Pemex Sales

Source: Secretary of Energy, with information provided by Pemex for the Informe of the Federal
Government. Combined Economic Statistics of S.H.C.P. and Criterios Generales de Política
Económica 1997.

**Table 8.9 Budgeted Revenues of Federal Government of Mexico
and Federal Tax Contribution of Pemex, 1980-1996 (Millions of pesos)**

| Year | Budgeted Revenues of Federal Government of Mexico (1) | Federal Tax Contribution of Pemex (2) | Proportion of Pemex (2/1) |
|------|------|------|------|
| 1980 | 683.8 | 162.0 | 23.7 |
| 1981 | 935.3 | 238.0 | 25.4 |
| 1982 | 1,532.3 | 327.0 | 21.3 |
| 1983 | 3,181.2 | 1,496.0 | 47.0 |
| 1984 | 4,974.7 | 2,376.0 | 47.8 |
| 1985 | 7,990.5 | 3,734.0 | 46.7 |
| 1986 | 12,670.3 | 5,107.0 | 40.3 |
| 1987 | 32,973.6 | 14,702.0 | 44.6 |
| 1988 | 65,505.9 | 24,327.0 | 37.1 |
| 1989 | 90,204.4 | 29,435.0 | 32.6 |
| 1990 | 117,710.3 | 35,736.0 | 30.4 |
| 1991 | 147,458.2 | 43,889.0 | 29.8 |
| 1992 | 180,322.6 | 52,335.0 | 29.0 |
| 1993 | 194,813.0 | 55,409.0 | 28.4 |
| 1994 | 215,301.2 | 58,662.0 | 27.2 |
| 1995 | 280,144.4 | 102,999.0 | 36.8 |
| 1996 | 376,411.0 | 154,339.6 | 41.0 |

Source: Secretary of Energy of Mexico, with data of Anuario Estadístico of
Pemex and Combined Economic Statistics of S.H.C..P.

**Figure 8.5 Petroleum Industry Percent Contributions to
Mexico Federal Government Revenues**

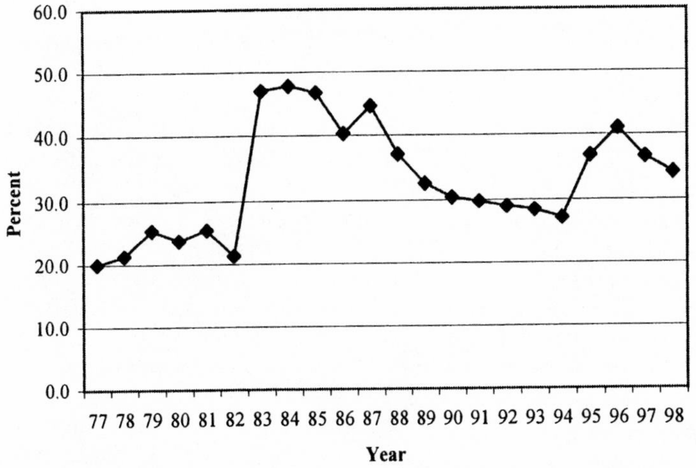

Year

Source: Secretaría de Energía, INEGI, 1998.

From the standpoint of Pemex, profit is substantially diverted to the federal government. As seen in Table 8.9, the proportion of Pemex's gross income contributed to the federal government over the past two decades has varied between 21 to 48 percent. This has several important ramifications. First, it tends to make the Federal government budget highly dependent on fluctuations in Pemex revenues and profits, which in turn depend to a great extent on worldwide changes in the petroleum markets. For instance, in 1998 the federal budget had major cutbacks with substantial layoffs three times. The source of these cutbacks was largely a fall in world oil prices during the year. Currently, a change of one dollar in the world price of oil implies a one billion-dollar change in federal government expenditures.

Second, the very high payout of profits to the federal government reduces the capacity of Pemex to reinvest its profits. It is hampered by restrictions on technological advance, exploration, and infrastructure investments for this reason. The worrisome element here is that as the petroleum industry becomes more competitive globally, Pemex may lack internal investment resources and not be able to accomplish technological and other advances that it needs in order to remain world competitive in refining, petrochemicals, and general business functions.

Pemex's subsidization of the Mexican federal government produces a situation of unusual influence of this one government entity. That factor has in turn stimulated widely reported corruption within the company. It also puts Mexico at risk with an undiversified "portfolio" of income sources for the federal government. This can lead to unanticipated jolts to governmental planning and strategies, such as occurred in 1998. It may also lead to temptations for more corruption in the case of excess in times of oil prosperity.

## Venezuela: A Global and Contrasting Competitor

In Latin America, Venezuela is comparable in many respects to Mexico and is even more richly endowed in petroleum and natural gas resources. This section looks at Venezuela as a competing oil producer and compares how it is similar or different from Mexico.

The giant oil reserve of Venezuela is located in the Orinoco Belt, 140 miles southeast of Caracas. It is serviced by a huge new oil industry complex located coastally on the Caribbean in José.

Historically, Venezuela had a very large foreign oil industry for most of the twentieth century. It nationalized its oil industry in the mid 1970s. The dominant national oil company that emerged, analogous to Pemex, is Petroleos de Venezuela (PDVSA). As seen in Table 8.3, PDVSA is the ninth largest oil firm worldwide, with revenues in 1997 of 34.8 billion dollars (Kahn 1998). Since 1993, Venezuela has opened up its nationalized oil industry and done so to a much greater extent than Mexico. As a result, prominent first world oil companies have been lured, including Arco, Conoco, TOTAL from France, Chevron, British Petroleum, and Mobil. Joint ventures are encouraged, for instance between PDVSA and Mobil in the Calmett, Louisiana refinery, and between Shell and PDVSA for a 50:50 refinery project in Deer Park, Texas, U.S.A (Poole 1998).

In Venezuela, as in Mexico, the federal government depends greatly on the oil industry. In fact, the oil industry provides nearly 60 percent of the federal budget, even higher than in Mexico. The dependence of Venezuela on world oil industry fluctuations parallels Mexico. What differs is the greater opening up of the oil industry in recent years to modern co-ventures with companies from advanced nations. Compared to Mexico, this opening up has served to greatly update the Venezuelan petroleum industry, making it more world competitive over time.

## Natural Gas

Mexico is richly endowed in natural gas, and currently produces over one trillion cubic feet (TCF) of natural gas annually. As seen in Table 8.10, Mexico is fifteenth in the world in natural gas production. At the same time, the nation is restricted in its development and use of this resource by several factors. In the southeast, there is the difficulty in extracting "wet" natural gas that is mixed in with petroleum deposits. A second constraint is inadequate distribution infrastructure to support the domestic market for natural gas. This constraint is being gradually overcome through programs of privatization.

There are two main forms of natural gas available in Mexico (U.S. Energy Administration 1998). The first category of natural gas is "associated gas," that is mixed in as part of the petroleum resource. It occurs in the southeastern states of Tabasco, Campeche, and Chiapas, as well as offshore Campeche (see Figure 8.6). The problem is that the natural gas production depends on the level of petroleum output. Since natural gas is mixed with petroleum, extraction becomes difficult. As pressures in the Cantarell field drop, less and less natural gas occurs as part of the mix.

The second form of natural gas is located in the dry fields located predominantly in the Burgos Basin, a huge natural gas deposit underlying the northeastern states of Tamaulipas, Nuevo Leon, and Chihuahua. Over the next ten years, Pemex plans to increase substantially production in the Burgos Basin.

## Figure 8.6 Production of Petroleum and Natural Gas and Its Liquids, by State, 1995

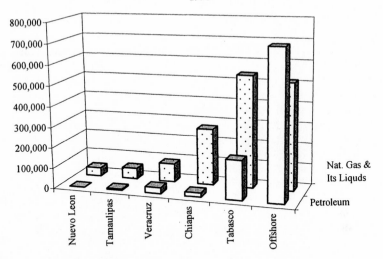

Note: on the y axis, the units are in millions of barrels per day for petroleum and in millions of cubic feet for natural gas and its liquids.
Note: Not shown is the Other State Category that consisted in 1995 of 109 millions of barrels per day of petroleum and 26,316 cubic feet of natural gas and its liquids.
Source: INEGI, 1996.

## Table 8.10 World Natural Gas Reserves, 1997

| Nation | Natural Gas Reserves (billions of barrels) | Percent of World total |
|---|---|---|
| Former USSR | 1,939.3 | 37.46 |
| Iran | 812.2 | 15.69 |
| Qatar | 244.8 | 4.73 |
| United Arab Emirates | 203.6 | 3.93 |
| Saudi Arabia | 191.5 | 3.70 |
| United States | 166.5 | 3.22 |
| Venezuela | 143.0 | 2.76 |
| Algeria | 138.9 | 2.68 |
| Indonesia | 135.9 | 2.63 |
| Norway | 123.3 | 2.38 |
| Nigeria | 109.7 | 2.12 |
| Australia | 83.5 | 1.61 |
| Malaysia | 79.1 | 1.53 |
| Canada | 68.1 | 1.32 |
| **Mexico** | **63.9** | **1.23** |
| Netherlands | 62.3 | 1.20 |
| Kuwait | 52.7 | 1.02 |
| Total Top 12 nations | 4,618.3 | 89.21 |
| World Total | 5,176.6 | 100.00 |

Source: World Oil, 1999.

The U.S. Energy Administration (1998) estimates that Pemex plans a natural gas increase from 0.5 to 1.5 TCF from 1997–2001. Yet, the company does not have the technological strength to provide for this large growth, so it needs private companies to drill the many hundreds of new wells needed. These include Schlumberger, as well as the Mexican producers Compañía Mexicana de Exploraciones and Perforadora Méxicana (*U.S/Mexico Business* 1997). A problem with this strategy is the potential exhaustion of the Burgos field. There may be a parallel here to the long-term depletion of the offshore petroleum fields in the southeast through over drilling and over producing discussed earlier.

The market for natural gas consumption in industrialized cities of the north is large and growing. However, there are competitive pressures, since tariff benefits to Mexican supplied natural gas manufactures to are disappearing and will be reduced from 10 percent in 1994 to 0 percent in 2002. This will stimulate U.S. natural gas producers, especially those in Texas, to seek markets in Mexico. For example, the Salamayuca natural gas driven plant in Chihuahua is being supplied by U.S. producers through a pipeline from El Paso.

Another important trend in natural gas is the national program of distribution system privatization. Having modern distribution systems for natural gas will overcome the traditional reliance on fuel oil, which is delivered by truck and exacerbates many problems of environmental contamination, especially air pollution (Blake and Rowland 1995).

Privatization has progressed fairly well, and important foreign and domestic companies have invested in projects to build distribution systems. Mexican natural gas concessions for the period 1996-98 reflect active gas distribution development in cities throughout the center and border regions of Mexico (Poole, 1998; McKinlay 1998). As seen in Table 8.11, firms that are involved include Mexican, U.S., and European companies. The five-year investment totaled around $2 billion.

In Mexico City, between 1995 and 2000, a one billion dollar investment will develop a natural gas distribution system to serve about 650,000 customers (Poole 1998). However, this massive construction project is constrained by obstacles including earthquakes, traffic pressures, land subsidence, and resistance to tearing up old buildings and streets. In Monterrey, Repsol, a Spanish energy firm, has invested a quarter of a billion dollars over a five year period to implement a modern network to serve about 300,000 customers (Poole 1998).

The process is continuing. One estimate is that from 2000 to 2005, there will be investment of an additional 800 million dollars. New cities planned to receive licenses include Tijuana, Tecate, Ensenada, as well as San Luis Potosi, Zacatecas, and Aguascalientes, and the large cities of Puebla and Guadalajara (Rodríguez Lopez 1999).

Natural gas offers great potential in Mexico to provide energy for heating, industrial, and other uses that are inexpensive and nonpolluting. Changes taking place depend on developing national sources of supply especially the Burgos field and addition of U.S. supply favored by NAFTA tariff reductions. The supply remains predominantly dominated by Pemex. By contrast, the transport and distribution of natural gas is undergoing rapid privatization. The largely foreign developers are motivated by the growing population and industrial markets, yet are subject to constraints of antiquated city infrastructure and natural obstacles.

Liquid gas, mainly propane and butane, is utilized and consumed substantially in Mexico. In fact, ninety five percent of Mexican consumers utilize liquid gas for home use. This is equivalent to natural gas use that is prevalent in other countries. Mexico currently has net import of liquid gas to satisfy this domestic demand.

**Table 8.11**

**Mexican Metropolitan Natural Gas Network Concessions, 1996-1998**

| Concession | Firm awarded concession | Investment over 5 years |
|---|---|---|
| Federal District | NA | Approx. $500 million |
| Cuautitlán-Texcoco (Mexico City N and E of Fed. Dist.) | NA | Approx. $500 million |
| Five concessions in Bajio Region, Tijuana-Tecate-Ensenada, Quertaro-San Juan del Rio, Torreon-Gomez Palacio-Lerdo and Puebla-Tlaxcala | NA | Approx. $300 million |
| Monterrey | Repsol (Spain) | $220 million |
| Chihuahua | Enova/Pacific Enterprises (U.S.) | $50 million |
| Toluca | Repsol (Spain) | $31.6 million |
| Mexicali | Enova/Pacific Enterprises (U.S.) | $25 million |
| Hermosillo-Guaymas-Empalme | KN Energy (U.S.)/ Grupo Marhnos (Mexico) | $20 million |
| Reynosa-Matamoros-Valle Hermoso | Gaz de France (France)/Bufete(Mexico/ Mexigas (Mexico) | $19 million |
| Tampico-Ciudad Madero-Altamira | Houston Industries (U.S.)/ Gutsa (Mexico) | $18 million |
| Ciudád Juarez | Gas Natural de Juárez | NA |
| Piedras Negras | Compañía Nacional de Gas | NA |
| Nuevo Laredo | Reposal | NA |

Source: Poole, 1998; McKinlay, 1998.

This sector is in process of being deregulated. This will open up what is now an exclusively domestic market to foreign entrants. This has already happened in a number of other Latin American nations in collaboration with U.S. and European companies, including Dow Chemical, Chevron, and the Spanish firm, Repsol (Shields 1998).

The net balance of trade in liquid gas is likely to continue importing in the future (Shields 1998). In 1997, Mexico imported liquid gas of 73 million barrels per day, while it exported only 5 million barrels per day.

## Refining and Petrochemicals

The Mexican energy industry is weak in refining and petrochemicals. This reflects the dominance of Pemex in petrochemicals and Pemex's somewhat antiquated condition, as well as lack of investment by the Mexican government. Refining and petrochemicals have rather sophisticated chemical processing requirements making older plants less competitive. The result is that most refining and petrochemical production from Mexican petroleum is done in the United States. This represents a classical dependency relationship between an advanced and peripheral or semi-peripheral country.

There are six major Pemex refineries, and four of them are old and in substantial need of upgrading (U.S. Energy Information Administration 1998). Those are Cadereyta, Ciudad Madero, Minatitlan, and Salina Cruz. Currently, there is not a program to privatize ownership of Pemex refineries. Refining is considered too "upstream" by the Mexican government to be included in the privatization programs. Rather, a program has been launched of agreements with international groups of companies to modernize refineries (Shields 1999). For instance, the Cadereyta refinery is being modernized by an international consortium of Synkyong (Korean), Simens (German), and Tribasa (Mexican). The Ciudad Madero and Salamanca refineries are also in process of being modernized through private contracts. This program has been successful in part because it doesn't threaten national ownership of upstream components.

A larger and more significant portion of refining involves Pemex agreements to refine in the U.S. Agreements are being established with companies in the U.S. including Shell, Mobil, and Clark U.S.A. For instance, a one billion-dollar agreement is that Pemex provides Shell with heavy crude oil. Shell in turn does the refining and produces 256,000 barrels per day. A major amount of gasoline from the refinery is provided to Pemex (U.S. Energy Information Administration 1998). Another example is an agreement with Clark USA that Pemex provides petroleum supply in the form of heavy crude to a major coking plan in Port Arthur, Texas. These agreements are characterized by low quality crude petroleum being provided to sophisticated U.S. refineries, which compensate Pemex with money and/or with refined product. These agreements lead to much more productive refining than Pemex can currently accomplish domestically.

In petrochemicals, the current Mexican leader is also a part of Pemex -- Pemex Petroquimica. It has 59 primarily petrochemical plants located in nine petrochemical complexes (U.S. Energy Information Administration 1998). The plants mainly produce eight petrochemicals, including butane, ethane, propane, and naphtha. These plants are largely outmoded. There are also over 60 secondary Pemex petrochemical plants.

The Mexican government, with the cooperation of Pemex, is offering a program of privatization of these plants. The program calls for privatization of the Pemex basic petrochemical plants with 51 percent Pemex ownership and 49 percent private ownership. Also there may be some privatization of the secondary industry (U.S. Energy Information Administration 1998). However, this privatization program has not worked. The reason is that bidders and potential bidders have less interest in 49 percent ownership and the lack of control. No major petrochemical deals have taken place. Some companies such as Grupo Alfa entered into the bidding process, only to pull out with concerns over the lack of control (Shields 1999).

The problem in petrochemicals comes down to the aging and noncompetitive state of the petrochemical industry and the lack of ability to either modernize or, up to now, privatize the sector. At the same time, there is the potential to turn around Pemex and domestic petrochemicals and make them more productive. Levy (1998) points to the following steps that could reverse the trend in the Pemex petrochemical sector: (1) improve the health of the finance and technology sectors supporting petrochemicals, (2) implement better transfer pricing mechanisms and re-constitute the supply chain links of the petroleum sector from twenty years earlier, (3) increase the regionalization of the petrochemical industry in a way to advance regional economies, and (4) develop better financial and economic strategy for the sector (Becerril 1998).

## Electrical Power

Mexico's large electrical power capacity built up rapidly during the past fifteen years, as Mexico became more populous and industrialized. Generally management and performance of the power industry has been successful. In the early 1990s, Mexico began to make arrangements to obtain some power from independent power produces in the U.S. However in 1999, a gradual process of opening up this sector was potentially catapulted forward with President Zedillo's proposal to privatize the entire Mexican power industry, mostly to foreign firms.

In 1997, Mexico had 36,000 Megawatts (MW) in electrical capacity, which compares to 710,000 MW in the U.S. (U.S. Energy Information Administration 1998). Mexico's installed capacity per thousand population was 0.37, versus 2.64 in the U.S., a seven-fold difference. As seen in Table 8.1, Mexico's energy is mostly petroleum and gas, with some coal (about 8 percent), substantial hydroelectric (25 percent), and minor renewable sources. This energy capacity has been historically developed by the Comisión Federal de Electricidad (CFE), which is one of the ten largest electrical generation organizations in the world. The Zedillo Administration has encouraged CFE to achieve nearly complete coverage of Mexico and increased population electricity coverage by about 12 percent, so that when Zedillo leaves office in 2000, energy coverage should be 97 percent (Moncada 1997). Another accomplishment is the narrowing of geographical coverage, so only about 12 percent of the Mexican land surface will not have electricity by 2000.

As seen in Table 8.12, Mexico's installed electrical production capability is located predominantly as hydro in the southern region, and as thermoelectric energy in the border states. It is interesting from a world systems theory perspective that these areas represent all three levels of development. However, vast amount of energy produced flows to the core areas of the country.

Foreign firms have been allowed to contract on construction and to sell power to CFE as independent power producers (IPPs). Some examples of foreign IPPs are GE, Central Power and Light, San Diego Gas and Electric, El Paso Energy, and AES Corp from the U.S., and Nickimen from Japan (U.S. Energy Information Administration). These tend to be utility firms based in the U.S. border states. In addition, connections are planned to be established between the U.S. and Mexican power grids in Arizona and Texas making power more easily transferable.

Besides independent production, several other options for private firms are currently possible including co-generation with CFE, self-generation, and small-scale rural production. Since 1992, Mexican firms have been allowed to develop and construct their own electrical generation capacity, referred to as self-generation. For instance, the steel firm Alto Hornos de México is building its own large and modern coal plant for electrical generation in the state of Coahuila, which will have a 360 MW capacity (Moncada 1997[1]). Several other major firms are planning self-generation including Cemex and Alpek-CSW[2]. Small rural production projects are less than 1 MW and done by small agricultural-based enterprises.

Foreign firms that have been involved in construction contracts often teamed with Mexican firms, including Nissho Iwai and Nichemen (Japan), Siemens (Germany), and Abengoa (Spain), as well as a number of U.S. firms. Mitsubishi was the contractor for the Cerro Prieto IV geothermal plant in Mexicali.

In 1999, the entire situation for electrical production was turned upside down by the Zedillo Administration proposal to completely privatize the electrical sector. Privatization was to be planned in the remaining Zedillo term and implemented by the next administration. The proposal is subject to approval by the Mexican legislature. This proposal from Energy Minister Luis Téllez is somewhat surprising given the generally good performance of CFE for several decades. The government rationale refers to the rapidly increasing electricity demand and need to raise multi-billions of dollars in investment to

---

[1]   Alto Hornos is rated as the 24th largest Mexican 500 (Expansión, 1998).

[2]   Alpek was the 22nd largest 500 in 1997 (Expansión, 1998).

**Table 8.12 Installed Electrical Energy Capacity, Mexico, 1985-1989**

| No. | State | 1985 Inst. Elect. Energy Capacity Total Cap. | % of Nation | 1989 Inst. Elect. Energy Capacity Thermoelectric | Hydroelectric | Total Cap. | % of Nation | Per Capita | Capacity Growth, 1985-1989 |
|---|---|---|---|---|---|---|---|---|---|
| 2 | Baja California | 938 | 5.00 | 1,100 | 0 | 1,100 | 4.51 | 0.0664 | 14.7 |
| 3 | Baja California Sur | 192 | 1.00 | 222 | 0 | 222 | 0.91 | 0.0604 | 13.5 |
| 4 | Campeche | 181 | 1.00 | 168 | 0 | 168 | 0.69 | 0.0340 | -7.7 |
| 5 | Coahuila | 1,066 | 5.00 | 1,291 | 66 | 1,357 | 5.56 | 0.0735 | 21.4 |
| 6 | Colima | 1,200 | 6.00 | 1,900 | 0 | 1,900 | 7.79 | 0.3617 | 36.8 |
| 7 | Chiapas | 3,509 | 17.00 | 0 | 3,929 | 3,929 | 16.10 | 0.2448 | 10.7 |
| 8 | Chihuahua | 954 | 5.00 | 954 | 19 | 973 | 3.99 | 0.0401 | 2.0 |
| 9 | Distrito Federal | 148 | 1.00 | 148 | 0 | 148 | 0.61 | 0.0018 | 0.0 |
| 10 | Durango | 415 | 2.00 | 415 | 0 | 415 | 1.70 | 0.0308 | 0.0 |
| 11 | Guanajuato | 907 | 4.00 | 907 | 0 | 901 | 3.69 | 0.0228 | -0.7 |
| 12 | Guerrero | 1,094 | 5.00 | 37 | 1,638 | 1,675 | 6.87 | 0.1260 | 34.7 |
| 13 | Hidalgo | 1,786 | 9.00 | 1,886 | 4 | 1,986 | 8.14 | 0.1054 | 10.1 |
| 14 | Jalisco | 217 | 1.00 | 62 | 154 | 211 | 0.86 | 0.0068 | -2.8 |
| 15 | Mexico | 1,497 | 7.00 | 1,458 | 340 | 1,528 | 6.26 | 0.0191 | 2.0 |
| 16 | Michoacan | 482 | 2.00 | 80 | 457 | 533 | 2.18 | 0.0278 | 9.6 |
| 18 | Nayarit | 4 | 0.00 | 2 | 2 | 5 | 0.02 | 0.0010 | 20.0 |
| 19 | Nuevoleon | 1,078 | 5.00 | 1,030 | 0 | 1,030 | 4.22 | 0.0332 | -4.7 |
| 20 | Oaxaca | 156 | 1.00 | 0 | 156 | 156 | 0.64 | 0.0103 | 0.0 |
| 21 | Puebla | 460 | 2.00 | 38 | 431 | 469 | 1.92 | 0.0218 | 1.9 |
| 22 | Queretaro | 79 | 0.00 | 298 | 2 | 300 | 1.23 | 0.0308 | 73.7 |
| 23 | Quintana Roo | 29 | 0.00 | 194 | 0 | 194 | 0.80 | 0.0262 | 85.1 |
| 24 | San Luis Potosi | 821 | 4.00 | 729 | 20 | 720 | 2.95 | 0.0369 | -14.0 |
| 25 | Sinaloa | 1,193 | 6.00 | 656 | 163 | 819 | 3.36 | 0.0452 | -45.7 |
| 26 | Sonora | 164 | 1.00 | 1,205 | 256 | 1,601 | 6.56 | 0.0932 | 89.8 |
| 28 | Tamaulipas | 1,227 | 6.00 | 1,197 | 32 | 1,198 | 4.91 | 0.0547 | -2.4 |
| 30 | Veracruz | 588 | 3.00 | 417 | 92 | 569 | 2.33 | 0.0106 | -3.3 |
| 31 | Yucatan | 261 | 1.00 | 227 | 0 | 277 | 1.14 | 0.0232 | 5.8 |
| 32 | Zacatecas | 17 | 0.00 | 17 | 0 | 15 | 0.06 | 0.0012 | -13.3 |
| | National Total | 20,663 | | 16,638 | 7,761 | 24,399 | 100.00 | | 18.1 |
| | Mean | 646 | 3.13 | 537 | 250 | 989 | 3.00 | 0.0519 | 10.9 |

Definition: Electrical energy capacity values are shown in megawatts.  AGUASCALIENTES, MORELOS, TABASCO, and TLAXCALA are zero values.  The per capita column is the ratio of the total megawattage in 1989 to total population 1990.

Note: National totals exclude mobile plants. AGUASCALIENTES, MORELOS, TABASCO, and TLAXCALA are zero values.

Source: INEGI, 1986 Anuario Estadistico, Table 2.2.5, 1991 Anuario Estadistico, Table 2.3.3.

provide new capacity. Given the high demand, rolling blackouts might occur, unless capacity is expanded.

Mexican energy capacity increased from 1973 to 1995 at 6.4 percent annually, which is high compared to advanced nations, which are in the range of 1.5 to 3.5 percent (Moncada 1997). At that rate of increase Mexican energy capacity would add another 36,000 MW over the period 1997 to 2008. The outcome of the Zedillo Administration's request for privatization is still unknown. Whether done by CFE or through privatization, this huge increment of development calls for enormous investment and effort.

## Privatization of the Mexican Petroleum Industry

The privatization of the Mexican petroleum industry has proceeded significantly. However, it has been constrained by fundamental concerns for Mexican sovereignty in certain segments that are "off limits." The trend in privatization that took place since the Miguel de la Madrid Administration of 1982-88 has affected many economic sectors besides petroleum, including steel, railroads, seaports, airports, and banking. The overall success rate in Mexico of privatization has been mixed. Petroleum so far has not been highly successful. There have been worse cases in other sectors, including highways and banking. Steel was generally successful. In highways, corruption has essentially brought construction to a halt. In banking, the process may have proceeded too quickly, without enough managerial capacity to run the privatized banks well, so many banks suffered early failures.

The Mexican government has consistently rejected the idea of privatizing the petroleum industry, in particular Pemex. However, beginning in the Carlos Salinas Administration of 1988-94, the efforts to privatize the petrochemical industry increased. Upstream production was classified as responsibility of the state, while downstream products increasingly were opened up to be divested from public ownership. In 1992, Pemex was re-organized into a holding company with four affiliates; the petrochemical affiliate was authorized for the alternative of establishing joint ventures with private firms including foreign ones. One year later, Pemex designated 60 secondary petrochemical plants for privatization including by foreigners (Teichmann 1995). In October of 1995, the Zedillo administration attempted 100 percent privatization of the petrochemical sector. However, substantial political opposition eliminated that idea.

A new plan was introduced by the Salinas Administration in 1997 to privatize 49 percent of Pemex's secondary petrochemical plants, leaving 51 percent in the hands of Pemex. Secondary refers to plants that tend to be more "downstream." That plan was approved and put into effect. However, it has encountered problems and lacks acceptance. These include the unattractiveness of multinational firms to enter the small Mexican marketplace without control; the fact that a private firm entering the market is competing directly against Pemex, which is also one of its suppliers; the large amount of bureaucracy and legalities; and the difficulty in operating a "public/private" firm (Wright 1997; Shields 1997). In addition, most petrochemical plants are deteriorated (Shields 1998). There have been almost no takers to this program of minority ownership. Many foreign and domestic firms closely examined the program, only to pull out (Shields 1999). The prospects are dim, given minority ownership provisions.

The stalled situation with privatization of petrochemicals should be contrasted with the good progress on privatization of natural gas transport and distribution that was discussed earlier. The reason for the better natural gas outcome is that natural gas is not regarded presently as critical for the national energy system, since it is a relatively new form of energy for Mexican consumers (Wright 1997). Mexico has tended to rely on liquid gas. Pemex does not consider natural gas yet to be substantial and hence the lowered resistance. However, as natural gas may become more important in the future, it likely will gain more visibility and appear more threatening to proponents of nationalization and to Pemex.

## Environmental Problems Aggravated by Energy Uses

Along with Mexico's large energy resource and increasing production are environmental problems aggravated by their use. These include air pollution from energy plants, water consumption and pollution including oceanic pollution, waste disposal, destruction to marine life, oceanic and onshore oil spills, and the environmental problems accompanying urbanization prompted by energy resource development. There are agreements and plans to mitigate or control certain elements of the energy resource development. Overall, the measures taken up to now are limited in controlling environmental impacts and damages. Since parts of the energy sector have foreign participants, the responsibility for this environmental damage lies partly also with the foreign players.

The electrical generating sector involves hundreds of power generating plants utilizing different technologies, but all of which have polluting effects. The national distribution of these impacts is shown in the distribution of installed thermoelectric energy capacity by state in 1989 (see Table 8.12). Two fifths of this capacity is located in the northern border states, much of it close to border cities. For instance, a huge coal plant is located only several miles from the U.S. – Mexico border city of Piedras Negras. Major thermal plants are located in Tijuana, while Mexicali has a large geothermal generating capacity. The air pollution and water demands of these border plants causes degradation of air quality in the border cities and reduces an already limited water supply. There is similar impact from the ten percent of capacity in the State of Mexico and Federal District. A positive event was the closing of a large thermal generating plant in the middle of Mexico City in the early 1990s due to its adverse environmental impacts. Several less populous western states have large thermal capacity in particular Colima, Sinaloa, and Hidalgo, accounting for another quarter of thermoelectric capacity. Air pollution effects in these states impact on dispersed populations, rather than large cities. The hydroelectric capacity, which is much less polluting environmentally, is mostly in the south especially in the states of Chiapas and Guerrero.

Pollution effects from petroleum are immense. They are mostly concentrated in the Gulf oil states of Campeche and Tabasco. A very detrimental effect is ocean pollution through drilling and pipeline losses that have impacted the marine life of a large area of ocean adjacent to Campeche. Particularly affected have been species of shellfish. Also threatened are mollusks, crustaceans, many invertebrates, and coral biota (Expansión 1998). A secondary problem in the oil states of Campeche and Veracruz is pollution from urbanization stimulated by petroleum facilities. The new petroleum-based cities have discharged large amounts of household wastes, as well as some industrial and agricultural wastes, into water bodies.

There have also been explosions in petroleum facilities, including in Plátano y Cacao in Tabasco in 1985 and 1995 and in Cactus in Chiapas in 1996 (Expansión 1998). Many conditions similar to those causing the explosions remain in other facilities (Expansión 1998).

Some government plans have been put into place, but with varying success. Although there has been progress in government initiatives to control air pollution in Mexico City (Mumme 1991), pollution levels remain high by international standards (United Nations 1994). A new government program, the National Environmental Program of 1996-2000 is making a 13.3 billion-dollar investment to further mitigate the problem (U.S. Energy Administration 1998).

Standards regulating power generation and the petroleum sector have been less successful. For instance, the NOM-85 and NOM-86 standards approved in 1994 provided regulations to limit air pollution and to regulate fossil-based fuels and gasses. However, three years later the standards proved unattainable and had to be delayed (Shields 1998). Some petroleum pollution is not currently regulated, in part because extraction-ecological systems are so complex that they are not understood.

## Conclusions

This chapter has examined the energy sector in Mexico and its relationship to the global economy. The nation has a vast resource in petroleum and natural gas. The resource is being extracted for domestic consumption and exported mainly to the U.S. Technology available for higher level processing of the resource is limited for a number of reasons. As a consequence, some higher level processing is being outsourced to foreign contractors in Mexico, while most of it is being performed in the U.S. Ironically, processed petroleum products are then sold back to Mexico. Even some types of gasoline are sold back to Mexico after being processed in the U.S. For natural gas, there is increasing privatization and foreign involvement. This is fundamentally due to lack of perceived direct competition with Pemex because natural gas is new.

Mexico's electrical generation is mostly thermoelectric i.e. petroleum-based and coal-based. There is a large hydroelectric capacity in the south. The electrical generation has begun to have private foreign sellers. Although the CFE has done a good job on the whole, the Zedillo government perceived demand increasing so rapidly that it proposed to privatize entirely the electrical sector. Whether this proves acceptable or practical is yet to be determined.

The environmental externalities of energy production are large. They are especially damaging in the petroleum sector, where there is less regulation and also less understanding of the complex processing and ecological systems involved. Foreign firms must be included in assessing the environmental costs and cleaning up the environmental damages from the energy sector.

# 9

## Maquiladoras

- **Introduction**
- **History**
- **Current Size and Economic Impact**
- **Regional Distribution**
- **Social and Health Disadvantages**
- **Relationship with the U.S.**
- **Trends: The Future**
- **Conclusions: Comparison of Maquiladora Manufacturing with Non-Maquiladora Manufacturing**
- **Case Study: Trico Components**
- **Short Case Study: Thompson**

## Introduction

Maquiladoras are a unique and important economic sector in Mexico. Maquiladoras are based on co-production that takes advantage of the relatively low cost of Mexican labor and close access to the huge U.S. marketplace. Maquiladoras historically have been based on special legal and trade arrangements between Mexico and the U.S., although other nations are now involved. The maquiladora sector forms a crucial part of the Mexican economy, having grown enormously since its founding in the 1960s, far surpassing early expectations. Currently it accounts for 2 percent of Mexican GDP and 14 percent of Mexican manufacturing production. Currently, one million Mexican workers are employed in maquiladoras. On the basis of exports, maquilas produced in 1996 a net trade balance of $6.4 billion. This is somewhat less but beginning to approach the order of magnitude of the net contribution of exports by the Mexican petroleum industry.

The maquiladora sector forms a particular variety of globalization, one that is unique and adapted to the joint geography and economic differences of Mexico and the U.S. It is not exclusively a form of globalization between those two nations, but to a lesser extent involves global links with Asia and Europe. This chapter examines the concept of maquiladora in relationship to globalization, its history, the sectoral size and scope, its regional distribution in Mexico, relationships with the U.S., and its sometimes adverse social and environmental impacts. The chapter includes several case studies, compares maquiladora and non-maquiladora manufacturing, and examines the future i.e. how they may change in the next 10 to 25 years and what effect globalization might have upon them.

A maquiladora is a "business established in Mexican territory that following contract, is linked with an enterprise based in a foreign nation to support industrial processes or services of transformation ... of raw materials of foreign origin imported temporarily and then exported... It also includes associated services" (SECOFI 1995). The concept of maquiladora implies legally based cooperation in production between foreign companies and domestic assembly/manufacturing largely dependent on foreign raw materials and/or parts. The maquiladora value chain steps include delivery of raw materials or parts; processing and assembly including addition of value; return of the finished product to the U.S.; export to another country; and/or sometimes consumption in Mexico. In the case of the U.S., there are often twin plants – one on the U.S. side and a "twin" on the Mexican side of the border. They cooperate in producing components in the U.S. co-plant, transporting them to the Mexican counterpart, which may be a short distance away, assembling the product in Mexico, and transporting the finished product back to the U.S. for shipment to U.S. consumers or for further export.

U.S. Customs regulations 9802.00.60 and 9802.00.80 historically have governed the maquiladora. They dictated that only the value-added portion would be taxed. There are corresponding Mexican laws allowing free import of certain raw materials and capital goods related to maquiladora manufacturing. The binational set of laws and regulations are changing and are discussed at the end of the chapter.

Embedded in the maquiladora concept is "shelter," implying that the U.S. (or other foreign) firm operates in Mexico through a Mexican firm that "shelters" or "protects" the U.S. firm from liabilities and other problems.

This leads to the classification of maquiladora operations into four categories:

1. *Shelter.* The Mexican company extends its manufacturing capability to a foreign cooperating firm at low cost. Manufacturing is usually located in a specialized industrial park.
2. *Subcontracting.* Other supporting Mexican firms subcontract portions of the maquiladora manufacturing process.
3. *Co-investment.* Sharing of investment in maquiladoras by Mexican and foreign partners.
4. *Domestic sales.* This is a new trend allowed by NAFTA permitting an ascending proportion of sales to occur within Mexico. It will reach 100 percent maximum by year 2001. However, the allowable maximum is rarely met.

The shelter aspect points to the fundamental justification of cost savings for maquiladoras. The major goal of establishing a complicated maquiladora arrangement is to sell products at lower cost and maximize profits. Domestic subcontracting is increasingly emphasized and encouraged by the Mexican government, since it provides a way to increase Mexican participation and benefit. It can also benefit the maquiladora company, especially if the subcontractor has high quality standards and locates near the maquiladora plant, reducing transport and cycle times. There are instances of subcontractors renting space inside a maquiladora plant. Co-investment is a form of spreading the risk and sharing in benefits, although it is sometimes difficult to trace the ultimate investors and/or benefits.

### History

The maquiladora sector was formed in the mid 1960s because U.S. firms sought low cost production. Early production was mostly of unfinished products, to be returned to the U.S. for finishing and consumption. The technological level of plants in Mexico was low to moderate.

The maquiladora sector grew rapidly from the start (see Figure 9.1). Between 1965 and 1970, the number of maquiladora workers increased by nearly seven fold from 3,000 to 20,327 (INEGI various years). About one quarter of today's maquiladora enterprises were established between 1966 and 1979 (Carrillo and Santibáñez 1993). Early arrangements were in the traditional model of a Mexican assembly plant coupled with a U.S. co-plant for design and production of components and storage of raw materials. The early period was characterized by some labor strikes. The problems of environmental pollution and urban overgrowth were not yet recognized. Early maquiladora companies were not conceived in terms of globalization but rather as a way to cut costs for U.S. products. In 1979, the first Asian maquiladoras arrived in Tijuana. They were initially Japanese firms that brought with them management and production standards of high efficiency and work discipline (Expansión 1997).

The period 1980 to 1988 was a time of continued rapid growth as well as improving plant technology in Mexico. Labor unrest lowered and there was greater acceptance of the maquiladoras as a "permanent" part of border manufacturing. There was more regional diversification especially to the broad northern region including Monterrey.

From 1989 to the present, the maquiladora tended towards modernization, globalization, and increasingly final manufacture in Mexico rather than intermediate assembly. The sector has continued to grow very rapidly, for instance the number of workers grew from 460,000 in 1990 to over one million in 1998. During the 1990s, some maquiladoras began to locate away from the border strip. This was abetted by NAFTA, which took away some of the border site advantage and encouraged more domestic consumption. The collective labor picture shifted to stronger unions that operate in close association with the Mexican maquiladora companies. This has lowered labor unrest overall. At the high end of the maquiladora industry in electronics manufacturing in Tijuana, modernization has been pronounced. Some of the larger and more sophisticated maquiladora plants especially in that city have now reached the level of world class production.

**Figure 9.1 Growth in the Maquiladora Sector, 1965-1996**

☑ Maquiladora Enterprises ☐ Maquiladora Workers

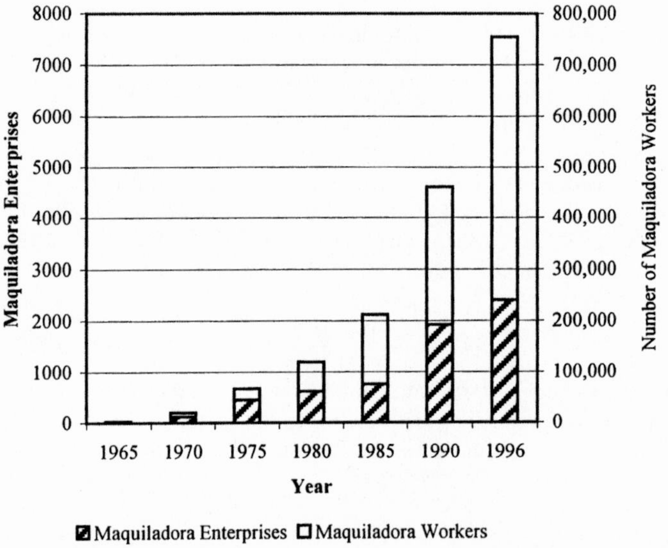

**Growth in Maquiladora Sector, 1965-1996**

|                          | 1965  | 1970   | 1975   | 1980    | 1985    | 1990    | 1996    |
|--------------------------|-------|--------|--------|---------|---------|---------|---------|
| Maquiladora Enterprises  | 12    | 120    | 454    | 620     | 760     | 1,920   | 2,411   |
| No. of Maquiladora Workers | 3,000 | 20,327 | 67,241 | 119,546 | 211,969 | 460,258 | 754,858 |

Source: INEGI, various publications.

## Current Size and Economic Impact

The maquiladora sector is a substantial contributor to the Mexican economy. In 1997 the sector imported raw materials totalling $36.3 billion and added value to the imports of $8.8 billion, which resulted in a total value of $45.1 billion (Secretaría de Comercio 1998). This represented 39 percent of Mexico's exports and 24 percent of its imports. The full value is equivalent to one eighth of Mexican Gross Domestic Product (GDP).

Among major economic sectors, maquiladoras are moving into first or second place in terms of the net proportion of Mexican export. In 1996, the net trade balance contributions from the major sectors were $9.9 billion from the oil industry, $6.4 billion from maquiladora, and $3.5 billion from tourism (INEGI 1997).    It is almost certain that for 1998, an adverse year for petroleum with the lowering of oil prices, the maquiladora was the largest economic sector in net contribution to the balance of foreign trade.  As shown in Chapter 4, Mexico is receiving substantial foreign direct investment involving import of capital equipment as well as the large import of certain consumer goods especially from the U.S. Hence, the petroleum and maquiladora net trade contributions are essential to maintain Mexico's overall balance of trade.

For the maquiladora sector, the value added in Mexico forms the net difference between imports and exports.  Table 9.1 shows the value added by the various aspects of maquiladoras in 1997.

**Table 9.1 Value Added to Maquiladora Sector, 1997**

| Component of Value Added | Value in Billions of U.S. Dollars |
|---|---|
| Workers salaries and benefits | 4.4 |
| Energy and diverse costs | 2.5 |
| Raw materials and packaging | 0.8 |
| Profits and other | 1.1 |
| Total | 8.8 |

Source: INEGI, 1997.

It is a bargain that the salaries and benefits only total $4.4 billion, given the much higher salary costs in the U.S. or other advanced nations.  It is clear that in most respects this is very efficient production.  The domestic raw materials contribution is very small relative to the overall size of the sector, a point discussed later.

Maquiladora exports in 1997 were predominantly sold to the U.S. The balance of trade between the U.S. and Mexico was favorable to U.S. in the early 1990s, but shifted in favor of Mexico in the second half of the decade.  In 1996, Mexico exported $74.2 billion to the U.S., and the U.S. imported $54.7 billion into Mexico, resulting in a trade balance favorable to Mexico of $19.5 billion. The contribution of the maquiladora sector to the U.S.-Mexico trade balance is substantial, and more so for Mexico than the U.S. Whereas the maquiladora sector proportion of Mexican trade was 24 percent of imports and 39 percent of exports in 1996, the sector's proportion of U.S. trade was 9.3 percent of imports and 2.5 percent of exports (see Figure 9.2).  Given the size of the U.S. economy, a trade contribution of nine percent overall is astounding.  This percentage reflects that maquiladora products (TVs, refrigerators, auto parts, textiles, etc.) are primarily keyed to serve the U.S. consumer.

As seen in Table 9.2, the maquiladora sector contributes multi-billions to the Mexican economy.  It accounts for substantial parts of national economic indicators, including the external sector of the economy, current account balance, raw materials consumed, and manufacturing employment.

In respect to co-investment, the ownership of the maquiladora sector is somewhat evenly divided between the U.S. and Mexico.  Of maquiladora enterprises, 43.2 percent are Mexican, 38.4 percent U.S., 12.8 percent joint U.S.-Mexican, 1.7 percent Japanese, and 3.9 percent other. The maquiladora concept has built into it collaboration between foreign and Mexican businesses.  It is perhaps surprising that the majority of maquiladora enterprises are Mexican owned.  The percentage of enterprises, however, is somewhat deceptive since the largest maquiladora companies are predominantly foreign owned.  Since the value of maquiladora industry production is heavily skewed towards a few large firms, the maquiladora industry measured this way is foreign dominated.

**Figure 9.2 Percent of Maquiladora Sector
Imports and Exports Between the U.S. and Mexico, 1996**

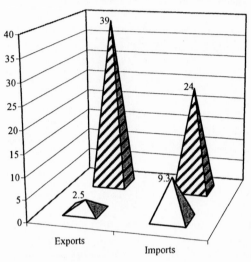

From Mexico to U.S., as
Proportion of Mexican Total

From Mexico to U.S., as
Proportion of U.S. Total

Source: INEGI, 1997.

The maquiladora industry currently employs about one million workers (Secretaría de Comercio 1998). The growth of this employment base was shown in Figure 9.1; further increases are projected. Eighty five percent of current maquila workers are located in the six northern border states. This implies that about eleven percent or more of the workforce of the border states is employed in the maquiladora industry. The economic impact on border families is enormous. For instance, a significant proportion of border region families have some income from the maquiladora. The gender balance of the maquiladora workforce depends on the product. For instance, at the worker level, 57 percent are female and 43 percent male, and the worker segment constitutes 81 percent of the maquiladora workforce (El Financiero International 1998). By contrast, the administrative and engineering production personnel, constituting 7 and 12 percent, of the maquiladora workforce, are predominantly male. The tendency for maquiladoras to employ more female workers has been noted by a number of prior studies (Sklair 1993), although some investigators differ on this point (Stoddard 1987). There are a number of justifications given by various parties for the gender imbalance. Some industry commentators have pointed to businesses seeking women's greater dexterity and manual skills, while others have noted the cost savings of lower salaries paid to women, and their supposedly more compliant work attitudes. This is an area of controversy, as well as changes as the sector matures, alters its product mix, and becomes more sensitive to women's issues.

Table 9.2 The Maquiladora Sector and Its Importance in the National
Economy, 1980-1995

| Concept | 1980 | 1985 | 1990 | 1995 |
|---|---|---|---|---|
| | External Sector | | | |
| Petroleum Export | 10.3 | 14.7 | 9.7 | 8.4 |
| Value Added Export (Maquiladora) | 0.8 | 1.3 | 3.6 | 6.1 |
| Tourism | 2.1 | 2.0 | 3.9 | 5.0 |
| | Current Account | | | |
| Total | (10.4) | 0.8 | (7.5) | (0.7) |
| Without Maquiladora | (11.2) | (0.5) | (11.0) | (5.6) |
| | Production | | | |
| PIB | 194.8 | 184.4 | 244.5 | 259.5 |
| Manufacturing | 43.1 | 43.1 | 55.6 | 51.2 |
| Maquiladora Sector | 0.8 | 1.3 | 3.6 | 5.0 |
| as percent of Total PIB | 0.4 | 0.7 | 1.5 | 1.9 |
| as percent of Manufacturing | 0.9 | 1.6 | 2.6 | 9.8 |
| | Raw Materials Consumption | | | |
| Total Raw Materials Consumption in the Maquiladora Sector | 1.8 | 3.9 | 10.7 | 21.6 |
| Percent of Foreign Origin | 98.3 | 99.2 | 98.2 | 98.5 |
| Percent of Domestic Origin | 1.7 | 0.9 | 1.8 | 1.5 |
| | Employment (thousands) | | | |
| Total | 20,280.0 | 21,955.0 | 22,584.0 | 23,372.0* |
| Manufacturing | 2,441.0 | 2,451.0 | 2,507.0 | 2,282.0* |
| Maquiladora Sector | 120.0 | 212.0 | 460.0 | 600 |
| as percent of Total | 0.6 | 1.0 | 2.0 | 3 |
| as percent of Manufacturing | 4.9 | 8.6 | 18.4 | 26 |

* 1994.
Note: Monetary Figures are adjusted to billions of 1995 U.S. dollars.
Source: Mendiola, 1997, drawing on data provided by Banxico, INEGI, CIMEX-WEFA.

Currency cycles affect the maquiladora industry in several ways. A strong peso weakens the sector's outputs and revenues, whereas a strong dollar strengthens them. This is seen by contrasting weakness in the maquiladora sector during the Salinas Administration (1988-94) when the peso was strong, with the strength of the sector during the Zedillo Administration (1994-2000) i.e. that occurred after the peso fell in November 1994. During the cycles of currency strength or weakness, there also may be shifts away from more expensive manufacturing towards cheaper products such as textiles where the maquila industry started in the 1960s.

In summary, the maquiladora sector is huge and based on low cost, mostly due to salary savings of the value added to raw materials and/or parts. The sector has grown very rapidly over 35 years, and along with petroleum accounts for the largest proportion of net exports from Mexico. The sector primarily is associated with the U.S., in terms of co-production, co-investment, imports of raw materials, and markets for maquila products. Other foreign nations involved to a much lesser extent are Japan, Korea, and several European countries. The industry noticeably influences even the giant U.S. economy through its nine percent contribution to U.S. imports. It also influences the Mexico border region through employment and influences on families and has indirect effects on other sectors of the economy. Social, health, and environmental impacts are discussed later.

## Regional Distribution

The regional distribution of maquiladoras in Mexico influences output and productivity of the sector as well as the inter-relationship of maquiladoras with the United States and other countries. Maquiladoras started in the 1960s, in cities along the U.S.-Mexico border. Although today the preponderance continues to be located along the border, fourteen percent of maquiladoras are now located south of the border states (Secretaria de Comercio 1998). This percentage is growing and is being encouraged by NAFTA.

It is important first to ask: Why the predominantly border location? The border has the disadvantage of being cut off topographically and in transport from the major population centers of Mexico. In particular, Mexico City, with a population today estimated at 17 million, has by far the largest metropolitan consumer base in the nation. In addition, Mexico City is the most prosperous city in Mexico (Pick and Butler 1997). Also, the border is cut off from the large consumer markets in Guadalajara, Puebla, and medium sized cities in the country's central flank and to a lesser extent in the south. A related minus is that many potential Mexican suppliers to the maquiladora sector are also located in Mexico City and other central metropolitan areas.

Border location must have advantages strong enough to offset these negatives. First, sitting along the border enables maquiladora companies to gain easy shipping access to the entire U.S. For maquilas with the traditional twin plant organization, there is great advantage to having the two co-plants located within an hour or so by vehicle of each other. This applies to the chapter case study of Trico Industries as well as to numerous other firms. Another advantage of border locations is the easy availability of U.S. suppliers. Today, an advantage also is the skilled labor force available in some border cities such as Tijuana. For certain higher level industries such as electronics, it is easy on the border to supplement Mexican skilled labor force with technical experts from the U.S.

As was pointed out in Chapter 3, Mexican western border states and cities are quite prosperous and economically developed by Mexican standards and by world standards (Pick and Butler 1994). This affords the advantage of locating in a more advanced and more educated environment, which supports maquila workers in becoming more skilled. It is important to underscore that the maquiladora industry is changing by requiring more skills appropriate for finished and higher quality products. At the same time, low cost of labor is a driving force. The modern border twin city labor markets offer skilled yet low cost Mexican workers and ready access to U.S. technical experts as well.

The distribution of maquiladora 1997 employment, shown in Table 9.3 and Map 9.1, points to dominance by cities in the three northern Mexico states of Chihuahua, Baja California, and Tamaulipas. These three states account for over 60 percent of maquiladora employment, especially in the cities of Ciudad Juárez, Tijuana, and Matamoros. The other border states account for nearly an additional quarter. This includes limited maquiladora employment in Monterrey. In terms of maquiladora plants, Tijuana dominates, followed by Ciudad Juárez and Mexicali (Figure 9.3).

The non-border states have 15 percent of maquiladora employment, with Durango, Jalisco, Aguascalientes, and Puebla accounting for half of it (see Map 9.1). The Federal District and State of Mexico have only 11,000 maquila workers, a tiny proportion of the 6.11 million workers in Mexico City in 1990 (Pick and Butler 1997).

**Table 9.3 Mexican Maquiladora Employment, 1998**

| State | Maquiladora Employment | Percent of Total |
|---|---|---|
| *Border States* | | |
| Chihuahua | 256,930 | 26.3 |
| Baja California | 207,801 | 21.3 |
| Tamaulipas | 149,689 | 15.3 |
| Coahuila | 88,296 | 9.1 |
| Sonora | 87,438 | 9.0 |
| Nuevo Leon | 43,448 | 4.5 |
| | | |
| *Non Border States* | | |
| Durango | 23,207 | 2.4 |
| Jalisco | 20,646 | 2.1 |
| Aguascalientes | 18,305 | 1.9 |
| Puebla | 17,413 | 1.8 |
| Yucatan | 13,187 | 1.4 |
| State of Mexico/D.F. | 10,832 | 1.1 |
| | | |
| Others | 38,188 | 3.9 |
| | | |
| Border States Subtotal | 833,602 | 85.5 |
| Total | 975,380 | 100.0 |

Source: Secretaria de Comercio, 1998.

**Map 9.1
Mexican Maquiladora Employment, 1998
(Percent of Total)**

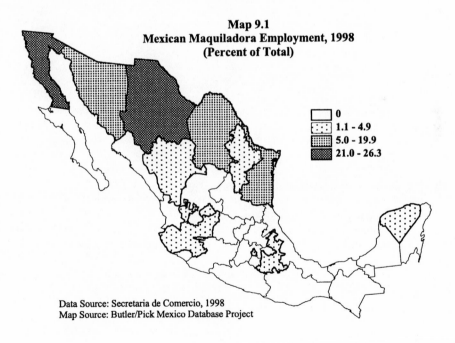

Data Source: Secretaria de Comercio, 1998
Map Source: Butler/Pick Mexico Database Project

**Figure 9.3 Number of Maquiladora Plants
by City in the Border States of Mexico, 1991**

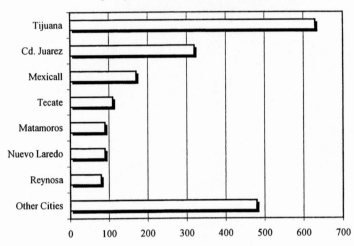

Source: INEGI, 1994.

Ciudad Juárez is the most important maquiladora location, having about 200,000 workers i.e. about a fifth of the national total. Its production emphasizes televisions, VCRs, clothing, telephones, appliances, and car parts. The large and moderately skilled maquiladora labor force grew rapidly through in-migration of mostly female workers from small towns in the north, but also from other regions. The infrastructure of these border cities is lagging as a result of this large in-migration. In utilities, government services, and schools, the city is inadequate for its burgeoning population (Quiñones 1998). The federal government has not stepped in to support the needed infrastructure, so that task falls to the city and state, which have limited resources. These cities also have serious problems in crime, vice, and narcotics that have garnered national attention both in Mexico and the U.S. (Rosen 1998). Ciudad Juárez typifies the problems and prospects of the maquiladora sector. Economically it is booming at near full employment and relatively high salaries and productivity; however, its social problems and costs are high and include in-migration of population without sufficient acculturation, poor infrastructure, lack of federal support, crime, and a generally fearful environment.

In second place is Tijuana. Its maquiladoras focus on electronics and technical products. It employed about 150,000 maquila workers in 1997. Like Ciudad Juárez, it is highly prosperous. It has been significantly influenced by NAFTA, so it in many respects resembles a "free zone." Among NAFTA indicators are its mixture of Mexican and U.S. ownership, its role as a transport corridor to the U.S., and its growing border commerce. In its maquiladoras, the attitude is prevalent of working towards world class quality standards, including training, ISO certification, and fast delivery of goods (Expansión 1997). It has become globalized to a greater extent than other border cities. On the other hand, Tijuana resembles Ciudad Juárez in its social and infrastructure problems. It also has an elevated crime rate, ties to narcotics (Golden 1999), and an infrastructure lagging behind its increasing population. The infrastructure problem is urgent but not as acute as in Ciudad Juárez, because Tijuana had more infrastructures in place prior to the maquila boom (Rosen 1998).

There are large regional differences in the extent of Japanese, Korean, and other foreign participation in the maquiladora industry. Of these, the Japanese presence is largest and may account for 5-7 percent of maquiladora plants in the border region (Carrillo and Santibáñez 1993). Table 9.4 reflects a survey study in the early 90s of the origin of capital in the two major maquiladora cities plus Monterrey.

**Table 9.4 Origin of Capital for Maquiladora Plants by City**

| Origin of Capital | Percent of Maquiladora Plants | | | |
|---|---|---|---|---|
| | Tijuana | Ciudad Juárez | Monterrey | Total |
| United States | 52 | 83 | 74 | 70 |
| Mexican | 36 | 8 | 22 | 22 |
| Japanese | 11 | 6 | 3 | 7 |
| Other | 1 | 3 | 1 | 1 |
| Total | 100 | 100 | 100 | 100 |

Source: Carrillo and Santibáñez, 1993.

Tijuana clearly has the highest Japanese presence. The "other" proportion is quite low – around one percent overall. "Other" is slightly higher at 3 percent in Ciudad Juárez. Hence, the role of Europe is very minor. Even the Japanese proportions are minor in comparison with U.S. origin of capital.

The geographical distribution of the largest maquila plants follows the patterns already noted of border location and concentration in the cities of Ciudad Juárez and Tijuana, as well as Matamoros (Expansión 1997). The fifteen plants shown in Table 9.5 and Map 9.2 accounted for $27.6 billion in maquiladora exports in 1996, about two thirds of the national total. There are eight billion-dollar plus plants, with the largest one the huge $7.9 billion Sony plant in Tijuana. These are all on or near the border, except for Motorola[1] in Mexico City. One of them, Trico Componentes, is discussed as a chapter case.

Mega-plants located in Tijuana tend to produce high end products including electronics and sophisticated mechanical goods. Trico Componentes in Matamoros produces less sophisticated windshield wipers for a large proportion of the U.S. auto industry. The giant Deltronics (GM) plant in Matamoros manufactures radios and radio flight equipment. The huge Motorola plant in Mexico City is based on full manufacture in Mexico, so its value added is 100 percent. The location distant from the U.S. border encourages this complete value added.

There are several other important dimensions to mention about the major 15 maquilas. First, the top 15's employment of only 37,600 workers appears small compared to total maquiladora employment in 1996 of 755,000. This is explained by the highly automated and robotic nature of many of these larger plants, reducing the need for workers. Products of the top 15 do not reflect the highly manual assembly processes of traditional

---

[1] Motorola was listed as number 92 in the Mexican 500 in 1997 (Expansión 1998).

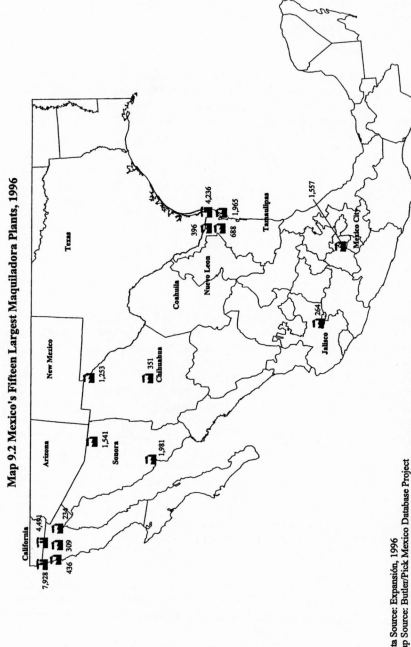

Map 9.2 Mexico's Fifteen Largest Maquiladora Plants, 1996

Data Source: Expansión, 1996
Map Source: Butler/Pick Mexico Database Project
Note: The number represents total exports 1996 in millions of dollars

**Table 9.5 Mexico's Fifteen Largest Maquiladora Plants, 1996**

| Rank | Maquiladora | Location | Total Exports 1996* | Value Added 1996* | Principal Products |
|---|---|---|---|---|---|
| 1 | Sony de Tijuana Este | Tijuana, Baja Calif. | 7,928 | 356 | TVs, monitors, boards |
| 2 | SIA Electrónica de Baja Calif. | Tijuana, Baja Calif. | 4,491 | 267 | Refrigerators, TVs, batteries |
| 3 | Deltrónicos de Matamoros | Matamoros, Tamps. | 4,236 | 391 | Radios, radio flight control devices |
| 4 | Daewoo Electronics de México | S. Luis Rio Colorado, | 1,981 | 134 | TVs, VCRs, monitors |
| 5 | Trico Componentes | Matamoros, Tamps. | 1,965 | NA | Windshield wipers |
| 6 | Motorola de México | Mexico City | 1,557 | 1,557 | Semiconductors, radio antennae |
| 7 | Maquilaas Teta Kawi | Empalme, Sonora | 1,541 | 298 | Auto seat belts, disposable clothing, cell phone batteries |
| 8 | Elamex | C. Juarez, Chih. | 1,253 | 203 | Electonics and medical products |
| 9 | Ensambladora de Matamoros | Matamoros, Tamps. | 688 | 52 | Cablevision converters |
| 10 | Juguetrenes | Tijuana, Baja Calif | 436 | 102 | Plastic toys |
| 11 | Whirlpool de Reynosa | Reynosa, Tamps. | 396 | 59 | Cable harnesses |
| 12 | Coleman Manuf. de México | Chihuahua, Chih. | 351 | 37 | Fire alarms, CO detectors, thermostats |
| 13 | Comair Rotrón de México | Tijuana, Baja Calif. | 309 | 119 | Power source ventilators |
| 14 | CP Clare Mexicana | Guadalajara, Jalisco | 264 | 68 | Switches, suppressors |
| 15 | Mabuchi de México | Tijuana, Baja Calif. | 234 | 14 | Foam products |
| Total | | | 27,630 | 3,657 | |
| Average | | | 1,842 | 261 | |

* in millions of dollars.
Source: Expansión, 1997.

**Table 9.5 Mexico's Fifteen Largest Maquiladora Plants, 1996 (Continued)**

| Rank | Market Destination | Percent Domestic Raw Materials | No. of Workers | Percent Admin./ Technical | Percent Foreign Owned |
|---|---|---|---|---|---|
| 1 | U.S., Canada, Panama | 0.10 | 6,202 | 33.9 | 100 |
| 2 | California | 0.00 | 3,658 | 27.0 | NA |
| 3 | U.S. | 0.00 | 5,081 | 16.7 | 100 |
| 4 | U.S. | 11.45 | 1,797 | 33.5 | 100 |
| 5 | U.S. | 0.06 | 2,974 | 19.0 | 100.0 |
| 6 | U.S. | 4.82 | 2,236 | 41.8 | 99.8 |
| 7 | Michigan, Arizona, Alabama | 0.00 | 3,500 | 9.1 | 0.0 |
| 8 | U.S., Canada | 0.00 | 3,562 | 20.3 | 49.0 |
| 9 | NA | 0.02 | 586 | 47.6 | 100.0 |
| 10 | U.S. | NA | 2,106 | 31.9 | 100.0 |
| 11 | Ohio, Ind., Tennessee, Arkansas | 0.00 | 1,120 | 9.7 | 100.0 |
| 12 | Texas | 1.43 | 1,127 | 25.2 | 100.0 |
| 13 | California | 0.57 | 2,771 | 8.0 | 100.0 |
| 14 | U.S., Belgium, Canada, Sweden | 2.01 | 808 | 16.1 | 100.0 |
| 15 | California | 53.97 | 108 | 21.3 | 100.0 |
| Total | | | | | |
| Average | | 5.32 | 2,509 | 24.1 | 89.2 |

maquiladoras, such as textiles and clothing. In fact, clothing tends mostly (55 percent) to be in small maquila plants, whereas electronics is mostly (51 percent) in very large or huge plants (Carrillo and Santibáñez 1993).

Finally, it is important to emphasize the predominant market destination of products. That is the U.S., regardless of maquiladora country of ownership, size, or regional location. Some maquiladoras serve markets in particular U.S. states. The U.S. states selected relate to border plant location. Serving a target state usually implies that the specific maquiladora plant is located along the border directly to the south of that state.

Ownership of the 15 largest plants is 89.2 percent foreign, mostly U.S. Although many maquiladoras are Mexican owned, the huge ones accounting for two thirds of production are foreign owned. This may have to do with economies of scale. For very large plants, a major U.S. or Asian company can develop a world class plant and provide extensive worker training so the plant can operate and compete at world class levels. At the same time, a large plant reduces overhead cost per product and increases worker efficiency.

## Social and Health Disadvantages

Foreign observers have been concerned about social and health conditions in the maquiladora industry (Quiñones 1998). Thus, the maquiladora industry has been criticized for engendering social and health problems for its workers. There is concern about workplace health, where workers labor in small, noisy work areas, often without adequate ventilation or environmental controls. There have been reports of high levels of pollutants in some plants, causing respiratory and other illnesses.

Another area of concern is for the social environment of the border's rapidly growing urban areas, fueled by the high inmigration of maquiladora workers. Women workers, who are in the majority in maquiladoras, often migrate from small rural towns at a young age of 18 to 20. They may fall prey to the social problems in large and sometimes dangerous and even threatening cities such as Ciudad Juárez (Quiñones 1998; Rosen 1998) or Tijuana. Among the social problems are vice, narcotics, and crime (Golden 1999). These cities have grown so rapidly that their public health and public safety infrastructure is lagging (Quiñones 1998). Another problem for the female maquiladora worker is role adjustment within her family where she may no longer fit the traditional stereotype, leading to marital stress (Quiñones 1998).

Worker unrest and workplace issues have been mostly restrained in the last ten years (Bacon 1998). However, unrest has occasionally spilled over into protests or strikes. For instance, a strike on working conditions occurred in 1998 at the Han Young maquiladora plant in Tijuana. The plant is a subcontractor for a giant Hyundai maquila plant. Eventually the strike was broken by the local government, and strikebreakers were allowed in, although the strike's ultimate resolution is still pending in Tijuana courts.

These are problems that can occur in any workplace, but they appear to be amplified in the maquiladora plants and adjoining cities because of lack of regulations, and enforcement existing regulations, deficient infrastructure, and neglect. They must be regarded as a part of the social costs of this industry. Similar social costs have been in studies of globalization (Sassen 1998). Sassen posits that women bear proportionately more of the costs. This topic will be returned to and discussed further in the final chapters of this book.

## Relationship with the U.S.

The relationship of the maquiladora industry to the United States is complex, consisting of legal, regulatory, economic, market, transporting, and environmental aspects, among others. The maquiladora was established on legal grounds to be suitable to the U.S. and Mexico. Some other dimensions have taken longer to become known and recognized. The original legal/regulatory framework was specified to serve U.S.-Mexico maquiladoras. It has been replaced by the more general framework of NAFTA that will presumably be combined with yet undetermined new regulations from various governments.

The maquila economic relationship between the two nations is reflected in the exports and imports that have already been mentioned. Table 9.2 underscored the maquiladora's increasing importance relative to Mexican GDP and to its manufacturing sector. Maquila production, i.e. the Mexican value added plus domestic raw materials, currently represents 2 percent of Mexican GDP, and ten percent of Mexican manufacturing. For the U.S., the total value of maquiladora production entering the U.S. represents only 0.6 percent of U.S. GDP, while maquiladora raw materials being exported to Mexico comprise 2.5 percent of all U.S. exports. Thus the economic impact on Mexico is much larger than on the U.S. This has to be gauged in terms of a U.S. economy that is 23 times larger than Mexico's.

The economic relationship between the two nations in the maquiladora sector is reflected in the components of maquila production. First of all, the proportion of value added has decreasing. As seen in Table 9.6, the vast majority of production value consists of imported raw materials. These are predominantly from the U.S. The trend over the past two decades is to increase the portion of foreign raw materials. The portion of domestic raw materials, currently at 1.5 percent, has been fairly steady over the past 16 years. This proportion is surprisingly small for an industry that is now over thirty years old. In other parts of the world with similar co-production arrangements such as Malaysia, the proportions of domestic raw materials are much higher. Again, it is important to ask why Mexico's proportion is so low, given that NAFTA has raised the allowable domestic percentage every year to reach 100 percent in year 2001. The real reasons may be largely business ones, i.e. businesses appreciate the quality, reliability, and availability of U.S. raw materials so much as to justify their overwhelming use.

Albeit small overall, the proportion of domestic raw materials varies regionally and by industry. As seen in Table 9.7 and Figure 9.4, the domestic proportion of raw materials is much lower in the border region than in the rest of the nation, which averages six percent. Also in certain industry sub-sectors such as chemicals and services-footwear, the portion of domestic raw materials in non-border areas reaches as high as 60 percent. Although still quite low on the average, this reinforces that distance to the U.S. favors Mexican supply.

The remaining component of value added declined over the 16 years from 30 to 18 percent of gross added value of production. What happened is that foreign raw materials displaced value added by 12 percent; in other words, imported components are both more complex and of higher quality and need less assembly, i.e. value added. This points to increased dependence on the U.S. and its pre-assembled components.

The market aspects of the maquiladora relationship are not discussed here, due to lack of space. However, the largest market for maquila products has always been the U.S., but the Mexican market offers future potential, especially when it becomes more affluent. There are a limited number of non-U.S. overseas markets particularly in Canada and Europe.

**Table 9.6 Raw Material and Value Added Components
in Maquiladora Production, 1980–1996**

| | Year | | | | |
|---|---|---|---|---|---|
| | 1980 | 1985 | 1990 | 1995 | 1996 |
| Content that is Imported | | | | | |
| Raw Materials Imported* | 1,748 | 3,816 | 10,483 | 21,315 | 28,292 |
| Percent Imported Raw Materials (of GMVP) | 68.5 | 74.6 | 73.7 | 79.9 | 80.2 |
| Content that is Domestic* | 803 | 1,300 | 3,743 | 5,351 | 6,976 |
| Raw Materials that are Domestic* | 30 | 35 | 192 | 322 | 543 |
| Percent Domestic Raw Materials (of GMVP) | 1.2 | 0.7 | 1.3 | 1.2 | 1.5 |
| Value Added* | 773 | 1,266 | 3,551 | 5,029 | 6,433 |
| Percent Value Added (of GMVP) | 30.3 | 24.7 | 25.0 | 18.9 | 18.2 |
| Gross Value of Maquiladora Production (GVMP)* | 2,550 | 5,116 | 14,226 | 26,666 | 35,268 |
| Percent of Non-Manufacturing Services in the Maquiladora Industry that are Domestic | 10.2 | 21.3 | 30.8 | 52.0 | 59.7 |

* in millions of dollars.
Source: Modified from INEGI and Banixco Data in Expansión, 1997.

**Figure 9.4 Use of Domestic Raw Materials,
Maquiladora Industry, 1975-1991 (in percent)**

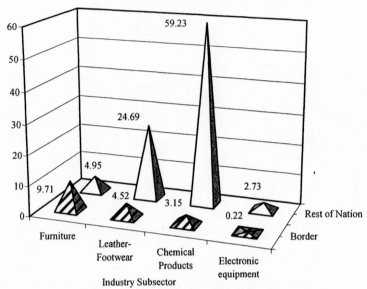

Source: INEGI, various years.

**Table 9.7 Use of Domestic Raw Materials in the Maquiladora
Industry by Sub-Sector, 1975-1991**

|  | Percent of Domestic Raw Materials | |
| Subsector | Border | Rest of the Nation |
| --- | --- | --- |
| Food | 15.46 | NA |
| Furniture | 9.71 | 4.95 |
| Services | 5.46 | 53.46 |
| Leather-Footwear | 4.52 | 24.69 |
| Chemical Products | 3.15 | 59.23 |
| Toys | 0.84 | NA |
| Tools, Non-electrical equipment | 0.42 | 2.73 |
| Electronic equipment | 0.22 | 2.73 |
| Other | 0.99 | 46.25 |
| Total | 0.90 | 5.79 |

NA = not available.
Source: Modified from Zepeda, 1996.

There are inevitable environmental interchanges between Mexico and the U.S. This reflects the fact that pollution is not restricted by national borders. Among the maquiladora-related sources of pollution are water and air pollution. There is both sewage base water pollution and pollution from toxic metals especially lead, mercury, chromium, nickel, and others (El Financiero 1998). In Tijuana, problems have become acute including pollution of shared waterways and disperson of poorly treated exudates in an ocean outfall.

Air pollution in the larger border cities, especially Tijuana and Ciudad Juárez, affects neighboring U.S. cities' airsheds and vice versa. Exchanges of water pollution in the El Paso-Ciudad Juárez metropolitan zone have been documented for years and are causing controversies (Bath 1986).

Although this chapter does not concentrate on environmental aspects, this area represents one of the costs of globalization. It will be referred to in the capstone discussions of globalization in the final chapters.

The two nations of Mexico and the U.S. are bound together cooperatively in maquiladora production. Other nations are involved to a lesser extent. Economically, the U.S. dominates this exchange, since it originally provides up to four fifths of the product as components and raw materials. Finally, there may be changes in the mix of domestic and foreign raw materials, as well as in markets as NAFTA becomes more fully implemented.

## Trends: The Future

While maquiladoras have grown rapidly, they have also changed in terms of product mix, location, training/education, and technology. This final section looks at trends influencing the future of the maquiladora industry.

One important trend is the phasing out of old U.S. customs regulations on tariffs and value added. There will be elimination of old customs for maquiladoras by 2001 in order to adhere to the General System of Preferences of NAFTA. For foreign-owned maquiladoras not belonging to NAFTA, old rules will stay in place i.e. there can be temporary importing of raw materials, equipment, and plant machines for purposes of production. There is also phased elimination of restrictions on sales in the Mexican domestic market, so that some maquiladoras will increase their sales emphasis in Mexico. Overall, these changes will encourage a maquila to do business more like a regular manufacturing company. There is still a difference having to do with incentives of maquiladora firms in the new sense, yet to be provided by the Mexican federal government. If a maquiladora currently has a close "twin plant" type of relationship with a U.S. counterpart, they will be encouraged to continue to do business as before, maintaining a good business relationship even if some federal tax breaks are eliminated.

Maquiladoras as part of globalization have social and environmental costs. The very cost cutting that is at the heart of the justification of maquiladoras also reduces possible expenditures for higher wages, a better workplace, and an improved environment. This counter-trend has been noted by commentators on globalization (Sklair 1993). In the case of maquiladoras, it is coupled in the border with rapid urban growth, which adds to the challenge to mitigate crime and poor education, as well as to control environmental contamination.

Important future trends that may impact maquila are the following (modified from Mendiola 1995):

- Significant development of maquiladoras elsewhere in Mexico beyond the border.
- Increased product specialization of maquiladoras in different regions.
- Increased use of domestic raw materials and components.
- Enhanced efforts at employee skills training in key business areas.
- Transfer of technology from the U.S.
- Shift of some maquiladoras away from a focus on Mexico and the U.S. to an enlarged focus encompassing international sub-contracting.

All these trends point towards a maturation of the maquiladora sector. They point to border centers of world class excellence in manufacturing, including quality control and advanced technology. However, these advances will only be possible if substantial foreign direct investment continues to flow into Mexico.

### Conclusions: Comparison of Maquiladora with Non-Maquiladora Manufacturing

This section examines the similarities and differences between maquiladora and non-maquiladora manufacturing. As seen in Table 9.2, the maquiladora proportion of Mexican manufacturing revenues grew from 0.9 to 9.8 percent over the 15 years starting in 1980-1995. The percentage of manufacturing employment rose from 4.9 percent to 26.3 percent during the same period. However, there are many exciting and progressive things happening with non-maquiladora manufacturing. This includes world class production by top firms like IBM/Mexico and HP/Mexico. There are also many average and some underperforming firms in the manufacturing sector.

An important question to ask is, what are the similarities and differences between the maquiladora and non-maquiladora sectors. At first glance, many would regard the sub-sectors as so different that seeking any common ground are not possible.

*Similarities between Maquiladora and Non-Maquiladora Manufacturing include the following:*

- *Cost reduction.* Both types of production benefit by lower costs in Mexico i.e. compared to advanced countries.

- *Pressure to reduce delivery times.* In general, transport costs have been reduced, as customers demand quick delivery. This is a common problem. Having suppliers close at hand solves it. This is true in maquilas by the tendency to locate suppliers within a plant or at least in Mexico within an hour of the plant. Suppliers are both Mexican and U.S. This is seen in the plants of Guadalajara, where suppliers have been lured there to form a Mexican "Silicon Valley."

- *Cooperation.* Maquilas tend to cooperate with each other, including sharing certain information, exchanging advice and expertise, sharing some suppliers, etc. Some newly arrived maquilas are not "socialized" and are staying aloof. This cooperative concept applies to non-maquila export oriented sectors. For instance, it applies to a certain extent in Mexico's "Silicon Valley".

*Differences between Maquila and Non-Maquiladora Manufacturing are the following:*
- *Legal status.* The maquila is under the "shelter" arrangement with a contract.

- *Scale.* The world class plants of leading non-maquilas have a huge scale. There are able to be more sophisticated in production because of economies achieved from the scale. Again, this reflects the "pilot" status of maquilas. When they "graduate," i.e. outgrow maquila status, they become full-fledged.

- *Innovation.* The world class plant is more innovative. The reason is due to scale and to competitive pressures. Innovation comes from creativity, energy, and education of the production workforce. The maquila level of production innovation is moderate. However, it is not the very low cost-saving of the original maquila concept several decades ago. That extreme cost saving approach now applies to production in other places, such as China and Malaysia.

- *Greater tendency to ship product into the U.S.* Maquila firms tend to supply the U.S. market. This is tied to the common need to reduce delivery times. The maquila location at the border means delivery times to the U.S. market. However, some maquilas are shipping to customers in other countries.

- *Different tax treatment.* A Shift in the tax and tax regulation in the year 2001 will occur, when NAFTA rules will apply to the maquila. However, it is expected that the Mexican government will step in by some means to maintain the difference. It may not be taxes, but in some way, it will compensate to give maquilas equivalent advantage. The maquila sector is too huge and important not to do so.

### Case Study: Trico

Trico Componentes was the fifth largest Mexican maquila plant in 1996 (Expansión 1998). It manufactures wipers and wiper blades and its market is the major U.S. automakers as well as many third party firms (see Table 9.5 and Map 9.2). In 1996, it exported $1.96 billion in products and employed 2,974 workers (In Figure 9.5). Trico follows the traditional pattern of co-twin plants near each other on the two sides of the border. Trico's Brownsville manufacturing plant produces nearly all of the components for its Mexican plant in Matamoros. In particular, the U.S. plant does metallurgy, casting, stamping, and manufacture of wiper blade arms. It also is the distribution center for shipping wipers and blades worldwide. Trico headquarters are located in Buffalo, New York, which is connected by a Manufacturing Resource Planning (MRP) system with the border twin plants. An MRP system does integrated tracking of the manufacturing process and all its component parts from raw materials through to final customer product.

Every morning sixteen large semi-trailer trucks arrive at the Brownsville Trico plant and load them with Trico components. They carry these components nine miles across the border to the Trico Componentes plant located in a modern industrial park in Matamoros. There, the components are assembled into wiper blades, blades, and blade motor assemblies. At the end of each day, the trailer trucks carry finished products back the same nine mile route to the U.S. Trico plant. From that plant, the major global auto companies come every few days to pick up batches of new products. The whole turnaround from raw materials to finished product and delivery takes only about five days.

Trico is remarkable in dominating the U.S. automotive market. The border twin plants manufacture 62 million blades, arms, wiper, motor assemblies, and other items per year. Trico has 80 percent of the U.S. market for blades and arms and 45 percent of the market on motor assemblies. Its customers include Ford, Chrysler, ITT Automotive (sells to GM and Toyota), CME (sells to Honda), Nissan, and ASMO (sells to Toyota and Chrysler). It also sells to leading service entities and private labels such as Pep Boys, Carquest, Atlas, Wheels, Might, Advance, etc.

**Figure 9.5 Trico**

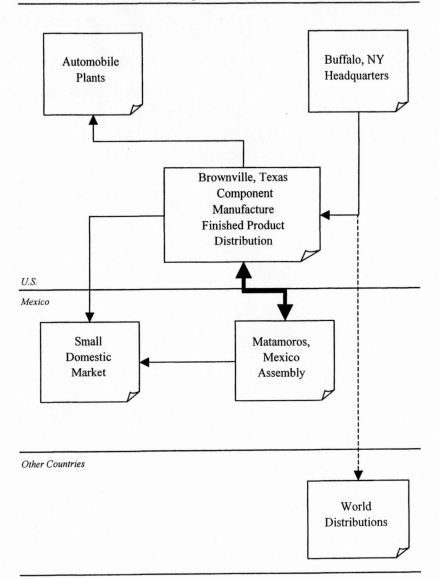

The Trico Matamoros plant consists of 355,000 square feet in an industrial park setting. The work environment is open i.e. not partitioned. Work areas are cramped, noisy, and fairly warm. Workers form 52 teams or Kaisans, and work in a coordinated manner within one team. They work in one of three 8 hour shifts. They make a fairly good Mexican salary up to $2,750 per year, the result of union pressure for higher wages. In spite of the "good" wages, it is meaningful to compare the $2,750 to the wage of the average U.S. Trico worker of over $25,000. Mexican workers are required to have ninth grade education, and Trico helps them finish high school.

Of Trico's 2,974 employees, 81 percent are line workers, 5 percent are technical, and 14 percent administrative. By gender, hourly workers are 80 percent female, generally in the age range of 18-22 years; technical workers are 35 percent female; while only 3.3 percent of high level management is female. This gender imbalance is typical of many maquiladoras. It is due in large part to management lowering costs by hiring very young women as workers. Historically, as seen in Figure 9.6, women have dominated maquiladora employment, even though the gender gap has narrowed somewhat. Predominantly male managers, with one exception, live in Brownsville and commute to the Matamoros plant daily.

**Figure 9.6 Manual Workers in Maquiladora Industry,
Mexico, 1989-1996**

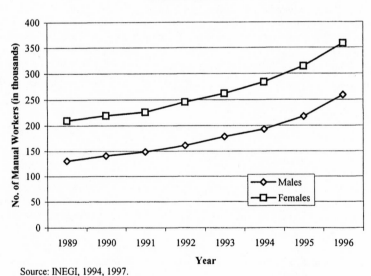

Source: INEGI, 1994, 1997.

There are several trends affecting Trico plants for the future. One is increased automation. The Matamoros plant already has several sections including painting that are automated and more are planned. This corresponds to a trend for the large maquilas to become more robotic, using advanced in technology over time. Likewise, the Brownsville warehouse is starting a conversion to robotics in 1899, with the first step of complete bar coding.

Another trend is increasing emphasis on quality control standards. This is typical of many maquila plants aspiring to reach world standards such as ISO 9000 and ISO 14000. ISO refers to quality control standards maintained by the International Standards Organization and increasingly adopted by companies seeking world class or nationally dominant competitive positions. Currently the Mexican Trico plant is in testing for ISO 9000, and it plans to move in 1998 to ISO 14000. It will be continuing this quest for higher and higher quality standards in the future. One motivating factor is that Trico products are being installed in vehicles, most of which already meet world class quality standards for export.

The amount of Mexican supply to Trico Matamoros is extremely small – only about $1 million per year, compared to $1.5 billion in imported raw materials. The reason is obvious – wiper blade components are not available at sufficiently high quality standards from Mexican companies but can be conveniently and inexpensively shipped in daily from U.S. sourcing in Brownsville.

Trico reflects a traditional maquiladora arrangement on a large scale. It adheres to the concept of co-producing companies, one on each side of the border. The arrangement is very much governed through a detailed legal contract. The plants are very productive and have reasonable working conditions by Mexican standards, although not by U.S. standards. Trends for the future include increased automation, adoption of higher quality standards of manufacture, and a shift towards more sales to the Mexican domestic market. NAFTA changes are not likely to disrupt the business plan and operations very much. The Trico Matamoros/Brownsville twin plants seem to be working well as a business and for the major stakeholders as well as for employees.

### Short Case Study: Thompson

Another successful maquiladora plant is that of Thompson S.A. of France in Ciudad Juárez. The plant produces 4 million television sets annually, and employs 4,000 workers. Previously, it did not perform final assembly of TVs, a job done at the Bloomington, Indiana Thompson plant. More recently, the Bloomington operations have been closed; the 1,100 workers in Bloomington were released, and 1,200 new workers were hired in Juárez to staff the operation.

The Juárez plant for Thompson is part of its global production strategy. It can produce at world class standards, supplying mostly the U.S. marketplace.

Thomson has focused on developing its staff in the Ciudad Juárez plant. It has provided some housing and shopping, and educational amenities. It actively encourages education and training.

The plant is highly productive, increasing the average yearly worker's productivity from $7,000 to $12,000 in 1997. The plant is the most efficient of all Thompson's major plants including those in France and Beijing. It has been able to reduce the total manufacture time for a TV set from 2 weeks to four hours. This in turn has been an important factor in lowering the price of a standard TV from $800 to $200.

This mini-example demonstrates another successful maquiladora operation. The success is due to strong and growing markets, management foresight in providing education and housing advantage to staff, and an emphasis on the latest technology. It is interesting that most of the same observations apply both for French firm, as was true for an U.S. form. The point about non-U.S. companies is that they too have access to very low labor costs and to the huge U.S. market. By organizing and managing well, they overcome any disadvantage of not being a NAFTA member country.

# 10

# Tourism

- **Introduction**
- **Tourism in the World**
- **Tourism Growth and Development in Mexico**
- **Tourism Exchange Between Mexico and Elsewhere**
- **The Spatial Patterns of Tourism in Mexico**
- **Local Impacts of Tourism**
- **Conclusions**
- **Case Study: Hoteles Presidente Inter Continental**

## Introduction

Tourism is an important part of the Mexican economy and of its exchange with other countries. This is made possible because Mexico is endowed with great natural settings, cultural history, appealing climate, archeological sites, and artistic accomplishments. Tourism is both domestic and national, and the two categories differ in their geographical thrust and features. Tourism, like oil, is a national asset that encourages positive international exchange. The Mexican government has developed its assets through federal funding of programs over many years. At the same time, private investment, much of it Mexican, has contributed to its long-term success. Federal programs have had some problems and setbacks, but on the whole have been successful in stimulating tourism to become a key economic sector and source of foreign exchange.

Mexican international tourism represents a form of interaction largely between semi-peripheral Mexico and a single core nation, the United States. It also can be understood in terms of the division of Mexico discussed in Chapter 3 into regional parts that are advanced, semi-peripheral, and peripheral. Most long-term international tourism occurs in the peripheral or semi-peripheral parts of the nation, while short-term international tourism occurs mainly in advanced areas. Domestic tourism occurs in all developmental areas, but is oriented towards more historically important zones. Within tourist categories, some tourists favor beaches and enjoyment, while others have more serious cultural interests.

Aspects of tourism examined in this chapter include tourism in the world perspective, growth and development of tourism in Mexico, tourism exchanges, and the spatial distribution of tourism. A case study of international tourism, Hoteles Presidente International, highlights the role of the private sector and international versus domestic tourism. The case shows the pressures of the global marketplace on the tourist industry, and how global and domestic management and market strategies intersect. Finally, tourism policy is addressed and how it has served Mexico.

## Tourism in the World

Tourism is a worldwide phenomenon, and it is important to recognize how Mexico fits into that pattern. International tourism has been growing, with worldwide tourist arrivals expanding from 69 million in 1960 to 612 million in 1997 (see Figure 10.1 with data from World Tourism Organization 1999). This implies an annual 5.9 percent growth rate in these arrivals over the past four decades, a rate far exceeding the world population growth rate over that period of 1.9 percent.

In the past ten years, international tourism growth moderated somewhat and in the late 1990s averaged about 4.4 percent annually. Comparing world regions over the past two decades, Europe decreased slightly, by 6 percent on a worldwide basis, and the Americas declined by 9 percent of total, while East Asia and the Pacific grew five fold and the "other" category doubled. This points towards large increases in regions not traditionally popular or known, and some proportionate decline in traditional favorites.

World hotel capacity also increased since mid century and in 1996 totaled 25.6 million bed-places (World Tourism Organization 1997). The rate of increase in bed-places is slower over the past two decades than tourist arrivals. Bed-places increased by 58 percent from 1980 to 1996, or at a rate of 2.9 percent annually. The U.S. dominates in bed-places, with 23 percent of the world hotel total, even though it has only 7.5 percent of the world's tourist arrivals. This may reflect substantial business travel in the U.S., as well as some unused hotel capacity.

**Figure 10.1**
**Growth in International Tourist Arrivals Worldwide, 1960-1997**
**Millions of International Arrivals**

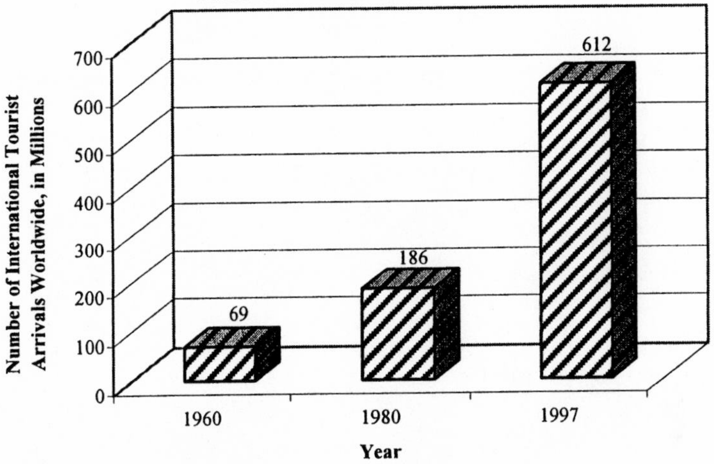

Source: World Tourism Organization, 1999.

Globally, tourism is centered in France, the U.S., Spain, Italy, China, the U.K, Mexico, Canada, and three Eastern European nations of Hungary, Poland, and the Czech Republic (see Table 10.1). The top 15 tourism nations include one peripheral nation, China, and one semi-peripheral nation, Mexico. The presence of these two nations is due to a combination of population size, and extent of tourist attractions. This is also reflected in Mexico and China being near the bottom of the list in terms of arrivals per capita. Volume of tourism in the developing world is driven by large and growing populations in these regions as well as by greater tendency of travel.

Another view of world tourism is economic. International tourist revenues and the net account of revenues minus expenditures, seen in Table 10.2, reveal that the U.S. and Europe account for about three fifths of world tourism revenues, while Mexico, Central America and South America only account for five percent. Of this, Mexico represents only 1.6 percent. Mexico's world tourism revenue proportion is half its share of world tourist arrivals. This is due to Mexico's lowered pricing of tourism versus the worldwide mix, which consists mostly of advanced nations with stronger economies and currencies.

Looking at the net travel account balances (see Figure 10.2), developing economies have a positive revenue flow, while advanced economies have a negative revenue flow (World Trade Organization 1997). Transitional economies are nearly even. Developing economies have profitable tourism balances since some of them possess rich natural and cultural offerings for tourism. Developing economies have increased their net account surpluses over time, due in part to those nations moving forward in governmental planning and policies to develop tourist infrastructure and facilities. The expanded international tourist demand comes largely from advanced nations. Mexico is an example of this including the efforts of its government arm FONATUR and the increasingly global

#### Table 10.1 Principal World Tourist Destinations, 1996

| Rank | Nation | Number of Arrivals 1996 (in millions) | Percent of World's Arrivals | Population 1998 (in millions) | Arrivals Per Capita | Per Capita Rank |
|------|--------|---------------------------------------|------------------------------|-------------------------------|----------------------|------------------|
| 1 | France | 61.500 | 10.36 | 58.8 | 1.046 | 7 |
| 2 | United States | 44.791 | 7.54 | 270.2 | 0.166 | 14 |
| 3 | Spain | 41.295 | 6.96 | 39.4 | 1.048 | 6 |
| 4 | Italy | 35.500 | 5.98 | 57.7 | 0.615 | 8 |
| 5 | China | 26.055 | 4.39 | 1242.5 | 0.021 | 15 |
| 6 | United Kingdom | 25.800 | 4.35 | 59.1 | 0.437 | 11 |
| 7 | Mexico | 21.428 | 3.61 | 97.5 | 0.220 | 12 |
| 8 | Hungary | 20.670 | 3.48 | 10.1 | 2.047 | 2 |
| 9 | Poland | 19.420 | 3.27 | 38.7 | 0.502 | 10 |
| 10 | Canada | 17.345 | 2.92 | 30.6 | 0.567 | 9 |
| 11 | Czech Republic | 17.205 | 2.90 | 10.3 | 1.670 | 4 |
| 12 | Austria | 16.641 | 2.80 | 8.1 | 2.054 | 1 |
| 13 | Germany | 15.070 | 2.54 | 82.3 | 0.183 | 13 |
| 14 | Hong Kong | 11.700 | 1.97 | 6.7 | 1.746 | 3 |
| 15 | Switzerland | 11.097 | 1.87 | 7.1 | 1.563 | 5 |
| | Total - Top 15 | 385.517 | 64.93 | 2019.1 | 0.191 | |
| | World Total | 593.745 | | 5926 | 0.100 | |

Source: Secretaria de Turismo, 1996; World Population Data Sheet, 1998.

#### Table 10.2 International Tourist Revenues, 1995-96

| Regions | International Tourist Revenues (millions of dollars) | | Percent of World Tourist Revenues | Population (millions) | Percent of World Population |
|---------|------|------|------|------|------|
| | 1995 | 1996 | 1996 | 1996 | 1996 |
| Africa | 6,980 | 7,670 | 1.80 | 763 | 12.66 |
| The Americas | 100,225 | 106,308 | 25.01 | 801 | 13.30 |
| North America | 75,313 | 79,998 | 18.82 | 399 | 6.61 |
| Central America | 1,530 | 1,567 | 0.37 | 35 | 0.57 |
| Caribbean | 12,537 | 13,392 | 3.15 | 37 | 0.61 |
| South America | 10,845 | 11,351 | 2.67 | 331 | 5.49 |
| Mexico | 6,164 | 6,894 | 1.62 | 98 | 1.62 |
| Asia (other than East) | 3,646 | 3,963 | 0.93 | 1,954 | 32.43 |
| East Asia and the Pacific | 73,411 | 82,158 | 19.33 | 1,499 | 24.88 |
| Europe | 207,351 | 216,913 | 51.03 | 728 | 12.08 |
| Middle East | 7,285 | 8,037 | 1.89 | 182 | 3.02 |
| Total | 398,898 | 425,047 | 100.00 | 6,025 | 100.00 |

Source: Secretaria de Turismo, 1996.

marketing reach of tourism companies in Mexico. These trends are reflected in the Hoteles Presidente case study.

Currently, Mexico has about 21-22 million yearly tourist visits; 12.4 million of them are border visits of 24-72 hours (see Table 10.3). The remaining nearly nine million are international tourists, coming largely from the U.S. In addition, there are 67 million short border excursions yearly. Although the international component constitutes one tenth of tourists, it accounts for two third of tourism revenues (see Figure 10.3). Distant visits that are longer term are much more expensive than 1-3 day border visits.

**Figure 10.2**
**Net Travel Account Balances by Level of Development,**
**1988-1996, in Millions of U.S. Dollars**

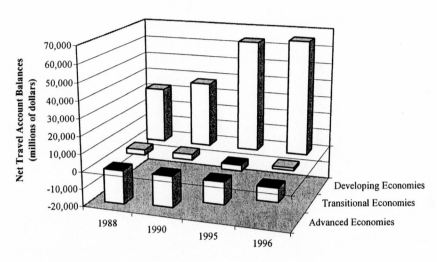

Source: World Trade Organization, 1997.

**Table 10.3 Composition and Revenues of International Tourism in Mexico, 1996**

| Category of International Tourist | Number of Tourists | Percent of Tourists | Tourist Revenues* | Percent of Revenues |
|---|---|---|---|---|
| International Tourism Visits | 8,994,000 | 10.02 | 4,632,000 | 67.19 |
| Border Visits 24-72 hours | 12,378,000 | 13.79 | 641,000 | 9.30 |
| Border Excursions Less than 24 hours | 66,748,000 | 74.36 | 1,531,000 | 22.21 |
| Transit Passengers on Ships | 1,639,000 | 1.83 | 90,000 | 1.31 |
| Total | 89,759,000 | 100.00 | 6,894,000 | 100.00 |

* millions of dollars.
Source: Bank of Mexico Survey, 1997.

Mexico's totals pale next to the world's 594 million annual tourist arrivals. Mexico must be put in the context of this huge and growing world tourism industry. It has done well in this global context, in spite of the ups and downs of the Mexican economy. The next section examines the history of twentieth century Mexican tourism and explores the crucial role of the federal government in stimulating it.

## Tourism Growth and Development in Mexico

Tourism was present in Mexico, even in Spanish colonial times. During the 1910s and 1920s, tourism was constrained by disruptions of the Mexican revolution, by lack of sufficient tourist infrastructure, and by the dearth of a large Mexican middle class to act as a

**Figure 10.3**
**Propositions of Number of Tourists and Tourist Revenues, 1996**

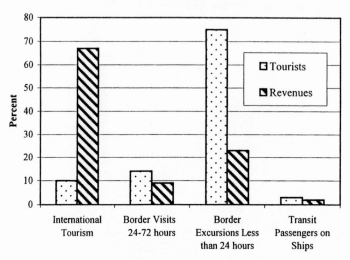

Source: Secretaria de Turismo, 1998.

source of domestic tourists. In the aftermath of the revolution, Mexico returned to some normalcy and its tourism potential began to blossom. Another trend during the 20s and 30s was the popularity of "indígenismo," a movement to return to Mexico's Indian or indigenous roots. This led to many outcomes such as government projects to shift the educational system to include more indigenous content and restoration of some sites from ancient civilizations (Nolan and Nolan 1988). These restorations stimulated the tourist market.

Another trend was the development of the transportation system. From 1930 to 1960, Mexico's transport system expanded and eventually opened up the entire nation to tourism. Two milestones of 1930 were the opening of a paved section of the Pan American Highway between Laredo, Texas, and Monterrey, Nuevo Leon, and the opening of a paved highway between Mexico City and Acapulco (Nolan and Nolan 1988). Pan American Airways started regular air service between the U.S. border and Mexico City in 1930. By 1936, the Pan American Highway extended from Laredo all the way to Mexico City (Nolan and Nolan 1988).

In the 40s and 50s, highways and air service continued to expand. By mid century, Mexico City became the hub of all tourist transport for Mexico. In the 60s, roads were built that opened up the center of Mexico, i.e. the Bajio Region to tourism (Nolan and Nolan 1998). Market interest in the center region was mostly domestic. The beach resort of Acapulco was opened up for large scale development in the 40s and 50s, and by 1950 had grown to prominence as Mexico's leading resort of that era. Transport and infrastructure continued to improve in the tourism areas of Mexico. During the second half of the century, rural areas became increasingly modern in utilities including energy and water supply, as well as in communications i.e. availability of phones. The transport network continued to expand and modernize. A milestone in 1984 was the completion of all links along the Pacific highway route from the U.S. to Guatemala (Nolan and Nolan 1998).

In the late 60s, the federal government brought forward a master plan for tourism that sought to develop the country's tourism over the long term. Along with this, the government promoted tourism at many levels and through many channels. This program has continued for the past thirty years, and remains vital today. The success of large scale planned tourism has depended on cooperation between the federal government and an active private tourism sector (Clancy 1999). Neither one nor the other could have succeeded alone.

The first major sign of the federal government's interest in tourism occurred in 1967. The government sponsored coastal resort development to supplement tourism. To select a new resort site for development, the national bank Banco de México sifted through numerous possible locations utilizing computers (Nolan and Nolan 1988). The computer study identified Cancún, then an unknown island with beaches, as the best location. Although it took nine years before the first hotels opened in Cancún in 1976, Cancún has grown vastly. Today Cancún has 20,000 hotel rooms and receives 2.3 million visitors per year (Secretaría de Turismo 1998).

The planned tourism development was spearheaded by the national tourism trust, FONATUR (Fondo Nacional de Fomento al Turismo), as well as by SECTUR (Secretaría de Turismo). The first set of resorts planned and developed in the 70s and 80s consisted of Cancún, Ixtapa-Zihuatanejo, Puerto Escondido, Los Cabos, Loreto, and Bahías de Huatulco (Nolan and Nolan 1988; Clancy 1999). These were located in the southeastern Yucatán Peninsula (Cancún), southern states (Ixtapa, Puerto Escondido, Huatulco) and northern state of Baja California Sur (Los Cabos, Loreto). The states involved of Quintana Roo, Oaxaca, and Baja California Sur were among the least populated and/or poorest in the nation. Referring to the world systems theory approach, these resorts are in the periphery or semi-periphery of Mexico. At the same time, the financial investment, loci of corporate control, and the preponderance of the tourist visitors come from core nations or the advanced part of Mexico.

The role of FONATUR has been to plan an overall national growth in tourism; encourage and develop infrastructure, both basic and tourist; provide financing opportunities and incentives; and seek investors in new projects (FONATUR 1999; Clancy 1999). FONATUR has invested in infrastructure, including transport, communications, and utilities for massive resort complexes.

The success of FONATUR is seen in its financial, construction, and job results over the last quarter century (Table 10.4).

**Table 10.4**
**FONATUR-Related Investment, Rooms Built, and Jobs Created, 1974-1998**

| Cumulative Indicator, 1974-1998 | Amount |
|---|---|
| Financial investment by FONATUR | 53.0 (billion pesos) |
| Total investment generated | 104.2 (billion pesos) |
| New rooms financed by FONATUR | 116,600 (rooms) |
| Rooms funded by private and other non FONATUR financing | 73,400 (rooms) |
| Rooms remodeled by FONATUR | 51,630 (rooms) |
| Jobs created | 336,000 (jobs) |

Source: FONATUR, 1999

FONATUR's program has been the dominant driver for hotels and associated infrastructure. For example Mexico in 1997 had a total of 382,364 hotel rooms (World Tourism Organization 1997). The rooms financed by FONATUR constituted 30 percent of them, and those with FONATUR-connected private funding added another 18 percent. Thus, nearly half of the nation's hotel rooms were derived directly or indirectly from FONATUR!

A project of this scale must be viewed from the standpoint of national development, rather than that of individual projects and locales. Some of the benefits of the FONATUR project become more apparent from this standpoint. From the 50s through the 70s, the Mexican economy was based on the approach of "import substitution." The problem was that starting in the 1980s import substitution faltered, partly due to competition from other countries. The balance of trade in the late 1980s began to shift away from Mexico. Another problem since the mid century in Mexico has been the increasing concentration of population in Mexico City (Unikel 1977; Pick and Butler 1997). FONATUR's initiatives helped to solve both problems: first by reducing the import-export gap and second by distributing jobs and population to remote areas away from large cities (Clancy 1999).

FONATUR initially faced huge problems in acceptance of its concepts. In spite of all its investment in infrastructure i.e. utilities, transport, and government services, the problem was lack of confidence that such large investment could succeed in remote regions. FONATUR initially could not find investors willing to invest (Clancy 1999). FONATUR and the federal government had to resort to purchasing and operating a hotel chain, Nacional Hotelera, in order to get things started. It also had to sweeten the investment package for outside investors, both by guaranteeing and subsidizing loans (Clancy 1999). As seen in the Table 10.4, FONATUR ended up providing about half of the financing itself. It also built three fifths of the hotel rooms, with the rest sponsored by outside investors. External investment was essential, and that investment also helped to stimulate external tourism.

Besides the federal level, there has also been limited state and local investment in tourism. State governments have promoted and encouraged tourism, with a view helping local and regional tourist markets (Van Den Berghe 1994, 1995). At the local -- city and municipio -- levels, tourism has been supported more from private rather than governmental sources. Such entities as tourist companies, bus firms, hotel chains, private guide services, and local architectural preservation associations have contributed (Van Den Berghe 1994). The main problem here is that the states and localities, especially the smaller ones, have very limited resources (Pick and Butler 1994).

Over the years, the FONATUR program weathered a number of economic perturbations and shocks including the debt crisis of 1982, the peso devaluation of 1994, and the subsequent 1995-1997 "crisis," i.e. deep recession. In the midst of all this, FONATUR had changes as well. In the privatization wave of the 1990s, the government's Hotelera chain was privatized. In its planning and initiatives of the 90s, FONATUR has had to take into account globalization. This has included globalization of tourist markets, the hotel business, and financing. In spite of changes, the long-term strategy has generally been successful, and continues to be. Negative aspects have included local opposition to FONATUR and environmental costs. However, groups opposing the national development plan have been unable to coalesce into a unified national front of opposition. Under its national plan, FONATUR continues to develop tourism further, an aspect discussed later under tourism policies.

## Tourism Exchange Between Mexico and Elsewhere

Tourism exchange is substantially between U.S. and Mexico. Both nations' tourist sectors are among the largest in the world (see Table 10.1) and both have significant natural, cultural, and historical advantages for tourism. It helps that these neighbors have a very long and fairly open border for tourist visits. Although the Mexican population is concentrated in the center of Mexico away from the border, substantial U.S. population is located in Texas and California near the border and having good tourist access to Mexico.

It fits into the economic strategy of Mexico to facilitate tourist exchange with the U.S., since Mexico's tourism sector serves to advance the balance of trade and foreign exchange. Although binational tourism exchange appears small in monetary terms vis a vis the U.S. balance of trade, it is major for Mexico.

Culture also plays a role in the exchange. The U.S. population is becoming increasingly Hispanic in composition. Many Mexican-Americans return to Mexico as tourists, and this ethnic group is expected to become larger in the future. Thus, although it does not represent national economic strategy, tourism to Mexico is favored in the long term by these population and cultural factors.

Impediments to tourism exchange are present and are discussed later under tourism policy. These include cycles of unrest or delinquency mostly in Mexico, pollution, economic downturns in both nations, and scattered occurrences of unfriendliness. However, they have not risen to the level of major disincentives. Overall, the economies of both nations favor tourism exchange, aided by the Mexican federal government actively fostering it.

For Mexico, the U.S.-Mexico exchange dominates in both arrivals and departures. As seen in Table 10.5, 94 percent of tourist arrivals in Mexico in 1997 were from the United States. Mexico is nearby, affordable, and offers great offerings in rich tourist activities. Border proximity of the U.S. is also a factor; for instance three fifths of tourist visits are border ones of 1-3 days. There is a tiny amount of tourism from the rest of the Americas and from Europe, and very little from elsewhere. In a parallel manner, about 90 percent of Mexican international tourists prefer to visit the United States. A mere five percent prefer Europe and four percent the rest of the Americas.

The preference of Mexican tourists for the U.S. may be puzzling, since the cost is potentially high. However, most Mexican visitors go to the border or to California and Texas, and utilize less expensive tourist options. Ten years ago, the same patterns were present. The U.S. accounted for 84 percent of Mexican tourism visits and the U.S. border accounted for 63 percent (Market Facts of Canada 1989). In the same study, the profile for Mexican travelers to the U.S. is interesting. Destinations were mostly "short haul," with any convenient means of transport utilized. The average length of trip was 22 days, with a mean of 3.4 people traveling. Five sixths of trips were independent and did not involve a travel package. About a third of the Mexican travelers planned their trip alone, without any outside information. Three quarters of trips were booked less than three weeks in advance (Market Facts of Canada 1989). The picture is of convenient, inexpensive, quickly arranged trips planned solely by the travelers and often involving visits to relatives and friends. The U.S. destinations are largely southwestern and urban. This pattern contrasts with that of U.S. tourists. U.S. tourists were primarily drawn to sea and surf, away from cities and family ties, while Mexican tourists had more family and city oriented, cost-effective travel. The contrast reflects fundamental differences culturally as well as economically. The study affirms that family connections of Mexican tourists with Hispanic population in the United States are very important.

**Table 10.5 Tourist Arrivals and Departures,**
**Mexico and United States, 1997**

| | | | | |
|---|---|---|---|---|
| *Tourist Arrivals 1997* | | | | |
| *Origin* | *To Mexico* | *Percent* | *To United States* | *Percent* |
| North America | 18,562,362 | 95.92 | 23,560,000 | 41.93 |
| *U.S.* | *18,193,715* | *94.02* | | |
| *Mexico* | | | *8,433,000* | *15.01* |
| Americas-Other | 378,624 | 1.96 | 4,583,272 | 8.16 |
| Europe | 346,530 | 1.79 | 10,734,881 | 19.11 |
| Middle East | NA | NA | 205,636 | 0.37 |
| Asia | NA | NA | 8,436,715 | 15.02 |
| Region Not Specified | 63,511 | 0.33 | 233,972 | 0.42 |
| Total | 19,351,027 | 100.00 | 56,187,476 | 100.00 |

| | | | | |
|---|---|---|---|---|
| *Tourist Departures 1997* | | | | |
| *Destination* | *from Mexico* | *Percent* | *from United States* | *Percent* |
| North America | 8,528,644 | 90.54 | 35,155,092 | 53.28 |
| *U.S.* | *8,433,000* | *89.53* | | |
| *Mexico* | | | *18,193,715* | *27.57* |
| Americas-Other | 366,376 | 3.89 | 7,802,707 | 11.83 |
| Europe | 472,587 | 5.02 | 16,875,255 | 25.58 |
| Middle East | 9,693 | 0.10 | 357,151 | 0.54 |
| Asia | 39,577 | 0.42 | 5,326,984 | 8.07 |
| Region Not Specified | 2,403 | 0.03 | 465,389 | 0.71 |
| Total | 9,419,280 | 100.00 | 65,982,578 | 100.00 |

Source: World Tourism Organization, 1999.

Mexico is seen to be significant but not dominant as sender and recipient of tourism to and from the United States. As with the maquiladora industry, for tourism the close proximity of a very large advanced nation and a large semi-peripheral nation stimulates a great deal of exchange in both directions. As seen in Table 10.5, Mexican tourists arrive in the U.S. in numbers about equal to European and Asian tourists. Likewise, U.S. tourists depart for Mexico about as much as they do for Europe and the rest of North America. As was evident for manufacturing and many other topics discussed in this book, the U.S. is much more important for Mexico than Mexico is for the U.S.

The economic strength of tourism for both nations is seen by comparing tourism earnings and spending of the five most important economies in the Americas -- the United States, Canada, Mexico, Argentina, and Brazil (World Tourism Organization 1997). The U.S. and Mexico stand out as the nations strongest in tourism revenues and profits. Both nations are in a "net profit" stance for the tourism sector in the late 90s. Argentina likewise is in a net profit stance, but Canada and Brazil have net losses. For 1996-97, the U.S. earned 75.1 billion dollars, with a 26.3 billion profit, while Mexico earned 7.6 billion dollars and had a 4.2 billion profit. The U.S. may be more of an exception than Mexico here, since most advanced nations are in a "net loss" position (World Tourism Organization 1997).

In broad context, the U.S. and Mexico resemble each other in tourist exchange (see Table 10.6). During the 1990s, both nations' arrivals by air grew, whereas arrivals by road and sea tended to decline. Also similar are the roughly equivalent percent increases in

**Table 10.6 Changes in Tourism Indicators, United States and Mexico, 1990-97**

| Tourism Indicator | Mexico 1990 | Mexico 1997 | Mexico Change 1990-97 | Mexico Ratios per Million Persons (1) | United States 1990 | United States 1997 | United States Change 1995-97 | U.S. Ratios per Million Persons (2) | Ratio of Column (1) to (2) |
|---|---|---|---|---|---|---|---|---|---|
| Tourist arrivals-Overnight visitors (Thousands) | 17,176 | 19,351 | 11 | 198 | 39,363 | 47,754 | 21 | 177 | 1.12 |
| Cruise Passenger Arrivals | 890 | 2,253 | 60 | 23 | NA | NA | NA | NA | NA |
| Arrivals by air (Thousands) | 4,313 | 6,978 | 38 | 72 | 19,789 | 29,402 | 49 | 109 | 0.66 |
| Arrivals by road (Thousands) | 12,859 | 12,373 | -4 | 127 | 13,324 | 12,356 | -7 | 46 | 2.78 |
| Arrivals by sea (Thousands) | 5,935 | 5,994 | 1 | 61 | 550 | 453 | -18 | 2 | 36.67 |
| Arrivals by leisure, recreation and holidays (Thousands) | 386 | 774 | 50 | 8 | 13,485 | 22,354 | 66 | 83 | 0.10 |
| Arrivals by business and professional (Thousands) | 72 | 126 | 43 | 1 | 2,915 | 4,728 | 62 | 17 | 0.07 |
| Number of rooms in hotels and similar establishments | 333,547 | 382,364 | 13 | 3,922 | 3,033,000 | NA | NA | NA | NA |
| Number of bed-places in hotels and similar establishments | 667,094 | 764,728 | 13 | 7,843 | 5,459,400 | NA | NA | NA | NA |
| International tourism receipts (Millions of U.S. $) | 5,467 | 7,595 | 28 | 78 | 43,007 | 73,268 | 70 | 271 | 0.29 |
| International tourism expenditure (Millions of U.S. $) | 5,519 | 3,892 | -42 | 40 | 37,349 | 51,220 | 37 | 190 | 0.21 |

Source: World Tourism Organization, 1999.

leisure arrivals and business/professional arrivals. A difference is that the U.S. increased its international tourism receipts from 1990-97 by 70 percent, more than twice Mexico's increase of 28 percent. The larger increase reflects the strong dollar and weak peso during this period. Paralleling this was a drop for Mexico in international tourism expenditures by 42 percent, compared to a gain of 37 percent for the U.S. This reflects the declining Mexican tourist visits overseas and the reduced tourist spending overseas, due to a weakened economy, peso devaluation, and recession. In summary, both countries experienced healthy tourism sectors in the 1990s with Mexico reflects somewhat weaker.

### The Spatial Patterns of Tourism in Mexico

The spatial distribution of tourism in Mexico is highly variable by region and state. Tourist destinations may be classified into categories, including grand cities, traditional, planned, interior, and border. Planned locations are coastal resorts planned and developed by FONATUR over the past thirty years. Traditional represents the older coastal resorts. The grand cities are the three largest of Mexico, in particular Mexico City, Guadalajara, and Monterrey. The interior cities consist of cities in the interior of Mexico that are older and less commercial.

The spatial patterns for tourism reveal groupings of cities than have great variation in the arrangement and types of tourism. The 1996 grouped data for the 31 largest tourist centers, representing ninety percent of the national total, are given in Table 10.7 (Secretaria de Turismo 1998). The corresponding map is shown in Map 10.1, where the sizes of symbols represent the total tourist arrivals. Examining the map, it is clear that the planned tourist centers are located in the beach and surf locations in the southeast, south, and in Baja Sur. The traditional tourist centers are also in beach and surf locations along Mexico's coastlines. The planned resorts, compared to the traditional ones, are in more remote and unpopulated parts of the nation. The grand cities and interior cities are predominantly in the interior, central section of the nation, while the border cites are widely spaced across the full extent of the U.S.-Mexico border. The areas in Mexico most deficient in tourism are the "oil states" of Campeche and Tabasco, the state of Chiapas, and most of the northern states, except for the immediate border strip and Baja Sur. These areas tend to be less accessible by transport and away from the major population centers. They have mountains, deserts, and jungles that constrain tourist development and interest. How the spatial locations relate to the world systems theory perspective is discussed in the conclusion section.

The "foreignness" varies by type of center. For the planned tourist centers, three quarters of tourist visits are by foreigners. However, the other types are much lower, with traditional and grand cities types at a quarter and a fifth foreign, and the interior and border types at 16 percent. All the planned sites of FONATUR are foreign oriented. The highest "foreignness" is for Los Cabos in Baja Sur and Cancún in Quintana Roo. These appear not too different in composition from some U.S. tourist spots, such as ones in Hawaii or Southern California. The federal planning for these "foreign" beach resorts has paid off handsomely on an economic basis. Nevertheless, there are environmental and social negatives that will be discussed later. From a balance of trade standpoint, foreign visitors contribute positively to the balance of trade and also have higher per capita and per trip expenditures than domestic tourists.

Tourism in the traditional and grand cities, amounting to three fifths of total tourism, is predominantly Mexican. Because Mexico is a highly centralized nation (Pick and Butler 1997), there is obviously a draw to the national capital. It has important cultural attractions,

### Table 10.7 Tourist Volumes in Major Tourist Locations, 1996

| Tourist Centers (city, state) | Rank Order* | Number of Rooms | Tourist Arrivals National | Tourist Arrivals Foreign | Total | Percent Foreign |
|---|---|---|---|---|---|---|
| Bahias de Huatulco, Oaxaca | 30 | 1,846 | 116,230 | 43,099 | 159,329 | 27 |
| Cancun, Quintana Roo | 2 | 19,754 | 472,902 | 1,832,636 | 2,305,538 | 79 |
| Ixtapa Zihuatanejo, Guerrero | 18 | 4,131 | 232,200 | 151,634 | 383,834 | 40 |
| Loreto, Baja Sur | 31 | 435 | 15,037 | 37,989 | 53,026 | 72 |
| Los Cabos, Baja Sur | 15 | 4,072 | 68,173 | 479,390 | 547,563 | 88 |
| Acapulco, Guerrero | 3 | 15,756 | 1,576,018 | 336,205 | 1,912,223 | 18 |
| Cozumel, Quintana Roo | 26 | 3,184 | 71,036 | 231,931 | 302,967 | 77 |
| La Paz, Baja Sur | 29 | 1,336 | 156,720 | 51,860 | 208,580 | 25 |
| Manzanillo, Colima | 17 | 2,827 | 321,747 | 75,942 | 397,689 | 19 |
| Mazatlan, Sinaloa | 9 | 6,585 | 529,964 | 193,459 | 723,423 | 27 |
| Puerto Vallarta, Jalisco | 7 | 8,134 | 384,904 | 490,994 | 875,898 | 56 |
| Tuxtla Gutierrez, Chihuahua | 27 | 1,724 | 268,629 | 29,087 | 297,716 | 10 |
| Veracruz, Veracruz | 5 | 5,552 | 1,202,765 | 50,551 | 1,253,316 | 4 |
| Villahermosa, Tabasco | 16 | 2,081 | 354,445 | 43,273 | 397,718 | 11 |
| Federal District | 1 | 40,188 | 5,748,795 | 1,640,765 | 7,389,560 | 22 |
| Guadalajara, Jalisco | 4 | 11,712 | 1,462,097 | 145,414 | 1,607,511 | 9 |
| Monterrey, Nuevo Leon | 6 | 6,624 | 879,999 | 172,872 | 1,052,871 | 16 |
| Puebla, Puebla | 11 | 3,451 | 561,196 | 89,724 | 650,920 | 14 |
| Cuernavaca, Morelia | 20 | 2,023 | 306,457 | 59,078 | 365,535 | 16 |
| Durango, Durango | 19 | 1,534 | 371,373 | 5,764 | 377,137 | 2 |
| Guanajuato, Guanajuato | 28 | 1,810 | 240,891 | 34,429 | 275,320 | 13 |
| Hermosillo, Sonora | 22 | 4,131 | 314,819 | 33,771 | 348,590 | 10 |
| Merida, Yucatan | 12 | 4,043 | 338,879 | 284,047 | 622,926 | 46 |
| Morelia, Michoacan | 14 | 2,886 | 509,947 | 24,636 | 534,583 | 5 |
| Oaxaca, Oaxaca | 13 | 3,266 | 392,593 | 161,833 | 554,426 | 29 |
| Queretaro, Queretaro | 21 | 2,227 | 338,828 | 10,584 | 349,412 | 3 |
| San Luis Potosi, San Luis Potosi | 25 | 2,418 | 293,789 | 18,853 | 312,642 | 6 |
| Zacatecas, Zacatecas | 24 | 1,322 | 327,331 | 12,760 | 340,091 | 4 |
| Tijuana, Baja California | 8 | 4,448 | 639,012 | 178,304 | 817,316 | 22 |
| Ciudad Juárez, Chihuahua | 10 | 2,777 | 641,977 | 79,361 | 721,338 | 11 |
| Reynosa, Tamaulipas | 23 | 2,106 | 311,250 | 37,203 | 348,453 | 11 |
| Total for Cities Shown | | 174,383 | 19,450,003 | 7,037,448 | 26,487,451 | 27 |
| Grand Total | | 190,405 | 21,906,314 | 7,469,235 | 29,375,549 | 25 |

Source: Secretaria de Turismo, 1998.

* The rank order represents the ordering in total tourist arrivals. This number appears on the corresponding map.

**Map 10.1**
**Major Tourist Centers, By Type and Tourist Arrivals, 1996**

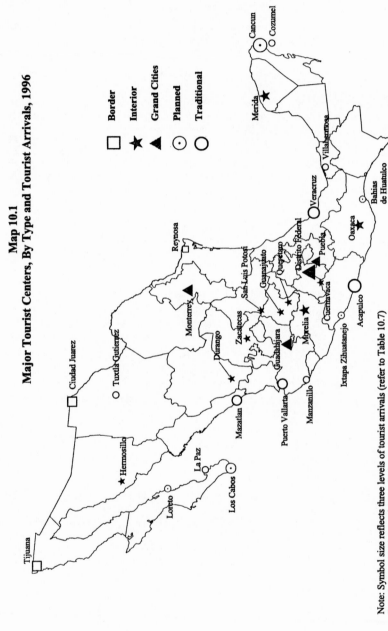

Note: Symbol size reflects three levels of tourist arrivals (refer to Table 10.7)
Data Source: 1996 Anuario Estadistico
Map Source: Butler/Pick Mexico Database Project

the most population, vast entertainment venues, as well as most of the government and corporations. Some of this applies to the other grand cities. The traditional locations are mostly older resorts, more keyed to middle class Mexicans, from language, cultural, and transport accessibility standpoints.

The interior and northern border draw six times as many Mexicans as foreigners. Mexicans visit the major interior locations for many reasons including their great historical and cultural importance, visits to family, and need to escape the major cities to quieter, safer, and more colonial environments. The reason for the low proportion of visits by foreign "tourists" to the border despite its U.S. proximity relates to the lack of enduring features to hold Americans more than a short period in Mexican border cities. Rather, there is preference for short excursions of less than a day that are not classified as "tourist." Instead of staying overnight in a border city, foreigners largely prefer these day excursions (see Table 10.3). This may also reflect large U.S. populations visiting the other side of border cities, such as San Diego – Tijuana and El Paso – Cuidad Juárez.

The patterns of transport to tourist centers differ by center type. For instance, 57.1 percent of air seats were occupied by foreigners to the centrally planned beach resorts, whereas the proportion was only 25-27 percent to the grand cities and colonial cities, and only 0.6 percent to the northern border (Secretaría de Turismo 1997). This reflects a tourist infrastructure that is oriented to certain kinds of tourists for certain regions. Other facts of supporting structure are similarly specialized; for instance flight services, support services, and airports serving Cancún emphasize different comfort and diet patterns than those for Veracruz or Ciudad Juárez.

## Local Impacts of Tourism

In addition to its national impact, tourism impacts vary in their local nature and for various regions and cities in Mexico. For instance, impacts on hotel jobs are local, while financial impacts may be distant or foreign. Environmental impacts are local, but transport impacts are mixed - local and distant. Tourism information shows tourist visits, hotel, and transport data, but does not provide data on local impacts including financial. Such impacts must be inferred based on particular locations.

This section discusses the delicate but crucial interrelationship between tourism and the local community and the local and regional impacts of tourist development. Case studies are cited that build on the classification in the previous section. The local and regional impacts are not only felt for planned development and mega-projects, but also for all the tourist types ranging from grand cities to the border. Nearly two million Mexicans work in the tourist industry, equivalent to eight percent of the national workforce. Besides the workers, there are many organizations interacting with local tourism, including service firms, transport companies, food and beverage enterprises, and unions. The global elements play a role in local tourism. Some companies are international and global. Tourists may be international, and they may or may not adopt the outlook of a typical international tourist.

Local impacts are too complex a topic to cover in its entirety with respect to Mexico, and furthermore much of it hasn't been studied. This chapter section discusses two cases from the literature of local impacts of tourism development; one of the planned resort of Bahías de Huatulco and a second of the interior city of San Cristóbal (Long 1993; Camacho 1996; and Van Den Berghe 1994). They will be discussed and related to the world systems theory perspective.

Bahías de Huatulco has already been mentioned as one of the planned resorts of FONATUR. It is perhaps the largest of all FONATUR's planned projects. Its current size is 1,846 hotel rooms and 159,000 annual visitors. It is projected to reach 30,000 hotel rooms and 2 million yearly visitors by the year 2018 (FONATUR master plan, cited in Long 1993). It is an area comprising nine bays in southeastern Oaxaca state. FONATUR began to develop Santa Cruz Huatulco in 1984. It previously had a tiny population of 735 in the city of Santa Cruz, which consisted mainly of farmers and fisherman (Long 1993). In 1986, the small town was displaced and moved to the other side of a hill, so that the original site could be utilized as a coastal tourist element in the planned project. The residents underwent drastic social changes, including facing the inmigration of young workers and tourist personnel, adapting to changes in the type of housing structures built, and enduring sharp rises in land prices (Long 1993).

There have been strong social impacts on the local residents. They expressed little support for the project, and not much support for FONATUR's handling of the development project (Long 1993). The local citizenry divided into groups that on the surface either accepted the project or resisted it. In response, FONATUR tried to reduce the problems by introducing mitigation efforts. The mitigation included job training programs, provision of medical, health, and police services, the building of the town of La Crucecita, new schools, public assemblies, and recreation support services (Long 1993). The mitigation efforts were not initially successful, but over time, the population gradually "adapted" to the realities of the mega-project and benefited by FONATUR's mitigation efforts (Long 1993). For instance, the longer people lived in the new "artificial" town of La Crucecita, the greater their acceptance of that town concept.

Another perspective on Huatulco is provided by an anthropological case study (Camacho 1996) in which the investigator worked in two multinational hotels posing as a maid and as an English teacher. The study is valuable in demonstrating large gaps in stratification even verging on segregation among hotel workers. For one hotel, initial stifled dissent blew up into a full-fledged worker strike that broke away from union control.

The conflict started from hotel worker stratification accentuating differences between non-union management and unionized low level workers. The management level consisted of higher level managers, mostly males, and mid level service personnel, with mixed gender balance. Below were the unionized workers serving as maids, janitors, and repairmen. The low level was more female. All levels had attire that clearly connoted strata (Camacho 1996). The case shows a sharp separation of union and non-union personnel, with non-union personnel having separate entrances, low quality of food, and even separate bathrooms from management (Camacho 1996).

The workers finally struck in one hotel over a dispute about union leaders pocketing a large proportion of tips. Union leaders sided with management and the dispute eventually was settled (Camacho 1996).

In this case, the multinational hotel chains had essentially moved former peasants with low education into low level hotel industry jobs, in which they were not given many choices and limited means of dissent. High level managers came in from outside and were regarded as if they were "foreigners" from a different world. The Huatulco case demonstrates the interplay of global and local elements for planned tourism in a peripheral region of Mexico. There is the classical theoretical element of drawing from the periphery to satisfy the needs of the core (Shannon 1992). The low-level workers suffered from many aspects of social change at every step. They were displaced from their town site and forced to adapt to an "artificial" city. They suffered economically as the standard of living in the region increased. There were clear problems of job maldistribution and social stratification, with the more educated and skilled managers even verging on segregation. At the same time, the multinational elements of tourists and hotel companies benefited, and the government was largely successful in developing a new region of great potential prosperity. To offset the social problems FONATUR offered its program of mitigation, which in essence attempted to give some of the benefits of the semi-periphery to former peripheral citizens. It has had mixed success.

Another case study that relates to interior tourist centers and the tension between commercial and eco-tourism is the well known study of San Cristóbal by Van Den Berghe (1994). That anthropological field study was performed in the late 1980s in the interior city of San Cristóbal in the highlands of Chiapas. The investigator surveyed nearly 200 tourists. The annual tourist volume was moderate at about 136,000, about half Mexican.

There were two groups of tourists, one a younger group called "eco-tourists," who were more oriented towards longer stays, enjoying the culture, meeting the local people, staying in local hotels and getting good value (Van Den Berghe 1994). By contrast, the other group was older, much more transient, often part of tourist travel groups, and with much less interest in local people and customs. The research also identified a group of middlemen, termed "ladinos," who brokered interactions of various kinds between the local Indians and the tourists. Foreign and domestic tourists acted differently. Among other things, the Mexican domestic tourists were more interested in western-standard hotels and modern accommodations with shorter stays, while the young, foreign eco-tourists were interested in more primitive and locational experiences (Van Den Berghe 1994).

There were large differences in the impacts of eco-tourists versus "commercial" tourists. For instance, eco-tourism created less social tension than "normal" commercial tourism. Van Den Berghe identified the following as causes of tension: transience, inter-ethnic differences, language differences, and wealth differences (termed "asymmetry"). These were reduced but not eliminated for the eco-tourists versus commercial tourists. For instance, eco-tourists had more interactions with the natives because they were much less likely to be travelling in groups. A great image from the study is that of commercial tourists entering San Cristóbal under the aegis of the agency Caravanas, in convoys of 15-20 oversized vehicles following a leader (Van Den Berghe 1992). Those tourists meet the stereotype of the commercial tourist, where interactions with locals are clearly delimited.

Van Den Berghe advocates the concept of ethnic tourism or eco-tourism. "Ethnic tourism is really much more profitable and beneficial to a greater number of people than it seems at first blush, and it produces little environmental or cultural pollution. Conversely, the manna of luxury coastal tourism brings much less than it seems: many profits are expected; it benefits far fewer people; and its environmental and cultural costs are staggering" (Van Den Berghe 1992).

This literature case points to the role of different types of tourists, who have different perceptions and appreciation of tourist environments. The contrasts are between eco-tourist and commercial tourist, and between foreign and domestic tourists. Generally, the interchanges are less harsh than in the Huatulco case. For instance, the scale of tourism had not displaced the natives to the extent of Huatulco. The presence of middlemen emphasizes that natives are appreciated in their native aspects, in contrast to the massive conversion of the natives into tourist workers, as occurred in Huatulco. The good aspects of this case are the potential of harmonious interchanges, without exploitation, between core and periphery elements. Although that was not achieved with certain categories of commercial tourists, the case does hold out hope. Another point is that the advanced core is less present in San Cristóbal than in Huatulco, including such aspects as massive modern hotels, an airport, and hotel managers who are removed from natives.

The end of chapter case is different there again. It illustrates a major hotel chain that straddles the business boundary between international and domestic tourism.

## Conclusions

Tourism represents one of the key assets of Mexico. It is based on the inherent advantages of a nation endowed with rich cultural and natural features. It is enhanced by proximity to a huge U.S. market of tourists seeking a variety of short-term and long-term visits. The increased sunbelt concentration of U.S. population with growing Mexican ethnicity also favors tourist flows. The Mexican government since the 1960s has taken a proactive role in fostering large scale planned tourism.

The chapter has highlighted the growth in tourism worldwide, as well as in Mexico as a semiperipheral nation. Developing nations today tend to have positive tourist exchange balances and Mexico is a good example. One result is that tourism ranks along with petroleum and maquiladoras as one of the three largest sources of income for the Mexican economy.

Besides positive economic benefits, there are negative elements that must be weighed. These include cultural impacts, pollution effects, bad images created by crimes and delinquency, relegation of local resident workforce menial tasks, and changes in the land pricing of tourist locations.

Another world systems theory perspective is that of the division of Mexico into core, semiperiphery, and periphery. From the perspective of world systems theory, a semiperipheral nation, Mexico, has exchanged natural resources and low cost labor for foreign investment. This is analogous to other exchanges of resources between the core and semiperiphery. Minerals might be another example. Many tourist features fit well into this framework. For one thing, the locus of planned tourist development, accentuating export exchange, is in the periphery and semiperiphery within Mexico. The Mexican government is playing a classic development game, of trading its "resource" base for financial benefits. By contrast, border tourism demonstrates huge volume and low costs of visits. It is largely keyed to the closeness of the U.S. southwest with the Mexican border region. In terms of the parts of Mexico, this is more of an exchange between equals. Much of the Mexican border region is advanced for that nation. It is not the equivalent of the U.S. border, but comparable in many aspects of exchange.

It is important to consider also the patterns of the Mexican domestic tourist, which are focused on the interior and traditional resorts -- older areas, many with great cultural importance. If Mexico expands its middle class, domestic tourism may become more important.

The case studies illustrate a number of aspects of this complex situation. The Huatulco case highlights that the advanced-peripheral exchange may involve displacements and tensions between different tourism players including managers, lower level workers, and the tourists themselves. It shows that mitigation efforts can be beneficial and are probably essential for larger scale planned development. The San Cristóbal case highlights an interior tourist center smaller in scale and reduced in its impacts on cultural and traditional features. Yet there are threats that may grow and eventually destroy intact native culture. A different aspect is the differentiation among tourists, who may be commercial or ecologically sensitive, foreign or domestic. The distribution of tourist types may influence the impacts and ultimately the success or failure of tourism in a location.

The Hoteles Presidente case demonstrates the business pressures on a luxury hotel chain. There are competing interests of globalization, domestic market, and global versus local owners. In spite of countervailing forces, the company seems to have adapted to the stresses and strains and to have reached a satisfactory compromise, including a split between local asset management and global operational management.

Tourism is a complex feature of Mexico. It has positive and negative elements that are different to various stakeholders. It has been and will continue to be a key element in the growth and development of the country.

## Case Study: Hoteles Presidente Inter-Continental

Hoteles Presidente (H-P) is a leading hotel chain in Mexico that is privately controlled. It has a close collaboration with Inter-Continental Hotels Corporation, a global hotel chain. This case study examines the history and current structure of Hoteles Presidente, its relationship globally and locally, its relation to international and domestic tourists and markets, and the tradeoffs that it faces between global and domestic needs.

Hoteles Presidente currently owns seven luxury hotels (see Map 10.2). Two are in grand cities, namely Mexico City and Guadalajara, and the others are in planned resorts. The chain had 2,564 rooms and an annual budget of about $180 million in 1997.

The company was founded by a Mexican businessman in the late 1950s. After falling into financial difficulties, the chain was purchased in 1972 by the federal government. The government operated it for 13 years, as a chain of 28 hotels that were mixed in quality and size. This government period illustrates FONATUR'S plan at the time of running some hotel chains to stimulate its national tourism plan. The company was re-privatized in 1985. Four Mexican families purchased control of the chain. The government hoped that privatization would further stimulate tourism. The chain became more oriented towards luxury markets; in 1988, many lower level hotels were sold off, leaving a grouping of luxury hotels. The management felt that it would be important to associate with a global hotel chain, in order to strengthen the company's international exposure and brand name exposure. Hoteles Presidente linked up with Stouffer Hotels, part of Nestle, from 1991 to 1993.

After breaking up with Stouffers, Hoteles Presidente floated for nine months while it looked for a new global association. The company's management felt it could not endure without global recognition. It was able to form a new association with the global chain of Inter-Continental Hotels in late 1993. Inter-Continental Hotels has about 200 hotels in 75 countries, mostly luxury category. H-P retained the management of Mexican hotel assets, while Inter-Continental assumed hotel operating responsibility. There was a complex agreement regarding the financial and corporate relationships, but essentially Inter-Continental was paid about half of profits and other fees in exchange for its operating role. H-P management cites market diversification as the major advantage to this association, in particular the ability to attract customers from the international marketplace, diversifying away from domestic clientele. There is also a strategic advantage of having access to world class competencies. This is especially applied to use of Inter-Continental's worldwide reservation system, IC Global II. That system is analogous to having access to a worldwide airline reservations system -- it attracts and maintains customers, travel agents, and other intermediaries.

In 1998, Inter-Continental was taken over by Bass PLC from the UK, which controls Holiday Inns and has a total of 2,600 hotels and 450,000 rooms i.e roughly equivalent to the entire hotel capacity of Mexico. Geographically, Bass/ Inter-Continental is located in London, while Hoteles-Presidente management is located in Mexico City, and the hotels are in Mexico City, Guadalajara, and planned resort areas.

In spite of the Inter-Continental linkage, the Mexican hotels are staffed nearly 100 percent by Mexicans. Out of the 3,000 employees of Hoteles Presidente, only 32 are foreigners including two hotel managers, several executive chefs, the Director of

**Map 10.2**
**Hoteles Presidente Inter-**
**Continental Hotels and Resorts, 1999**

Data Source: Hotels Presidente
Map Source: Butler/Pick Mexico Database Project

Marketing, trainers, sales managers, and several others. Nationalities of the foreign employees include a variety of European backgrounds, Canadian, and Israeli. About one third of the workforce is temporary and half is unionized, but unlike the Huatulco case, there have been no labor disputes or unrest for the past ten years. The 659-room Mexico City Hotel Presidente Inter-Continental forms a hub in this network. All strands come together in this flagship hotel that houses the domestic asset management firm, national operating management from Inter-Continental, and the management team for the chain's largest hotel.

Understanding and responding to customers have been major challenges to Hoteles Presidente. For instance, management interviews indicated that the international customer, at 70 percent of the chain's market, is very different in tastes and interests than the domestic customer. The profile for the international customer is someone who likes to reserve far ahead of time, is used to multiple seatings in restaurants, likes canned fruit juices, and books conventions far in advance. The domestic customer is opposite on all of these characteristics including preferring fresh juices, and reserving conventions sometimes only weeks in advance. Hoteles Presidente seeks to serve both of these customers, and has had to train its staff to service both. At the same time, the entire chain is being brought up to world class hotel quality standards, from computers to water quality to comfort. The customer mix from year to year also influences the company's financial flows since a weak peso may favor a higher proportion of foreign visitors and imply purchasing relatively more goods and services domestically.

The upshot of this corporate case includes the need to balance global and local concerns and viewpoints. There are a lot of diverse stakeholders here. They include British multinational executives, private family owners in Mexico City and their hired asset managers, Inter-Continental's Mexico-based operating management, a large number of skilled and unskilled Mexican workers, and a customer base ranging from the Middle-Eastern and European global travelers to wealthy Americans and well-off Mexican nationals. Additional stakeholders are the minority owners of the asset company, Bancomer, a leading Mexican bank discussed in Chapter 5, and FONATUR. Hoteles Presidente represents a balancing act between domestic and foreign interests and markets, government and business, and private versus public needs. Although the firm has been well managed and has avoided major labor unrest seen elsewhere, the key issue of identity remains. Right now the firm is relying mainly on an associated global brand name to establish identity. A challenge for a firm managed in the advanced core cities of Mexico City and London is to be sensitive to hotel locations that are outside of the core, with many in the periphery. The deep key to success may be cultural. Can the gaps be bridged between managers and workers having different outlooks, and customers varying in cultural attitudes? Can the hotels full mostly of wealthy foreigners relate well to the mostly low-level and native hotel workforce? So far things have been working well.

# 11

# Agriculture

- **Introduction**
- **Agriculture Exports & Imports**
- **Ejidos, Ejidatarios, and Article 27 of the Mexican Constitution**
- **Agricultural Industry**
- **Agriculture in Mexico and the Environment**
- **Future Prospects**
- **Conclusions**
- **Case Study: Maseca/Gruma**

## Introduction

Nature and man have treated the potential for agriculture in Mexico harshly. In addition, centuries of misuse and neglect hamper the productive use of an inhospitable landscape (Cole and Sanders 1970). Only about one-third of Mexico has relatively level land. The remaining two-thirds consist of high and barren mountains, steep hillsides, and deep and rock barrancas. In addition, the level land is not always favorable to intensive agricultural use. In the North, a large portion of level land is arid and semi-desert and needs irrigation to be productive. The south has level land but much of it is shallow, leaches easily, and is not suitable for large-scale agriculture. A further problem is uneven rainfall, which supports jungles in some areas and only cacti and lizards in others. Drought and forest fires also influence agricultural production (Burke 1998b). Using river water for irrigation is made difficult because most rivers and streams have their origin near oceans and the rivers drop abruptly to them. Finally, less than twenty percent of land is suitable for agriculture.

Nature's handicaps have been exacerbated by cultivation techniques that have eroded and depleted the utility of the land. Much of the land surface that was verdant in the 16th century was destroyed by the utilization of the plow and overgrazing after the Spaniards brought domesticated animals to Mexico. In addition, the depletion of forests for use for firewood and charcoal has led to extensive deforestation. Farmers with limited capital were more likely to grow corn and had more problems getting credit and less likely to have purchased seeds, fertilizer, and pesticides, or use a tractor. Their land tended to be of lower quality (Lopez et al. 1995).

The rate of change from traditional to modern agricultural practices has been slow except in the north and west. Thus, many subsistence farms and farm workers still exist. Rural areas continue to send their "surplus" population to the cities, while the urban labor force contributes to the sustenance of rural relatives.

Some of Mexico's most serious problems arise from the physical environment within which its inhabitants live and work (Whetten 1948). Internal struggles in Mexico have centered on the problem of land, its distribution, and use. Agrarian reform and the land tenure system are the scarcity of tillable land available for agricultural uses.

The total available cropland is little more than ten percent of the country. Thus, a relatively large proportion of Mexico is unsuitable for agricultural pursuits. In addition, there is a lack of adequate rainfall in many areas with level and potentially tillable land. Mexico has experienced frequent and severe droughts, which have threatened crop production many times (Liverman 1990).  Who is able to use the arable land has historically been an important issue both from a social and a production perspective.

As shown on Figure 11.1 and Table 11.1, the Mexican population up until 1960 was primarily rural. Since that time, however, the country has become progressively urban in character. The percentage of rural population in Mexico has steadily decreased from one-third in 1980 to 27 percent in 1995. Currently, the agriculture labor force is primarily male – 85.8 percent to 14.2 percent female.

Mexican states with the highest levels of agricultural employment are among the poorest. Forty one percent of paid agricultural workers in 1996 earned less than the daily minimum wage of 25.4 pesos ($3.34 dollars).  However, 31.2 percent were unpaid i.e. received no pay at all (Ernesto Zedillo Administration, III Informe de Gobierno 1997). Many of the unpaid workers are family members.  This percentage is much higher than the 12.3 percent for the nation as a whole.  Compared to other economic sectors, agricultural

**Table 11.1 Urban and Rural Population, Mexico, 1900-1990**

| Year | Urban | Rural |
|------|-------|-------|
| 1900 | 28.3 | 71.7 |
| 1910 | 28.7 | 71.3 |
| 1921 | 31.2 | 68.8 |
| 1930 | 33.5 | 66.5 |
| 1940 | 35.0 | 65.0 |
| 1950 | 42.6 | 57.4 |
| 1960 | 50.7 | 49.3 |
| 1970 | 58.7 | 41.3 |
| 1980 | 66.3 | 33.7 |
| 1990 | 71.3 | 28.7 |
| 1995 | 73.5 | 26.5 |

Source: Estadisticas Historicas de Mexico, 1985; INEGI, 1992a; INEGI, 1998.

**Figure 11.1**
**Urban and Rural Population Mexico: 1900-1990**

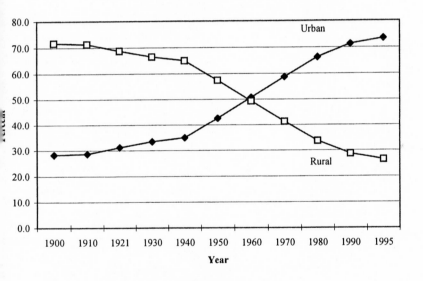

Source: Estadisticas Historicas de Mexico, 1985; INEGI, 1992a; INEGI, 1998.

workers are underpaid on a nationwide basis. The average daily pay in the years 1996-97 for the agricultural sector workers was 46.5 pesos daily i.e. $5.99, which compares to 79.8 pesos i.e. $10.29 per day for the nation (Ernesto Zedillo Administration, III Informe de Gobierno 1997). However, this sharp differential also depends greatly on the size of enterprise. For instance, as seen in Figure 11.2, pay for agricultural workers in medium and large size enterprises was roughly equivalent to the pay rates for all workers in micro and small businesses.  In other words the industrial-agricultural income gap is nearly entirely compensated for by altering the size of enterprise.

Mexico at times cannot produce enough food to feed its population currently at 100 million. This means that Mexico is sometimes a net agricultural importer and other times a net exporter. As seen in Figure 11.3 and Table 11.2, agricultural exports and imports have tended to increase in absolute value from 1987 to 1996. The agricultural net balance of trade has fluctuated in plus and minus directions from year to year. Recently, it was negative in 1992, neutral in 1993, negative in 1994, very positive in 1995, very negative in 1996, and positive in 1997. This reflects a composite of economic, political, and agricultural trends.  For example, the positive level in 1995 reflects the advantage of the 1994 peso devaluation, i.e. that lower prices abroad of Mexican products led to much higher volume exports.  In 1997, the trade was somewhat positive, which reflected a balancing of Mexican agricultural strengths and weaknesses in the developing NAFTA environment.  Imports of agricultural products to Mexico are primarily from the U.S. (70 percent), followed by Canada (7 percent). The agricultural sector was 20 percent of PIB in 1950 (Europa Editions 1999), but had declined to 12.2 percent of PIB by 1970, and was only 5.7 percent of PIB in 1997 (see Figure 11.4). The decline is due to greater diversification of the Mexican economy, including in manufacturing, commerce, service, and communications sectors.  The total agricultural PIB in 1997 amounted to 21.8 billion U.S. dollars. This pales in comparison to U.S. agricultural GDP, yet is important as a means to preserve Mexican self-sufficiency.

Whetten (1948) identified several agricultural regions in Mexico and there is substantial concentration of crops by region and in some instances by state (also see Scott 1982).

**Table 11.2 Agricultural Balance of Trade for Mexico, 1987-1997**

| Year | Total Exports | Total Imports | Net Balance of Trade | Agricultural Exports | Agricultural Imports | Net Agric. Balance of Trade |
|------|---------------|---------------|----------------------|----------------------|----------------------|------------------------------|
| 1987 | 27,600 | 18,812 | 8,788 | 1,543 | 1,108 | 435 |
| 1988 | 30,692 | 28,082 | 2,610 | 1,670 | 1,774 | -104 |
| 1989 | 35,171 | 34,766 | 405 | 1,754 | 2,003 | -249 |
| 1990 | 40,711 | 41,593 | -882 | 2,162 | 2,071 | 91 |
| 1991 | 42,688 | 49,966 | -7,278 | 2,373 | 2,130 | 243 |
| 1992 | 46,196 | 62,129 | -15,933 | 2,112 | 2,858 | -746 |
| 1993 | 51,886 | 65,367 | -13,481 | 2,504 | 2,633 | -129 |
| 1994 | 60,882 | 79,356 | -18,474 | 2,678 | 3,371 | -693 |
| 1995 | 79,542 | 72,453 | 7,089 | 4,016 | 2,644 | 1,372 |
| 1996 | 96,000 | 89,469 | 6,531 | 3,592 | 4,671 | -1,079 |
| 1997 | 52,420 | 50,329 | 2,091 | 2,412 | 2,030 | 382 |

All monetary values are in millions of dollars.
Source: III Informe de Gobierno, Mexico, 1997.

*The Northwest*

This is an arid zone of large-scale mechanization and irrigation along a thousand mile coastal strip between the Gulf of California and the Sierra Madre Occidental, plus parts of Baja California.

**Figure 11.2**
**Average Daily Salary - Agricultural Sector vs. Overall Economy, Mexico,**
**1996-97**

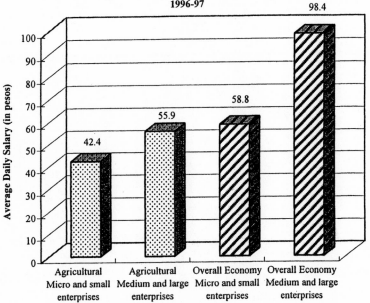

Note: micro and small enterprises are between 1 and 100 workers.
Medium and large enterprises are 101 or more workers.
Source: III Informe de Gobierno, 1997.

**Figure 11.3**
**Agricultural Net Balance of Trade Mexico, 1987-1997**
**(in millions of dollars)**

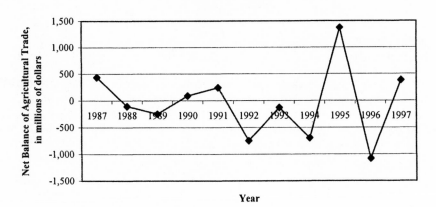

Source: III Informe de Gobierno, Mexico, 1997.

**Figure 11.4**
**Agricultural PIB as a Percent of Total PIB, Mexico, 1970-1997**

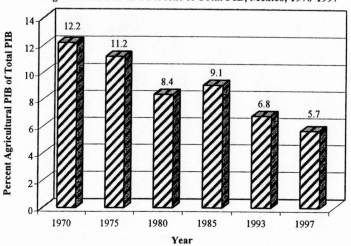

Data Source: Banamex, 1998.

### The North

The rest of the north of the country is generally arid; it is only cultivable with irrigation except for the eastern portions near the Gulf of Mexico. Mechanization has taken place in this region with tractors and reapers being extensively used. Wheat and cotton are major crops. Almost two-thirds of agricultural credit in 1960 went to the large, private owners in the pacific north and north. The north and northwest also are the areas that have been most productive with irrigation. In many of these areas, rainfall is less than three inches per year so irrigation is an absolute necessity. Historically, with few exceptions, irrigation has been undertaken only for larger plots of land. Irrigated land from 1940 though 1960 was about equally divided between ejido and non-ejido land. Irrigated land has expanded over the years. This has been true despite the shift of budgets from agriculture and land reform to an emphasis on industrialization. In the north, increases in agricultural production would have been impossible without irrigation. Up through 1958, over two-thirds of federal government funds for irrigation were spent in the north and west. Not too surprisingly these also are the regions with highest output per agricultural worker. Over 99.9 percent of alfalfa is grown in Guanajuato and Chihuahua. Another prominent crop of this region is asparagus.

### The Central Plateau

The Central Plateau is an area of mixed rainfall and irrigated farms. Farms are generally small. Previously this was the most productive region in Mexico but now has been surpassed by the northern regions. Slash and burn is still used as a means of preparing fields for planting and the crops depend upon rain to grow. Many fields in this and the south region have been depleted of nutrients necessary for productive yields.

*The South*

The south is tropical and has very few systems of irrigated water control. In this region, sugar cane, coffee, bananas, pineapples, and rice are grown. Most cultivation is at a subsidence level. Examples of crop concentration are shown in Tabasco and Quintana Roo producing 62 percent of achiote. Similarly, half of the avocado production for all of Mexico is in Michoacan. Over 99 percent of cocoa production is in Tabasco and Chiapas. Thirty-four percent of sugar cane, 25 percent of mango, and 38 percent of oranges are grown in southern states.

The regional distribution of agricultural PIB, measured as proportion of PIB in agriculture for each state, is concentrated in the north central as well as in Chihuahua, Michoacan, and Oaxaca (see Map 11.1 and Table 11.3). The north central states and Chihuahua are especially important for livestock and grain production. From a transport and distribution standpoint, the heavily agricultural states tend to be away from population centers, yet some are positioned for export to the southwestern and western U.S. while others domestically serve Guadalajara, other western cities, and even Mexico City. These agricultural producing states tend to be semi-periphery ones and they supply the core in the U.S. and both core and semi-periphery in Mexico. On the other hand, the periphery, located in the distant south, is producing mostly for itself and to a lesser extent for the other development levels.

As seen in Table 11.3, on a statewide basis agricultural PIB dropped by nearly half from 1970 to 1993. This parallels the national decline in agricultural PIB. As seen in Map 11.2, the largest proportionate drops occurred in the major urban states of Federal District and Nuevo Leon, as well as in a mixture of medium level and poorer states. Several formerly richly agricultural states in 1973, including Chiapas, Quntana Roo, and Campeche dropped considerably, while others such as Zacatecas, Sinaloa, and Yucatan maintained their agricultural nature. The strong state differences over the 23 years emphasize the many forces impinging on the size and extent of agriculture in Mexico, including urbanization, competition from the tourism sector, the private sector, and federal government initiatives.

Mexico's food production is hampered by the problems of outdated agricultural technology, insufficient infrastructure, federal bureaucracy, lack of access to financing, debt build-up, poor soils, poor transport capability, adverse weather conditions, and subsistence farming. Over 70 percent of Mexican farms are subsistence or community farms. Mexico has over 27 million productive hectares but many have inadequate rainfall and less than 7 million have access to irrigation water. As seen in Table 11.4, irrigation supply and capacity are greatest in the northwest region, consisting of Sinaloa and Sonora. This is logical because of its arid environment. The south region, on the other hand, has the lowest irrigation, due largely to its bountiful water sources. Most of the irrigation is in the northern tier of states including the border states with the U.S. Although this is positive for northern agriculture, it puts pressure on the scarce water supply systems in the border region of increasing urban demographic growth.

**Table 11.3 Agricultural PIB as a Proportion of State PIB, 1970-1993**

| No. | State | 1970 | 1993 | Difference, 1970-1993 | Proportionate Difference, 1970-1993 |
|-----|-------|------|------|------------------------|-------------------------------------|
| 1 | Aguascalientes | 19.2 | 6.8 | -12.4 | -64.6 |
| 2 | Baja California | 8.2 | 6.3 | -1.9 | -23.2 |
| 3 | Baja California Sur | 21.4 | 4.2 | -17.2 | -80.4 |
| 4 | Campeche | 29.9 | 9.0 | -20.9 | -69.9 |
| 5 | Coahuila | 9.7 | 3.5 | -6.2 | -63.9 |
| 6 | Colima | 26.4 | 5.2 | -21.2 | -80.3 |
| 7 | Chiapas | 31.0 | 8.7 | -22.3 | -71.9 |
| 8 | Chihuahua | 14.7 | 18.4 | 3.7 | 25.2 |
| 9 | Distrito Federal | 0.3 | 0.1 | -0.2 | -66.7 |
| 10 | Durango | 25.5 | 17.4 | -8.1 | -31.8 |
| 11 | Guanajuato | 21.2 | 9.8 | -11.4 | -53.8 |
| 12 | Guerrero | 19.5 | 10.5 | -9.0 | -46.2 |
| 13 | Hidalgo | 16.1 | 9.0 | -7.1 | -44.1 |
| 14 | Jalisco | 17.2 | 8.7 | -8.5 | -49.4 |
| 15 | Mexico | 6.2 | 2.7 | -3.5 | -56.5 |
| 16 | Michoacan | 24.7 | 17.5 | -7.2 | -29.1 |
| 17 | Morelos | 20.6 | 11.7 | -8.9 | -43.2 |
| 18 | Nayarit | 31.3 | 20.6 | -10.7 | -34.2 |
| 19 | Nuevoleon | 5.3 | 1.4 | -3.9 | -73.6 |
| 20 | Oaxaca | 25.9 | 18.9 | -7.0 | -27.0 |
| 21 | Puebla | 14.6 | 9.0 | -5.6 | -38.4 |
| 22 | Queretaro | 17.9 | 4.6 | -13.3 | -74.3 |
| 23 | Quintana Roo | 33.5 | 1.7 | -31.8 | -94.9 |
| 24 | San Luis Potosi | 16.8 | 12.8 | -4.0 | -23.8 |
| 25 | Sinaloa | 29.0 | 22.8 | -6.2 | -21.4 |
| 26 | Sonora | 29.5 | 13.5 | -16.0 | -54.2 |
| 27 | Tabasco | 19.5 | 7.5 | -12.0 | -61.5 |
| 28 | Tamaulipas | 14.1 | 9.7 | -4.4 | -31.2 |
| 29 | Tlaxcala | 11.6 | 8.6 | -3.0 | -25.9 |
| 30 | Veracruz | 19.4 | 10.4 | -9.0 | -46.4 |
| 31 | Yucatan | 11.7 | 9.1 | -2.6 | -22.2 |
| 32 | Zacatecas | 29.8 | 25.6 | -4.2 | -14.1 |
|  | Nation | 12.2 | 6.8 | -5.4 | -44.3 |

Source: Banamex, 1998.

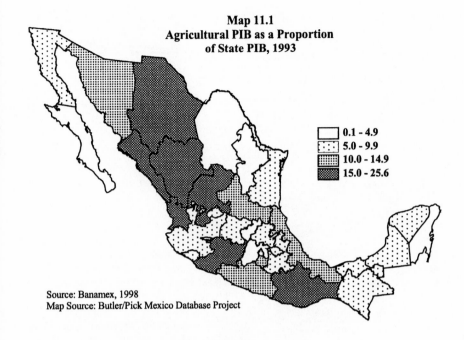

**Map 11.1**
**Agricultural PIB as a Proportion**
**of State PIB, 1993**

0.1 - 4.9
5.0 - 9.9
10.0 - 14.9
15.0 - 25.6

Source: Banamex, 1998
Map Source: Butler/Pick Mexico Database Project

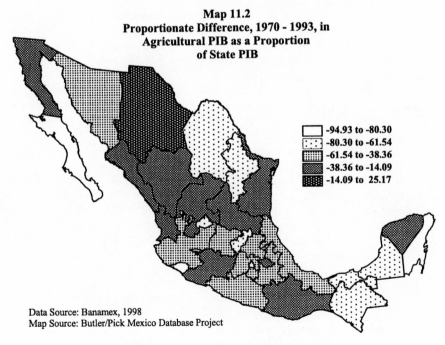

**Map 11.2**
**Proportionate Difference, 1970 - 1993, in**
**Agricultural PIB as a Proportion**
**of State PIB**

-94.93 to -80.30
-80.30 to -61.54
-61.54 to -38.36
-38.36 to -14.09
-14.09 to  25.17

Data Source: Banamex, 1998
Map Source: Butler/Pick Mexico Database Project

**Table 11.4 Location of Irrigated Agriculture in Mexico, 1997**

| Region | Volume of Irrigated Water Supplied* | Total Capacity for Irrigation* | Percent Utilization |
|---|---|---|---|
| Northwest | 7,752 | 25,154 | 30.8 |
| North Central | 3,547 | 10,771 | 32.9 |
| Northeast | 2,579 | 10,459 | 24.7 |
| Central | 3,317 | 6,642 | 49.9 |
| South | 1,457 | 1,478 | 98.6 |
| Others | 7,470 | 21,497 | 34.7 |
| Total | 26,122 | 76,001 | 34.4 |

\* in millions of cubic meters.

Source: Banamex, 1998.

Note: Northwest districts are in Sinaloa and Sonora. North Central districts are in Chihuahua, Coahuila and Durango. Northeast districts are in Tamaulipas. Central districts are mostly in Aguascalientes, Guanajuato, Hidalgo, Jalisco, Michoacan, Puebla, Queretero, and Zacatecas. South districts are in Guerrero, Oaxaca, and Chiapas.

Currently, agriculture production in Mexico is by commercial agricultural enterprises, organized ejidos, cattle ranchers, and locally organized basic food producers, among others (Barkin 1998). Mexico is no longer a nation of peasants working in a system of rain-fed agriculture raising maize (Barkin 1992). The Mexican government has systematically intervened in the agricultural sector by establishing programs aiding in the financing, production, and distribution of output. In 1930, however, over 70 percent of credits were to large, private farmers even though they accounted for only 3.8 percent of individuals served (Cole and Sanders 1970). In addition, large landowners also had better access to private bank loans. Between 1940 and 1960, agricultural production more than tripled and livestock output doubled (Cole and Sanders 1970). These increases were accomplished with a reduction of the economically active population engaged in agriculture and a consequent migration of the rural population to urban centers.

Land under cultivation has gradually increased. However, productivity in the agricultural sector has not increased over recent years. In 1994, Mexico had 12.1 percent of its land under cultivation (Banamex 1998). This is similar to the world as a whole at 10.3 percent, but is double the proportion for Latin America and the Caribbean of 6.2 percent (Banamex 1998). Mexico is ahead of Latin America and this is due to its large population of consumers and its long history of developing agriculture, among other things.

Mexico is important for livestock and grain crops. The most important grain crop produced is maize. In 1997, the nation produced 19.8 million tons of maize (see Table 11.5). Other grain crops of importance are sorghum (6.5 million tons), wheat (3.8 million tons), beans (1.5 million tons), and rice (448 thousand tons). Other significant crops are barley and sugar (Europa Edition 1999). Faced with a doubling of population from 1970 to 1997, Mexico's grain production has generally kept up (see Table 11.5). This reflects productivity increases in grain crops as well as some expansions in land under grain cultivation. On a per capita basis for specific crops, over the past three decades, maize and sorghum production have increased, while wheat, beans, and especially rice have declined. Major fruits and vegetables produced are citrus, strawberries, apples, pears, cucumbers, limes, mangoes, melons, tomatoes, and pineapples (Europa Editions 1999).

**Table 11.5 Production of Major Cultivated Crops in Mexico, 1970-1997**
(in thousands of tons)

| Year | Population | Maize | Maize in tons per thousand persons | Sorghum | Sorghum in tons per thousand persons | Wheat | Wheat in tons per thousand persons | Beans | Beans in tons per thousand persons | Rice | Rice in tons per thousand persons |
|---|---|---|---|---|---|---|---|---|---|---|---|
| 1970 | 48,225,238 | 8,879 | 184.1 | 2,747 | 57.0 | 2,676 | 55.5 | 924 | 19.2 | 405 | 8.4 |
| 1980 | 66,846,833 | 12,374 | 185.1 | 4,126 | 61.7 | 2,785 | 41.7 | 935 | 14.0 | 445 | 6.7 |
| 1990 | 81,249,645 | 14,635 | 180.1 | 5,978 | 73.6 | 3,931 | 48.4 | 1,287 | 15.8 | 394 | 4.8 |
| 1995 | 91,158,290 | 18,353 | 201.3 | 4,170 | 45.7 | 3,468 | 38.0 | 1,271 | 13.9 | 367 | 4.0 |
| 1997 | 94,695,274* | 19,819 | 201.3 | 6,533 | 45.7 | 3,805 | 38.0 | 1,508 | 13.9 | 448 | 4.0 |
| Percent Change 1970-1997 | 89.0 | 123.2 | 209.3 | 137.8 | 69.0 | 42.2 | 40.2 | 63.2 | 15.9 | 10.6 | 4.7 |

* Estimated by authors.

Source: III Informe de Gobierno, modifed by Banamex, 1998.

With respect to NAFTA exporting, fruits and vegetables have benefited the most, especially cucumbers, limes, and mangoes (Rodriguez and Burke 1999). Coffee has been important in the 1980s and 1990s as an export crop. Livestock amounts to about one third of the agricultural sector output. As seen in Figure 11.5, beef has historically been the most important item but grew only slightly in the 1990s; on the other hand, chicken production grew substantially in the 1990s in line with population growth and in spite of a U.S. ban on beef imports since 1994 (Banamex 1998). For a maritime nation, Mexico has a minor fishing industry – its total fish production in 1998 was only 1.09 million tons (Banamex 1998).

In respect to agricultural trade, Mexico is the third largest importer of U.S. agricultural products and the second largest supplier of agricultural products to the U.S. The U.S. is much more important to Mexico than the reverse. While Mexico purchases less than 10 percent of U.S. production, the U.S. buys almost 80 percent of Mexican agricultural exports in any given year. The U.S. especially dominates agricultural imports from Mexico. Thus, globalization of agriculture has not influenced Mexico to become fully integrated in world markets because of the dominance of the U.S. market for Mexican agricultural products. The impact that changing regulations will have (e.g., NAFTA) is yet to be seen.

A discussion of current influences upon agriculture in Mexico covers a wide range of topics, including globalization and NAFTA. Thus, there are a variety of changes occurring in the world and in Mexico impacting the agricultural sector. A few of these alterations are increasing urbanization, rural to urban migration patterns, corporate agriculture, grazing, irrigation and water use, maquiladoras, and environmental protection, among others. However, possibly more important than all of these other factors may be the change in Mexico's Constitution Article 27 in respect to ejido land tenure and property rights. These changes have implications far beyond any impacts of trade flows between the two countries (Schulthies and Williams 1992).

### Agriculture Exports and Imports

Mexico is substantially like many other semi-periphery countries in being challenged to meet the food needs of its population (Knight-Ridder 1996). Thus, Mexico has fluctuated between a net importer and a net exporter of agricultural products. During most of the 1990s, it increased imports, especially of agricultural products. During 1998 the imports of grain to Mexico increased extensively as a result of drought and heat, a drop in international prices, and a growth in domestic demand (Senzek 1998). Estimates of imports range from the 6 million tons of grain by the government to 14 million tons by peasant marketing organizations (Burke 1998:12). Part of the problem may be related to the federal budget that has reduced its former 12 percent budgetary proportion for agriculture to five percent. There appears to be little technical support for small farmers, a lack of credit opportunities, accompanied by worldwide price drops. Farm product exports have decreased percent wise as maquiladoras as more import.

The main agricultural exports in 1995 were fruits, melons, coffee and tea. The main fruits exported were mangos (U.S.), bananas (U.S. and Bermuda), grapes (U.S.), melons (U.S), and strawberries (U.S.). Also, over 75 percent of crude coffee exports was to the U.S. and virtually all decaffeinated coffee was exported to the U.S. (INEGI 1996).

Total imports in 1995 were $72,453,000 compared to $79,542,000 in exports (see Table 11.2). Agricultural imports were $2,644,000, compared to agricultural exports of $4,016,000. Thus, that year, Mexico exported more agricultural products than it imported. Primary import products under Mexican census categories are (1) wheat and mixtures of

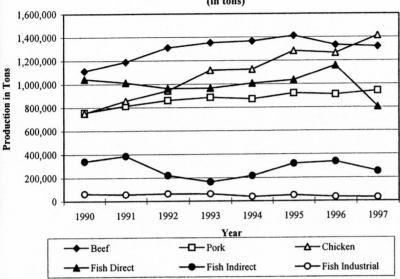

**Figure 11.5**
**Production of Meat and Fish, Mexico, 1990-1997**
**(in tons)**

Source: Banamex, 1998.

wheat and rye (which includes other such as sorghum) and (2) soybeans. Value under the wheat category included 6,079,000 peso or 43.2 percent and 5,286,000 peso for soybeans, for a total of 37.5 percent. Thus, wheat and soybeans accounted for 80.7 percent of agricultural imports to Mexico in 1995. The vast majority of wheat, corn, and rice imports were from the United States, with Canada contributing 461,000 peso. The unpredictably of agricultural trade patterns is seen by 1991 and 1994 being net importing years (see Table 11.2).

In 1998 additional agreements were reached regarding a new system for declaring certain areas in Mexico as being free of diseases carried by animals and plants. This agreement allows the free flow of more agricultural products between the U.S. and Mexico (El Financiero 1998).

### Ejidos, Ejidatarios, and Article 27 of the Mexican Constitution[1]

Beginning in 1917, land reform was used in Mexico to distribute land resources to the peasants. By 1965, over 46.5 million hectares had been expropriated from large farms and given to 2.3 million previously landless peasants, or ejidatarios who now lived on ejidos. An ejido consists of land to which the members have property rights. Part of the land may be an individual plot and part communal. Ejidatarios commanded over half of the total agricultural land by 1970 and over half of Mexico's farmers lived on ejidos (Stavenhagen

---

[1]   This section relies heavily upon Vallodolid (1995). For a more extensive discussiono of land tenure in prior years, see Cole and Sanders (1970).

1986; Hertford 1971). Over 80 percent of all ejido plots have been classified as info-subsistence and they are too small to provide full employment and an adequate income for a peasant family (Stavenhagen 1986: 263). Since individual plots could not be sold or leased, yet could be bequeathed to descendents, this led to land fragmentation. Land fragmentation, in turn, reduces the potential agri-business productivity and adoption of modern technology.

The Mexican Agrarian Code prohibited the sale or rent of ejido farms. Around 1949 and 1950 the Mexican government subsidized certain crops such as corn, chiles, eggs, etc., in an effort to stabilize prices and support farm incomes. These subsidies neither increased output nor reduced the poverty of subsistence farmers (Heath 1987). Throughout this era, crops always were more important than meat and dairy production.

Beginning around 1940, there was a steady increase in irrigated cropland and the use of fertilizers. The harvested area continues to grow and from 1941-1946 through 1983-1986, harvested areas more than doubled as did per capita domestic output. During the same period, output tons increased six-fold. Corn typically has accounted for around one-third of the arable land area and one-quarter of the total value of crop outputs in Mexico. However, the growth of imports in percent and tonnage far outpaced domestic production. For example, the import percent went from 1.9 percent in 1941 to 21.2 percent by 1986. Similarly, import tonnage in 1941 was 42,000, while this grew to 2,837,000 tons in 1986 (Heath 1987:265).

There has been growth in the number of ejidos and communal units. Their population expanded 1970-1995 from 2.2 to 3.5 million, a 60 percent growth. By contrast, Mexico's rural population increased by only 17 percent between 1970 and 1990. This demonstrates the process of fragmentation of ejidos and communal units. The magnitude of the ejido and communal land is also apparent in terms of tenancy of productive land. On the basis of tenancy by productive land area, 32 percent of land area in 1991 consisted of ejido and communal land (see Figure 11.6). The largest proportion of productive land, about two thirds, was private land while colonia and public lands accounted for only three percent. The distribution of productive land holding by states (see Table 11.6 and Map 11.3) reveals a dramatic difference in ejidos and communal land holding, ranging from only eight percent in Nuevo Leon to 78 percent in Morelos. The small ejidal and communal lands in the northern border states is due to the reduced agriculture in those states at the time that ejidos were formed. States with higher ejidal/communal percentages were ones that historically were heavily agricultural. The level of ejidal/communal land tenency is a rough indicator of the extent that a state is bound by more traditional agricultural practices versus others states that may be better able to transition to modern, privatized agriculture.

In 1992, Article 27 changed Mexico's agricultural land policy. Its major impact was on small landholders as well as ejidos and ejidatarios (people who work on collectively-owned ejido lands). This land formerly assigned to individual households could not be sold or leased but had to be passed to heirs. The 1992 amendments allow ejido land to be sold or rented, or to be utilized as collateral in obtaining financial funding. Further, the amendments stopped the redistribution of land (Europa Editions 1999). However, Amendments to Article 27 threaten to obliterate the very existence of ejidos and have great implications for their future as well as for agricultural production in Mexico. Many Mexican farmers will be rendered landless and their land will be taken over by larger corporate farms. This amendment allows parcelized ejido lands, by decisions of the majority of ejidatarios, to be rented and in some instances to be sold to other farmers and transnational and domestic corporations. This is a major change from the 1917 Mexican Constitution that did not permit the sale or rental of ejido land. Despite the Constitution

# Map 11.3
## Productive Land Area and
## Land Tenancy by State, Mexico, 1991

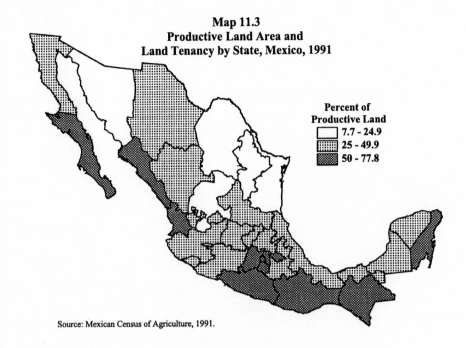

**Percent of**
**Productive Land**
☐ 7.7 - 24.9
▦ 25 - 49.9
■ 50 - 77.8

Source: Mexican Census of Agriculture, 1991.

# Figure 11.6
## Land Tenancy in Mexico, 1991

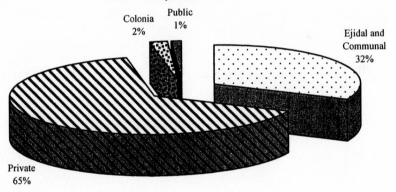

Colonia
2%

Public
1%

Ejidal and
Communal
32%

Private
65%

Source: INEGI, Census of Agriculture, 1991.

engendering ejidos, it took a number of years for ejidos to become established. In 1934, 93 percent of land was still owned by private landowners and 7 percent by ejidos. By 1970, however, 43 percent of farmland had been redistributed from large landowners to rural families. The revised Constitutional changes allow consolidation of land holdings that were interspersed with private holdings. The impact of this change will be greater in some states than others since the percent of population living on ejidos varies substantially (see Map 11.4). Still more than 27,000 ejidos exist; however, 30 percent of them are yet to be legally defined which undoubtedly will create problems as some of them attempt to privatize (Burke 1998c). The national program to certify and give land titles to persons living in ejidos is well underway. The program is "Programa de Certificacion de Derechos Ejidales y Titulación de Solares Urbanos (PROCEDE). By 1998, about 70 percent of ejidos had been certified, and one third had completed the entire process and been granted titles. The effort to certify and legally document the ejidos nationally has been very time consuming and challenging. The cartographic and database elements are being directed by INEGI.

The anticipated results of Article 27 are as follows: (1) the development of large landholdings producing economies of scale, (2) encouraging foreign investment to promote large-scale corporate farming, (3) making larger landholders more secure since their lands no longer can be expropriated by the government, and (4) potentially increasing agricultural production.

Critics believe that the amendments also will accelerate the exodus of the rural population to cities and increase economic inequalities in rural Mexico. Changes accompanying Article 27, along with NAFTA may assist in what Barkin (1992) argues, "Only a small elite will be able to take advantage of the many productive opportunities offered by Mexico's integration into the largest economic bloc in the world via NAFTA..." (Barkin 1992). The results so far point to limited commercialization of ejido property and limited ejido self autonomy and industrial development. At the start of 1996, only six farm cooperatives had elected disincorporation (U.S. State Department 1999). This may reflect the lack of financial experience among ejido leadership.

Several recent programs of the Ernesto Zedillo Administration have included agriculture. In 1996, most federal government price supports for agriculture began to be eliminated. In its place, the government developed state-specific goals to increase use of up to date technology and equipment in order that state productivity would increase (U.S. State Department 1999).

Another important program to stimulate agriculture is Procampo. Instead of the prior price supports, Procampo provides a direct subsidy to the 3.5 million farmers based on the acreage they own. The purpose of the program is to enhance the income of small producers and provide assured direct support. Procampo also encourages conversion of farm facilities for greater productivity.

Among other federal farm and rural programs are the following:
- Alliance for rural areas. This program is designed to enhance agricultural productivity through irrigation technology, rural infrastructure, better seed quality, milk, restoring saline soils, better information systems, etc.
- Shared agricultural programs. These are programs shared between the federal government and states, municipios, and other entities.

**Table 11.6 Productive Land Area and Land Tenancy by State, Mexico, 1991**

| No. | State | Productive Land Area | Ejidal | Communal | Ejidal and Communal | Private | Colonia | Public |
|---|---|---|---|---|---|---|---|---|
| 1 | Aguascalientes | 354 | 27.7 | 0.1 | 27.8 | 71.9 | 0.0 | 0.6 |
| 2 | Baja California | 1,848 | 27.4 | 0.3 | 27.7 | 29.5 | 5.8 | 0.3 |
| 3 | Baja California Sur | 2,713 | 64.1 | 0.0 | 64.1 | 43.7 | 6.2 | 15.9 |
| 4 | Campeche | 1,932 | 42.5 | 0.2 | 42.7 | 51.8 | 1.3 | 4.1 |
| 5 | Coahuila | 9,355 | 10.3 | 0.4 | 10.7 | 87.4 | 1.2 | 0.7 |
| 6 | Colima | 398 | 47.1 | 0.2 | 47.3 | 48.0 | 0.0 | 4.7 |
| 7 | Chiapas | 4,002 | 46.9 | 5.0 | 51.9 | 46.1 | 1.4 | 0.6 |
| 8 | Chihuahua | 17,751 | 24.3 | 1.3 | 25.6 | 70.8 | 3.2 | 0.3 |
| 9 | Distrito Federal | 24 | 26.6 | 30.6 | 57.2 | 42.4 | 0.0 | 0.4 |
| 10 | Durango | 6,175 | 32.2 | 16.4 | 48.6 | 50.0 | 1.1 | 0.2 |
| 11 | Guanajuato | 1,997 | 27.7 | 0.1 | 27.8 | 71.9 | 0.0 | 0.4 |
| 12 | Guerrero | 1,632 | 58.6 | 14.7 | 73.3 | 25.7 | 0.4 | 0.5 |
| 13 | Hidalgo | 1,048 | 37.9 | 6.0 | 43.9 | 55.5 | 0.3 | 0.3 |
| 14 | Jalisco | 4,856 | 23.2 | 4.8 | 28.0 | 71.6 | 0.1 | 0.4 |
| 15 | Mexico | 993 | 44.5 | 8.9 | 53.4 | 45.0 | 0.0 | 1.7 |
| 16 | Michoacan | 3,405 | 27.6 | 5.1 | 32.7 | 67.0 | 0.1 | 0.3 |
| 17 | Morelos | 204 | 71.4 | 6.4 | 77.8 | 21.6 | 0.2 | 0.5 |
| 18 | Nayarit | 1,147 | 47.8 | 10.5 | 58.3 | 40.0 | 0.0 | 1.8 |
| 19 | Nuevoleon | 4,381 | 6.7 | 1.0 | 7.7 | 90.9 | 1.0 | 0.4 |
| 20 | Oaxaca | 3,016 | 27.0 | 44.1 | 71.1 | 28.5 | 0.0 | 0.3 |
| 21 | Puebla | 2,234 | 23.2 | 2.6 | 25.8 | 72.1 | 0.0 | 2.1 |
| 22 | Queretaro | 660 | 24.4 | 0.7 | 25.1 | 73.3 | 0.9 | 0.7 |
| 23 | Quintana Roo | 1,291 | 69.1 | 0.0 | 69.1 | 29.0 | 0.0 | 1.9 |
| 24 | San Luis Potosi | 2,496 | 33.2 | 2.8 | 36.0 | 59.6 | 4.0 | 0.5 |
| 25 | Sinaloa | 2,241 | 59.5 | 5.8 | 65.3 | 33.5 | 0.4 | 0.7 |
| 26 | Sonora | 12,292 | 13.5 | 1.2 | 14.7 | 81.7 | 1.4 | 2.1 |
| 27 | Tabasco | 1,723 | 42.6 | 0.1 | 42.7 | 48.5 | 8.3 | 0.5 |
| 28 | Tamaulipas | 5,956 | 22.1 | 0.1 | 22.2 | 75.4 | 1.6 | 0.8 |
| 29 | Tlaxcala | 241 | 56.6 | 0.0 | 56.6 | 43.3 | 0.0 | 0.1 |

| Table 11.6 Productive Land Area and Land Tenancy by State, Mexico, 1991 (Continued) |         |      |      |      |      |      |      |
|-------------------------------------------------------------------------------------|---------|------|------|------|------|------|------|
| 30 Veracruz                                                                         | 5,992   | 41.2 | 1.5  | 42.7 | 49.9 | 7.2  | 0.2  |
| 31 Yucatan                                                                          | 1,946   | 29.7 | 0.1  | 29.8 | 67.6 | 0.0  | 2.6  |
| 32 Zacatecas                                                                        | 4,042   | 20.1 | 0.3  | 20.4 | 78.1 | 1.0  | 0.5  |
| Mexico                                                                              | 108,346 | 27.7 | 4.0  | 31.7 | 65.1 | 2.0  | 1.2  |

Source: Mexican Census of Agriculture, 1991.

## Map 11.4 Ejido Lands of Mexico City

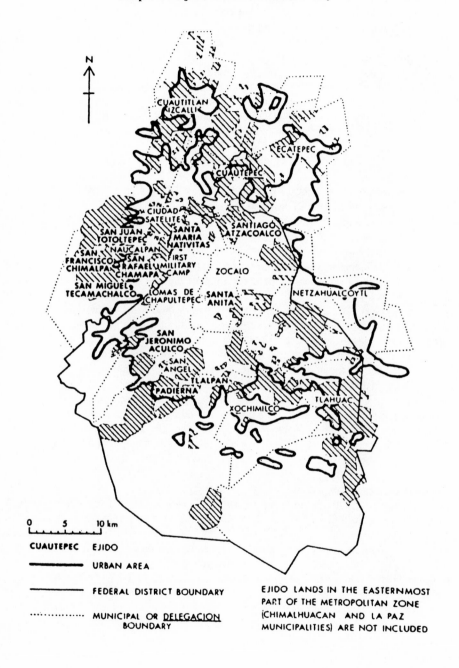

N

CUAUTITLAN
IZCALLI

ECATEPEC

CUAUTEPEC

CIUDAD
SATELITE

SAN JUAN
TOTOLTEPEC

SANTA
MARIA
NATIVITAS

SANTIAGO
ATZACOALCO

NAUCALPAN

SAN
FRANCISCO
CHIMALPA

SAN
RAFAEL

FIRST
MILITARY

CHAMAPA    CAMP          ZOCALO

SAN MIGUEL
TECAMACHALCO

LOMAS DE
CHAPULTEPEC

SANTA
ANITA

NETZAHUALCOYTL

SAN
JERONIMO
ACULCO

SAN
ANGEL

TLALPAN

PADIERNA

TLAHUAC

XOCHIMILCO

0        5        10 km

**CUAUTEPEC**    EJIDO

━━━━━━━━     URBAN AREA

━━━━━━━━     FEDERAL DISTRICT BOUNDARY

·············     MUNICIPAL OR <u>DELEGACION</u>
                 BOUNDARY

EJIDO LANDS IN THE EASTERNMOST
PART OF THE METROPOLITAN ZONE
(CHIMALHUACAN AND LA PAZ
MUNICIPALITIES) ARE NOT INCLUDED

- Federal institutionalized programs. These include programs to strengthen judicial actions, provide legal help to solve rural conflicts, give training, provide dispute resolution, and regularize rural property.

Overall, there are twenty or more federal programs, which have the intent to strengthen, regularize, and make agriculture more productive. The success of the programs varies and depends on complex circumstances including the economy, attitudes, climate, and global markets. It is important to note that the federal government today does not intend to do everything. One example discussed later is the potential to establish new types of alliances between agri-businesses and producers.

## Agricultural Industry

Mexican agricultural industry became large-scale in the second half of the twentieth century. Earlier in Mexican history, small farms predominated with limited technology and productivity. Today, many companies support an increasingly sophisticated agricultural industry in Mexico. The industry is predominantly domestic. As seen in Table 11.7, among the top 15 agricultural companies, only Nestle is foreign-owned. Some of the companies have significant presence overseas e.g. the worldwide bread products company Bimbo, while others serve largely domestic markets e.g. the chicken producer Bachoco. Overall, the sales of the top 15 companies totaled 9.6 billion dollars in 1997, which compares to Mexico's 21.8 billion dollar agricultural sector. Most of the top 15 firms are headquartered in the Mexico City area, although four firms are located in the north central border region as well as one each in Durango and Jalisco. The companies are mostly conservatively run without substantial debt, which when present tends to be domestic.

Roughly half of the agricultural sector is corporate, which underscores that Mexican agriculture is shared by huge numbers of small farms and production units. Nevertheless, the Mexican agricultural industry and companies are very important since agriculture is in process of opening up to greater private investment and trade. This section discusses Nestle as an example of a foreign multinational with a special market role, examines two instances of food trade situations in sugar and avocados, and looks at the corporate alliances as a mechanism to link together agricultural industry and producers. Another example of major agri-business, the tortilla grupo of Maseca/Gruma, is analyzed as the chapter case study.

Nestle plays an important role in Mexican agriculture by filling multiple gaps in markets and products that is only possible from a global multipurpose firm. It is important to point out that Nestle is the world's biggest food manufacturing firm, with 1998 sales of $71.7 billion and 232,000 employees. It produces diverse lines of food products including instant coffee and other beverages, prepared dishes and frozen foods, chocolate and candy products, baby foods, milk products, pasta, ice cream, pharmaceuticals, ophthalmic products, bottled water, and many others (Wright Investors Service 1999). Nestle's special importance derives from the rest of the Mexican agricultural industry being largely domestic and having limited technology and range of sophistication of products. Hence, Nestle serves to fill in numerous gaps in the market with a variety of often more advanced products. It is for that reason that the Nestle brand name can be seen in many different settings in Mexico.

**Table 11.7 Mexico's Fifteen Largest Food Companies, 1997**

| Position* | Name | Location | Ownership** | Sales (in dollars) | Debt (in dollars) | Ratio Debt to Equity |
|---|---|---|---|---|---|---|
| 14 | Grupo Industrial Bimbo | Mexico D.F. | domestic | 2,345,562 | 511,482 | 0.292 |
| 28 | Nestle | Mexico D.F. | Switzerland | 1,467,507 | 311,343 | 0.353 |
| 29 | Gruma | Monterrey, Nuevo Leon | domestic | 1,371,947 | 658,716 | 0.380 |
| 58 | Grupo Industrial Lala | Gomez Palacio, Durango | domestic | 669,148 | 83,944 | 0.283 |
| 63 | Grupo Industrial Maseca | Monterrey, Nuevo Leon | domestic | 578,237 | 118,727 | 0.189 |
| 65 | Sigma Alimentos | Monterrey, Nuevo Leon | domestic | 572,710 | 198,172 | 0.533 |
| 67 | Bachoco | Mexico D.F. | domestic | 556,606 | 86,409 | 0.143 |
| 86 | Ganaderos Productores de Leche Pura | Cuautitlan-Izcalli, Mexico | domestic | 419,908 | 32,142 | 0.404 |
| 96 | Grupo Herdez | Naucalpan, Mexico | domestic | 312,748 | 124,141 | 0.458 |
| 115 | Pasteurizadora Laguna | Torrean, Coahuila | domestic | 237,377 | 26,118 | 0.451 |
| 118 | Grupo Minsa | Tlalnepantla, Mexico | domestic | 232,572 | 93,596 | 0.321 |
| 119 | Corporacion Azucarera de Lala | Corporacion Azucarera de Tala, Tala, Jalisco | domestic | 220,471 | 150,950 | 0.764 |
| 124 | Grupo Azucarera Mexico | Mexico D.F. | domestic | 207,253 | 399,923 | 2.023 |
| 130 | Beta San Miguel | Mexico D.F. | domestic | 191,839 | 139,619 | 0.386 |
| 132 | Tablex | Toluca, Mexico | domestic | 188,929 | 43,228 | 0.204 |
| Average | | | | 638,188 | 198,567 | 0 |

* Position in Sales in Expansion 500.

** Majority ownership domestic or foreign country. Domestic firms are privately owned.

Source: Expansion 500, 1999.

**Table11.7 Mexico's Fifteen Largest Food Companies, 1997 (Continued)**

| Position* | Name | Location | Debt-Pesos | Equity-Pesos | Percent Foreign Debt | No. of Employees | Year of Founding |
|---|---|---|---|---|---|---|---|
| 14 | Grupo Industrial | Mexico D.F. | 4,047,922 | 13,866,005 | 73 | 57,383 | 1945 |
| 28 | Nestle | Mexico D.F. | 2,464,000 | 6,977,000 | 24 | 6,272 | 1930 |
| 29 | Gruma | Monterrey, Nuevo | 5,213,144 | 13,702,297 | 91 | 12,384 | 1949 |
| 58 | Grupo Industrial | Gomez Palacio, | 664,338 | 2,345,193 | 2 | 7,461 | 1950 |
| 63 | Grupo Industrial | Monterrey, Nuevo | 939,614 | 4,974,310 | 48 | 3,495 | 1949 |
| 65 | Sigma Alimentos | Monterrey, Nuevo | 1,568,356 | 2,941,857 | 74 | 10,330 | 1980 |
| 67 | Bachoco | Mexico D.F. | 683,848 | 4,774,005 | 60 | 10,090 | NA |
| 86 | Ganaderos | Cuautitlan-Izcalli, | 254,374 | 629,896 | 93 | 2,735 | 1970 |
| 96 | Grupo Herdez | Naucalpan, Mexico | 982,462 | 2,143,694 | 61 | 4,376 | 1991 |
| 115 | Pasteurizadora | Torrean, Coahuila | 206,697 | 458,283 | 0 | 2,856 | 1950 |
| 118 | Grupo Minsa | Tlalnepantla, Mexico | 740,731 | 2,308,376 | 72 | 1,468 | NA |
| 119 | Corporacion | Corporacion | 1,194,637 | 1,564,639 | 24 | 861 | 1990 |
| 124 | Grupo Azucarera | Mexico D.F. | 3,165,034 | 1,564,639 | 30 | 2,996 | NA |
| 130 | Beta San Miguel | Mexico D.F. | 1,104,959 | 2,861,169 | 21 | 1,801 | NA |
| 132 | Tablex | Toluca, Mexico | 342,114 | 1,680,525 | 52 | 2,347 | 1979 |
| Average | | | 1,571,482 | 4,186,126 | 48 | 8,457 | |

Nestle in Mexico consists of three parts: Nescalín, which manages and controls in Mexico the major segments of the international product lines; Nestlé México, which prepares, mixes, produces, buys, and sells foods and drinks of domestic origin; and Manantiales La Asunción, a Mexican subsidiary that focuses on treating, purifying, preparing, marketing and distributing mineral water and juices. Manantiales may be regarded as a specialty unit, adapted to the Mexican marketplace that suffers from major water quality problems. The Nescalín part supports the special role of Nestle as "filling in the gaps," while Nestlé México offers the company special domestic niche opportunities. A niche example was Nescalin's acquisition in 1995, i.e. right after the peso crisis, of the major Mexican chocolate manufacturer, Azteca. In summary, Nestle in Mexico mainly is a sophisticated multinational, but also acts to provide some major local products such as chocolates and bottled water.

The chapter next turns to the trade roles for the agricultural industry. It does this by examining two examples of industry sectoral trading situations, both involving the U.S. and Mexico. The first example is the Mexican sugar sub-industry. That industry sector accounted for 5.2 million tons of sugar production in 1998. About one third of the Mexican sugar production is incorporated into soft drinks by bottlers. The problem is that the U.S. market has shifted rapidly to dominance by corn syrup-based producers that eliminate sugar from soft drinks.

In 1996, there was a step-change in U.S. corn syrup imports to Mexico; in particular, corn syrup imports increased from 20,000 tons to 350,000 tons. This increase delivered a direct threat to the Mexican sugar industry. In response, the Mexican export agency, SECOFI, reacted by imposing temporary tariffs. The U.S. in turn bitterly opposed these tariffs.

The NAFTA agreement had limited Mexican sugar exports to the U.S. to 25,000 tons, so it was not possible for Mexico to retaliate for the intrusion of corn syrup through heightened U.S. exports. After the year 2000, the limit on Mexican sugar exports will be raised to 250,000, but that future date did not help with the current dispute.

This ugly and often bitter dispute is continuing to unfold. For example, U.S. sugar producers are not happy with the situation and many feel that the dispute is a trick to increase limits on Mexico-to-U.S. sugar exports. Another factor is that some U.S. brands in Mexico including Pepsi prefer to retain the traditional sugar content. Nevertheless, the situation is foreboding. There are forecasts that if U.S. corn syrup imports continue, some Mexican sugar refineries may need to be closed. The dispute is complicated enough that it may well end up being resolved at the World Trade Organization. This example demonstrates the potential of cultural clashes involving products, consumer tastes, government regulation, and the dangers of an overly competitive environment.

A second example of an industry trade dispute concerns the recently approved opportunity to export Mexican avocados to the U.S. The dispute centers around Mexico's role as the world's largest avocado producer, and the long-time ban on sale of Mexican avocados to the U.S. Mexico accounts for one third of the world production of 2.3 million tons of avocados (El Financiero 1998). The Mexican avocado is largely the prized Hass variety and furthermore has special features of good taste, high nutrition, and generally high quality. Not surprisingly, Mexican avocado production and consumption are the highest in the world. Mexico internally consumes 94 percent of its production, while exporting 6 percent.

Although Mexico is the world's largest exporter of avocados at 27 percent the U.S. banned its export to the U.S. for eighty-three years. The reason was that the Mexican avocados did not meet the phytosanitary norms for the U.S. It is curious that Mexican avocados have been sold for years in large quantities in seven leading western European countries and currently at a volume of 20,000 tons. Finally, in 1997, the U.S. agreed with Mexico that it could sell annually to the U.S. 6,000 tons of avocados i.e. only about one percent of Mexican production. The zones of origin and destination were carefully chosen. North of the boarder, the market destinations are restricted to 19 northeastern states, whereas for Mexico export can take place from only four municipios in the state of Michoacan. The municipios were selected on the basis of U.S. Dept. of Agriculture approval of their phytosanitary conditions.

One of the interesting points is that, once the market regulations lifted, there has been only slight penetration of Mexican exports to the U.S., in particular less than one percent of its total avocado production of 800,000 tons per year. Another point is that pressures have also been building up from California and Florida producers. That pressure has served to restrain U.S. approval of large import increases. The limiting is done through inspection by U.S. agricultural specialists of farms and plantings mostly in the state of Michoacan. A side effect of this detailed inspection process is the stimulus for the Michoacan facilities to incorporate higher technology.

Many of the embedded problems of Mexican agriculture are evident in this dispute. For example, the avocado producers in Michoacan lack technical skills in cultivation; there is weak commercial structure; and the markets have historically been unstable and subject to change. Another aspect has been the Mexican avocado's phytosanitary problems, which have gotten into the thick of the dispute. Since the avocado ban was lifted in November of 1997, the problems have gotten worse rather than better. For instance, U.S. avocado producers are considering dumping avocados at low prices. There have also been financial problems and climatic downturns including frosts (El Financiero 1998).

It is difficult to tell where this dispute is heading and how it will end. Mexican producers are urging the U.S. to further relax its import restrictions, while U.S. producers consider dumping and U.S. phytosanitary regulators continue to be strict. The lesson here is that the potential for enhanced trade can be greatly limited by conflict among government and business.

The technological and business innovation gap is not only present between the U.S. and Mexico, but also present between Mexican firms including the top 15 and the farmer-producers. Many of the producers are still struggling with the ejido system and quite primitive agricultural methods. Many are still hand tilling the soil and using primitive financial mechanisms. These "campesinos" stand in contrast to the preponderance of U.S. production, which is mechanized, advanced, and large-scale. The Mexican federal government has increasingly pulled out of the overly regulated environment of the mid 20th century and has given the private sector the potential to innovate with new arrangements and forms of financing, exchange, and organization. However, the problem persists of the huge gap in capabilities and attitudes between "campesinos" and agro-business firms.

An example of this is the lack of success of agrobusiness-producer alliances in Mexico. Firms such as Bimbo, Maseca, and Herdez have tried to set up collaborations with producers that assure "just in time" delivery of products at the agreed time and place to the agrobusiness. Such alliances are commonplace in Europe and to a certain extent in the U.S., where they have increased efficiency and productivity. Sometimes the alliances are called "clubs of production" (Ramírez Tamayo 1999).

The success has been very limited. For instance, Maseca set up an alliance arrangement between itself and corn producers that utilized unorthodox sources of credit to make up for credit deficiencies rampant with its producers (Ramirez Tamayo 1999). However, the scheme came apart when the federal government starting setting the price of corn three months later than usual. Bimbo has such an alliance working with Sonoran wheat producers, but the resultant financial savings are limited. Herdez has tried but been unable to establish such an alliance (Ramírez Tamayo 1999). Clearly, the potential for agricultural advance is stymied through the backwardness of rural producers, as well as the market and financial problems.

Another related problem is distribution of agricultural products. Distribution is hampered by a largely inadequate transportation systems discussed in Chapter 7. If producers' goods are not assured of getting to the business destination, or if other free-lance intermediaries ("coyotes") take too large a percentage of profits, the types of systems described will not work, nor will international systems of exchange. One place that this appears is in warehousing of food products, since the warehouse structure is antiquated. An example of the potential here is a large-scale refrigerated warehouse being installed in Tuxpan, the Mexican gulf coast city (McCosh 1999). The 3,200 square meter warehouse costing $2.5 million will allow Mexican producers to deposit smaller orders for long-term preservation. Orders can be mixed and merged and delivered in a "just in time" manner. This example demonstrates the potential for well-planned technological advance to improve the efficiency and success of domestic or international agricultural exchanges.

### Agriculture in Mexico and the Environment

Current environmental problems related to Mexican agriculture are as follows (Ozuna and Williams 1993):
- Inefficient irrigation practices resulting in a 65 percent loss of irrigation water and poor crop productivity levels due to the flooding of crops, land salinity, and erosion.
- Groundwater aquifers are being severely depleted resulting in the presence of arsenic in the water. In other areas, depletion has led to the intrusion of salt water rendering the groundwater unfit for human and agricultural uses.
- The use of water containing effluents or industrial waste causing soil degradation and contamination of crops.
- Misuse of pesticides resulting in contamination of groundwater and surface water that has negatively impacted aquatic life, wildlife, and human health.
- Degradation and erosion of available pastureland as a consequence of overgrazing and other forms of mismanagement.

These negative impacts of agriculture on the environment are not being alleviated and they are expected to continue well into the future resulting in further environmental degradation.

### Future Prospects

Mexico has made unilateral efforts to open its economy that has led to a significant increase in Mexico agricultural trade with the United States, although so far there has been mixed results for individual crops (Rymer-Zavaka 1998). As a legal document, the

NAFTA agreement between Mexico and the U.S. preempts state laws and renders all inconsistent states' trade rules and regulations unconstitutional (Boadu 1991). A further issue is trade with the European Union (Senzek 1998b).

In comparison with the U.S., Mexico apparently has comparative advantage in the production and export of feeder cattle, horticultural products, and citrus. The U.S. has a similar advantage in the production and export of breeding and slaughter livestock, dairy productions, most feed and food grains, and probably cotton (Schulthies and Williams 1992). The removal of tariffs is not likely to influence greatly the export-import relationship between the two countries. This is because most tariffs have already been removed and because of long established relationships of production and consumption. However, international markets apparently have reduced Mexico's share of the coffee market (Martinez 1997) and sugar imports from the U.S have created turmoil in the Mexican sugar industry (Salaman 1997).

Several potential influencing factors, however, are (1) the recent change in land tenure laws in Mexico that might result in the development of larger scale agriculture formerly occupied by ejidatarios (Article 27, 1992) and (2) a potential growing market in Mexico for dairy products and meat from the U.S.

Agricultural trade between the U.S. and Mexico is likely to continue growing. Most of this growth will be a result of changes in Mexico, especially in respect to policy and infrastructure changes, labor force availability, foreign investment, utilization of technology, and market demand. Potential limiting factors are the land tenure system of ejidos, limited water resources, domestic and international markets and pricing, and Mexican and local governmental policies. Also, corn and beans raised mainly by small farmers and peasants may be replaced by non-traditional crops. On the other hand, agribusiness production is finding an expanded market in the U.S., probably as a result of NAFTA.

One major implication of changes in Mexico is a reduced demand for labor on larger farms that are technologically oriented. That is, there will be displaced agricultural workers. Whether these workers can be absorbed into the labor market is questionable. This may result in more undocumented immigration to the U.S. and/or migration to the cities in Mexico. Potential counteracting factors are the need for foreign investment in agricultural production by foreign investors and Mexican investment in the inefficient infrastructure, especially in transportation modalities. Thus, expanding agricultural trade depends on (1) the access of the U.S. trucking industry to Mexico, (2) relaxation of constraints at border crossings, and (3) the need to modernize and expand the Mexican transportation infrastructure.

Another future scenario may result in more foreign direct investment in Mexico (e.g., from the U.S.) in food processing thus reducing exports from the U.S. to Mexico. So far, these production facilities have been for the local Mexican markets rather than for export to the U.S. These relationships, of course, are tied to many multinational corporations, both U.S. based and others, e.g., Nestle.

Another potential impact upon Mexican agriculture is the privatization of warehouses. This has occurred recently (1997) and its importance is still not known (Martinez 1997). The tortilla business in Mexico is a billion dollar business and substitution of non-traditional agriculture, privatization of warehouses, imports of grains, decline of contribution to the national gross product of agriculture, and agribusiness may influence upward basic food costs for the average Mexican (see Rudino 1998; Humble 1997; Zellner 1995).

Mexico is labor-rich but land-poor in respect to desirable and available agricultural land. This implies that future agricultural development in Mexico will have great influence on the human population. For example, the utilization of technology undoubtedly will result in greater production but a reduction in the agriculture labor force. This could result in unemployment and a push for illegal immigration to the U.S. It also implies a reduction in ejidos. The growth of efficiency in the agricultural sector will result in an even more massive rural to urban migration that already has influenced the growth of Mexican cities. These rural migrants to the cities have the lowest educational and skill levels in Mexico and most likely will become part of the ever-expanding informal labor force (see Chapter 12).

Mexican agriculture has fared poorly under NAFTA according to many at a 1998 conference attended by representatives from the U.S. and Canadian embassies as well as economists and agronomists from Mexico (Burke 1998a). Whether such a conclusion will continue in the future remains a matter of conjecture.

## Conclusions

Agriculture has been important in the history of Mexico and today provides sufficiency but not a surplus for the Mexican population. Mexican agriculture is dominated by maize, livestock, coffee, and fruits and vegetables. It is closely tied to the U.S. agriculture through competition and cooperation in certain products and markets and though penetration of some of each nation's products into the other's markets.

Spatially, Mexico's major agricultural producing regions are in the northwest, central west, and south, in areas removed from the large cities and consumer bases. This points to well know deficits in the transportation and distribution systems.

Historically, Mexico put reliance on small ejido and communal based agriculture, but inefficiencies built into that system have led to changes that are sometimes controversial. The pace of change is much slower than expected from ejido-based to corporate-based agriculture. This has perpetuated an economic gap in wages and profits between the urban and rural areas, and may be one of the drivers of the huge rural to urban migrations of the twentieth century.

From the standpoint of world systems theory, the agricultural situation in Mexico illustrates a divide between traditional third world agriculture (periphery) and the performance of some of the large corporations and government partners (advanced). This divide fits somewhat with the geographic divisions of Mexico outlined earlier in the book. The ejido-based traditional agriculture is located in the periphery and semi-periphery; the government setting policies and agro-corporate headquarters are located mostly in Mexico City and somewhat in Monterey. Mexican agriculture is subject to a great deal of fluctuations that depend on such volatile factors as world markets, the weather, the peso exchange rate, and federal administration leadership initiatives. Hence, it is difficult to generalize into the future. The conclusion may be that agriculture is slowly but steadily moving away from its longtime ejido tradition and becoming more open and somewhat more international.

## Case Study: Maseca/Gruma

Gruma is the world's largest corn flour producer and one of the biggest tortillas manufacturers. It is headquartered in Monterrey and produces corn flour, wheat flour, and tortillas. Gruma, the parent firm of Maseca, is the domestic subsidiary and the leader along with Minsa of the Mexican corn tortilla marketplace. Gruma is the third largest Mexican agricultural company, while Maseca is the fifth largest. They are both among the top 65 firms in Mexico (Expansión 1999). The combined revenues of the two companies of $1.95 million compares to the agricultural leader Grupo Bimbo. The major tortilla competitor of Maseca, Grupo Mina, is half the size of Maseca and much smaller than the combined firm. This case study examines the role of the government, traditional tastes, and foreign trends in the enlargement of Maseca/Gruma to become an international company, while still dominating domestic marketplaces.

An important element in understanding these companies is the distinction between a traditional maize dough or "nixtamal" (sometimes called "masa") tortilla and a modern corn flour one. Corn flour is the key ingredient in the modern corn flour tortilla. The modern process is based on the simple principle of mixing corn with water. By contrast, the traditional process utilizes "nixtamal" dough. In the nixtamal-based process, the corn flour is mixed with lime first and then the "nixtimal dough" is made in a more complex manner. The traditional process has several disadvantages. It produces maize dough which has shorter shelf-life than the corn flour product. The nixtamal process is more complex and slower, and produces lower yields, in terms of tortillas per kilogram (Case 1999). Offsetting these disadvantages is the plus for the traditional tortilla of strong market and taste acceptance in Mexico, and even more so among the more populous lower classes.

Gruma and Maseca were founded in 1949 and have grown rapidly since then. Gruma has emphasized R&D from its founding and has the advantage that it can plan and develop strong technology and processes for the entire product chain from corn through flour, dough, and tortillas. This is a strategic advantage over less comprehensive firms that only deal with part of the production chain. A recent example of its technology edge is that Gruma has installed the SAP enterprise resource system in all of its areas at an investment cost of around $15 million (Gruma Corporate website 1999). The SAP system integrates in one software system all the major business functions worldwide.

The companies have benefited by closeness at times to the federal government. For example some sources have alleged that the founder of Gruma took advantage of close links with former Mexican President Carlos Salinas to win favors and government contracts including preference for CONASUPO contracts (U.S./Mexico Business 1999). CONASUPO handles commodities for the Mexican government. There were also claims about subsidies incorrectly allocated to certain flour stocks being resold as animal feed (U.S./Mexico Business 1999). In recent years of the Ernesto Zedillo Administration, the government has put in quotas and price controls that have adversely affected Gruma and Maseca, along with other corn flour firms.

In the domestic market, there are several large companies such as Maseca, Minsa, and Bimbo that produce packaged corn flour tortillas, as well as an estimated 50,000 smaller firms that emphasize the traditional maize dough tortilla and serve local markets. The government had subsidized tortilla production for many decades, which satisfied the palettes of the populace and served to check the domestic growth of the large firms. However, in 1997 the Zedillo Administration started a phase-out of the subsidy. This has been highly controversial since it not only goes against the food tastes of Mexicans but it raises the cost of living for the poor. The Zedillo Administration offered two offsetting initiatives: (1) the new poverty program Progresa started in 1997 emphasizes nutrition and may make the modernized tortilla more appealing and (2) the 1999 agreement of the Zedillo government and citizen groups instituted vitamin and mineral enrichment of corn flour tortillas. For some everyday Mexicans, the nutritional enrichment may be the offset for the loss of the traditional tortilla subsidy.

Gruma is the international parent of the conglomerate. In the early 1970s, Gruma started selling its products in Central America. By 1976, it was starting to sell products in the U.S. marketplace. In the late 1980s and early 1990s, Gruma expanded its operations in Central America, particularly Honduras, El Salvador, and Guatemala. It has grown in the U.S. markets so it now has the largest tortilla market share. Recently, it has also moved into northern South America and Europe. For instance, it is building a $50 million tortilla factory outside London.

Gruma has benefited by the great popularity of tortillas in the U.S. That popularity is the result of the high and growing proportion of Mexican population, especially in California, Arizona, Texas, Miami, and Chicago. The market for tortillas is magnified by major chain producers, such as Pepsi-subsidiary Taco Bell, which Gruma sells to. For instance, in 1996, Taco Bell utilized 5.2 billion tortillas in 4,800 restaurants (Bruner 1997). Grupo Gruma can also market very large amounts of tortillas through its subsidiary, the supermarket Mission Foods, which is located in states that have large Mexican-origin population. However, way beyond Mission Food, tortillas are sold in nearly every supermarket in the U.S. Studies have shown that they are popular with Latinos as well as non Latinos (Brunere 1997). Overall, this market is rapidly expanding with huge growth potential and Gruma/Maseca is poised as the key producer.

Gruma has recently expanded its product lines to wheat flour, canned food, snacks, and manufacturing of machinery to produce tortillas and snacks. It has taken advantage of its technology edge in this expansion. In addition it has partnered in wheat flour production with ADM (Archer-Daniels-Midland Co.), a leading multinational grain company.

It is clear that the corn flour/tortilla business is very complicated and closely involves everyday Mexicans, the federal government, overseas consumers, entities in the U.S. and the Americas as well as Europe. This case illustrates the impact on Mexican industry of the changing Mexican demographic composition of the U.S. In a way, Gruma products have followed the wave of migration and received the added ripple affects of U.S. non-Latino adopters. The case also illustrates the advantages of technological advances to market leadership both in Mexico and the U.S. Gruma's technology has been strategically blessed to be integrated across the entire production cycle i.e. all the way from corn to packaged tortilla. The case highlights a number of chapter themes i.e. that big agri-companies are usually separated from little local producers, that the Mexican government recently got out of the way of managing markets, that corn and its byproducts constitute Mexico's leading agricultural commodity, and that the Mexican and U.S. agricultural/food sectors are closely intertwined.

# 12

## The Informal Sector

- **Introduction**
- **The Informal Sector and Globalization**
- **What Is the Informal Sector?**
- **Activities that Make Up the Informal Sector**
- **The Magnitude of the Informal Sector in Mexico**
- **The Informal Sector in the Mexican Labor Force – STPS Studies**
- **Informal Micro-Businesses – INEGI Surveys**
- **Illustrations of the Informal Sector in Mexico**
  - Tianguis
  - Ambulantes Vendedores
  - Marias or Street Vendors
- **Structural Organization**
- **Children in the Street Sector**
- **Lezama's Study of Woman Street Vendors in the Mexico City Historic District**
- **Conclusions**
- **Mini Case Study: The Informal Labor Force in Ciudad Juarez and El Paso**

## Introduction

Historically in discussions of the labor force in peripheral countries there has been an evolution from preoccupation with unemployment to the identification of *employment* as being an important problem (Moser 1978). This led to a focus on the "informal sector" of employment and the notion of a "dual labor market" into the formal and informal sectors. This interest has cut across disciplines with an ancillary of confusion in definitions (see Bromley 1978a; 1978b). In the United States, as elsewhere, the informal sector is not included in official estimates of the Gross Domestic Product of a country; in the United States the estimate is that one in four dollars is "off of the books." To a large degree, this sector has been ignored because it has not been perceived as a problem until relatively recently.

There are very high percentages of workers in the 'informal economy' in Latin America and Mexico (see Figure 12.1). The informal economy is characterized by all kinds of economic activities, many of them unregulated and uncontrolled by the state, regardless of their legality (Castells and Henderson 1987). In Mexico the informal sector has been called "the subtreanean" economy (CEESP 1987). While this concept applies to drugs and other illegal activities, it primarily refers to undeclared waged work, unpaid taxes, lack of compliance with health and safety regulations, and so on. This employment sector is particularly vulnerable to low pay, exploitation, subcontracting, and decentralized production and other activities. Much of the informal labor force is female. In Mexico, estimates vary but a recent one by a knowledgeable observer made an estimate of that the informal economy represents 10 percent of PIB (Jarque, cited in EI Financiero 1997).

Implications of the informal sector range from uncollected taxes; reductions in small business registration; family structure and childrearing; over-estimates of poverty, unemployment, and underemployment; bureaucratic corruption, distortion of official statistics of the national accounts; and the political economy.

In respect to potential policy, it is imperative that many conceptual problems associated with the idea of an informal sector be solved before policy recommendations are made.

## The Informal Sector and Globalization

At its broadest definition, the informal sector does not register with formal authorities but it still may have available private or public institutional credit.

Sassen (1994: 106-107) suggests that the informal labor force is linked to globalization in that (1) it meets the demands of those involved in the process by making available small enterprises at the local level, including services and products and (2) these small enterprises are linked to global corporations by assisting them in maximizing profits via the use of sweatshops and home-work. The informal labor force also is linked to globalization by its increasing demand for low-cost services and products being produced by an expanding low-income population. Even street vendors may "represent but one link in a nationwide distribution chain of smuggled and stolen property" (Foote 1987).

Another perspective focuses on the dual labor market as arising from the need of larger firms to reduce costs and gain in flexibility. That can be accomplished through smaller and less formal organizations.

**Figure 12.1 Informal Labor Force in Selected
Latin American Countries**

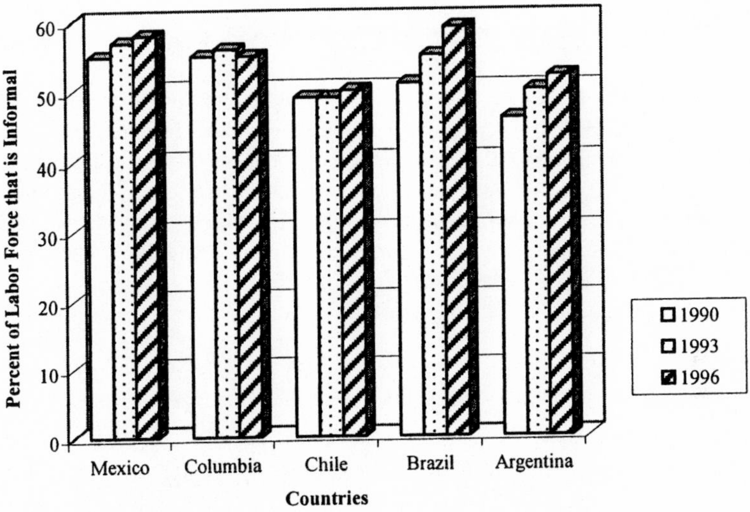

Source: Secretaría del Trabajo y Previsíon Social. 1995. Tendencias de la Estructura
Económica y el Sector Informal en México. México, D.F.: Secretaría del
Trabajo y Prevision Social.

## What Is the Informal Sector?

The informal sector includes the whole array of goods and services that generally are
ignored in official statistics. Obviously, this includes illegal or criminal activities, bartering,
work performed by households for themselves -- virtually anything that could be done by
someone else if paid enough.

According to the United Nations (1987), informal activities are characterized by:
a.   Ease of entry;
b.   Reliance upon indigenous resources;
c.   Family ownership of enterprises;
d.   Small scale of operation;
e.   Labor-intensive and adapted technology;
f.   Skills acquired outside the formal school system; and
g.   Unregulated and competitive markets.

Our investigation of the informal sector in Mexico suggests that several of these
characteristics do not adequately describe the informal labor force in Mexico. They are
problematic when their opposites are considered; that is:

a.  Difficult entry;
b.  Frequent reliance on overseas resources;
c.  Corporate ownership;
d.  Large scale operation;
e.  Capital-intensive and often utilizing imported technology;
f.  Formally acquired skills, often expatriate; and
g.  Protected markets (through tariffs, quotas, and trade licenses).

In addition, in some instances informal labor force data from some countries exclude non-agricultural enterprises, illegal and criminal activities, begging, and sometimes domestic work is not included. On the other hand, small businesses using paid labor are included when the owner and workers operate at a subsidence level. The conclusion that must be made is that the informal labor force is open to a variety of conceptual definitions. In this chapter, we attempt to clarify what definition is being used for the data and discussion (see U.S. Dept. of Labor 1992:13a-13c).

Some of the problems that exist in use of the dichotomy of informal/formal labor force are:

(1) It is a very crude and simple classification; (2) There are inadequate guidelines for classification purposes; (3) Policy prescriptions rely upon the dual classification; (4) Often the informal is assumed to take place only in urban areas; (5) Other sectors need to be defined; (6) There is little consideration of the future of the informal dimension; (7) There is confusion as to the relationships among informal, households, families, people, activities and enterprises; (8) An individual may have an association with different sectors in their daily routine across time, and (9) A tendency to associate informal status with being poor and uneducated (Bromley 1978a; 1978b).

In Mexico there is a need to distinguish between the marginal (marginalidad) and informal (informalidad) labor sectors and their multiple definitions (Savari 1996).

### Activities That Make Up the Informal Sector

Activities of those involved in the informal sector include the following (CEESP 1986):

a.  Workers or employees who are not registered – off of the books); this may include those who are 'moon lighting;' avoiding paying taxes and/or to social security;
b.  Contraband merchandise sales;
c.  Illegal gaming;
d.  Work by undocumented immigrants;
e.  Traffic in illegal drugs;
f.  Bartering of goods and services;
g.  Prostitution and other illegal sexual activities;
h.  Usury financial services;
i.  Transactions that could be taxed but are not reported (domestic work, rental of automobiles, houses, etc.)'
j.  Non taxed import and exports; and
k.  Corruption and graft payments.

*Who is in the Informal Sector?*

Data for Mexico in 1988 suggest that in municipios of 100,000 and more inhabitants, about one in three men (31.2 percent) are involved in the underground economy while two in five women are (38.2 percent) (El Sector 1993: 51).

By age, the heaviest concentration in the informal sector is for those aged 20-29. By marital status, those who are not married (vs. all other categories) are more likely to be in the underground economy than the married. About two-thirds of workers participating in the underground economy have not completed primary schooling.

The vast majority of informal jobs are in the service and commerce sectors followed by the manufacturing sector. Within the service sector, virtually all domestics are in the informal labor force. In the commerce sector they are making tortillas, doing laundry, selling-to-go, vending ice cream, etc. As might be expected, almost half of those in the underground economy have incomes below the minimum legal salary ("Salario Minimo"), in contrast to about one-fifth in the formal economy. They are also likely to work more hours.

## The Magnitude of the Informal Sector in Mexico

There are a number of different ways of calculating the extent of the informal sector on the gross national product (PIB). One way in Mexico is to survey nationally the number of micro-businesses, estimate the combined revenues of the businesses, and extrapolate that to estimate a fraction of GDP. This is made feasible by regular surveys of micro-businesses started by INEGI in 1994 (INEGI 1995, 1996).

In the United States, the underground economy has been estimated to range from 3 to 40 percent, depending on the definition used. If only illegal activities are counted, the percentage is less than if all activities not added into national accounts are considered. In Mexico, beginning around 1974, and depending on the year since, estimates range from ten to as high as almost forty percent of the PIB being from the subterranean sector (Centro 1987; El Financiero 1997). The size of the informal labor force in terms of the economy was estimated by INEGI at 10 percent of PIB (Carlos Jarque Uribe, cited in El Financiero 1997). The informal economy was defined as businesses with less than five persons and without registration.

In Mexico there is a need to distinguish between the marginal (marginalidad) and informal (informalidad) labor sectors and their multiple definitions (Savari 1996). Over one-third of those in the informal labor force (35.1 percent) in 1980 were in the commerce, restaurant, and hotels and one-fourth were involved in community, sales, and personal services.

Estimates in 1996 placed the percent in the informal labor force (subterranea) approximating between forty and sixty percent (Guiterrez 1997; Foote 1997; Martinez 1997). In number of persons this means around 20 million! In the commercial sector the estimate in 1996 was that almost forty percent of persons were in the informal sector. In employee numbers, this amounted to 2,214,574 of 5,057,910 persons. The commerce sector represented 19.7 percent of PIB in 1996 (Economic Commission for Latin America and the Caribbean 1997). Some estimates show this percentage increasing rapidly by the year 2000 to contain almost forty-four percent (Perez 1997).

Figure 12.2 shows that the formal and informal labor force (i.e street vendors or *vendedores ambulantes*) percentages have raised slightly between 1988 and 1993. However, Figure 12.2 also shows substantial change from 27 to 43 percent of labor force between 1993 and projections for the year 2000. This figure illustrates the growth in vendedores ambulantes has been constantly growing since 1988 and is expected to have continued growth. While increasing in number, Figure 12.3 shows variation in classification in informal employment has remained relatively stable from 1990 to 1996 among independent workers, domestic service, and small businesses (Perez 1997).

**Figure 12.2**
**Labor Force: Formal Commercial and**
**Vendedores Ambulantes**

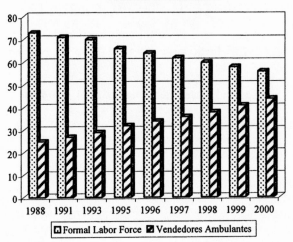

Source: Perez, 1997.

This estimate indicates that the informal proportion of the labor force is even higher if small business services and domestic services are included. For 1996, this large estimate is 59 percent. Within this 59 percent, the largest proportion were independent workers (32 percent), followed by small business (21 percent), and domestic service (4 percent). This emphasizes that the most common form of informal labor force is independent work. This corresponds more fully to the street vendors and informal individual service people that are prevalent especially in Mexican cities. Small businesses are not surprisingly a substantial proportion, while domestic service is not so commonplace.

One possible surrogate measure of the informal sector illustrating the minimum level may be the "other and not specified" categories in the labor force. If so, the level in 1990 would be, at a minimum, over eleven percent (Pick and Butler 1994). Other estimates for Mexico are closer to 20 percent (CEESP 1987: 89).

### The Informal Sector in the Mexican Labor Force: STPS Studies

The informal labor force can be considered in terms of the entire workforce and in fact in terms of the entire population of age 12 and older. One of the most in depth studies of the Mexican informal labor force was conducted the Secretaría del Trabajo y Previsión Social (STPS) for the years 1988 to 1993 (STPS 1995). In that study, "informal" was defined by fairly complex criteria: (1) domestic work, (2) non-salaried and contract workers in establishments of 5 or fewer employees, (3) independent workers, except professionals, (4) workers receiving no pay, except professionals (STPS 1995).

The study was based on three large national surveys of employment conducted by STPS in 1988, 1991, and 1993. The framework of this study views the population 12+ as consisting of economically active population and economically inactive population (see Table 12.1). The economically active population consists nearly entirely of the major categories of formal employed and informal employed. The economically inactive population includes the categories of students, housewives, retired persons, incapacitated persons, and "others" (STPS 1995).

### Figure 12.3 Informal Employment, 1990-1996

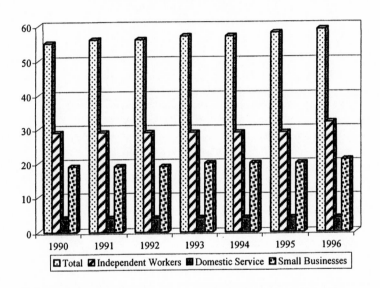

Source: Perez, 1997.

The results revealed that in 1993 about half of the population 12+ was economically active and half inactive. Within the economically active portion of 15.1 million workers, 9.1 million were formal employed workers and 5.8 million were informal employed workers. Hence, 39 percent of the employed labor force was informal. Overall, this segment represented one fifth of the population 12 years and older. This type of analysis places the informal labor force in the larger context of the population as a whole. Informal labor force becomes one of the four largest categories for adult population. This underscores its importance in Mexico, including as an economic force.

The same study carefully compared the age, education, gender, and occupations between the informal and formal labor force. In all cases there were large differences. This helps in understanding that the formal and informal labor forces must be regarded differently.

**Table 12.1 The Size of the Informal Sector and Other
Categories of Economically Active and Inactive Population, 1993**

|  | *No.** | *Percent* |
|---|---|---|
| *Economically Active Population, 12+* | 15,705 | 54.99 |
| Employed | 15,120 | 52.94 |
|     Formal | 9,142 | 32.01 |
|     Informal | 5,781 | 20.24 |
| Agricultural laborer | 197 | 0.69 |
| Interns | 94 | 0.33 |
| Unemployed | 491 | 1.72 |
| *Economically Inactive Population, 12+* | 12,853 | 45.01 |
| Students | 4,897 | 17.15 |
| Housewives | 6,639 | 23.25 |
| Retired persons | 544 | 1.91 |
| Incapacitated persons | 282 | 0.99 |
| Others | 491 | 1.72 |
| Total Pop. 12+ | 28,558 | 100.00 |

Source: Secretaría del Trabajo y Previsión Social, 1995.

* in millions.

In age distribution, the STPS results for 1993 indicated that the informal sector had relatively more teens and older (50+) population than the formal sector. For instance, teens (i.e. age 12 to 19) comprise 17 percent of the informal sector but only 10 percent of the formal sector. At the opposite end, older persons (50+) comprise 18 percent of the informal sector but only 10 percent of the formal sector. It may be that the lengthy economic crisis of the 1980s reduced jobs in the formal economy, and the jobs eliminated were for the young and old. The informal economy filled in.

As seen in Table 12.2, low educational level is linked with high informal participation, while higher schooling has low informal presence. In the middle levels of schooling i.e. 1 to 6 years, there is between 49 and 63 percent informal presence. Even though the rate of informality drops at the secondary schooling level of 10 or more years i.e., there is still a surprisingly high informal presence i.e. of one fifth. This reflects the economic pressures towards the informal labor force even for a more highly educated population.

**Table 12.2 Educational Distributions for the Formal and Informal Sectors, 1993**

| *Level of Schooling* | *Percent of Formal Sector* | *Percent of Informal Sector* | *Rate of Informality* |
|---|---|---|---|
| No schooling | 1.7 | 7.7 | 74.1 |
| 1-3 years | 4.4 | 11.8 | 62.9 |
| 4-5 years | 2.9 | 7.0 | 60.8 |
| 6 years | 17.7 | 27.1 | 49.2 |
| 7-9 years | 36.1 | 31.2 | 35.4 |
| 10 or more years | 37.3 | 15.2 | 20.5 |
| Total |  |  | 38.7 |

* The rate of informality is the ratio of informal workers to total workers.

Source: Secretara del Trabajo y Previson Social, 1995.

The gender ratio of the two sectors differs, with the informal sector much more balanced. For instance, in terms of proprietors of micro-businesses, 46 percent of proprietors in the informal sector are women, compared to only 16 percent in the formal sector. The greater opportunities for women proprietors in the informal sector may stem from lack of governmental regulation and educational barriers.

The differences in the informal versus formal sectors are accentuated in looking at differences in occupations. The raw numbers and percent distributions of 27 occupational categories reveal considerable differences ranging between 1 and 100 percent in the extent of informality (see Table 12.3). For the total labor force, the average rate of informality was 39 percent. Among the major categories with high rates of informality were domestic services (100 percent) cleaning and laundry services, repair services, and retail commerce, all above 65 percent. This singles out commerce as especially oriented towards informal. Not surprisingly street vendors are 99 percent informal.

Highly formal sector occupations include metals/machinery/glass, mining, financial/educational/medical services, sewing/fabrics, and paper and wood products. These are older industries and services that have more tradition associated with them and higher levels of education in the case of finance/education/medical.

The vast occupational differences in informality help to explain Mexico's informal sector. In certain niches in the economy, work is predominantly done independently, sporadically, and at low or no pay. There is lack of government regulation. In other niches, work is done in larger groups and regulated. The informal occupations have easier entry, which are available to the large populations affected and displaced by succeeding economic crises that have typified the 1980s and 1990s.

### Informal Micro-Businesses: INEGI Surveys

INEGI recognized the information gap on informal micro-businesses and instituted a regular national survey in 1994 in order to provide more information on informal as well as formal micro-businesses. Nearly all the firms surveyed had five or fewer employees. "Informal" was determined quite differently than for STPS or other surveys. A variety of registration criteria could be applied to determine extent of informality. INEGI identified "informal" through the presence or absence of business registration i.e. whether a firm was registered with the federal government, municipal government, trade unions, or industry groups. Once a micro-business was established as informal, workers in the business are likewise classified as informal.

The range of registration status is shown in Table 12.4 for 1994 and 1996. In 1996, the percent of micro-businesses with no registration of any kind was 63 percent! If total lack of registration is utilized to define informal, most micro-businesses fall into the informal sector. From 1994 to 1996, the informal sector grew by 14 percent, or 460,000 workers. This huge increase was the result of two factors. First, the economy worsened in 1995 following the peso crisis of late 1994. Second, the Mexican labor force in the 1990s grew by about one million net new workers per year (Pick, Butler, and Gonzalez 1993), and regardless of the crisis, there were not enough formal jobs to absorb this population increment.

When registration of micro-businesses occurred, it tended to be at the state, municipio, or trade union level; federal registration was surprisingly low. The registration results by economic sector reveal that the highest non-registered sectors are construction, manufacturing and services; commerce is moderate; and transport has the most registration (see Table 12.5). This may be surprising, since some studies have pointed to commerce as the major constituent of informal sector. However, many studies such as of ambulantes have over-emphasized commerce and not included construction and manufacturing, since they are not done in the street. Manufacturing's high informal percentage may be due to

**Table 12.3 Comparison of Occupations of the Informal and Formal Labor Force, 1993**

| Occupation | No. of workers in formal sector | Percent of formal sector | No. of workers in informal sector | Percent of informal sector | Rate of Informality* |
|---|---|---|---|---|---|
| Domestic services | 0.0 | 0.00 | 509.4 | 8.81 | 100.00 |
| Articles of palm and wicker | 0.1 | 0.00 | 0.5 | 0.01 | 91.23 |
| Grinding of mixtamal and tortilla | 10.7 | 0.12 | 63.7 | 1.10 | 85.57 |
| Cleaning and laundry services | 70.1 | 0.77 | 332.0 | 5.74 | 82.56 |
| Repair services | 203.7 | 2.23 | 773.2 | 13.37 | 79.15 |
| Retail commerce | 767.6 | 8.40 | 1,838.9 | 31.81 | 70.55 |
| in established site | 765.2 | 8.37 | 1,462.0 | 25.29 | 65.64 |
| street vendor | 2.4 | 0.03 | 376.9 | 6.52 | 99.36 |
| Hotels and restaurants | 324.3 | 3.55 | 393.4 | 6.80 | 54.82 |
| Furniture | 84.8 | 0.93 | 95.7 | 1.66 | 53.04 |
| Transport | 392.1 | 4.29 | 430.7 | 7.45 | 52.35 |
| Construction | 489.7 | 5.36 | 414.8 | 7.18 | 45.86 |
| Grinding of wheat and bread | 85.6 | 0.94 | 61.8 | 1.07 | 41.92 |
| Clothing | 193.7 | 2.12 | 117.8 | 2.04 | 37.81 |
| Metal products | 183.1 | 2.00 | 108.1 | 1.87 | 37.12 |
| Deserts, ice cream | 22.2 | 0.24 | 12.1 | 0.21 | 35.34 |
| Printing | 134.2 | 1.47 | 63.2 | 1.09 | 32.02 |
| Entertainment serices | 214.3 | 2.34 | 76.1 | 1.32 | 26.21 |
| Leather and shoes | 168.1 | 1.84 | 44.3 | 0.77 | 20.86 |
| Drinks and tobacco | 310.4 | 3.40 | 60.1 | 1.04 | 16.21 |
| Chemicals and rubber | 455.6 | 4.98 | 82.9 | 1.43 | 15.40 |
| Paper and wood products | 96.4 | 1.05 | 11.9 | 0.20 | 10.94 |
| Sewing and fabrics | 113.5 | 1.24 | 13.3 | 0.23 | 10.48 |
| Financial, education, medical services | 2,425.9 | 26.53 | 217.3 | 3.76 | 8.22 |
| Mining | 26.3 | 0.29 | 1.1 | 0.02 | 4.13 |
| industries | 569.8 | 6.23 | 6.9 | 0.12 | 1.20 |
| Other Occupations | 1,800.7 | 19.70 | 52.0 | 0.90 | 2.81 |
| Total | 9,142.8 | 100.00 | 5,781.1 | 100.00 | 38.74 |

* The rate of informality is the ratio of informal workers to total workers.

Source: Secretaria del Trabajo y Prevision Social, 1993.

lack of regulations for manufacturing and at the same time the often medium to high educational levels of informal manufacturing workers. The high rates for construction may stem from lack of regulation of this industry in Mexico, while transport is more regulated.

The surveys reveal many features of informal micro-businesses, in comparison to formal ones. In size, informal micro-businesses consist mostly of a single worker (77 percent). This relates to the independence and lack of control of the informal sector. Only a tiny proportion of informal micro-businesses had more than three employees (see Figure 12.4).

### Table 12.4 Registration Status of Micro-Businesses, 1994-1996

| Type of Registration | 1994 | | 1996 | | Percent Change 1994-1996 |
|---|---|---|---|---|---|
| | Percent | Number | Percent | Number | |
| Trade Union | 10.34 | 377,697 | 10.67 | 381,576 | 0.33 |
| Industry Group | 8.48 | 309,602 | 5.81 | 207,892 | -2.66 |
| Municipio or State Treasurer | 16.70 | 609,768 | 13.77 | 492,283 | -2.93 |
| Treasurer of the Federal District | 5.54 | 202,456 | 9.58 | 342,594 | 4.04 |
| SECOFI | 1.74 | 63,615 | 2.92 | 104,479 | 1.18 |
| Secretary of Health | 6.41 | 234,090 | 6.85 | 244,794 | 0.44 |
| Other Registrations | 1.29 | 47,270 | 2.60 | 93,012 | 1.31 |
| No Registration | 49.50 | 1,807,743 | 63.46 | 2,269,131 | 13.96 |
| Total | 100.00 | 3,652,241 | 100.00 | 3,575,587 | |

SECOFI = Secretaria de Comercio y Fomento Industrial.

Note: the data are based on entire sample of micro-businesses in INEGI Surveys of of 1994 and 1996.

Source: INEGI, 1996, 1997.

### Table 12.5 Registration of Micro-Businesses by Sector, 1994-1996

| Economic Sector | 1994 | | | 1996 | | |
|---|---|---|---|---|---|---|
| | No. of Micro-Businesses | No. Not Registered | Percent Not Registered | No. of Micro-Businesses | No. Not Registered | Percent Not Registered |
| Construction | 135,498 | 118,831 | 87.70 | 146,535 | 135,967 | 92.79 |
| Manufacturing | 485,429 | 339,777 | 70.00 | 415,939 | 307,711 | 73.98 |
| Services | 1,273,161 | 835,591 | 65.63 | 1,586,540 | 1,144,006 | 72.11 |
| Commerce | 1,034,497 | 467,679 | 45.21 | 1,238,574 | 640,879 | 51.74 |
| Transport | 161,667 | 45,865 | 28.37 | 188,003 | 40,568 | 21.58 |
| Total | 3,090,243 | 1,807,743 | 58.50 | 3,575,587 | 2,269,131 | 63.46 |

Source: INEGI: 1996, 1997.

Another aspect is the location of informal micro-businesses. Mostly informal work is done in the home of clients or the home of the workers (see Table 12.6). Although the perception is that informal work occurs in the street, commerce is only 28 percent of informal micro-businesses. The large informal segment of manufacturing and services are more likely to occur in homes.

For the segments that occur in the street, there are a variety of arrangements of varying permanency. Perhaps the most "permanent" is the fixed or moveable stand of a tianguis (5.7 percent). Much less permanent are goods or services offered from a motorcycle, bicycle or motor vehicle (4.3 percent). Anyone observing a typical Mexican crowded city street can notice the moving variety of places and locations for goods and services.

Some other aspects of the informal micro-businesses relates to the influence of the family, the tax implications, lack of accounting books, sources of credit, and the education of owners. These micro-businesses are only 30 percent family run, which implies more sole practitioners. This again may be due to the INEGI survey's greater breadth and inclusion of manufacturing and construction. Since informal micro-businesses have little registration, one implication is that very few taxes are paid. This in turn is a cause of the open conflict with the government and with established merchants that has engulfed downtown street vendors in Mexico City in recent years (Berman 1998). In fact, the federal government has started to question whether street vendors should not be approached to pay their share of income taxes (Berman 1998). This may be difficult since over half of the micro-businesses do not keep any books, and only a quarter has accounting records.

An important stimuli to informal micro-businesses is the sources of credit to start. As seen in Table 12.7, the largest credit source is from suppliers. This points to the need for further research to determine that the suppliers are, what their role is, and describe the entire supply chain. Most of the rest of the credit comes from friends and relatives; there is a very small proportion (ten percent) from banks and savings institutions. Conforming to other studies of the informal sector, the INEGI study reveals lower average education for the informal sector, but nevertheless a significant segment of secondary or even college educated. This further reflects job market pressures stemming from the peso crisis and mounting numbers of workers.

**Figure 12.4 Micro-Business Size by Registration Status**

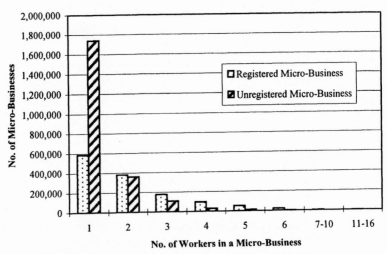

Note: the data are based on entire sample of micro-businesses in INEGI surveys of 1994 and 1996.

Source: Secretaría del Trabajo y Previsión Social. 1995. Tendencias de la Estructura Económica y el Sector Informal en México. México, D.F.: Secretaría del Trabajo y Prevision Social.

**Table 12.6. Distribution of Locations for Micro-Businesses, 1996**

| Type of Location | No. | Percent |
|---|---|---|
| Mechandise, foods, or services offered at the home of clients | 867,387 | 38.9 |
| Mechandise, foods, or services offered at home without a special installation | 412,776 | 18.5 |
| Street vendor | 182,950 | 8.2 |
| Improvised stand in a public street | 138,749 | 6.2 |
| Mechandise, foods, or services offered at home with an improvised installation | 129,942 | 5.8 |
| Stand that forms part of a tianguis (fixed or moveable) | 126,319 | 5.7 |
| Improvised stand or street vender in a market or tianguis | 95,267 | 4.3 |
| Fixed or semi-fixed stand in a public way | 86,008 | 3.9 |
| Merchandise, foods, or sevices offered from a motocycle, bicycle, or motor vehicle | 83,008 | 3.7 |
| Merchandise, foods, or seviced offfered from a van, mini-bus, or collective taxi | 75,922 | 3.4 |
| Other | 29,431 | 1.3 |
| Total | 2,227,759 | 100.0 |
| Without a fixed location | 2,089,750 | 93.8 |
| With a fixed location | 138,009 | 6.2 |
| Total | 2,227,759 | 100.0 |

Source: INEGI, 1997.

**Table 12.7 Types of Loans Received to Start a Micro-Business, by Registration Status, 1996**

| Type of Loans to Start the Operation | Not Registered | Percent | Registered | Total |
|---|---|---|---|---|
| Bank loan | 9,930 | 6 | 69,638 | 79,568 |
| Savings institution loan | 9,853 | 6 | 10,215 | 20,068 |
| Loan from friend or relative | 56,722 | 34 | 67,523 | 124,245 |
| Small private loan | 8,935 | 5 | 14,271 | 23,206 |
| Credit from Suppliers | 69,477 | 42 | 132,868 | 202,345 |
| Other | 11,339 | 7 | 10,069 | 21,408 |
| Total receiving a loan | 166,256 | 100 | 304,584 | 470,840 |
| Percent receiving a loan | 7.3 | | 23.3 | 15.2 |
| Total not receiving a loan | 2,102,875 | | 1,002,643 | 3,105,518 |
| Total | 2,269,131 | | 1,306,456 | |

Source: INEGI, 1997

## Illustrations of the Informal Sector in Mexico

As shown on Figure 12.5, there is substantial variation in the formal and informal labor force in Mexico by size of workplace. The vast majority of workers in the informal sector work alone or with a maximum of five workers, whereas the majority of those in the formal labor force work in facilities with 51 or more workers.

Another substantial difference between the informal and formal labor force is by sex of owner. As shown in Figure 12.6, the formal labor force is almost completely male whereas the informal labor force is almost equally participated in by each sex.

Earnings by participation in the formal and informal labor force for 1993, as shown on Figure 12.7 when compared with earnings in 1988, indicates that there was a general uplifting in both the informal and formal labor force, but with a larger increase upward for those in the informal sphere.

**Figure 12.5 Occupation by Formal/Informal Status and Size of Workplace**

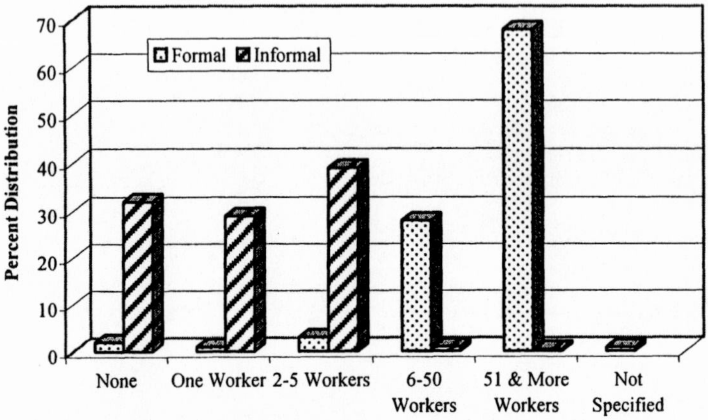

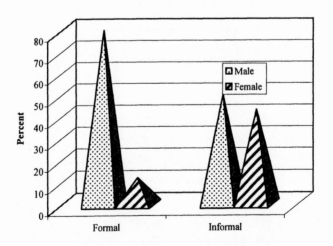

Source: Secretaría del Trabajo y Previsión Social. 1995. Tendencias de la Estructura Económica y el Sector Informal en México. México, D.F.: Secretaría del Trabajo y Prevision Social.

**Figure 12.6 Small Business by Sex of Owner**

Source: Secretaría del Trabajo y Previsión Social. 1995. Tendencias de la Estructura Económica y el Sector Informal en México. México, D.F.: Secretaría del Trabajo y Prevision Social.

**Figure 12.7 Population in Formal and Informal Labor Sectors by Income**

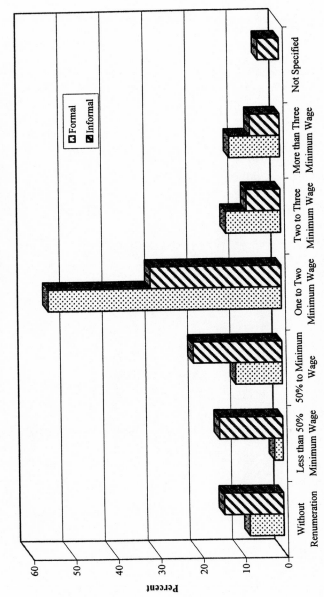

Source: Secretaria del Trabajo y Previsión Social. 1995. Tendencias de la Estructura Económica y el Sector Informal en México. México, D.F.: Secretaria del Trabajo y Prevision Social.

Some cities such as Monterey are low in informal labor force, which reflects a strong metropolitan economy and high educational levels. A study of the percent in the informal labor force in Mexico compared Mexico City, Guadalajara, Monterrey, and combined 42 other cities. The results shown on Figure 12.8 demonstrate that there is some variation but that most cities have at least one in four persons in the labor force being in the informal sector. Another perspective shows that of the total informal labor force in Mexico, 22 percent is concentrated in Mexico City (see Figure 12.8).

In Mexico the informal sector has been analyzed by different governmental organizations. However, these analyses rely substantially upon demographic and structural analysis. Additional questions about the informal sector in Mexico imply that the UN characterization has some severe limitations. Several of these questions revolve around how much organizational structure there is, who settles disputes, who is in control, and if control is exerted by others.

It is readily apparent by observation in cities in Mexico that there are several different types of involvement in the informal structure. These types and associated dimensions imply that much research needs to be accomplished beyond a structural and statistical analysis. For example, at least three different types of the informal labor force have been identified: (1) *Tianguis* which are highly organized in several ways; (2) *Vendedores Ambulantes* involving substantial movement, but in a systematic manner; and (3) *Marias* – street vendors with weak or no organization.

**Figure 12.8 Informal Labor Force by Cities and Percent of Total**

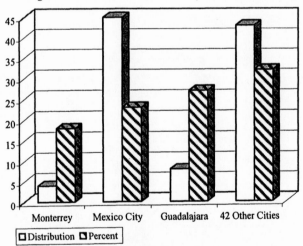

Note: Distribution represents the percent of total population of all 45 cities. Percent is the percent of the labor force that is informal.
Source: Secretaría del Trabajo y Previsión Social. 1995. Tendencias de la Estructura Económica y el Sector Informal en México. México, D.F.: Secretaría del Trabajo y Prevision Social.

*Tianguis*

Tianguis involves persons who appear to be substantially organized. They may be in different locations on different days; however, they return to the same spot is a particular location, and there appears to be little conflict with those who might want the same location. They also may be paying taxes, receiving governmental recognition, and may have management. This suggests a certain amount of control and structure.

*Vendedores Ambulantes*

In urban areas, many persons under this classification are involved in manufacturing activities and in commercial and service industries. In rural areas, they also are in marginal positions, often involved in small scale manufacturing.

*Marias or Street Vendors*

Perhaps the most visible of those in the informal sector are the marias. These are the women and a few men who are highly visible on the streets selling dolls, native artifacts, and sometimes small food items. However, while it may appear on the surface that marias are not organized in any systematic fashion, they have certain areas staked out defining their territory and little conflict appears between them and others who might want to claim their territory; that is, there is consistency in place and time.

Street vendors hawk everything from chewing gum to stereos. One estimate places the number as approaching one million (Foote 1997).

## Structural Organization

Clearly, the informal structure exists within the framework of governmental knowledge, and, some would argue, with governmental protection. Some believe that the government has 'rented' out the public space sidewalks for private commercial use although this practice is prohibited by the Mexican constitution. There may be kickbacks or 'fees' to government officials, ranging from $200 to $1,500 for a sliver of a sidewalk. In addition, there are many other economic processes associated with street vendors in a variety of ways. Street vendors may have undercut retail prices by as much as 70 percent driving stores out of business by the hundreds if not thousands.

In Mexico City at the behest of regular storeowners, the police have attempted to remove street vendors. One such episode used 3,500 policemen to sweep the city center clean of the unlicensed (Berman 1998). In full riot gear, the police prohibited street peddlers from setting up shop. The fallout from this sweep and other attempts to rid the city of street competition to the regular stores undoubtedly had political repercussion in the mayoral election and will continue to do so in future elections since the vendors have been affiliated with the PRI.

In a study of 60 street vendors in the center of Mexico City, Solis (1995) examined, among other things, the organizational structure and external relationships of the vendors. She found that nearly all the vendors (88 percent) belonged to a street vendor organization. The primary role of the vendor organizations was to defend the physical street location of work. A secondary role was to provide special assistance in times of need, for example if goods were stolen. In addition, some of the organizations had the broader goals to dignify the role and status of the street vendor. There were also economic linkages to other businesses based on supplier credit. Sixty percent of stands had received credit from suppliers. This implies a close relationship with suppliers and a form of risk sharing between the supplier and vendor (Solis 1995). A substantial proportion of the supplier relationships extended further since 37 percent of the merchandise was of foreign or of mixed foreign/domestic origin. This supplier aspect is important for the present book, since it shows that there are international supply chain linkages for parts of the informal sector.

### Children in the Street Sector

A recent report counted 13,373 minor street children working in eight of the centrally located delegations in the central part of Mexico City (UNICEF 1996). Some of these children were under the age of five (see Figure 12.9). In a comparison by age, the younger street children were more likely to be female while progressively age-wise they were male – nearly half and half at ages under five were female while at ages 16 and over four out of five were male. Most of these children were street vendors (ca. 58 percent) while over a fourth, all Indians, were street beggars. Other activities were windshield washers, actors, and street porters (see Figures 12.10 to 12.12).

### Lezama's Study of Women Street Vendors in the Mexico City Historic District

A study by José Luis Lezama in 1991 characterized a group of women street vendors in Mexico City's Historic District located near the Zocolo in the heart of the old part of the city. This study reveals details about work structure of informal street workers as well as their social and family characteristics. Lezama conducted a survey of 66 women in January of 1991. The respondents were involved in selling goods including clothes, shoes, fake jewelry, games, electrical items, and foods. The study also focused in further on a group of women who worked "double work days," i.e. worked in the street and performed substantial child and domestic care.

The overall profile of the women was young, in unions, having significant numbers of children, and with a range of education. Three fifths of the women were between 20 and 39 years old, and three fifths were in unions. Three quarters had children and nearly a half had three or more. Further, supporting other studies mentioned in the chapter, there was significant proportion of more highly educated. Although 30 percent of the women had no education or incomplete primary schooling, 27 percent had completed secondary school and 5 percent were preparatory level. This again reflects the pressures of the economic crises, in this case from the 1980s debt crises.

There was a lot of pressure on this group. For instance in one third of cases, the street vendor respondent was the only family breadwinner. In length of work, 70 percent worked 8-11 hours daily, and 5 percent 12 or more hours. In addition to street vending, 45 percent of the women were engaged in domestic work and 32 percent in care for children (Lezama 1991).

A high proportion of the women were migrants to Mexico City. In fact, 50 percent had arrived in Mexico City in the past ten years. This demonstrates that many women migrants to Mexico City, mostly from rural areas, ended up in low-paying street occupations.

Lezama (1991) further studied a subsample of 12 women who (1) worked 8-11 hours as informal street vendors, and (2) cared for children and did domestic work. This subsample was younger and slightly more educated than the sample as a whole. The subsample reflects the even greater work and familial stresses present for certain segments of the informal labor force.

**Figure 12.9**
**The Street Children Population in Mexico City, 1995:**
**Minors per Political District**

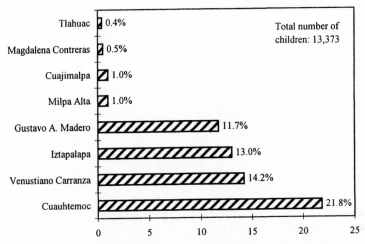

Source: Economic and Social Research Division of BANAMEX. Based on data from
UNICEF. DIF. DOF. II Censo de los niflos y niflas de la caffe. Ciudad de Mexico.
Mexico 1996.

**Figure 12.10**
**The Street Children Population in Mexico City, 1995:**
**Minors per Classification**

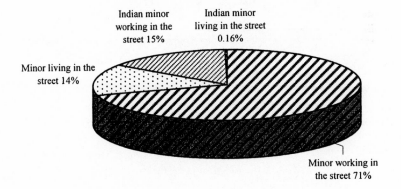

Source: Economic and Social Research Division of BANAMEX. Based on data from
UNICEF. DIF. DOF. II Censo de los niños y niñas de la calle. Ciudad de Mexico.
Mexico 1996.

**Figure 12.11**
**The Street Children Population in Mexico City, 1995:**
**Minors by Sex and Age**

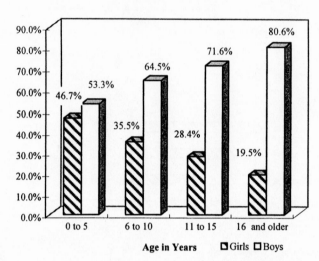

Source: Economic and Social Research Division of BANAMEX. Based on data from
UNICEF. DIF. DOF. II Censo de los Niños y Niñas de la Calle. Ciudad de Mexico,
Mexico, 1996.

**Figure 12.12**
**The Street Children Population in Mexico City, 1995:**
**Minors by Major Activity**

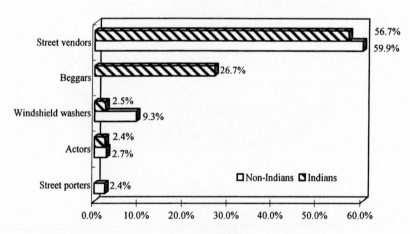

Source: Economic and Social Research Division of BANAMEX. Based on data from
UNICEF. DIF. DOF. II Censo de los Niños y Niñas de la Calle. Ciudad de Mexico,
Mexico, 1996.

It is noteworthy that 56 percent of the women were associated with an organization of street vendors. However, there was also uncertainly about the political confrontations that whirl around the vendor environment, including from the government and from competing licensed merchants.

Lezama ascribed the motivation of the women to "economic reproduction," a term that refers to the desire to perpetuate economic gains, even small ones, for the next generation. The motivation is noteworthy because of the extent of work and "doubling up" of work that often occurred. He regards these street vendors as being at the center of complex economic forces (Lezama 1995). For instance, there are the cost pressures of capitalism, even international ones, on the goods being sold; there are political and governmental stresses and conflicts related to physical space and competition in the city center; and there are pressures from the complex organizational structures that control the physical space i.e. vendor organizations. In addition, the vendors are part of often large family structures that include many economic exchange mechanisms. The study is valuable in revealing the complex interplay of players and forces that impact this segment of the informal marketplace.

## Conclusions

The informal sector in Mexico is very large and influential. It consists of workers in the range of 6-8 million who perform economic tasks and account for about 10 percent of PIB and 40 to 50 percent of the workforce. The informal sector is specific occupationally and emphasizes particular service and commerce occupations but also has substantial manufacturing and construction presence. Informal work tends to be done by individuals or small groups of up to three persons. Although the popular informal image of the street vendor or "ambulante," recent broader studies have shown that the largest location for the informal sector is in homes i.e. the homes of clients or informal workers themselves.

There are some generalizations that are possible about the characteristics of informal workers including that they are less educated, have more females, and include both more young and more older people. The sources of credit are mostly through suppliers and personal/familial contacts, rather than the formal credit system. Informal workers and businesses tend to have no registration and not to pay taxes or fees. Informal commercial workers tend to be members of organizations that provide them with some basic support specially regarding territorial claims.

The motivation for the informal sector stems from a variety of complex factors. First, the poorer segment of the urban populations have looked to the informal sector as a means of "economic reproduction," i.e. a way to provide some economic benefits to their children of the next generation (Lezama 1991). A substantial portion of these poor urban populations are migrants from rural areas into the cities; they lack other options and find the informal sector a means of entry and often long term livelihood. Second, at the individual level, the economic crises that have typified the 1980s and 1990s combined with the growing working age population have displaced many workers and those workers have often been forced to enter the informal labor force. This applies even to some persons of high education. Third, competitive and cost cutting pressures in the economy have made the informal labor force attractive to both buyers and sellers. Some of these pressures are international or global ones. Finally, constraints and problems of the formal sector such as high taxes, excessive regulations, administrative prohibitions and bureaucratic corruption encourage movement to the informal sector (CEESP 1987).

These same motivations can lead to conflict in some cases. For instance, the cost cutting and competitive factors can pitch street vendors against licensed formal-sector merchants in the same neighborhoods. Government may in the future seize on the magnitude and visibility of parts of the informal sector to impose taxation programs.

The focus of this book is on the world system and globalization. How does the informal labor force relate to these themes? Sassen (1994) and others have pointed out that the informal labor force provides smaller but essential support functions for the larger global enterprises to succeed. Some of the global manufacturing that is growing in Mexico depends on complex supplier chains that are based on small services, commercial exchange, and even some minor products supplied by the informal economy. One example certainly is the international tourism industry. Informal service workers are essential to that industry and many are informal. Informal commerce plays a role as well.

Although the maquiladora industry receives its high tech components and supplies from outside of Mexico, it benefits by the low costs provided by small, informal services and commercial exchanges. The transformation and global "opening" that is occurring in the Mexican economy is driven partly by domestic cost advantages and some of them stem from the informal sector.

Another book theme feature is that as the Mexican economy modernizes and opens up, shocks and crises are occurring, such as for example the peso crisis of 1994. The informal sector provides a "cushion" to absorb some of these shocks, in particular as an alternative source of livelihood for displaced workers, in absence of a well developed government social welfare system.

There is a paucity of studies and a great deal that remains unknown about this major part of the labor force and economy. Most analyses have been relatively unsophisticated and have not explored more subtle nuances of the informal labor sector, definitional problems, and interactions with economic change. More surveys and research studies are needed to help to elucidate the complex factors impacting this sector and to shed more light on the sector's role in the process of Mexican economic transformation.

### Mini Case Study: The Informal Labor Force
### in Ciudad Juárez and El Paso

A book by Kathleen Staudt (1998) covered the informal economies at the U.S.-Mexico border for the cities of Ciudad Juarez and El Paso, Texas. Here, however, we only present a brief summary of it related to the informal labor force. She argues that informal self-employment is a less than ideal household support strategy. She points out that informality offers flexibility but it also bring meager earnings and lacks security. According to her, female workers on both side of the border earn equal amounts and these are comparable to male earnings on the Mexican side but not for males on the U.S side. (In all instances the earning are meager). Since maquiladora workers make less than the poverty wage, she believes that those in the informal labor force are doing as well as those in the formal labor force. Informals maintain a calculated distance from governments. They melt into the background as much as possible. She reports that the informals only feign compliance with rules and regulations but ignore them as much as possible. She notes that they have virtually no voice in policy that affects them. She illustrates that informality in the labor force is part of the everyday lives of most persons on both sides of the border. The families involved pursue multiple income-generating strategies with multiple household workers.

Stoudt's data for Ciudad Juárez suggests that almost thirty percent of the labor force is self-employed and that almost half do not have social security. Income from informal work is essential for survival from many Mexican border households. Street vendors make up a large segment of the informal labor force but used clothing has the major share with home-based women buying in the U.S. and selling in Mexico. Thus, at the border, part of the informal labor force activities involve Mexican women crossing the border into the U.S. to purchase clothing (rope usada), shoes, etc., for which there is a likely market in Mexico. These products are brought back across the border by fayuqueras and then sold from their homes where space has been set aside to display them. Profits are generally good, one successful trip equals one-week wages in a maquiladora. Used clothing stores abound on the U.S. side with home stores located on the Mexican side.

# 13

---

## The Mexican 500

- **Introduction**
- **Mexican Corporations**
  - Number of Corporations
- **Location of the Mexican 500**
  - Concentration by State
  - Concentration in Mexico States and Major Cities
- **Privatization**
- **Mexico's Top Corporations**
- **Foreign Ownership of the 500**
- **Mexican Corporations in Latin America**
- **Conclusions**

## Introduction

This chapter expands work reported by us in *Mexico Megacity* (1997) and *The Mexico Handbook* (1994). Earlier chapters in this volume examined Mexico's place in the world system and quite firmly established that while contemporary Mexico is a semi-periphery nation -- in the middle level of development, earlier analyses placed it in the periphery. Mexico's current international relationships are substantially with core nations. Via international corporations, Mexico now has extensive interaction with a variety of nations, including the U.S., Germany, England, and Asian countries. In addition, several major domestic Mexican enterprises are becoming global by expanding their corporate activities worldwide, including expanding into Latin American. Nevertheless, the United States remains Mexico's primary international partner in multiple ways already shown in earlier chapters. A similar relationship exists for the Mexican 500, i.e. the nations 500 largest enterprises.

In this chapter we focus on the extensive privatization of the Mexican corporate world in some detail since it has influenced the 500. As we noted in earlier chapters, Mexico has undergone vast change in respect to direct foreign investment since 1986. Using the perspective of world systems theory applied within Mexico, this chapter illustrates the concentration of economic activities by state, within state, and within cities. Thus, this chapter reinforces conclusions of earlier chapters of the domination of Mexico City for corporate headquarters and other activities; it is clearly the core economic sphere of influence in Mexico. A similar concentration of the 500 is demonstrated. Privatization and the North America Free Trade Agreement (NAFTA) influenced changes in the Mexican 500 between 1986 and 1997. The extensive relationships alluded to in previous chapters between Mexican and U.S. corporations are examined in this chapter by focusing on the 500s. In addition, since many Mexican 500 enterprises are multinationals, another important feature of this chapter is examining Mexican national corporations that are transnational in character.

Data utilized in examining the Mexican 500 are from a variety of sources, including Mexico's commercial, economic, population and housing censuses for a variety of years, and from publications by Mexican banks. However, the major Mexican source is various years of Expansión; the editors of that journal have been extremely accommodating in allowing access to their information and data. Finally, the *Fortune 500* is used for comparison purposes. In exploring corporations in Mexico note that the U.S. concept of a corporation is roughly equivalent to a S.A.C.V. (Sociedad Anonima Constituida) in Mexico.

In previous chapters we examined Mexican corporations in various sectors. In this chapter focus on Mexican corporations in 1986 and changes that have taken place since that time up through our analysis of 1997. It is anticipated that subsequent analyses will demonstrate the votality of the economic situation in Mexico with the emergence of alliances, mergers, and further penetration of foreign firms into Mexico as well as Mexican firms expanding outside of Mexico.

## Mexican Corporations

The unadjusted corporation value, for Mexico, in thousands of pesos in 1986 is reported on Table 13.1. The total unadjusted corporation value in 1986 was 142.4 billion pesos. Since this was prior to the great wave of privatization in Mexico, many large 'corporations' were still nationalized and hence not included in this table. Table 13.1 also illustrates the total unadjusted corporate value in 1997 after substantial privatization had taken place in Mexico.

**Table 13.1 Unadjusted Corporation Value, 1986 and 1997**

| No. | State | Commercial Corps. | Industrial Corps. | Other Corps. | 1986 Total | Unadj. Corp. Value Per Capita, 1986* | 1997 Total |
|---|---|---|---|---|---|---|---|
| 1 | Aguascalientes | 238,649 | 264,978 | 299,094 | 802,721 | 1,115.40 | 581,374 |
| 2 | Baja California | 1,525,949 | 1,158,171 | 1,668,272 | 4,352,392 | 2,620.60 | 5,694,660 |
| 3 | Baja California Sur | 142,289 | 46,319 | 162,291 | 350,899 | 1,104.30 | 678,661 |
| 4 | Campeche | 127,390 | 99,991 | 215,254 | 442,635 | 827.10 | |
| 5 | Coahuila | 1,377,279 | 4,033,782 | 2,074,153 | 7,485,214 | 3,795.10 | 35,206,414 |
| 6 | Colima | 149,037 | 3,428 | 135,535 | 288,000 | 672.10 | 497,077 |
| 7 | Chiapas | 182,972 | 48,822 | 114,219 | 346,013 | 107.80 | |
| 8 | Chihuahua | 968,057 | 3,168,894 | 1,053,703 | 5,190,654 | 2,125.70 | 11,513,471 |
| 9 | Distrito Federal | 2,003,127 | 178,404 | 8,251,423 | 10,432,954 | 1,266.80 | |
| 10 | Durango | 268,295 | 436,892 | 435,524 | 1,140,711 | 845.40 | 17,816,053 |
| 11 | Guanajuato | 497,430 | 963,289 | 1,105,999 | 2,566,718 | 644.50 | 642,734 |
| 12 | Guerrero | 139,041 | 51,468 | 143,484 | 333,993 | 127.40 | 448,687 |
| 13 | Hidalgo | 237,638 | 141,887 | 200,079 | 579,604 | 306.90 | 2,232,713 |
| 14 | Jalisco | 2,252,671 | 905,449 | 1,405,637 | 4,563,757 | 860.60 | 39,751,071 |
| 15 | Mexico | 2,149,096 | 2,300,684 | 14,738,578 | 19,188,358 | 1,954.80 | 35,394,932 |
| 16 | Michoacan | 162,720 | 144,318 | 434,957 | 741,995 | 209.10 | 274,753 |
| 17 | Morelos | 328,562 | 154,426 | 473,804 | 956,792 | 800.60 | 108,081 |
| 18 | Nayarit | 162,354 | 404,948 | 770,044 | 1,337,346 | 1,621.70 | |
| 19 | Nuevoleon | 3,927,714 | 46,199,435 | 10,862,204 | 60,989,353 | 19,682.00 | 277,277,966 |
| 20 | Oaxaca | 203,815 | 81,013 | 285,285 | 570,113 | 188.80 | 520,745 |
| 21 | Puebla | 837,512 | 1,036,353 | 1,033,155 | 2,907,020 | 704.50 | 32,134,003 |
| 22 | Queretaro | 627,584 | 722,391 | 435,470 | 1,785,445 | 1,698.40 | 2,643,060 |
| 23 | Quintana Roo | 385,131 | 86,711 | 124,521 | 596,363 | 1,209.00 | 253,516 |
| 24 | San Luis Potosi | 654,048 | 127,002 | 1,382,524 | 2,163,574 | 1,080.10 | 3,847,556 |
| 25 | Sinaloa | 632,474 | 551,859 | 1,407,773 | 2,592,106 | 1,176.10 | 3,370,664 |
| 26 | Sonora | 926,089 | 580,291 | 918,571 | 2,424,951 | 1,329.80 | 1,097,929 |
| 27 | Tabasco | 264,045 | 53,098 | 533,792 | 850,935 | 566.60 | |
| 28 | Tamaulipas | 251,491 | 104,262 | 222,519 | 578,272 | 257.10 | 5,428,513 |
| 29 | Tlaxcala | 79,436 | | 26,479 | 105,915 | 139.10 | 1,478,884 |
| 30 | Veracruz | 424,519 | 206,795 | 1,103,542 | 1,734,856 | 278.50 | 11,403,053 |
| 31 | Yucatan | 499,532 | 1,897,953 | 986,881 | 3,384,366 | 2,483.10 | 189,033 |
| 32 | Zacatecas | 144,649 | 41,320 | 422,568 | 608,537 | 476.80 | 381,975 |
| | National Total | 22,770,595 | 66,194,633 | 53,427,334 | 142,392,562 | 1,752.50 | 490,867,578 |

**Table 13.1 Unadjusted Corporation Value, 1986 and 1997 (Continued)**

| | | | | | | |
|---|---|---|---|---|---|---|
| Mean | 711,581 | 2,135,311 | 1,669,604 | 4,449,768 | 1,633.60 | 18,180,281 |
| Median | 356,847 | 206,795 | 503,798 | 1,239,029 | 853.00 | 1,669,604 |
| S.D. | 849,244 | 8,234,488 | 3,290,936 | 10,989,922 | 3,399.10 | 53,259,050.04 |
| C.V. | 119.35 | 385.63 | 197.11 | 246.98 | 208,070.00 | |
| Minimum | 79,436 | 3,428 | 26,479 | 105,915 | 107.80 | 108,081 |
| Maximum | 3,927,714 | 46,199,435 | 14,738,578 | 60,989,353 | 19,682.00 | 277,277,966 |

Definition: Values shown are in thousands of pesos. The ratios are the total value of corporations to the 1990 total population.

Source: INEGI, 1988-1989, Anuario Estadistico, Table IV.7.1.

Note: *Not adjusted. Multiplied by 1000.

As also shown on Table 13.1, there is variation in state by type of corporation – commercial, industrial, or other. The major states for commercial corporations are Nuevo Leon, Mexico, Jalisco, the Federal District and Baja California. They all are centers for major commercial enterprises and markets. The major state with industrial corporation values is Nuevo Leon and it overwhelms the rest of the nation—this single state accounts for 70 percent of industrial corporation value. This reinforces the importance of Monterrey as the headquarters of substantial parts of Mexico's private industry. Coahuila and Chihuahua are in remote second and third place, each having 4-6 percent of the nation's industrial corporation value. The value of "other" corporations, again, is dominated by Nuevo Leon, along with the State of Mexico and the Federal District.

In 1986, the state of Nuevo Leon had a value of corporations per capita far surpassing any other state – 19,682 pesos vs. an average of 1,752 pesos for the nation. In addition, except for Yucatan, the dominance of the northern border region and central part of the country is readily apparent. Map 13.1, illustrates the very low corporation value in the pacific south region. Its total corporation value was only 1.25 billion pesos, under one percent for the total nation! (see Map 13.2)

**Map 13.1**
**Unadjusted**
**Corporation Value in Pesos,**
**Per Capita, 1986**

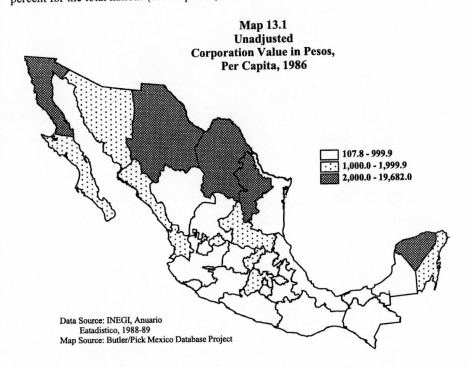

107.8 - 999.9
1,000.0 - 1,999.9
2,000.0 - 19,682.0

Data Source: INEGI, Anuario
Eatadistico, 1988-89
Map Source: Butler/Pick Mexico Database Project

*Number of Corporations*

In 1988, there were 20,634 corporations (S.A.C.V.s) in Mexico. The number of corporations increased greatly, especially in the Federal District, between 1986 and 1988. This may have been the result of the advent of the Salinas Administration and the beginnings of opening the economy. The number of corporations per 1,000 persons in 1986 and 1988 shown on Table 13.2 illustrates that there was large variation among states, as shown by a coefficient of variation of 219 in 1988. In contrast to value of corporations, the Federal District dominated in absolute and per capita number of corporations. Other states with a relatively large ratio of corporations were San Luis Potosi, the Bajas, Nuevo Leon, and Quintana Roo. There were several clearly discernible regional patterns. The border region consistently had a large number of corporations in 1986 (see Map 13.3). The south region had a very small number of corporations per capita, with a total of only 514 corporations. The gulf region also had a low prevalence of corporations per capita. Maps 13.4 and 13.5 show these data in 1993 and 1997.

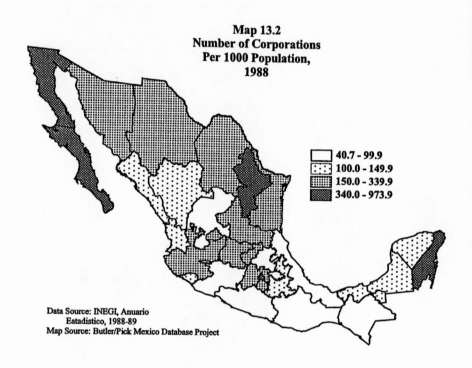

**Map 13.2**
**Number of Corporations**
**Per 1000 Population,**
**1988**

40.7 - 99.9
100.0 - 149.9
150.0 - 339.9
340.0 - 973.9

Data Source: INEGI, Anuario
Eatadistico, 1988-89
Map Source: Butler/Pick Mexico Database Project

## Location of the Mexican 500[1]

This section explores the location of the Mexican 500 in 1986 and 1997 by state, within states, and in Mexico City. During the eleven year period great economic changes took place in Mexico, including opening up of the economy, extensive privatization of nationally owned enterprises, and North American Free Trade Agreement (NAFTA). Accompanying these changes during this era was extensive concentration of the major corporations in Mexico located in the Federal District and within several municipios within the Federal District.

### Concentration by State

Data for 1986 demonstrate that the number of total corporations and value of corporations are distinctly different measures. In 1986, the largest number of major corporations were located in the Federal District (see Map 13.5). On the other hand, the

---

[1] For more extensive discussion of the Mexican 500 in 1986 see Pick and Butler (1994) and for the Mexican 500 in 1993 see Pick and Butler (1997).

## Table 13.2 Number of Corporations, per 1,000 Population, 1988 and 1996

| | | 1988 | | 1996 | |
|---|---|---|---|---|---|
| No. | State | Number of Corporations | Number of Corporations Per 1,000 Persons | Number of Corporations | Number of Corporations Per 1,000 Persons |
| 1 | Aguascalientes | 184 | 0.2557 | 218 | 0.3029 |
| 2 | Baja California | 734 | 0.4419 | 764 | 0.4600 |
| 3 | Baja California Sur | 125 | 0.3934 | 92 | 0.2895 |
| 4 | Campeche | 65 | 0.1215 | 42 | 0.0785 |
| 5 | Coahuila | 452 | 0.2292 | 448 | 0.2271 |
| 6 | Colima | 52 | 0.1214 | 85 | 0.1984 |
| 7 | Chiapas | 140 | 0.0436 | 26 | 0.0081 |
| 8 | Chihuahua | 478 | 0.1958 | 451 | 0.1847 |
| 9 | Distrito Federal | 8,021 | 0.9739 | 1,591 | 0.1932 |
| 10 | Durango | 152 | 0.1126 | 181 | 0.1341 |
| 11 | Guanajuato | 664 | 0.1667 | 696 | 0.1748 |
| 12 | Guerrero | 198 | 0.0756 | 123 | 0.0469 |
| 13 | Hidalgo | 146 | 0.0773 | 94 | 0.0498 |
| 14 | Jalisco | 1,590 | 0.2998 | 746 | 0.1407 |
| 15 | Mexico | 1,611 | 0.1641 | 1,218 | 0.1241 |
| 16 | Michoacan | 215 | 0.0606 | 130 | 0.0366 |
| 17 | Morelos | 198 | 0.1657 | 166 | 0.1389 |
| 18 | Nayarit | 84 | 0.1019 | 82 | 0.0994 |
| 19 | Nuevoleon | 1,465 | 0.4728 | 1,264 | 0.4079 |
| 20 | Oaxaca | 176 | 0.0583 | 112 | 0.0371 |
| 21 | Puebla | 607 | 0.1471 | 583 | 0.1413 |
| 22 | Queretaro | 275 | 0.2616 | 240 | 0.2283 |
| 23 | Quintana Roo | 323 | 0.6548 | - | 0.1014 |
| 24 | San Luis Potosi | 338 | 0.1687 | 243 | 0.1213 |
| 25 | Sinaloa | 288 | 0.1307 | 289 | 0.1311 |
| 26 | Sonora | 488 | 0.2676 | 481 | 0.2638 |
| 27 | Tabasco | 159 | 0.1059 | 162 | 0.1079 |
| 28 | Tamaulipas | 518 | 0.2303 | 61 | 0.0271 |
| 29 | Tlaxcala | 51 | 0.0670 | 40 | 0.0525 |
| 30 | Veracruz | 585 | 0.0939 | 216 | 0.0347 |
| 31 | Yucatan | 200 | 0.1467 | 310 | 0.2274 |
| 32 | Zacatecas | 52 | 0.0407 | 73 | 0.0572 |
| | National Total | 20,634 | 6.8468 | 11,227 | 4.8267 |
| | | | | | |
| | Mean | 645 | 0.2140 | 352.00 | 0.1508 |
| | Median | 245 | 0.1556 | 199.00 | 0.1326 |
| | S.D. | 1,410 | 0.1964 | 394.00 | 0.1092 |
| | C.V. | 219 | 91.78 | 112.00 | 72.39 |
| | Minimum | 51 | 0.0407 | 26.00 | 0.0081 |
| | Maximum | 8,021 | 0.9739 | 1,591.00 | 0.4600 |

Definition: The number of corporations per 1,000 population is the number of corporations to the
total population 1990 multiplied by 1,000.

Source: INEGI, 1988-1989, Anuario Estadistico, Table IV.7.1.

major value of corporations was highest in Nuevo Leon and especially in Monterrey. In 1997, the Federal District and Nuevo Leon far surpassed the sum of sales by major corporations in all other jurisdictions. The other important states in number of corporations in 1988 and 1996 were Jalisco, State of Mexico, Coahuila, Puebla, and Guanajuato (see Table 13.2).

**Map 13.3**
**Mexico's 500 Major Corporations, 1986**

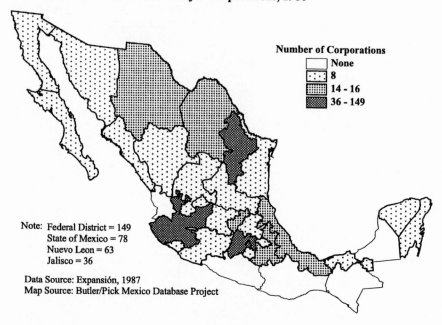

**Number of Corporations**
None
8
14 - 16
36 - 149

Note:  Federal District = 149
      State of Mexico = 78
      Nuevo Leon = 63
      Jalisco = 36

Data Source: Expansión, 1987
Map Source: Butler/Pick Mexico Database Project

**Map 13.4**
**Mexico's 500 Major**
**Corporations, 1993**

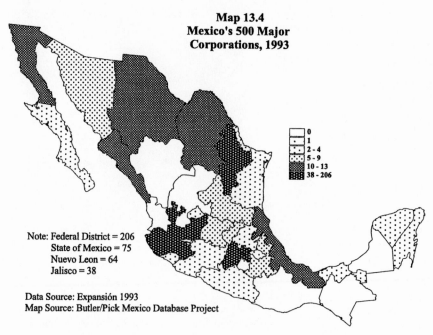

0
1
2 - 4
5 - 9
10 - 13
38 - 206

Note: Federal District = 206
     State of Mexico = 75
     Nuevo Leon = 64
     Jalisco = 38

Data Source: Expansión 1993
Map Source: Butler/Pick Mexico Database Project

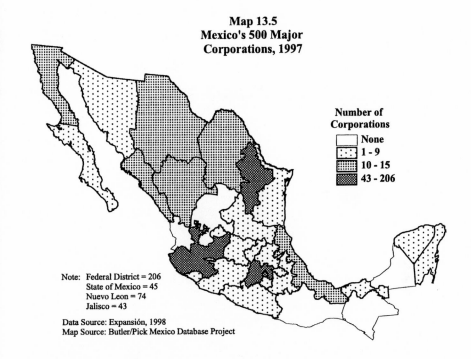

**Map 13.5**
**Mexico's 500 Major**
**Corporations, 1997**

Number of
Corporations
☐ None
░ 1 - 9
▦ 10 - 15
▨ 43 - 206

Note:  Federal District = 206
       State of Mexico = 45
       Nuevo Leon = 74
       Jalisco = 43

Data Source: Expansión, 1998
Map Source: Butler/Pick Mexico Database Project

Concentration of the Mexican 500 by state and the importance of Mexico City is illustrated by concentration of enterprises in the city in 1986; in fact, Mexico City has historically been the most important place in Mexico, well before the development of modern corporations. Thus, Table 13.3 and Map13.3 illustrate that in 1986 Mexico's largest corporations were not equally distributed throughout Mexico (*Expanión* 1987). Clearly, the Federal District with 149 headquarters dominated and equaled the total number in the State of Mexico (78) and Nuevo Leon (63), which totaled 141. Jalisco followed with 36 corporate headquarters.   There was a substantial drop in number with Chihuahua, Puebla, Queretaro, Coahuila, and Veracruz having a number varying from 14 and 15.  A few states (see Table 13.3) had between one and ten, while five states had no headquarters.  As shown on Map 13.3, four of these five states were located in the far South of Mexico,

Dramatic changes in location by state took place between 1986 and 1997. Table 13.3 presents data for 1986 and 1997.  However it should be specifically noted that the major changes in concentration of Mexican 500 corporations by state took place by 1993 (see Pick and Butler 1997: pp. 327 ff.). The most dramatic change was an increase in the Federal District from 149 major enterprises in 1986 to 206 in 1993, the same number as in 1997. Map 13.4 and 13.5 show that while the number in the Federal District remained the same between 1993 and 1997, there was a substantial reduction in the number of major corporations in the State of Mexico from 78 in 1986 to 45 in 1997. There was a slight increase in number of 500s in Nuevo Leon and Jalisco.  A major change took place between 1986 and 1997 with the state of Durango by then containing 15 of the 500.  Four of the states in 1986 that had no 500 corporations still did not in 1997; however, Guerrero had none in 1986 but had two in 1993.

We have noted previously that the Salinas Administration promulgated the 100 cities plan, which had as a goal decentralizing the population and economy from the over-concentrated Mexico City to medium sized cities throughout the nation. This plan intended to attract private corporations to medium sized cities. That plan failed during the early 1990s and instead of de-concentration there has been continued population and economic magnification in certain states and Mexico City.

Table 13.3 Location of Mexico's 500 Major Corporations, 1986 and 1997

| | Number of Corporations | |
|---|---|---|
| Location | 1986 | 1997 |
| Distrito Federal | 149 | 206 |
| State of Mexico | 78 | 45 |
| Nuevo Leon | 63 | 74 |
| Jalisco | 36 | 43 |
| | | |
| Chihuahua | 14-16 | 11 |
| Puebla | 14-16 | 9 |
| Queretaro | 14-16 | 5 |
| Coahuila | 14-16 | 11 |
| Veracruz | 14-16 | 13 |
| | | |
| Aguascalientes | 1-10 | 2 |
| Baja California | 1-10 | 12 |
| Baja California Sur | 1-10 | 2 |
| Colima | 1-10 | 3 |
| Durange | 1-10 | 15 |
| Guanajuato | 1-10 | 5 |
| Hidalgo | 1-10 | 2 |
| Michoacan | 1-10 | 2 |
| Morelos | 1-10 | 1 |
| Quintana Roo | 1-10 | 2 |
| San Luis Potosi | 1-10 | 6 |
| Sinaloa | 1-10 | 10 |
| Sonora | 1-10 | 5 |
| Tabasco | 1-10 | 4 |
| Tamaulipas | 1-10 | 4 |
| Tlaxcala | 1-10 | 4 |
| Yucatan | 1-10 | 2 |
| Zacatecas | 1-10 | 0 |
| | | |
| Campeche | 0 | 0 |
| Chiapas | 0 | 0 |
| Guerrero | 0 | 2 |
| Nayarit | 0 | 0 |
| Oaxaca | 0 | 0 |

Definition: Number and location of 500 Major Corporations found within primary
areas of Mexico City, Mexico State, Nuevo Leon, Jalisco, and three groups of the
remaining states.
Source: Expansión, 1987 and 1998.

## Concentration in Mexican States and Major Cities[2]

In 1986, there was further concentration within 108 municipios, with seven of them containing 28 percent of the total number of enterprises. In 1986, Mexico City proper

---

[2]  For a more extensive discussion and data on Mexico City, see Pick and Butler 1997.

contained 29.8 percent of them and the State of Mexico municipios surrounding the Federal District contained 15.5 percent; thus 45.4 percent of the total located in Mexico City. Of these 149 of the 500 were in the Federal District, virtually all of them were located in two delegations -- Miguel Hidalgo and Cuauhtemoc. In the State of Mexico, 42 of the enterprises were located in two municipios -- Ecatepec and Tlalnepantla, both immediately adjacent to the Federal District. In Nuevo Leon, 38 of 63 corporations were located in Monterrey and 12 were located in the municipio of San Nicolas de los Garza. In Jalisco, 22 of 36 enterprises were located in Guadalajara. In the states of Puebla and Queretaro, all top 500 were located in the two major cities. These several cities, then, contained 65 percent of the total major enterprises. Thus, the Mexican 500 in 1986 was located in a few states, within these states primarily in major cities, and in the major cities in a few concentrated districts (see Butler and Pick 1990; Pick and Butler 1998).

The concentration that existed in Mexico City in 1986 continued through 1993. Forty-one percent (206/500) of the major corporations were headquartered in Mexico City in 1993 and 21 percent (105/500) of them were located in the same two delegations of Cuauhtemoc and Miguel Hidalgo as they were in 1986. Sales and assets of the major corporations also were concentrated in Cuauhtemoc and Miguel Hidalgo.

Such concentration of major enterprises continued and was even more apparent in 1997, especially within the same districts in Mexico City.

## Privatization

One of the major changes in the Mexican economy over the past decade has been an emphasis on privatization. In 1986, for example, 154 of the Mexican 500 were state owned enterprises, ranging from food products, (N = 8), commercial corporations (N = 8), production of metal products (N = 5), and auto parts (N = 4). Other state owned endeavors included petrochemicals, minerals, and transportation-related industries. Of course, the major state owned enterprise was Pemex discussed earlier as a case study and Exportadora de Sal (ESSA), a mini-case study; both of these enterprises remain as state-owned. As shown on Table 13.4, by 1993, only six Mexican 500 were state owned; three of these state owned entities were state owned in 1986 -- Pemex (No. 1 at both dates); an enterprise exporting salt from Baja California, Sur (ESSA, No. 184); and a corporation transporting salt from Baja California Sur's ESSA (No. 409). Three new state owned endeavors not listed in 1986 were listed in the 1993 major 500 -- the Postal Service (No. 80); the production and importing of paper (No. 91); and a group concerned with hotels (No. 211).[3]

During the period of 1986 (see Figure 13.1 and 13.2) to 1993, private ownership increased from 73.1 percent in 1986 to 77.8 percent in 1993. Foreign ownership increased from 17.2 percent in 1986 to 20.9 percent in 1993. All of these increases were a result of a decline in state owned enterprises. In 1997, the distribution remained almost exactly the same as in 1993. The changes that took place in privatization were primarily between 1986 and 1993. Thus, stasis in ownership remained between 1993 and 1997. Six or seven enterprises were state owned in 1997.[4] Of the state owned in 1997, four of them also were state owned in 1993 -- Pemex (No. 1), production and importing paper (from #91 in 1993 to #122 in 1997), exporting salt (#184 in 1993 and #218 in 1997), and transporting salt (#409 in 1993 and #453 in 1997). The other state owned endeavors in 1997 500 were Pan

---

[3] For a full listing of the 500 in 1986 and 1993 *Expansión* 1987 and 1997).
[4] There is a slight discrepancy in data as presented on p. 335 in *Expansión* reporting six state owned enterprises while the actual listing of the 500 indicates that seven are state owned.

**Table 13.4 Mexican State Owned '500' Enterprises in 1986, 1993, and 1997**

| Firm | 1986 Position | Principal Activity | 1993 | 1997 |
|------|---------------|--------------------|------|------|
| Petroleos Mexicanos | 1 | Petroleum | | |
| Telefonos de Mexico | 4 | Communications | | |
| Altos Hornos de Mexico | 6 | Iron and Steel | | |
| CIA. Mexicana de Aviacion | 9 | Transport | | |
| Fertilizantes Mexicanos | 15 | Fertilizer | | |
| Aseguradora Mexicana | 19 | Financial Services | | |
| Siderurgica L. Cardenas Las Truchas | 21 | Iron and Steel | | |
| Compania Mindera de Cananca | 32 | Mining | | |
| Tereftalatos Mexicanos | 37 | Petrochemical | | |
| Minera Carbonifera Rio Escondido | 38 | Mining | | |
| Hules Mexicanos | 60 | Petrochemical | | |
| Distribuidora Conasupo Metropoli | 86 | Rubber | | |
| Exportadora de Sal | 99 | Mining | | |
| Constructosora Nal. De Carros de Ferpo | 100 | Transportation Equipment | 184 | 208 |
| Seruicio Pan Americana de Proteccion y Subs | 110 | | | |
| Rassini | 110 | Auto Parts | | |
| Industrias Conasupo Monterrey | 111 | Food | | |
| Conscorcio Minero B. Juarez P. Color | 113 | Mining | | |
| Telefonos del Noroeste | 114 | Communications | | |
| Industrias Conasupo Gomez Palacio | 119 | Food | | |
| Industrias Conasupo Tultitlan | 120 | Food | | |
| Tetraetilo de Mexico | 128 | Petrochemical | | |
| Motores Perkins | 141 | Auto Parts | | |
| Petroquimica Cosoleacaque | 157 | | | |
| Alimentos Blanceados de Mexico | 158 | Food | | |
| Algodonera Comercial Mexicana | 160 | Commerce | | |
| Industrias Conasupo Puebla | 167 | Food | | |
| Grupo Contelmex | 174 | Constraction | | |
| Industrias Conasupo Co. Obregon | 175 | Food | | |
| Arrendadora Internacional | 183 | Financial Services | | |
| Turboeactores | 207 | Professional Services | | |
| Dina Rockwell Nacional | 259 | Auto Parts | | |
| Industrias Conasupo Mexicali | 264 | Food | | |
| Caompania Operadora De. Est. de Serv. | 268 | Commerce | | |
| Envases Passini | 273 | Metal Production | | |
| Moto Diesel Mexicana | 320 | Auto Parts | | |
| Procesadora de Aceros Rassini | 323 | Metal Production | | |
| Tornillos Rassini | 324 | Metal Production | | |
| Torres Mexicanas | 335 | Metal Production | | |
| Prograsa | 356 | Printing/Publishing | | |
| Compania Mexicana de Exploraciones | 373 | Professional Services | | |
| Industria Conasupo Nvo. Laredo | 381 | Food | | |
| Acwros Rassini | 411 | Iron and Steel | | |
| Transportes Centrales | 417 | Transport | | |
| Instalacions Inmobiliros Fortudstn | 421 | | | |
| Estructuras de Acero | 436 | Metal Production | | |
| Transportadora de Sal | 474 | Transport | | 453 |
| Servicio Postal Mexicano | | Postal Service | | |
| Producto y Importado de Papel | | Paper | | 122 |
| Grupo Hotelero Brisas | | Hotels | | |
| Total | N = 64 | | N = 6 | N = 7 |

Source: Expansión, 1987, 1994, and 1997.

**Figure 13.1**
**Ownership of Enterprises: Mexico's 500, 1986**

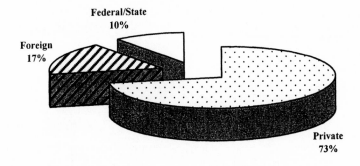

Source: Expansión, August 17, 1987.

**Figure 13.2 Ownership of Enterprises: Mexico's 500, 1997**

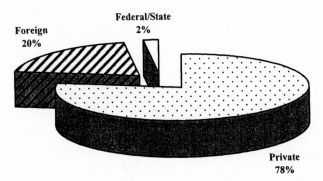

Source: Expansión, August 12, 1998.

American services and protection (#110), Petrochemicals (#157), and #421 -- installations for industry.

## Mexico's Top Corporations

Table 13.5 reports the principal activities of the 500 major Mexican enterprises in 1986 and 1997. There were increases in the number and percentages of major corporations involved in food/beverages, consumer products, and transportation. Declines were noted for mineral/metals, commercial activities, and financial/professional. The number and percentage of major corporations involved in oil/chemicals, construction, and communications/electrical remained virtually the same. At each year there were a number of enterprises that remained outside of this classification scheme.

Table 13.6 illustrates the top ten corporations in 1997 and 1998. The top two corporations remained the same -- Petroleos Mexicanos and Telefonos de Mexico. The next three in 1997 were U.S. automobile companies -- General Motors, Chrysler, and Ford, respectively. General Motors was 4th in 1993 and Chrysler was 5th. Ford was 3[th] that year. Newcomers to the 1997 list were Alfa y Subs, Cemex, Grupo Carso, and Volkswagen. Dropping out were Gigante, Grupo Modelo, Controlodora Comercial Mexicana, Grupo Industrial Bimbo, and Nestle.

**Table 13.5 The Principal Activities of the 500 Major Mexican Enterprises in 1986 and 1997**

| | 1986 | | 1997 | |
|---|---|---|---|---|
| *Principal Activity* | *Number* | *Percent* | *Number* | *Percent* |
| Minerals/Metals | 78 | 18.2 | 56 | 11.8 |
| Consumer Products | 61 | 14.2 | 94 | 19.8 |
| Food/Beverages | 61 | 14.2 | 86 | 18.1 |
| Commercial | 60 | 14.0 | 42 | 8.8 |
| Oil/Chemicals | 57 | 13.3 | 64 | 13.5 |
| Transportation | 41 | 9.6 | 69 | 14.5 |
| Construction | 25 | 5.8 | 28 | 5.9 |
| Financial/Professional | 24 | 5.6 | 14 | 2.9 |
| Comm./Electrical | 22 | 5.1 | 23 | 4.8 |
| Totals | 429* | 100.0 | 476* | 100.0 |

* The remainder of the 500 in both years did not fit any of these categories.
Source: Expansión, 1987 and 1998.
Note: These figures and percents were calculated by the authors.

The obvious dominant emphasis in 1997 was shown by five of the top ten being automobile and automobile parts related corporations; three of these automobile corporations were U.S. companies – General Motors, Chrysler, and Ford; one was a Mexican firm and one was a German firm. General Motors and Ford remained in the top ten also in 1998 (see Table 13.6). The main changes in 1998 compared to 1997 were the merge of Chrysler into Daimler Chrysler and the high rank of Volkswagen.

When examining enterprises in Mexico one must also be aware of major conglomerates or groups (Grupos). For example, Cemex was used as a case study in an earlier chapter. It consists of a number of companies, one of which is located in the U.S. (Sunbelt Ent.). Similarly, Pulsar was used as an example of a major corporation that is a conglomerate.

### Foreign Ownership of Mexican 500 Corporations

Mexico's major corporations have substantial foreign ownership. Table 13.7 shows the position of foreign owned 500 enterprises in 1986 and 1993. Table 13.8 lists top ten corporations in 1997, with their position and country origin of capital. In 1997, 130 of the top 500 were foreign owned – 26 percent. Of these, 92 or 18.4 percent had U.S. foreign capital and 6.2 percent had European capital. Of the foreign owned, the remaining had capital from a variety of counties including Japan (3), with Canada, Philipines, Chile, and Virgin Islands one each. Of the 130 foreign owned, 70.8 percent (92/130) had U.S. origin of capital and 23.8 percent was of European origin, most prominently from Germany.

Half of the top 50 enterprises in 1997 had foreign capital; of these, 22 of the 25 were U.S. corporations, and one German, Swiss, and Canadian, respectively. Figure 13.3 shows the origin of capital in 1986 and Figure 13.4 illustrates origin of capital in 1997. The major change noted is that Mexican capital origin increased from 62.5 percent in 1986 to 74 percent in 1997. The U.S. origin of capital increased during this time period from 23 to 26 percent. European origin of capital decreased as it did from all other countries.

Mergers and acquisition developments also influence rankings from year to year. As an example, Chrysler merged with Daimler of Germany and this corporation was ranked #4 in Mexico in 1998. Empresa La Moderna also purchased companies both in the U.S. and Argentina. As another example, Cifra merged with Walmart and immediately moved into

### Table 13.6 Expansión 500 Top Ten Mexican Companies, 1997

| Rank | Firm | Sales |
|------|------|-------|
| 1 | Pemex | 33,232 |
| 2 | Telmex | 7,643 |
| 3 | General Motors de Mexico | 7,250 |
| 4 | Chrysler de Mexico | 6,227 |
| 5 | Ford de Mexico | 4,919 |
| 6 | Cifra y Subs | 4,142 |
| 7 | Alfa y Subs | 4,111 |
| 8 | Cemex y Sub | 3,848 |
| 9 | Grupo Carso | 3,767 |
| 10 | Volkswagen de Mexico | 3,483 |

### Expansión 500 Top Ten Mexican Companies, 1998

| Rank | Firm | Sales |
|------|------|-------|
| 1 | Pemex | 26,050 |
| 2 | Telmex | 7,931 |
| 3 | General Motors de Mexico | 6,912 |
| 4 | Daimler Chrysler de Mexico | 5,720 |
| 5 | Cifra/Walmart y Subs | 5,218 |
| 6 | Volkswagen de Mexico | 4,563 |
| 7 | Cemex | 4,331 |
| 8 | Ford de Mexico | 3,900 |
| 9 | Alfa y Subs | 3,654 |
| 10 | Grupo Carso | 3,629 |

Source: Expansión, 1997 and 1998.

number 5 position in the 500 as opposed to being number 6 in 1997 (see Table 13.9 for overlaps). Also, Cemex and Volkswagen moved up, while Ford, Alfa, and Grupo Carso moved down.

Other factors influencing position in the 500 are joint ventures and alliances. Among the more recent prominent relationships between Mexico and U.S. corporations are Aeromexico and Delta Airlines; Mexicana and United Airlines; Banamex and CoBank; Modelo and Barton Beers Ltd.; Bulete with companies from the U.S., France, Canada, and UK; Casa Autrey with Twentieth Century Fox; Tablex with Miller Brewing; Enova with Proxima Gas; Televisa and NBC; Penóles and Newmont Gold; Minera Tayahua and Kennecot Exploration; Vitra with Unimin Corp.; Alpek with DuPont; Alfa and Celanese/Hoescht (Germany); Alfa with AT&T; Alestra and World Partners, among others. These relationships cover many sectors from food, glass, banking, and communications. Each of these mergers and alliances undoubtedly will have subsequent impact upon 500 rankings.

Table 13.7  Foreign Owned '500' Enterprises in 1986 and 1993

| Companies | 1986 Position | Descriptions | 1993 Position |
|---|---|---|---|
| Chrysler de Mexico | 2 | Automobiles | 5 |
| General Motors | 3 | Automobiles | 4 |
| Ford Motor | 5 | Automobiles | * |
| Volkswagen | 8 | Automobiles | * |
| IBM | 14 | Electronics | 14 |
| Compania Nestle | 18 | Food | 10 |
| American Express | 22 | Financial Services | 28 |
| Teleindustria Ericcson | 33 | Electronic Equipment | 48 |
| Industrias Fogografica | 39 | Other Manuf. | 77 |
| Xerox Mexicana | 42 | Commerce | 59 |
| Anderson Clayton | 43 | Food | 50 |
| Carton Papel de Mexico | 46 | Paper and Cellulose | |
| Kodak Mexicana | 48 | Commerce | 69 |
| Barcardi y CIA | 56 | Beverages | |
| Renault Industrias | 58 | Auto Parts | |
| Quimica Hoechst de Mexico | 63 | Chemicals | 92 |
| Bayer de Mexico | 66 | Chemicals | 63 |
| Hewlett Packard | 71 | Electronics | 47 |
| BASF Mexicana | 81 | Chemicals | 196 |
| ICI de Mexico | 87 | Chemicals | * |
| Unisys de Mexico | 90 | Commerce | |
| Uniroyal | 91 | Rubber | |
| General Foods de Mexico | 94 | Food | |
| Siements | 122 | Electronic Equipment | 71 |
| Mobil | 124 | Petrochemical | |
| Mem-Mex | 133 | Electronics | |
| Black and Decker | 143 | Electronic Equipment | |
| Componentes Mecanicos de Matamoros | 148 | Auto Parts | |
| Square D de Mexico | 149 | Machinery | 157 |
| Singer Mexicana | 159 | Machinery | 111 |
| Olympia de Mexico | 162 | Machinery | 217 |
| Sandoz | 163 | Pharmaceuticals | 167 |
| RIMR | 166 | Auto Parts | |
| AGA de Mexico | 168 | Chemicals | * |
| Grolier | 170 | Commerce | |
| Nichimen de Mexico | 201 | Commerce | |
| Fermentaciones Mexicanas | 215 | Chemicals | |
| SKF Mexicana | 219 | Commerce | |
| Upjohn | 222 | Pharmaceuticals | |
| Materias Primas | 224 | Commerce | |
| Grupo Camilar | 241 | Commerce | |
| Becton Dickinson | 243 | Pharmaceuticals | 185 |
| Berol | 247 | Pencils | 222 |
| Rio Bravo Electricos | 248 | Auto Parts | |
| Prove-Quin | 253 | Commerce | |
| Industrias Mexicanas Unisys | 255 | Electronics | |
| Editorical Cumbre | 269 | Printing/Publishing | |
| American Ref. Products | 270 | Electronic Equipment | 164 |
| Inmont de Mexico | 281 | Chemicals | |
| Sperry | 282 | Commerce | |
| Nashua de Mexico | 285 | Commerce | |
| Sandvix | 290 | Metal Production | |
| Federal Pacific Electric | 296 | Electronic Equipment | 256 |
| Laboratorios y Agencies Unidas | 300 | Food | 218 |
| NCR Industrial | 301 | Electronics | 174 |
| Deltronicos de Matamoros | 309 | Auto Parts | |
| Sonoce de Mexico | 310 | Paper and Cellulose | |
| Byron Jackson | 314 | Non Electronic Equipment | |

**Table 13.7  Foreign Owned '500' Enterprises in 1986 and 1993 (Continued)**

| | | | |
|---|---|---|---|
| Eds de Mexico | 317 | Professional Services | |
| Cajas Corrugadas | 318 | Paper and Cellulose | |
| SAF de Mexico | 326 | Food | * |
| Durr de Mexico | 328 | Non Electronic Equipment | * |
| Campbell's | 332 | Food | |
| Delredo | 354 | Auto Parts | |
| Quimica Sumex | 358 | Chemicals | 384 |
| Conductores y Componentes | 361 | Auto Parts | |
| Recold | 376 | Non Electronic Equipment | |
| Gestetner | 379 | Commerce | |
| Cableados de Juarez | 382 | Auto Parts | |
| Productos Darex | 401 | Chemicals | |
| Sistemas Elec. Y Commutadores | 429 | Auto Parts | 290 |
| G.F.T. de Mexico | 438 | Control Systems | |
| Delnosa | 445 | Auto Parts | |
| Degussa | 446 | Chemicals | 242 |
| Garlock | 452 | Minerals | |
| Louis Mulas Sucs | 453 | Commerce | |
| Burroughs Wellcome | 456 | Pharmaceuticals | |
| Cajas y Empaques | 459 | Paper and Cellulose | |
| Sinalopasta | 464 | Food | |
| A.C. Nielson Co. | 477 | Professional Services | |
| Quimica Knoll | 484 | Pharmaceuticals | 377 |
| Cutler-Hammer | 495 | Electronic Equipment | |
| Ediciones Larousse | 496 | Printing/Publishing | 320 |
| Firsche Dodge y Olcott | 497 | Chemicals | |

Source: Expansión, 1987, 1994, and 1998.
Note: Blank indicates not listed in the 500.
* Indicates may not have

Most major corporations are concentrated in Mexico City in the Cuauhtemoc and Miguel Hidalgo delegations and even more massed there are foreign owned entities. In 1993, the top ten corporations accounted for 49 percent of revenues and 51 percent of assets the Mexican 500. This disproportion at the top exceeds that of other North American countries. For example, the ratio of sales of the nation's top 25 corporations to the 500 is much higher in Mexico (68 percent) than in the United States (42 percent) or Canada (38 percent) (Expansión 1995). The converging of top corporations in the core of the Federal District also is associated with a disproportionate massing of services, especially high-end services and commerce. The inescapable conclusion is that there is a high concentration of major corporations and that this concentration will continue unabated well into the future. Another conclusion that can be drawn from this concentration of both domestic and foreign corporations into a small area within Mexico City is that it is being impacted by the globalization of the Mexican economy.

## Mexican Corporations in Latin America

The number one enterprise in Mexico is Pemex and it was the second rated corporation in Latin America in 1996. Telmex, General Motors, and Chrysler of Mexico also were in the top ten enterprises in Latin America in 1996. Ford was ranked 18th and Cemex number 24. Among banks, Bancomer, Banamex, and Serfin were ranked 3, 4, and 5 in Latin America in 1996. In 1996, six of the twelve largest multinationals in Latin America were Mexican, with Cemex being the leader ranked at number 6, with the others primarily concerned with food products.

**Figure 13.3**
**Origin of Capital: Mexico's 500 Major Enterprises, 1986**

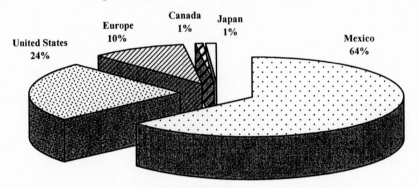

Source: Expansión, August 17, 1987.

**Figure 13.4**
**Origin of Capital: Mexico's 500 Major Enterprises, 1997**

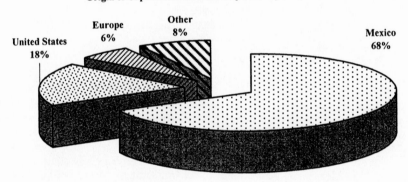

Source: Expansión, August 12, 1998.

## Conclusions

The top 500 Mexican corporations in 1986, 1993, and 1997 were influenced by substantial policy changes in Mexico. There has been extensive privatization of major government owned enterprises. On the other hand, origin of capital by the state has increased substantially for these entities giving the appearance of replacement of state-owned enterprises with some of them receiving state-subsidies. In essence this may mean the release of government control of them but with government funds allowing them to continue. If this conclusion has any weight, policy changes have led to a whole host of other issues about control and profits, foreign versus domestic ownership, and others

## Table 13.8 Mexico's Top Ten Corporations, 1993 and 1997

### 1993

| No. | Name | Business | Revenues* | Assets* | Capital Composition** | Origin of Foreign Capital | State/Municipio |
|---|---|---|---|---|---|---|---|
| 1 | Petroleos Mexicanos | Petroleum and Gas | 82,790 | 153,102 | State (100) | none | DF/Miguel Hidalgo |
| 2 | Telefonos de Mexico | Communications | 24,602 | 52,902 | ND | U.S. | DF/Cuauhtemoc |
| 3 | Cifra y Subsidiarias | Auto Service/Sales | 14,231 | 10,204 | Private (100) | none | DF/Cuajimalpa |
| 4 | General Motors de Mexico | Auto | 13,409 | 8,610 | Foreign (100) | U.S. | DF/Miguel Hidalgo |
| 5 | Chysler de Mexico | Auto | 11,153 | 4,544 | Foreign (100) | U.S. | DF/Miguel Hidalgo |
| 6 | Gigante | Auto Service/Sales | 7,944 | 5,231 | Private (51), Foreign (49) | ND | DF/Miguel Hidalgo |
| 7 | Controlodora Comercial Mexicana | Cement | 7,160 | 4,583 | Private (51), Foreign (49) | ND | DF/Cuauhtemoc |
| 8 | Grupo Modelo | Beverage | 5,106 | 8,234 | Private (99.98) | ND | DF/Miguel Hidalgo |
| 9 | Grupo Industrial Bimbo | Food | 5,097 | 4,148 | Private (100) | none | DF/Alvaro Obergon |
| 10 | Compania Nestle | Food | 4,205 | 2,762 | Foreign (100) | Switzerland | DF/Miguel Hidalgo |
| | Total - Top 10 | | 175,697 | 254,320 | | | |
| | Top 10 - Percent of Total | | 49 | | | | |

### 1997

| No. | Name | Business | Revenues* | Assets* | Capital Composition** | Origin of Foreign Capital | State/Municipio |
|---|---|---|---|---|---|---|---|
| 1 | Petroleos Mexicanos | Petroleum and Gas | 264,030 | | State (100) | U.S. | DF/ |
| 2 | Telefonos de Mexico | Communications | 60,724 | | Foreign (100) | U.S. | DF/ |
| 3 | General Motors de Mexico | Auto | 57,601 | | Foreign (100) | U.S. | DF/ |
| 4 | Chysler de Mexico | Auto | 49,474 | | Foreign (100) | U.S. | DF/ |
| 5 | Ford de Mexico | Auto | 39,080 | | Foreign (100) | U.S. | DF/ |
| 6 | Cifra y Subsidiarias | Auto Service/Sales | 32,909 | | Private (51), Foreign (49) | U.S. | DF/ |
| 7 | Alfa y Sub | Various | 32,659 | | Private (100) | Nati | Garze Garcia, NL |
| 8 | Cemex y Sub | Cement | 30,573 | | Private (100) | Nati | Monterrey, NL |
| 9 | Grupo Largo | Various | 29,931 | | Private (100) | Nati | DF/ |
| 10 | Volkswagen de Mexico | Auto | 27,669 | | Foreign (100) | Germany | Puebla, Pue |

Note: Cifra became Cifra/Walmart in 1998.
* in millions of 1993 new pesos.
** in millions of 1997 new pesos.
*** the number in parentheses is the percent of ownership.
ND = not determined.
Source: Expansión.

**Table 13.9 Overlaps in Lists of Largest U.S. and**
**Mexico Firms, 1997**

| *Fortune 500 Top Ten U.S. Companies, 1997* | | |
|---|---|---|
| *Rank* | *Firm* | *Sales\*\** |
| 1 | *General Motors* | 178,174 |
| 2 | *Ford* | 153,627 |
| 3 | Exxon | 122,379 |
| 4 | Wal-Mart\* | 119,299 |
| 5 | General Electric | 90,840 |
| 6 | IBM | 78,508 |
| 7 | *Chrysler* | 61,147 |
| 8 | Mobil | 59,978 |
| 9 | Philip Morris | 56,114 |
| 10 | AT&T | 53,261 |

| *Fortune 500 Top Ten U.S. Companies, 1998* | | |
|---|---|---|
| *Rank* | *Firm* | *Sales\*\** |
| 1 | *General Motors* | 161,315 |
| 2 | *Ford* | 144,416 |
| 3 | *Wal-Mart\** | 139,208 |
| 4 | Exxon | 100,697 |
| 5 | General Electric | 100,469 |
| 6 | IBM | 81,667 |
| 7 | Citigroup\* | 76,431 |
| 8 | Philip Morris | 57,813 |
| 9 | Boeing | 56,154 |
| 10 | AT&T | 53,588 |

Note: Companies in italics are overlapped in the U.S. and Mexico Top Ten Companies.
\* Cifra became Clifra/Walmart in 1998.
\*\* In U.S. dollars
Source: Expansión, 1998 and 1999.

Despite some efforts by national administrations to decentralize the population and economic activities, in fact there has been increased massing of major corporations in Mexico City and in particular small areas within the city. Our analysis shows that Mexico City is attracting in great numbers the major companies doing business in the nation, domestic and especially foreign enterprises. Thus, in addition to the centralized government decision making, corporate executive decision making also is taking place in a small central area of Mexico City. Mergers, alliances, takeovers by foreign firms of Mexican enterprises, and Mexican corporations becoming themselves multinationals is not expected to alter the concentration of major corporations in Mexico City and within small areas within the city. Our analyses indicate that most of these changes occurred between 1986 and 1993 and continued at least through 1997. Whether this trend has continued or not over the past several years remains to be examined.

Sassen (1991) postulated that advanced megacities would retain executive decision making and related services. On the other hand, manufacturing plants, middle level service offices, and support functions would move away from the megacity, even perhaps to another country. In Mexico, this explanation only partially fits. For major domestic, and especially foreign corporations, this is clearly the case and during the time period of 1986 through 1997 such influence has continued to grow. However, as shown throughout other chapters in this volume, Mexico City continues to have concentration of population, manufacturing, services, and other activities.

Our expectation for the next several decades is that while the government may continue to stress de-concentration of population and economic activities it will have little success. This is despite the growing importance of the increased industrial successes of Monterry and Guadalajara and growth in maquiladora industry along the U.S.- Mexican border. Corporation headquarters will continue to converge on Mexico City and this means that corporate decision making, both by domestic and foreign owned entities, will continue to be made in Mexico City.

# 14

# Growth and Development
# Outcomes and Policy

- **Introduction**
- **Population Growth and Distribution**
- **Migration to the United States**
- **Labor Force**
- **Technology**
- **Economic Growth**
  - **NAFTA**
- **Decentralization/Concentration**
- **Privatization**
- **Petroleum**
- **Tourism**
- **Maquiladoras**
- **Environment**
- **Drugs**
- **Inequality History Repeated Itself: the Diaz Era**
- **Conclusions**

## Introduction

This chapter identifies and discusses the important issues for the growth and development of Mexico over the last three decades and into future. It summarizes and draws out the larger book outcomes and asks what the policy implications are for Mexico. It is less focused on the world systems theory and other theoretical implications, which are emphasized in Chapters 15 and 16, and more on practical aspects.

The chapter starts by discussing Mexico's population growth. Mexico has undergone a huge demographic shift over the past 40 years, moving from a higher fertility, younger, more rural, and less economically productive society to a demographically slowing, somewhat older, much more urban, and more economically productive one. Health conditions have improved greatly, to the extent that its life expectancies approach those for the United States. The chapter examines what has led to the enlarged role of Mexican migrants in the United States and how this relates to the world economy themes of this book. The labor force is a crucial aspect supporting the economic transformations that have taken place and continue to. The key characteristics and change elements in the labor force are examined, including its relative youth and the growing yet limited role for women. The chapter asks what are the relationships between population changes and the opening up of the economy.

Mexico has grown economically over the past twenty years, albeit in fits and starts that have issued from a variety of stresses and strains. The Mexican PIB and PIB per capita have grown significantly. This has brought prosperity, although the benefits have been distributed unequally. Productivity has increased and especially so in manufacturing. The economy is production oriented, and has made great strides in enlarging its manufacturing sectors, both conventional and maquiladora.

The trends of decentralization and privatization are examined in the chapter. Mexico became overly centralized during the twentieth century. It has concentrated in one primate city a sixth of its population and inordinate proportion of its economy, financial institutions, manufacturing, political institutions, and most of the federal government and corporate headquarters. This extent of concentration has led to a need to decentralize, a need recognized by the federal government for the past two decades. However, in spite of clear need, little progress has been made and at the century's end, the nation if anything was more centralized (Garza 1999).

In the late stage of the De la Madrid Administration, a trend started toward privatization that eventually impacted major segments of the Mexican economy. This book has examined a number of these privatization efforts including in banking, communications, and transportation. The chapter asks what the benefits and drawbacks have been to privatization and why certain sectors have largely succeeded after been privatized, while others have failed. It recommends policy steps.

The chapter summarizes the major trends in the key export sectors of oil, tourism, and maquiladoras. It points to the growth of these sectors and to the successes realized as well as the problems and detriments encountered. Although the sectors differ greatly in the extent of foreign involvement, each of them in their own way has an underlying dilemma of the extent of autonomy versus outside control. How much do they serve the interests of Mexico, versus the interests of foreign investors, partners, and consumers? This is the flip side of the old import substitution economy, which avoided the risks of foreign interventions by blocking and sheltering domestic entities. In the new open economy, foreign investment is encouraged, but it may have downsides domestically.

Foreign investment has been one of the drivers in opening up the Mexican economy. Early in the process, it was one of the keys to ending the "import substitution" economy. Direct investment has focused primarily in manufacturing and has set the basis for multinational production and for infrastructure changes underlying this production. How can this investment best be regulated and channeled in the future? It is a key policy issue for Mexico.

Mexico has been blessed with one of the most bountiful natural environments in the world. However, in the rush to develop a modern and open economy, its rich ecological heritage has been given low priority. Many severe compromises have been made. The effects include pollution impacts, deforestation, erosion, reduction of water quality and supply, toxic chemicals, poor agricultural practices, and others. The relationship of environment with world economy trends is discussed.

A sector not examined heretofore in the book but one significant to the international and domestic economy is the narcotic drug trade. It increased in Mexico in the mid 1980s, due largely to the successful stoppage of drug flows into the U.S. through the Caribbean. The role of Mexican drug cartels has been largely to serve as traffickers of drugs from South America to the vast U.S. marketplace. The drug trade has had adverse impacts on crime, health, and sense of well being and security within Mexico. There are uncomfortable questions relating to possible government involvement, the role of the banking and finance industries, and collaborating networks within the United States. This area presents touchy issues and challenges for national and binational policy. For instance, should the stance of the Mexican government be that the Untied States is the responsible party, because of its market demands, or should Mexico take responsibility for the crisis? How much cooperation versus distancing should take place between the drug enforcement agencies of the two nations? The narcotic drug trade is added, albeit briefly, to this book's discussion because it also relates to Mexico and the world economy.

There are interesting parallels between today's economic opening up and the "open" Porfirio Diaz era in the late 19th and early 20th centuries. During that era, some of the trends seen today occurred in Mexico, and also closely involved the U.S. There are lessons that can be learned. The chapter draws comparisons to the current situation.

## Population Growth and Distribution

In the second half of the twentieth century, Mexico has undergone a transformation in its population in almost all respects, including size, vital rates, age structure, labor force, urbanization, and international migration to the U.S. Its change in fifty years is equivalent to what many advanced nations encountered in one to two centuries. However, similar rapid transformations took in the twentieth century in other developing nations. The demographic change in many ways underpins and relates to the economic change that has been the focus of this book.

As seen in Table 14.1 and Figure 14.1, the Mexican population increased from 13.6 million in 1900 to 25.8 million at mid century, and is very close to 100 million today. The second half of the twentieth century had four fold growth, which compares to two fold growth in the first half of the century. The population increase has been one of the underlying motivators for the growth in the size of the Mexican economy, but the economy has grown more rapidly still due to productivity increases. The primary driver of the population growth has been the sharp reduction in fertility in Mexico since the mid 60s. As seen in Table 14.2, Mexico's Total Fertility Rate (TFR) dropped from 6.95 in the late 60s to 3.10 in 1998, a reduction of fifty five percent in only thirty years. The Total Fertility Rate represents the average number of children born per mother. The large TFR drop was due to widespread adoption of modern contraceptive methods as they became more widely available. In Latin America, Potts (1999) has indicated a current contraceptive prevalence of around two thirds overall.

**Table 14.1 Population and Growth Rates of Mexico, 1900 to 2030**

| Year | Population (in 1000s) | Decennial Growth Rate | Source |
|------|---------------------|----------------------|--------|
| 1900 | 13,607 | | INEGI |
| 1910 | 15,160 | 11.4 | INEGI |
| 1921 | 14,335 | -5.4 | INEGI |
| 1930 | 16,553 | 15.5 | INEGI |
| 1940 | 19,654 | 18.7 | INEGI |
| 1950 | 25,791 | 31.2 | INEGI |
| 1960 | 34,923 | 35.4 | INEGI |
| 1970 | 48,225 | 38.1 | INEGI |
| 1980 | 66,847 | 38.6 | INEGI |
| 1990 | 81,250 | 21.5 | INEGI |
| 2000 | 99,582 | 22.6 | CONAPO (est.) |
| 2010 | 112,231 | 12.7 | CONAPO (est.) |
| 2020 | 122,107 | 8.8 | CONAPO (est.) |
| 2030 | 128,927 | 5.6 | CONAPO (est.) |
| | | | |
| 1995 | 91,158 | | INEGI |
| 2010 | 117,500 | | PRB (est.) |
| 2025 | 140,000 | | PRB (est.) |

Sources: INEGI, Estadisticas Historicas de Mexico, 1999; CONAPO, 1998; PRB, 1998.

**Table 14.2 Mexican Fertility Change, 1966 to 1998**

| Year | TFR-National Total | TFR*-Rural | TFR-Urban | Source |
|------|-------------------|-----------|-----------|--------|
| 1966-1970 | 6.95 | 7.96 | 6.08 | WFS |
| 1970-1974 | 6.48 | 7.90 | 5.93 | ENP |
| 1975-1979 | 5.24 | 6.67 | 4.45 | ENP |
| 1984-1986 | 3.80 | 5.85 | 3.47 (est.) | ENFES |
| 1990-1993 | 3.70 | NA | NA | PRB |
| 1998 | 3.10 | NA | NA | PRB |

Sources:  WFS = World Fertility Survey, 1976-77.

ENP = Encuesta Nacional de Prevalencia en el Uso de Metodos Anticonceptivos, 1979

ENFES = Encuesta Nacional de Fecundidad, 1987

PRB = Population Reference Bureau, 1990-1993, 1998

TFR = Total Fertility Rate

Today, there is potential for further contraception advances, lowering fertility further (Potts 1999). This would be of greater importance in the rural areas, where the TFR is much higher. Citing somewhat old data for 1987, Potts points to the potential through contraception and child spacing, to reduce Mexico's fertility by another 25 percent (Potts 1999).

Mortality is less important to Mexican demographic growth because the Mexican population is quite young, with a median age in 2000 of 24 years (U.S. Census Bureau 1999). The U.S. median age, by contrast is 36. Because Mexico has been very young over the past 50 years, mortality has not been an influential factor on population growth.

There has been a large increase in longevity during the second half of the twentieth century. As seen in Table 14.3, Mexican overall life expectancy in 1950 was 49, but it lengthened to 62 in 1970 and is estimated by the Population Reference Bureau at 72 years for 1998, a nearly 25 year increase in half a century! This life expectancy compares well with U.S. life expectancy in 1997, estimated at 76 years (Population Reference Bureau

**Figure 14.1 Population of Mexico, 1900 to 2030**

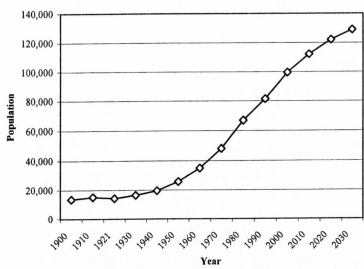

Source: INEGI, Estadisticas Historicas de Mexico, 1999; CONAPO, 1998; PRB, 1998.

1997). The advances in standardized mortality are due to a combination of factors including better medical care, improved sanitation, and better preventative health care (Pick and Butler 1998). There has been an epidemiological transition in Mexico in the second half of the century, paralleling its fertility transition. Also evident in Table 14.3 is that Mexican male life expectancy has consistently been about six years less than for females, a gender differential typical of most countries.

Age structure depends on the population growth and its change components. Over the past fifty years, Mexico has undergone substantial alteration in its age structure that has influenced its economy and the change tendencies discussed in this book. The extent of aging is indicated by the median age of the Mexican population, which increased from 18 years in 1980 to 24 years in 2000 and will increase further to an estimated 29 years by 2020 (U.S. Census 1999). Over that time period, the U.S. median age increased only from 30 in 1980 to an estimated 36 in 2000, and to a forecast 38 years in 2020 (U.S. Census 1999). The median age of the Mexico population forecast for 2020 will equal that of the U.S. in 1980. Eventually, Mexico will catch up, and, according to the U.S. Census, both populations will be equal by 2060 at 38 years median age (U.S. Census 1999).

**Table 14.3 Mexican Mortality Change, 1950 to 1998**

| Year | Crude Mortality Rate | Life Expectancy at Birth | | |
|------|----------------------|---------|------|--------|
| | | Overall | Male | Female |
| 1950 | 16.1 | 49 | 48 | 51 |
| 1960 | 11.5 | 59 | 58 | 60 |
| 1970 | 10.1 | 62 | 60 | 64 |
| 1980 | 6.3 | 66 | 63 | 69 |
| 1993 | 6.0 | 70 | 66 | 73 |
| 1997 | 4.5 | 74 | 70 | 77 |
| 1998 | 5.0 | 72 | 69 | 75 |

Source: Rabell et al., 1986 for 1950-1980; Population Reference Bureau, 1993 for 1993 and 1998; Banamex, 1998 for 1997.

This large alteration in Mexico's age structure is illustrated in Figures 14.2 to 14.4. They show that in 1970, Mexico had a very young population, i.e. large proportions of children and few elderly. Twenty five years later, in 1995, the age distribution moderated and was less bottom heavy with children and adolescents. By year 2020, CONAPO forecasts indicate a population that will have a large proportion of working age population 20-55, fewer children and adolescents and a larger proportion of elderly than in 1995 (CONAPO 1999).

This age structural pattern of change is a well known demographic outcome of fertility reductions. It occurred, for example, in the U.S. and European nations in the 19th and early 20th centuries.

Age structural change relates to the economic globalization processes examined in this book. When opening of the economy started in the mid to late 1980s, the Mexican population was half composed of children and adolescents. By the mid to late 1990s, these cohorts began to enter labor force age (see Figure 14.3) and to overload the job market, leading to several outcomes -- growth in the informal labor force and increased push for migration to the U.S. (see Pick, Butler, and Gonzales 1992). It is evident by comparing the forecast 2020 age structure and the 1995 one (compare Figures 14.4 and 14.3) that the rising labor force and its job market impacts just begin in the 1990s and should last until 2030 or later.

Mexico became more urbanized over the purview of this book. As seen in Figure 14.5, the urban proportion i.e. the percent of population living in places of 2,500 or more, became balanced at about 50 percent urban and 50 percent rural in 1960. However by the end of the century this proportion is three quarter urban and one quarter rural. The principal causes were the difficult conditions of Mexican peasant agriculture discussed in Chapter 11; the growing job opportunities in Mexico City (discussed in our prior book, see Pick and Butler 1997); job opportunities in Monterrey and Guadalajara, some coming from manufacturing as well as other companies discussed in this book; job opportunities in the maquiladora industry in northern cities (discussed in Chapter 9), and the draw of rural migrants to the United States. The extent of rural to urban flows has benefited many of the migrant families economically. Some of them have benefited through the opportunity to migrate to the U.S. For some migrants, this has led to naturalization and to U.S. citizenship.

Mexico's long term rural to urban migration trend has a number of adverse impacts including:

- Housing and lifestyle deficits in the large cities especially in the peripheral areas that have more migrant composition.
- Cultural losses, in particular loss of ethnic language and identity of indigenous origin people.
- Hard work conditions in the Mexican urban informal labor force approximating those of the rural origin areas.
- Often harsh economic conditions and marginal social status, and lack of government benefits and recognition for many migrants to the U.S.

Overall the population change has been immense over the past 30-40 years and has been an underlying structural factor affecting how globalization has occurred in Mexico. The next section examines more deeply one component of population change, migration to the U.S.

**Figure 14.2**

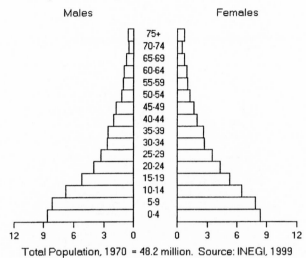

Total Population, 1970 = 48.2 million.  Source: INEGI, 1999

**Figure 14.3**

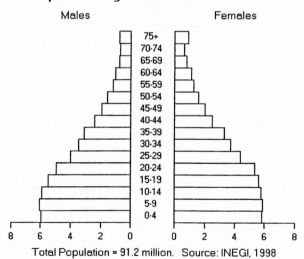

Total Population = 91.2 million.  Source: INEGI, 1998

**Figure 14.4**

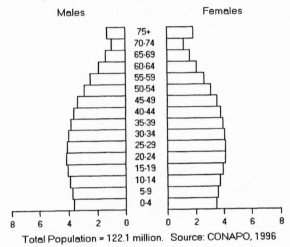

Total Population = 122.1 million.   Source: CONAPO, 1996

**Figure 14.5**
**Urban and Rural Population**
**Mexico: 1900-1995**

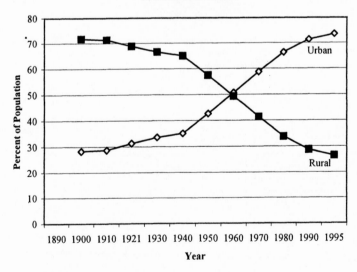

Source: Estadisticas Historicas de Mexico, 1985; INEGI, 1999.

## Migration to the United States

Migration flows to the United States reflect the demographic and economic transformations taking place in Mexico. It is a large scale process that warrants further discussion in relation to the book themes and findings.

As a result of forty years or more of migratory flows, there were between 7 and 7.3 million Mexican migrants resident in the U.S. in 1996 (Banamex 1998). This large population component was equivalent to 7.8 percent of the population of Mexico.

Of these U.S.-resident Mexicans, 4.7-4.9 million were legal residents and 2.3-2.4 million were illegal residents (Banamex 1998). The extent of illegal residents had been reduced by the one time conversion to U.S. citizenship of two to three million migrants flows from the Immigration Reform and Control Act (IRCA) of 1986. Estimates by decade of the net migration flow from Mexico to the U.S. are as follows:

**Table 14.4 Migration Flow from Mexico to U.S., 1960-1995**

| Period | Net number of Migrants from Mexico to U.S. |
|---|---|
| 1960-1970 | 260,000-290,000 |
| 1970-1980 | 1,200,000-1,550,000 |
| 1980-1990 | 2,100,000-2,600,000 |
| 1990-1995 | 1,390,000 |

Sources: U.S.-Mexico Binational Study on Migration, 1997; Banamex, 1998.

It is evident that flows increased in the 1980s and continued at high levels in the early 1990s, although they lowered somewhat in the mid 1990s (Banamex 1998). The reasons for some slowing may be that border crossing barriers in the U.S. have been amplified, so migrants are more cautious about crossings.

The Mexican migration destinations in the U.S. are concentrated in the states of California, Texas, and Illinois (Banamex 1998, citing U.S. Census figures). As a result, in 1990, 85 percent of Mexican migrants were located in these three states. There is some trend to a spreading out of the migrant population to the midwest, south and east (Passell 2000). Overall, the migrants tend to locate in more urban areas and ones that already have substantial Mexican population.

The Mexican migrants in the U.S. tend to have low education and low income. For instance, in 1996, 11 percent of families of recent migrants had incomes of less than $5,000. The temporary migrants tend to be young men working in agriculture, while the permanent residents i.e. possessing a "green card," were gender balanced, with only about a seventh in agriculture.

In terms of the present research, this very large volume of migration flow underscores structural weaknesses in the Mexican economy and its standard of living. In the book, these weaknesses have been noted frequently. They include the increasing poverty in the Mexican population that some estimate at over 50 percent; the nation's periodic severe economic crises; lack of availability of financing and credit (as seen in the banking crisis); wide wage differentials between the U.S. and Mexico (Massey 1998); and environmental, housing, and lifestyle deficiencies.

The appeal of the United States has been pointed to in two recent analyses of Mexican immigration to the U.S. in the context the economic integration of North America (Alba 1999; Massey 1998). Those investigators point to the underlying need of Mexican individuals and families to achieve economic well being and in particular wealth (Massey 1998). The opportunities for achieving capital accumulation were stimulated by the opening up of a North American integrated economy, following the 1994 passage of NAFTA. The opening up presented many new capital generating opportunities, some discussed in this book. However, what the NAFTA agreement did not address was the need to open up labor migration (Massey 1998). To the contrary, following the NAFTA agreement, the U.S. put into effect greater barriers to migration. The barriers have included more border patrol officers, special apprehension operations such as "Operation Hold the Line" in El Paso-Ciudad Juárez, increased sanctions on immigrants, and, in certain states, reduced welfare and government services (Massey 1998).

These studies point to the underlying motivation of U.S.-based migrants to return capital to families and relatives in Mexico. Studies at Banco de Mexico indicated that for 1997 and 1998, Mexican migrants to the U.S. transferred annually five billion dollars back to Mexico (study by G. Vera of Banco de Mexico, cited in Alba 1999). This yearly financial flow is of the magnitude of the Foreign Direct Investment in Mexico (compare with Table 4.1). In other words, the economic needs of a multitude of poorer migrant families are generating amounts of monetary return flow roughly equivalent to the Mexican infrastructure needs of U.S.-based corporations. Furthermore, the locations of FDI investment in Mexico have been in the advanced border and central parts, so that investment over time may serve to restrain local workers in the north Mexico from migrating to the U.S. By contrast, the region of origin of Mexico-to-U.S. migrants tends to be in more impoverished and rural areas of the nation, and in parts of the center and the south.

Alba points out that both federal governments appear to be comfortable with not having formal migration policies that will recognize the full flows, i.e. documented and undocumented (Alba 1999). There is "blindness" here, i.e. the two national governments have defined in great detail their open economic relationship, but have given scanty attention to their labor force relationship. The potential to formalize labor force flow policies may have to wait for the next round of integration treaties, in a way similar to a half century of experiences in European integration (Alba 1999).

Another aspect of Mexican migration to the U.S. is that it is a circular process that builds up over time (Massey 1998). Large Mexican migrant communities in the U.S. are established; migrants enter the U.S. workforce often starting at a low level; and migrants both return and transfer money back to Mexico. About 86 percent of undocumented migrants and 56 percent of documented migrants return to Mexico (Jasso and Rosenzweig, cited in Massey 1998). Once they have returned, these migrants generate motivation and interest in family and friends to further migrate to the U.S. Massey (1998) refers to this process as "social capital formation." The skills upgrading that takes place among Mexican migrants in the U.S. he calls "human capital formation." Increases in "human capital" represent a motivating factor, since the human capital formation may have a positive effect on future jobs and income streams of workers.

Massey (1998) sees the largest causes of Mexico-to-U.S. labor migration as desire to realize capital formation and human capital formation, and the push of social capital. On the other hand, he assesses binational wage differentials as much less important. In terms of the present research, North American market integration as a stimulus to Mexico-to-U.S. labor migration is important. We have pointed to the many ways that economic integration is taking place, with our emphasis on the integration within Mexico, i.e. in infrastructure projects, advances in manufacturing, foreign partners of Mexican firms, a Mexican auto parts industry that supports foreign-owned multinational auto manufacturing, etc. We have emphasized that the North American economic integration taking place within Mexico is driven by low domestic labor costs; the economic gain of the average Mexican worker is not emphasized. By contrast, the economic integration taking place in the U.S. has benefits of needing low skilled and low cost labor that cannot be supplied sufficiently by the U.S. labor force. Mexican workers can receive capital benefits by working in the U.S. that far exceed those possible in Mexico. There is a parallel here to what happened in Europe with labor migration of Turks to Germany. The economic integration benefits workers from peripheral nations occurred during their residence in the advanced economy, rather than at home. Another point is that the continuing trajectory of economic growth of Mexico outlined in this book will lead eventually to greater parity between the U.S. and Mexican economies and standards of living. When that happens, the causes for the labor migration will largely disappear. Thus, the transition or "opening-up" period must be viewed as a bridge (Massey 1998). Massey, among others, has called for the U.S. government to change its policies to encourage labor migration during this bridge era.

### Labor Force

Labor force is a vital element in the globalization processes discussed in this volume. Labor force, like population, has grown over the period of this study. As seen in Table 14.5 and Figure 14.6, the labor force in Mexico grew from 8 million in 1950 to an estimated 40 million in 2000, at a compounded annual rate during the second half century of 2.9 percent. The figure shows that the growth of labor slowed in 1990 and then continued its upward growth in the mid 1990s. The lowering in 1990 may have been due to census undercount, since the economically active population counted in the "Encuesta Ingreso-Gasto (EIG)" of 1989 was 26,043,000, two million higher than the census total one year later. Regardless of this irregularity, Mexico's labor force has grown rapidly. If we use the EIG figure for 1990, labor force increased in the 1990s by 1,254,000 net additions yearly. This volume is similar to the annual increment predicted in our study (Pick, Butler, and Ramirez 1992). This level of labor force expansion is overloading the Mexican labor market and leading to unemployment, a larger informal labor force, and outmigration to the U.S. Because of

**Figure 14.6 Growth in Labor Force, Mexico, 1950-2000**

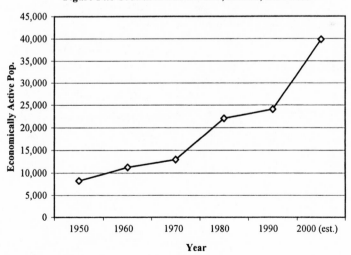

Source: INEGI, various years; Banamex, 1998.

built-in age structure determinants, this overloading aspect should be present for 30 or more years. It underscores that a major part of the labor force crisis in Mexico is demographic.

**Table 14.5 Growth in the Mexican Labor Force and Its Sectors, 1950-1995**

| Year | Population | Population Econ. Active | Population Econ. Active | Percent in Primary Sector | Percent in Secondary Sector | Percent in Tertiary Sector |
|------|-----------|------------------------|------------------------|---------------------------|------------------------------|-----------------------------|
| 1950 | 25,791 | 8,272 | 0.321 | 60.9 | 16.7 | 22.4 |
| 1960 | 34,923 | 11,253 | 0.322 | 54.6 | 19.1 | 26.3 |
| 1970 | 48,225 | 12,955 | 0.369 | 41.8 | 24.4 | 33.8 |
| 1980 | 66,847 | 22,066 | 0.317 | 37.0 | 29.0 | 34.0 |
| 1990 | 81,250 | 24,063 | 0.288 | 23.9 | 28.3 | 47.8 |
| 1995 | 99,582 | 39,833 | 0.400 | NA | NA | NA |
| 2000 | 91,158 | 35,759 | 0.390 | 22.6 | 24.5 | 52.9 |

Source: INEGI, various years; Banamex, 1998.

The labor force's sectoral composition has radically changed from 1950 to 1995, as seen in Figure 14.7. While the primary sector diminished, the secondary sector grew modestly, and the tertiary sector tripled in proportion. This labor force compositional transformation is integral to many of the trends noted in earlier chapters, such as the rising skill and educational levels of workers, the increase in the service sector, the raise in agribusiness, and the expansions in the information, accounting, and legal areas.

Mexico has a much lower labor force participation of women compared to the U.S. In 1996, the "Encuesta Nacional de Empleo" ("National Employment Survey") showed a labor force participation rate of women of 34.8 percent, an increase from 17 percent in 1970 (INEGI 1974). This compares to a U.S. female labor force participation rate in 1996 of 59.3 percent (U.S. Bureau of Labor Statistics). It is important to recognize that in 1970, the rate of labor force participation for U.S. women was only 43.3 percent. The advances of women in the labor force are continuing to rise in Mexico and can be expected to provide millions more women workers in the labor force in the early 21st century.

It is important to point out that many of the globalization trends and changes discussed here involve increased efficiency, computerization, and modernization of business processes that <u>reduce</u> rather than increase employment in the labor force. Examples have included the computerized manufacturing and delivery processes at Cemex, automated high tech plants of IBM/Mexico, and Maseca's automated manufacturing process that provides modern versus traditional tortillas. While globalization may help increase the size of the macro economy, this is offset to a certain extent by labor reductions stemming from these corporate efficiencies. Hence, it is likely that the growth pressures on both the informal labor force and migration to the U.S. will continue.

**Figure 14.7 Change in Economic Sectors, 1950-1995**

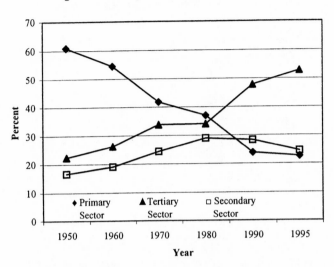

Source: INEGI, various years; Banamex, 1998.

## Technology

In the area of technology, Mexico has a small but productive domestic research and development capability, that is based on federal support largely through CONACYT (Consejo Nacional de Ciencia y Tecnología) and the national university, UNAM. Overall, Mexico depends for technology largely on advanced nations. As seen in Table 14.6, the level of Mexican scientific productivity is roughly equivalent to that of other leading Latin American countries, but is considerably behind the advanced nations. In terms of scientific publications per capita, Mexico in 1994 was two percent of the U.S., Canadian, and British levels, but comparable to Brazil and Venezuela, although trailing Argentina and Chile. One of the reasons for the gaps may be lower investment in R&D -- Mexico's proportion of GDP expended on R&D is much lower than for advanced nations, for example one eighth of the U.S's.

The domestic spending on R&D was $1.1 billion in 1995. It is largely channeled CONACYT. R&D focuses on the areas of basic research, applied research, encouraging human resources in science, postgraduate education, and administrative support for R&D. Although very limited by U.S. standards, CONACYT has a good reputation for developing research. Mexico awarded 488 doctorates in science and technology in 1995, much more than the 177 ten years earlier. Also in 1995, 3,538 patents were awarded in Mexico, but only six percent of them to investigators of Mexican citizenship (CONACYT 1995). This underscores Mexico's secondary position relative to foreigners' R&D.

A growing part of domestic encouragement of research is the "Sistema Nacional de Investigadores" ("National System of Researchers") or SNI. SNI is an organization of the best Mexican researchers in the country. It numbered 5,868 in 1995, and its members were 69 percent at the doctoral level. SNI provides salary stipends to its members, who need to

**Table 14.6 Comparison of R&D Expenditures and**
**Per Capita Publications, Selected Nations, 1993**

| Nation | R&D Expendit, 1993 | Percent of PIB, 1993 | Scientific and Technology Publications, 1994 | | Population 1995 |
| | | | Number | No. Per Million Pop. | |
|---|---|---|---|---|---|
| Germany | 37.15 | 2.48 | 48,172 | 587 | 82 |
| Canada | 8.38 | 1.50 | 31,054 | 1,035 | 30 |
| US | 166.3 | 2.66 | 257,896 | 981 | 263 |
| Spain | 4.56 | 0.88 | 14,109 | 362 | 39 |
| France | 26.43 | 2.45 | 38,044 | 656 | 58 |
| Italy | 13.21 | 1.31 | 23,420 | 411 | 57 |
| Japan | 69.1 | 2.73 | 54,902 | 439 | 125 |
| Mexico | 1.96 | 0.32 | 2,018 | 22 | 92 |
| United Kingdom | 21.57 | 2.19 | 52,959 | 898 | 59 |
| Argentina | NA | NA | 2,374 | 68 | 35 |
| Brazil | NA | NA | 4,387 | 28 | 159 |
| Chile | NA | NA | 1,169 | 84 | 14 |
| Venezuela | NA | NA | 615 | 28 | 22 |

Source: SEP, 1995

meet strict yearly publication standards. SNI has been growing in size and importance, and provides an incentive to science and technology achievement.

The domestic science establishment is highly concentrated in Mexico City, in line with so many other features. As seen in Table 14.7, 56 percent of SNI researchers were located in the Federal District and about 60 percent in Mexico City. Overconcentration in this case may have some synergistic benefits, given the limited number of top scientists; however, it also presents challenges to developing research broadly throughout Mexico.

Globalization processes are benefiting the technological advancement of the nation. Through transfer and foreign direct investment in the technology, it is possible for firms to skip rapidly to the latest cutting edge technology. Alestra represents a case company that has brought the latest cutting-edge technology from the U.S. to bear in Mexico quickly. In other cases, multinational corporations are encouraging some of these R&D centers to be located in Mexico. This is true of Deltronics R&D Center in Ciudad Juárez and HP's printer R&D in Guadalajara. DuPont utilizes advanced chemical technology in its plants in eastern Mexico, which is derivative from the U.S. IBM manufactures ThinkPad laptops in Guadalajara, but R&D comes from the U.S. and Europe. In all instances, the multinational firm can achieve economies in R&D, because Mexican engineers, scientists, and technical staff have lower compensation than their counterparts in advanced nations. Yet, for those instances, some key R&D foreign personnel tend to be brought in from overseas, even if for temporary stays. Cemex represents a firm that has taken a technological lead in its industry worldwide, and is using technology on a global basis to achieve efficiencies and enhance communications, on-time delivery, and corporate integration. At the same time, Cemex has largely derived its technology from best practice systems approaches of the Fortune 100 companies in the U.S.

Table 14.7 Geographical Location of SNI Investigators, 1995

Table 14.7 Geographical Location of SNI Investigators, 1995

| Location | Number | Percent |
|---|---|---|
| Distrito Federal | 3,309 | 56.4 |
| Morelos | 351 | 6.0 |
| Mexico | 325 | 5.5 |
| Baja California Norte | 195 | 3.3 |
| Puebla | 235 | 4.0 |
| Others | 1,453 | 24.8 |
| Total | 5,868 | 100.0 |

Note: SNI = Sistema Nacional de Investigadores.
Source: SEP, 1995

There are also counter-currents to the technology advancement of Mexico. For instance, many top Mexican scientists and engineers have left Mexico because they have not found it offers the necessary world class laboratories, funding, and other infrastructure for research. In the diffusion of computing and internet technology, Mexico is lagging the U.S. For instance, only one percent of the Mexican population actively utilized the internet in 1999 according to Microsoft/Mexico and only 4 percent of Mexicans own PCs, although this is likely to change rapidly in the future, especially as communications infrastructure gets modernized (Stevenson 1999). The overall technology picture is one of a small but growing domestic technology capability, yet of dependency on advanced nations and particularly the U.S. for the state of the art.

The Mexican government has fruitfully cultivated its domestic science and technology, given the economic and educational constraints. In the 21st century, it has the potential to invest more of PIB in R&D; to expand the promising SNI network to a much larger doctoral-educated segment; to encourage technology transfer to Mexico and growth of corporate R&D in Mexico; and to foster more alliances between advanced-nation and Mexican scientists. These steps will be easier if the economy is expanding and prospering.

## Economic Growth

The Mexican macro economy has had good overall growth over the past 30 years, but has also experienced abrupt ups and downs at times. These jolts are caused by several factors: the central dependence on petroleum, which utilized a world markets; a federal government which relies on six year planning cycles; susceptibility to government credit problems of different types; and public and private mismanagement in certain economic sectors.

The economy in the late 1990s has prospered in terms of PIB growth, international trade, growth in manufacturing, and even at the end of the decade by an upward tilt in world oil prices. At the same time, weaknesses remain including hidden unemployment and underemployment among the poor and in the informal sector, growing poverty, NAFTA-generated displacement of certain sectors and smaller businesses, an expanding labor force confronted with not enough job creation, and several distressed industries most notably banking. The irony is that a Mexico with upward trending macroeconomic numbers also has nagging economic problems for large segments of the population. This dilemma forms one of the rallying cries for the political left and has led to attention by the dominant PRI party to some of the same problems including poverty.

A driver of the economic growth of Mexico is the large foreign direct investment stemming partly from changes in the investment laws of the early 1990s. As was seen in Figure 4.1, FDI expanded from the 50s through the 1990s, with a dip in the mid 1980s. In the 1990s, as discussed in Chapter 4, the large FDI flows, averaging nearly $10 billion per year, stimulated manufacturing, both maquiladora and traditional. At the same time, in the 1990s, manufacturing productivity grew rapidly. For instance the index of manufacturing productivity per worker increased by 6.2 percent from 1991 to 1998, at one of the fastest rates worldwide and exceeding the U.S. by 1.7 percent (Banco de Mexico 1998). The manufacturing sector passed commerce in the mid 90s to become the largest part of PIB at about one fifth (see Figure 5.3). Since manufacturing is export-oriented, it has also bypassed petroleum to become dominant in exports. Although manufacturing represented only 31 percent of exports in 1980, it rose to 68 percent by 1990 and in 1998 was 90 percent.

Mexico's Producto Bruto Interno is 1998 stood at $415 billion, with the largest parts being manufacturing, followed by commerce and private sector services. Each of these sectors has been the focus of earlier chapters. The PIB grew in 1998 by 4.8 percent (Banco de México 1998) and it can be expected to continue to grow, set back at time by shocks such as the peso crisis of late 1994.

Mexico is tethered in trade to the U.S. In fact, in 1998, the U.S. received 87 percent of Mexico's exports, and Mexico's imports constituted 74 percent from the U.S. (CIA 1999). Relative to the U.S. economy of $8.8 trillion in GDP in 1998, Mexico's is much smaller, yet Mexico in the late 1990s moved into second place behind Canada as a U.S. trading partner Among other things, Mexico has the pluses of geographical proximity for the movement of goods and services. The upward curves of Mexico's imports and exports are even higher after NAFTA was passed in 1994 (see Figure 3.1). The balance of trade is more favorable to Mexico in times of economic stress in Mexico such as the mid 1980s and 1995-1996, since a weakened Mexican economy is a less attractive place to sell U.S. goods while export-oriented manufacturing costs in Mexico are even less.

Mexico's macroeconomic indicators should continue to grow over the long term. Yet, past experiences have shown that economic events in the U.S. can have profound short term impacts on Mexico and that Mexican mismanagement can lead to problems, such as the debt crisis of the mid 80s and severe peso crisis of the mid 90s.

On the surface, unemployment is low and average income good for a semi-periphery nation at $4,360 yearly. However, the large size of the informal sector and the large income inequality disguises some economic problems. We saw in Chapter 12 that up to 50 percent or more of Mexican workers are informal. This also implies that many of them are missed in counting the unemployed, which officially, i.e. for the formal economy, was only 3.2 percent in 1998 (Banco de México 1998). The large extent of poverty is another manifestation of the high income inequality. At the other end of the scale, the top ten percent of earners commanded 37 percent of income. However, at the very top this is even more distorted. In 1998, the ten most influential businessmen in Mexico controlled businesses which had combined wealth accounting for 15 percent of the country's PIB. The personal wealth of the ten is huge and equivalent to nearly 4 percent of PIB (studies by Jorge Basave Hunhardt, cited in Muñoz Valencia 1998). The other end of this imbalance consists of the estimated 30 million Mexicans who are poor (Centro de Estudios Economicos y Sociales, UNAM, cited in Philpott 1999). The problem of poverty looms large as a national issue that has to be solved in order to improve the overall prosperity of the nation.

In summary, over the long term the macro economy is doing well and growing, but that must be conditioned by the inequality of its benefits. While much wealth has been created at the top, the middle class has often been squeezed; and the extent of poverty is increasing. The impacts on the middle class were highlighted in the peso crisis of the mid 90s, in which the middle classes' income level was impacted, compounded with over-extension of credit. There are huge regional differences in the benefits, with the three major cities and parts of the border states benefiting the most. Poverty is manifest both in rural poverty highlighted in the south and in a huge informal economy that suffers from low income and often mediocre working conditions. The neo-liberal opening of the economy to the world has sprung forward the nation's macro-economic growth, productivity increase, and selective sectoral benefits, but at the same time it has displaced many traditional elements.

## NAFTA

What are the benefits of the now six year old NAFTA Agreement? Much has been written about NAFTA (a few examples are in Randall and Konrad, 1995; Jamar and Young 1999; McCosh 1999). This book has shown that many of the globalization and economic opening up trends that have occurred started prior to NAFTA going into effect. Some examples are the increases in manufacturing productivity, which started in the 1980s; the exponential growth of the maquiladoras starting in the late 1960s; federally master planned tourism beginning in the late 1960s; and large-scale federal privatization efforts that commenced in the 1989-1993 period. Thus, major parallel events, some preceding NAFTA, have influenced the economy to open up.

Overall, NAFTA has contributed many benefits. Among its benefits are the following (Jamar and Young 1999):

- Increase in export-oriented jobs in Mexico. Some have placed the number of such jobs created at 1-2 million (SECOFI, referred to in Jamar and Young 1999).
- Increase in aggregated trilateral trade (it grew by 76 percent from 1994-1999) As part of this, increasing U.S.-Mexico trade.
- Increase in FDI in Mexico from $3-4 billion per year pre-NAFTA to levels of around $10 billion per year afterwards (Jamar and Young 1999)
- Opening up of investment opportunities in Mexico.
- Stimulation of the export-oriented businesses and sectors in Mexico.

Some NAFTA weaknesses have also been consistently pointed to (Wallach and Sforza 1999; Jamar and Young, 1999). These include:

- Job displacement. Workers in particular impacted sectors may lose their jobs as a result of NAFTA. This impact is greater in smaller businesses and agricultural enterprises that cannot content with larger, efficient and sometimes global entities moving in.
- Environmental impacts. These include solid wastes, water pollution and supply, air pollution, and inadequate sewage disposal.
- Highway safety in the U.S. So far, this problem has been contained, since the Clinton Administration has restricted Mexican trucks from entering the U.S.
- Reduction in jobs in the U.S. Although this is clearly less than doomsayers predicted ahead of time, it is likely in the range of 200,000 workers yearly losing jobs (U.S. Dept. of Labor, cited in Jamar and Young 1999).
- Potential problems in agricultural products shipped into the U.S. The percentage of Mexican agricultural products imported from Mexico that are inspected is tiny, yet it the inspections indicate major contamination problems. (Wallach and Sforza 1999).

This is only a brief sketch of the advantages and disadvantages of NAFTA. The overall consensus is that NAFTA has contributed to a stronger macroeconomy for Mexico and also helped somewhat the large Canadian and giant U.S. economies. It has helped in creating jobs and investment opportunities in Mexico. However, on the flip side, NAFTA has presented detriments including job displacement in certain sectors in Mexico, environmental impacts especially in Mexico, and highway safety threats to the U.S.

Rather than discussing NAFTA in a separate chapter in this volume, we have felt its effects and processes were better examined under the specialized topics of manufacturing, maquiladoras, etc. Also, we contend that NAFTA is one of many parallel processes that have been transforming Mexico over the past thirty years.

## Decentralization/Concentration

Mexico is an overly primate nation, this is a country with too large a concentration of its population and economy in one huge megacity. Yet the federal government has put forward policies of deconcentration (Garza 1999). The problem has been lack of will and often resources to effect the deconcentration. There are several counter-examples and counter trends, however. For instance, studies have shown that Mexico City has spread out further geographically over the past 50 years and is continuing to spread out (Negrete 1999). This may represent an evolutionary type of deconcentration i.e. within the central region, but not yet extending to the whole nation. There are also several government agencies which serve as counter examples to the primacy trend. One is INEGI. It moved its headquarters in the late 1980s from Mexico City to Aguascalientes and has been very successful as an agency located away from the primate city. The rapid growth of the maquiladora industry, mostly in the border states, also constitutes a different kind of a counter-trend. However, it is also straddled with over-concentration of a different type i.e. in the two major border cities of Tijuana and Ciudad Juárez, although there is a gradual shift in the maquiladora away from those cites. De-concentration appears to be an urgent policy issue for the Mexican government to approach in the future. It may be difficult to resolve because of environmental and economic constraints.

## Privatization

Privatization has been a crucial although imperfect aspect of the Mexican economic transformation. Privatization is a trend started in the De La Madrid Administration and continues to evolve. Mexico increased its nationalized ownership during the era of import substitution in the 50s through 70s. However, in the debt crisis of the 1980s, the De La Madrid Administration started the privatization initiative by privatizing smaller firms. The underlying motivation was to raise needed investment capital. The pace accelerated greatly in the Salinas Administration. Whole industries were denationalized. There have been successes and failures. For instance, the telecommunications industry seems to have advanced in many respects after being privatized. Banking, on the other hand, deteriorated to a crisis stage following its re-privatization in 1992. The mixed success depends on the care taken by the government in planning high quality privatization. In the case of banking, for instance, care was not taken to insure high quality of management of the newly privatized banks. Rather, the banks were often taken over initially by speculators and inexperienced entrepreneurs who fell into serious mistakes or engaged in abuses.

The problem with these efforts has been that the government has tended to favor its political associates rather than conducting an open and impartial bidding process (Overman 1995). This was very evident in banking in the early 1990s and also in the failure of highway privatization in the mid 90s. In has been prevalent across the sweep of privatization. Among the adverse consequences are that industries may still be dominated by a few enterprises, and management performance and controls may be weak. For instance, in privatizing the telecommunications industry, Telmex was left as by far the dominant entity. Likewise in airlines, privatization and a subsequent merger left a dominant domestic airline consisting of Aeromexico and Mexicana. These adverse aspects are not confined to Mexico, but have surfaced in the worst examples in economies undergoing even more radical transformation, such as Russia. The resulting industries may not be competitive enough or have sufficiently broad ownership (Overman 1995). On the other hand, following privatization, the Mexican federal government has had a good record of not controlling or over-regulating (Overman 1995). Proponents of privatization point out correctly that the sale of companies has raised needed capital from private investors and that the funds can be re-directed to areas of need including public services and welfare.

Overall, benefits have stemmed from privatization, but they depend on specific industries and government administrations. The Mexican Congress has become aware especially through the banking crisis of the needs to monitor and regulate this process and may constitute somewhat of a government check and balance in the future. The federal government and Congress should consider instituting mechanisms for future privatizations that ensure an open and fair bidding process and do not preserve oligopoly or dominance by a few firms.

### Petroleum

Petroleum is a great national resource (see Chapter 8). Mexico possesses among the world's largest reserves of petroleum with 48 billion barrels of oil reserves and 64 trillion cubic feet of natural gas reserves. This puts Mexico in the category of one of the half dozen largest petroleum producing nations. It is not surprising that the government and people of Mexico regard petroleum as part of the national patrimony. However, this underlying cultural belief also presents Mexico with some of its biggest problems and challenges related to petroleum. Mexico has fiercely retained petroleum as nationalized, in order to protect this heritage from foreign intervention. The national oil entity, Pemex, with revenues in 1997 of 28.6 billion dollars, is one of the world's largest oil companies and the second biggest in Latin America. However, Pemex has not been managed efficiently.

The wave of privatization that swept through Mexico in the 1990s left petroleum still predominantly nationalized. Some trend towards privatization has occurred in some "downstream" realms including somewhat in petrochemicals and to a moderate extent in natural gas distribution.

The total petroleum part of PIB has dropped substantially since the import substitution era of the early 1980s, when it was nearly 14 percent. Today it is still significant at around two percent of PIB, but has the potential to increase as world petroleum prices may rise or as future efficiencies may increase production. Another reason for its drop in PIB proportion is that the rise of other dynamic sectors such as manufacturing has served to diminish petroleum's overall importance.

Pemex contributes a huge amount to Mexican exports, in 1997 for instance Mexico's net petroleum exports were $10.3 billion. Since nearly 90 percent is exported to the U.S., this is another instance where the Mexican-U.S. binational relationship dominates. With respect to binational balance of trade, the petroleum exports serve to offset many areas of U.S. strength in bilateral exports including electronic components, autos, and machinery.

Pemex is essentially part of the Mexican federal government and also one of the largest revenue sources for the government. For instance, in 1997 Pemex provided 37 percent of Federal government revenues, while the total of all taxes provide only 35 percent. However, this subsidizing of government may restrain Pemex from reinvestment and constrain productivity enhancement and modernization. As a result, Pemex is not able to retain world competitiveness, which may have future adverse effect.

Pemex has had a history of bureaucratic management and inefficiencies. There have also been claims of corruption, which stems in large part from the overly close connection of Pemex to the federal government.

Another important aspect of petroleum is its environmental impact, which is complex and large. It is important to mention that petroleum production is localized in the southeast of Mexico, especially in Campeche and Tabasco. These are areas of middle level development i.e. semiperiphery, yet their production largely serves advanced areas in Mexico or the United States. This constitutes dependency – of the southeast region as a dependent of the nation's rich center.

In the future, petroleum will continue as a national asset. There is the potential to put it to greater benefit.

Among the potential steps the federal government can take, short of privatization of its major production segment, are the following:

- Privatize the electrical generation sector. This has already been proposed to the Congress by the Zedillo administration.
- Invest in and develop more modern and competitive oil refining capability in Mexico.
- Reduce federal government dependency on Pemex profits. Rather, the federal government should broaden its sources of revenues including putting into place a more efficient federal taxation system.
- Involve more foreign investment and participation in the downstream aspects of the petroleum sector. Create incentives for this involvement that interest foreign firms over the long term.
- Improve the environmental regulation and control of petroleum-related impacts. This will require a complicated regulatory framework, since the environmental interactions in this area are often complex.

### Tourism

Mexico has many natural and historical features for tourism (see Chapter 10). As a result, the Mexican tourism industry has developed into one of the world's largest. In tourist arrivals, Mexico was in seventh place among nations in 1996. The pricing of Mexican tourism is lower than that of the other leading nations.

Tourism has a significant effect on Mexico's balance of trade. This is driven by international tourism revenues, which in 1996 were 6.9 billion dollars. Tourism is the third most important source of revenues for the trade balance, after petroleum and maquiladora.

In the late 1960s, the federal government realized the strategic potential of tourism for the nation. Led by the new agency FONATUR, it developed a long-term master plan to develop massive international tourism. Over the last third of the 20th century that plan was largely carried out. Tens of thousands of hotel rooms were built, financed by a combination of domestic and international funding. Huge new resorts were built that have been largely successful. The program is continuing to grow with the expansion of existing resorts such as Bahías de Huatulco, and some new resorts planned.

It is important to recognize that the states affected tend to be peripheral ones such as Quintana Roo, Baja California Sur, and Oaxaca. These areas experienced massive planned development for the first time, and the impacts have varied.

Case studies highlight positive as well as negative aspects of tourism. For the company Hoteles El Presidente/Intercontinental, Mexico has offered an opportunity to develop high-end tourism to suit both foreign and domestic tourists. The challenge has been to establish identity and brand recognition, which are viewed differently by domestic and foreign markets. The domestic Hoteles El Presidente firm has had to seek strong foreign partners over the past decade in order to compete and be recognized globally. The case of Bahías de Huatulco illustrates the positive and negative aspects of tourism. The development of the mega-resort displaced peasant workers and destroyed an old village yet offered some of the same workers menial but reliable jobs. The largely external investors and managers benefited and international tourists were offered an attractive resort.

Overall, tourism in Mexico has among positives and negatives for multiple stakeholders.

The positives are the following:
- Major source of revenues for the nation's balance of trade.
- Secondary and tertiary effects on the local economies in tourist regions.
- Source of local employment in key tourist zones including employment for many disadvantaged citizens.
- Advantages to investors from the growth and development of a very rich resource.

The negatives include:
- Losses to local culture and traditional ways of life.
- Environmental impacts on tourist regions, some of which were previously remote and even pristine.
- Stratification in tourist workforce with peasants at the bottom;
- Often there is prominent gender stratification.

The Mexican government and private partners have developed a rich resource of tourism in the 20th century. The question in the 21st century is how this feature can be further enhanced into an outstanding world leader in tourism, while mitigating and minimizing the inevitable cultural and environmental detriments. The challenge for government policy is to create an updated master plan for the next fifty years of tourist development that considers the need to develop and at the same time conserve the resource.

## Maquiladoras

Maquiladoras in Mexico grew rapidly during the past 30 years to become one of the two most important exports sectors (see Chapter 9). Today there are one million workers, and the annual sector generates over six billion dollars in value added. The total amounts imported and exported are totaled over 60 billion dollars in 1996.

The maquiladora is based on the advantages of low labor costs in Mexico, combined with access to components from the U.S. or other advanced nations and access for sales to the vast U.S. marketplace. Added to this have been tax benefits. However, these tax benefits are being eliminated in the year 2001, along with sales restrictions to the Mexican domestic market. Neither of these changes will dramatically affect the maquiladora sector, since labor force and proximity advantages will continue to be present. The Mexican government may step in and make up for some of the lost tax benefits.

As the maquiladora industry has expanded, its nature has also changed somewhat. Its locus moved partially away from the border. Its industry composition has shifted -- from original concentration in textiles to more electronics and auto parts. Today, in the western border especially Tijuana, there is a concentration of electronics firms including many of Japanese and some of Korean ownership. This change has implied an upgrading in the skill levels of some maquiladora workers.

As the maquiladora industry becomes more world competitive and utilizes higher skills, some may join the conventional manufacturing sector. On the other hand, low-end maquiladoras that cannot compete, even on a very low cost basis, have no choice but to move away from Mexico and relocate to parts of the world with much cheaper labor than Mexico, such as Malaysia.

There has been a tendency to develop maquiladora mega-plants that produce product that account for substantial amount of the U.S. market. In the case of Trico discussed in Chapter 9, the wiper blades produced constitute over half of the U.S. market. One SONY TV mega-plant in Tijuana produces nine billion dollars yearly, a significant part of the U.S. market. In fact, fifteen maquiladora mega-plants constitute two thirds of sectoral exports.

One of the persistent problems from the standpoint of Mexico has been the low proportion of Mexican raw materials and components used. On the average in the 1990s 1.5 percent of the maquiladora raw materials have been domestic. The value is much lower than for co-production arrangements in many other areas including Asia. The reason may be the close proximity of most of the maquila production plants to the U.S. -- this encourages U.S. supply, since it is so readily at hand. Another reason relates to the increasing prevalence in the maquilas of electronics production, which requires very high standards of components pointing to U.S. supply.

There are environmental, social, and health detriments. Environmentally, the maquiladoras cause water pollution, water consumption (i.e. in the very dry border region), air pollution, and toxic discharges, among other things. Health problems stem from the crowded, noisy, and sometimes contaminated work environment in the plants. Another aspect is the family disruption often caused for women working in the maquiladora. This may be expressed as marital strains, since the maquila worker is no longer following traditional role.

The maquiladora has been an economic motivator for growth of the Mexican border region. That region has been growing at rapid rates in the 20th century and continues to increase. One of the principal causes is the rapid rise of maquiladora employment opportunities. The growth has also causes positive spillover effects in the U.S. twin cities on the U.S. side.

On the other hand, the Mexican border cities have grown so rapidly that they are overburdened with infrastructure, government services, and public order and safety problems (Pick, Viswanathan, Hettrick, and Ellsworth 1999).

Among the major trends expected for the future are the following (Mendiola 1995):
- Development of more maquiladoras away from the border strip.
- Increased Mexican supply of raw materials and components.
- Greater opportunities for skills training of employees.
- Increased technology transfer from the U.S. to Mexico.
- Rising specialization of products. This will encourage sales not only to the U.S. market but also to global markets.

In sum, what these future changes point towards is an adaptation of the best parts of maquiladora to become more conventional. The Mexican federal government must take steps to recognize the changes taking place in this industry and to adopt support measures that are appropriate to ensure success for the 21st century. It needs to plan for a higher quality and more world competitive maquiladora industry. It needs also to figure out ways that the domestic suppliers and consumers will benefit to a greater extent.

## Environment

Mexico has a one of the richest ecological storehouses in the world. However, in the thrust to modernize, many environmental damages have occurred. The environmental impacts are heightened in Mexico City, which has experienced severe environmental deterioration. Yet, it also impacts regions distant from the capital such as the oil region, the tropical forests, and the border zones. Although federal government regulations have been strengthened, even to advanced standards, the real problem is the frequent inability to enforce the regulations. This stems from lack of budget and sometimes lack of will, inconsistency in political interests, and politically-based regional "planning".

Among the causes of the serious environmental problems of Mexico are the following:

- The massive rural to urban migration of the past fifty years has brought too many people into ciites and over-strained the capacity of the largest cities to control, regulate, and mitigate environmental hazards and threats.
- The emphasis on national economic growth, productivity gains, and export in the 1990s has led to enlarged environmental impacts i.e. through addition of factories, transport, pipelines, and infrastructure, that have lacked controls.
- The growing urban populations have put pressure on water and energy supply systems that have caused environmental damages.
- The petroleum industry as part of the federal government has proceeded in a largely unregulated way and yet the potential damages are highly complex and not easily remedied, i.g., oceanic pollution.
- The remote parts of the nation have had severe incursions due to opportunistic investors and projects. This has led to annual losses of forests of over one million acres per year and erosion problems (Mumme 1991).
- Environmental data are not collected systematically or provided freely, so the ability to analyze and understand the often highly complex environmental problems is limited.

Mexico City has the worst environmental situation. It is due in part to inadequate environmental planning and control measures in one of the world's largest cities with over 15 million inhabitants. Among its environmental problems are loss of lakes and woodlands, land degradation, devastation of plant and animal life, air pollution, water pollution, deficiencies in land use and housing, pressure on limited water supplies, land subsidence, and insufficient means of solid waste disposal (Mumme 1991; Pick and Butler 1997). In several of these area particularly air pollution, Mexico City is among the world's worst.

There are some interesting trends towards grass roots environmental opposition. In the 1990s, non-profit environmental groups became more prominent. Although not in the center of the national spotlight, these issues are emerging as important secondary ones in the new electoral environment of Mexico.

The government has taken formal steps to mitigate the environmental toll. The federal government has had an environmental secretariat since the De la Madrid administration in the 1980s. Currently the responsible agency SEMERNAP is providing a large array of programs to stall or reduce the hazards. However, the environmental problems are growing and the ability of the federal government to stop the tide is limited.

We regard the environmental area as being a downside of the economic opening up and globalization tendencies discussed in much of this volume. Federal budget resources have been limited and have been allocated more to stimulate production, manufacture, and export, rather than restrict the pollution impacts. The government has tried at times, but has been ineffective at significantly turning around the long-term rural to urban migration trend (Garza 1999); consequently the environment in the big cities is continuing to deteriorate.

There is potential for the government to provide better environmental quality. It can do this through allocating more funding and real clout to environmental education and regulation, and by steadily addressing some of the underlying causes noted above. It is not an easy pathway, but it hasn't been in advanced nations including the U.S. However, it is an important area of policy to preserve a natural heritage and improve the quality of life.

## Drugs

An area of "globalization" that has not been discussed in this book is that of narcotic drugs. This area is pointed out in this summary chapter since it is an important one for Mexico respected to its economic growth, political stability, public security, and quality of life. Regarding the economic aspects, drugs accounted for about 1.25 percent of GDP in 1988 (Estimates of Peter Reuter and David Ronfeldt, cited in Toro 1998). The level is probably higher today, since drug flows have increased over the past twelve years. The fact is that study of the actual amounts or percentages are not possible to obtain with much accuracy.

The rise in the Mexican drug trade was stimulated by the successful efforts in the mid 1980s of the U.S. to greatly inhibit the trading routes that went from Columbia through the Caribbean and into the U.S. often in Florida (Economist 1997; Toro 1998). As a consequence, a new principal route was established, from Columbia through Mexico and then into the U.S. over the border. Drug gangs developed in many cities, but especially in the Mexican border cities (Golden 1999) including Tijuana (Arellano Félix gang) and Ciudad Juárez (gang of the late Amado Carillo Fuentes and his successors). When the U.S. government, starting in the Reagan Administration, put more emphasis on reducing Mexican drug flow, the effects were mixed. Although the volume of traffic was reduced, the ironic flip side was that as prices increased, the revenues of Mexican drug cartels increased substantially, leading to great potentials for bribery and corruption within Mexico and larger, more amply financed operations. It is well known in Mexico that drug money has been used to infiltrate and influence government officials, police, transport companies, financial institutions, and other mainstream entities.

The Mexican federal government has offices and large budgets to combat the drug trafficking, since the late 1980s including a large portion of the Mexican Attorney General's budget (Toro 1998). The offices responsible in the federal government have shifted over the past decade and now are a shared effort of the Federal Direction of Security (DFS), Federal Judicial Police, and Attorney General (Astorga 1998). The success has been limited, many would shown by the large resources and continuing influence by the cartels.

Among the social costs have been rising security and safety problems; serious threats to certain constituencies; reduction in the profitability of some industries; increasing although still not worrisome addicted segment of the population; and instances of governmental corruption. There are also opportunity costs i.e. the billions spent in the drug trade could have been used for beneficial purposes.

We raise this problem area because it strangely and sadly fits into the broader themes of this book, i.e. of international opening up of the economy, of imports and exports, and of the world system relationships of an advanced nation and its consumer market with developing countries that supply a commodity. In the binational policy debates, both federal governments express deep concern about the problem. There have been claims and counter-claims of who is responsible for the problem and what the reach of national sovereignties are to repair the problem. Mexican leaders have pointed out that the root of the problem lies in the market demands of a large U.S. consumer base. U.S. leaders have stressed the supply routes principally go through Mexico and are not being constricted enough including not having enough cooperation inside Mexico. These arguments have been uncomfortable and difficult, and have led to diplomatic tensions at times.

We do not propose policy solutions in this very difficult area, but underscore that any lasting solution will need to be one involving binational cooperation, just as the "solutions" in the Caribbean in the 1980s had to be done cooperatively. We hope that the leaders of both governments will make progress in ameliorating this economic force and its detriments.

## Inequality History Repeated Itself: the Diaz Era

The era of the presidency of Porfirio Diaz lasted from 1885 to 1910 and was a time of general prosperity and foreign involvement in Mexico. It is a time that has been criticized because of the inequalities and overly capitalistic emphases. This section briefly discusses this era as a counterpart that has some similarities to the present.

The Porfiriate was an era of economic growth and prosperity. The Mexican PIB grew by 3 percent yearly (Catao 1998) and exports grew substantially. However, because Mexico started at such a low level of exports, by 1910, the ratio of exports to GDP was only 10.5 percent. This was much lower than for the other large Latin American countries of Argentina (22 percent) and Brazil (20 percent). Mexico exported predominantly products from mining especially copper, lead, silver, and oil. In a parallel to the present day, the refining of oil was done in the U.S. (Catao 1998). The regions of Mexico with the most foreign interactions were the Yucatan peninsula and the border states (INEGI 1994). The north is consistent with the present day, although the Yucatan is mainly tied to the exterior today through tourism. Another parallel of today was a labor force characterized by high mobility.

In another comparison to today, agricultural exports were not prominent and 85 percent of agricultural production was consumed domestically (Catao 1998).

There were social inequities that grew during the period, and eventually underpinned the Mexican revolution. This included a lack of landholding by the peasantry and high levels of poverty. Today, agriculture is widely owned through the ejido system, but the ejido system is gradually being changed by new laws. Largescale commerce was dominated by foreigners, although local commerce was controlled by Mexicans and Spanish (INEGI 1994). There are some parallels here. Mexico is beginning to see foreign presence in the larger areas of commerce, with Walmart's prominent position being one example of an emerging trend. Yet, the smaller areas of commerce were Mexican controlled, often through the informal economy.

In the Porfirian era, foreigners invested substantially in Mexico. For example, land was 25 percent owned by foreigners in 1910 (Catao 1998). There was large scale capital investment in the railroads and in other aspects of infrastructure (Catao 1998). This is similar to the privatization that influenced transportation and infrastructure during the 1990s, but often not successfully.

Banking enlarged and did so through *auto-prestamos* i.e. loans by banks to their own directors or immediate associates. In spite of this obvious conflict of interest, banking prospered during the era. This is in contrast with the recent experience, in which conflicts of interest and mismanagement in the re-privatization brought down the banking industry.

Overall, the Porfiriate was a time of economic expansion and international trade. It brought foreigners into the country to a much larger extent, but their successes were mixed. Under the surface, inequalities increased substantially, since the peasants were further removed from the standards of living of the wealthy. The era has been criticized often harshly as a time of rampant capitalism and lack of social concerns. Eventually, the situation was brought to a boiling over into the revolutionary period, which drew Mexico inward and ended this time of an open and growing economy. One of the lessons that may be learned from the Porfiriate is that government should avoid becoming too fixated on economic gain, while it ignores social class inequities. It also might indicate that there is nothing new about strong foreign and especially U.S. involvement and interactions with Mexico. The Porfiirate happened one hundred years ago, and many the cautions as well as opportunities again confront policy makers and leaders.

## Conclusions

This chapter has summarized the key findings of the book and related them to government policy and challenges for the future. There are many ways that the Mexican federal government can build on accomplishments and successes of the past twenty years, as well as reverse or mitigate certain detrimental tendencies. In many of the key areas discussed, the binational relationship with the U.S. emerges as the defining element. This was true in labor migration, technology transfer, imports/exports, petroleum, tourism, maquiladoras, and drug trafficking. The proximity has created a special and more important relationship. That relationship will continue as crucial to policy and decision making.

Many recommendations are made for government policy. It is important to note that the political environment may open up a lot in the early 21st century, with opposition parties at some point gaining control. Whichever party is in control and how ever much they perceive change as their mandate, effecting many of these policies will require determination and will. Many of the problems are not easy to solve, but will take steady, concerted efforts over many years to make headway. We respect how great these challenges are, and also are confident that leaders will emerge to tackle them.

# 15

---

# The Future

- **Introduction**
  - **Environment**
  - **Population**
  - **Technology**
  - **Organization**
  - **Culture**
- **Conclusions**

## Introduction

This chapter focuses on Mexico and Mexico City as they have been influenced by globalization. Before systematically examining Mexico and Mexico City in the larger global context in Chapter 16, this chapter emphasizes Mexico and Mexico City as they have been influenced by globalization. The points made about the environment, population, technology, and how the society is organized are based upon observations made by us, and knowledge obtained in writing this book, and from cited research. For those who may disagree with these judgments, they may effectively serve as hypotheses for future research endeavors.

*Environment*

We expect continued problems with the urban infrastructure. We have described substantial problems with the transportation infrastructure throughout Mexico. We do not predict any great changes in resolving them. Especially in Mexico City, and along the U.S.-Mexico border, there are severe pollution problems. The pollution existing in Mexico City, along the border, and elsewhere in Mexico will continue unabated in the mid-term. In these same regions, and in other cities with expanding populations, there are severe infrastructure deficits – in delivery of potable water, sewage disposal, lack of electricity, and other basic services. Our expectation is that they will become more severe in the future. Many of these deficits will become even more challenging in industrializing areas, e.g., along the border, because of the lack of environmental controls.

*Population*

While there has been a substantial reduction in fertility in Mexico, there will be continued population growth in the near term and it will be several generations before the population will become stationary; that is, replacement only. Currently, we have shown there is a need to generate one million new jobs/year for the next fifteen years because of children already born (Pick, Butler, and Ramirez 1992). There will be continued migration to Mexico City, other large urban centers, urban corridors, and the U.S. border region. This migration will persevere because of the excess fertility of rural regions in Mexico. There also will be a depletion of population in many rural areas despite higher rural fertility because of migration to urban areas and to the U.S.-Mexico border region. While Mexico's population is expected to continue to grow, some rural areas are expected to actually lose population.

Another major influence in many rural areas will be that former ejidatarios, especially from areas suitable for large-scale agriculture, will be migrating to urban centers because of Article 27 allowing sales of ejido land. Thus, the development of agribusiness on these lands will result in urban migration and also have the consequence of reducing the need for a rural labor force with mechanization. This impact, we emphasize, will vary by where there is a broad expanse of land and availability of water to make agribusiness mechanization profitable. Urban and border migration patterns also will be accompanied by international migration to the U.S., much of it undocumented. We anticipate continuation of two major flows associated with the Mexican population in the U.S. First, there will be a certain extent of re-migration that is Mexican migrants to the U.S. returning to Mexico. Second, Mexico will benefit economically since many migrants to the U.S. will be sending money back to their relatives remaining behind in Mexico.

The lack of environmental superstructure noted in the previous section will not be universally shared. There are emerging interest groups that are favorable to an improved environment, but they have not yet been important enough have electoral impact. Spatial differentiation of 'haves' and 'have nots' will increase throughout the country and within urban areas. While educational level in Mexico has shown a general upward ascent over the past forty years, the relative difference among states has remained constant. We have shown the immense extent of the informal labor force in Mexico. The magnitude of poverty, of the marginal population in Mexico, may be as large as thirty percent. Given the need to develop so many new jobs we have cited above, it is highly unlikely that without a huge infusion of capital they will be created. In addition, there are trends of increasing use of technology in manufacturing and agriculture reducing the need for a large labor force. Thus, there are virtually no indications of a reduction in the marginal population in Mexico. In fact, the proclivity is for a potential large increase.

*Technology*

An increased use of higher technology in manufacturing and agriculture will be accompanied by dispersal of factories and jobs with increasing differentiation between lower and higher level jobs. An enlargement in service positions and an increase in part-time work will produce a downsizing of the middle-class.

Increasingly those who will luxuriate in the international economy's impact upon Mexico will be those who have the opportunity for a higher level education and training. A base of world-class production exists in Mexico City, Guadalajara, Monterrey, and in some locations along the U.S.-Mexico border. Upper level job potentials exist and probably will enlarge in communications, automobiles, and industries amenable to robotics. In particular there will be a flourishing number of positions in telecommunication technology. Accompanying these telecommunications jobs will be widespread conflict over who is going to control telecommunication technology in Mexico. This friction undoubtedly will engender substantial job dislocations.

Despite possible growth in upper level positions, the vast majority of jobs will be at lower levels. Thus, overall employment will continue to be at the menial level. The lack of middle class employment opportunities will plague Mexico over the next decades. Even if such positions were to expand, there would remain problems of education and training. Thus the problem is at least twofold. First, to develop the necessary jobs and second to engender a well-trained and educated labor force. These two uncertainties will continue to plague economic expansion thus help continuing the marginalization of most of the potentially economically productive parts of the population.

*Organization*

We are convinced that Mexico is a semi-periphery country and that it will remain so; we do not see it becoming a core nation or reverting to a peripheral status; however, it undoubtedly is becoming an increasingly important player in Central and South America.
Mexico will receive expanded foreign direct investment accompanied by greater influence of its economy by the World Bank, the International Monetary Fund, and transnational corporations, increasingly from Asia, but especially those from the U.S. There will be continued expansion of alliances, mergers, and associations by Mexican corporations with foreign firms, especially those from the U.S. and Asian countries.

Notwithstanding all other influences, major tourism, financial, and "cultural" exchanges will continue to be dominated by the U.S. One consequence of this international influence, especially by the U.S., is a need to examine Mexican national control vs. dominance by international corporations, again especially those from the U.S. There is one future scenario we do not want to contemplate. That is, what would happen if there was an extensive economic turndown in the U.S.? Obviously, such a circumstance would have a major impact U.S. and Mexico and other international relationships. Unless such economic devastation occurs, economic influence by major U.S. corporations will grow substantially in the future.

The importance of foreign relationships to Mexico are underscored by recalling that many of the top 500 enterprises in Mexico are U.S. corporations, some of them having as large a "GDP" than the entire country of Mexico. Our examination of the interdependency of Mexico on core countries implies that much more examination is necessary assessing relationships among the poor and wealthy (nations, states, and areas), in this instance Mexico. We feel that we have just begun to understand the complexity of these exchanges. There is much that needs to be accomplished before we comprehend how economic structures within the nation exist with other nation-states and multinational enterprises. One arena in which these connections will be played out is in the communications industry. Transnational enterprises from several nations are vying to control the communications industry in Mexico. This sector is a major component of the globalization of the Mexican economy but at the same time is going to be a source of conflict over its control – within Mexico and at the international level. Currently there is regional variation in control over Mexico's long distance telephone system with Telmex dominating local calls. The emergence of other electronic media, including the internet, has resulted in countries other than the U.S. vying for dominance. This arena of contention may give a hint as to what extent other countries may be able to overcome the hegemony of the U.S. in the Mexican economy, or at least in some sectors.

Oil in Mexico is an important commodity. Yet much of it is refined in the U.S. If Mexico is to become oil independent it must develop its own refining capacity. To do so requires a huge capital investment, an investment not likely to be made in the near future. Further, this means that nothing will be accomplished in modernizing this capacity. On the other hand, it is clear that while extensive privatization has taken place in Mexico, especially up to 1993, the oil sector is not a candidate for privatization. If so, modernization of Pemex remains problematic without extensive external resources

At the national level, dependency on oil revenues will continue and result in constant variation in available resources to government because of international fluctuations in oil prices over which Mexico has very little influence. The Mexican federal budget then will be subject to conditions beyond its control since it will continue to depend upon oil revenues.

On the other hand, maquiladoras will continue to expand and increasingly become spread throughout Mexico. Possible alterations in this sector are tariffs that in the year 2001 are to be eliminated. Currently there appears to be little anxiety on either side of the border in respect to possible impacts of eliminating such tariffs.

As it is now, tourism will remain as one of the main contributors to the Mexican economy. There is little anticipation that the dominance of U.S. tourists will be altered in the future. In fact, there is a possibility of future tourist development in Mexico with expanded facilities oriented toward the U.S. market. In addition, there is a huge potential tourist potential in the large "Mexican" population in the U.S. Many second and later generations may have the urge to return to Mexico to visit relatives and for recreational purposes.

Neither the expansion of maquiladoras, tourism, or other economic developments will generate enough jobs for those who want them; there will be a deficit of jobs in Mexico for the potentially economically active population. This lack of jobs, of course, will continue to exert pressure on Mexican nationals to migrate to the U.S., legally and illegally.

There will continue to be hyper-concentration of Mexico's main financial activities in greater Mexico City and within specific areas within that city. As such, continued concentration of high-end and other service activities in Mexico City will be associated with an expanded globalization impact on the economy of Mexico and Mexico City. By their sheer economic power, political influence by major U.S. corporations will grow substantially. Environmental and other rules and regulations hindering economic expansion will fall to the wayside because of consistent violations will make them not enforceable.

In Mexico we anticipate little change in the core, semi-periphery, and periphery states and areas within cities in Mexico. That is, limited change in classification will occur. This is substantially because the north to south relative lack of education, poor training, and lack of resources will persist. The south's major natural resources will not aid it in overcoming its basic inequality.

We already noted that future agriculture increasingly will be controlled by agribusiness, where ample water is available. Nevertheless, the vast majority of Mexicans involved in agricultural pursuits will have very small plots of land having marginal subsidence farms. The informal labor force in Mexico will continue to be the dominant "sector." Yet, on the other hand, there will be ample opportunity at the top. Thus, there may the emergence of a u-shaped social structure with a relative decrease in the middle levels.

Increasing inequality among regions, cities, households, and families in Mexico will be accompanied by increases in the marginalization of the population; that is a lower quality of life for most Mexicans and an increasingly unequal distribution of income. Thus, inequality will continue and most likely will grow greater. The major possible mitigating factors in resolving most of the uncertainties in Mexico is the combination of a number of outstanding leaders coupled with the political will to overcome these major deficits.

The appearance of and perhaps reality of political democracy will continue; however, the increasing disparity between the haves and "have nots" will engender great conflict in Mexico unless this positive leadership is demonstrated.

*Culture*
Many of the cultural traditions in Mexico will hinder globalization. Among them is long-standing distrust of their northern neighbor. This wariness is constantly reinforced by those in the U.S. who have little knowledge of Mexico, many of whom also have no interest in increasing their knowledge or understanding.

Within Mexico there is still great variation. There is a wealthy-poor axis beginning at the U.S. border (excluding Mexico City and environs) to the poor south. Little change is expected in these socioeconomic levels. Other cultural differences are noted, some of which are related to indigenous status – Indian and non-Indian, but also region of residence, e.g., Chilangos, Nortenos, etc. Thus, cultural complexity and variation is great in Mexico and virtually all of these patterns will continue to exist; however, perhaps the most important cultural element emerging in Mexico is the extent to which "culture," literature, music, cinema, etc., is being influenced by its neighbor to the north – the gringos.

## Conclusions

The environmental, population, technology, organizational, and cultural dimensions presented in this chapter do not contemplate an overly optimistic view of the future in Mexico. Our usual optimism cannot replace what we consider an objective view of observations, research, and literature review. However, political will and outstanding leadership could advance Mexico at a more rapid pace and lead to more positive outcomes in the long term.

# 16

## Mexico and Mexico City
## In the Larger Global Context

- **Introduction**
- **Nation-State Developmental Levels: Cluster Analysis**
- **Mexico States Developmental Cluster Analysis**
- **Major Mexican Cities Developmental Cluster Analysis**
- **Mexico's World System Relationships**
  - **Transnational Corporate Penetration**
  - **Foreign Direct Investment**
  - **Exports and Imports**
  - **In-Bond Industry (Maquiladoras)**
  - **Privatization and Oil**
  - **Tourism**
  - **Other Flows and Exchanges**
- **Concluding Remarks**

## Introduction

Most analyses examining world system theory focus on nation-states (see Sklair 1999 and Shannon 1989 for reviews). Even so, world system theory may apply to other units of analysis such as cities and firms (Chase-Dunn 1985, 1998:259, 203) that are spatially differentiated. This implies that there are zones with boundaries. In addition, there appear to be different aspects of globalization, among them ecological, communications, cultural, and political. In this book we concentrated on nation-states and emphasized *economic globalization* as it influences Mexico. Economic globalization is defined as the expansion and intensification of international trade and investment (Manning 1999; Chase-Dunn 1999). Ultimately, another question must be answered: Does globalization[1] impact not only nation-states but also subunits within nations, such as cities and regions? Thus, chapters also accentuated states within Mexico cities and small areas within cities, especially Mexico City.

World system theory assumes that there are identifiable strata in the world's economic system. The theory does not necessarily require systematic patterns of development of nation-states such as divergence, convergence, or polarity.

However, convergence theory in economics obviously maintains that there is convergence. Part of the argument rests upon the assumption that modern technology allows poorer nations to become more like industrial nations. In contrast to convergence theory, dependency theory assumes continued divergence and polarization of the periphery from the core. This perspective also contends that there are powerful forces driving strata further apart. Thus, dependency theory assumes that wealthy nations (core) are enriching themselves at the expense of poor nations because only the core benefits from economic exchanges. This results in an increasing and continuing gap between the core and periphery. These orientations imply that inter-country disparity among nations and not inequality within nations is the major component of the world's total income inequality (Firebaugh 1999).

For recent decades, Firebaugh (1999) asks whether or not any convergence or divergence has taken place and whether it is related to the faster population growth of poorer nations. He assumes that slower income growth in poor nations may not be related to globalization at all but rather to their greater population increases, as seem for example in the swelling of the young, nonworking population. He points out that at the onset of the Industrial Revolution average income in the wealthiest nations grew to four times the level of the poorest nations but now differs by a factor of about 30. There is little difference of opinion that such a dramatic divergence took place.

The query now is "What has happened in more recent times?" This question is an important one in respect to the research presented in this book because different explanations have been offered as to whether or not change has transpired. Economists generally report that divergence has occurred. On the other hand, Firebaugh's (1999) analysis shows that when weights are applied for population growth, there were increases until 1975 and declines thereafter; as a result, there was little net change in inequality from 1960 to 1989. These results lead him to conclude that the centuries old rising inequality among nations leveled off between 1960 and 1989. Thus, the dependency thesis of a polarizing world receives no support. Further, no divergence or convergence has taken

---

[1]  Sklair (1999) distinguishes between globalization, i.e. global processes, as opposed to inter-nationalization, i.e. each country in its inter-national relationship. From his perspective we are studying Mexico's inter-nationalization.

place but rather there has been stability in the world's hierarchy of nations. Thus, both dependency theory and convergence theory do not receive support. Clearly, it is important to distinguish population-induced polarization from dependency-induced polarization.

Firebaugh's view is that population change accounts for the stability that has taken place since 1960. Thus, per capita income is a function of both changing income and changing population. Countries with rapid population increases are inherently disadvantaged. This explanation, we believe, is related to world cluster developmental levels reported in Chapter 3 and further explicated in this chapter. In addition, his explanation of stability in world system country rankings may apply to states in Mexico and small areas within cities in Mexico.

If Mexico is a typical example, and we believe that it is, we have shown that huge inequality exists within Mexico that must be taken into account. Our prior empirical analyses, as well as this volume, demonstrate that in Mexico huge inequality exists at the regional, state, municipio, city, and household levels (Pick, Butler, and Lanzer 1989; Pick and Butler 1994; Pick and Butler 1997, 2000).

Important questions remain for states and cities. That is, what changes have taken place over time? Has there been convergence, divergence, or stability and for what periods of time? Mexico is especially important in this regard because its economic development has been controlled for many years and under varying circumstances. First outsiders were encouraged, then excluded by import substitution, and subsequently once again incorporated into the economic system. Thus, for different economic regimes and time periods, the impacts of foreign and domestic investment, productivity, and population growth need to be analyzed. In addition, while population growth in Mexico has been rapid up until recently it is slowing in the 21$^{st}$ century.

In the remainder of this chapter we revisit Chapter 3 that placed Mexico and Mexico City in the larger global context. In that chapter we presented results of cluster analyses examining developmental levels in the world's nation-states, states of Mexico, municipios, and within in Mexico City. In reformulating our theoretical position in this chapter we rely upon research carried out to complete this book and further review of previous and emerging literature on globalization and Mexico.

Our focus initially on nation-states' developmental levels was undertaken on the assumption that this was only a first analytic step in understanding Mexico in the globalization process. We also believed that the world system perspective would prove to be very valuable in carrying out similar analyses for various units *within* nations – in this case, Mexico and, *within* cities of that nation. After accomplishing these first analytic operations, we assumed then it would be appropriate to emphasize networks delving into specific relationships among nations, especially for Mexico, and among various units within that nation; and in Mexico among the various states, municipios, and cities.

As we noted in Chapter 3, variables for the nation-state cluster analysis were selected on the basis of past development and world system research (see Chase-Dunn 1999: 365-366). Data were derived from the *World Bank* (1995) and *CIA* (1996). In our Mexico Database Project we have many additional nation-state variables that could have been used in the analysis.

In placing nation-states in a hierarchy, our results were substantially consistent with other research operating from several different perspectives illustrating that our cluster analysis approach was appropriated for these data. There are such large differences among nation-states that diverse analyses are to a large extent consistent. However, it still may be problematic as to what to label categories (see Snyder and Kick 1979: 1110).

## Nation-State Developmental Levels: Cluster Analysis[2]

World system theory makes the assumption that there is a hierarchy of nations; it also postulates that there is consistency among forces driving nations into various strata or levels. The theory also assumes that the hierarchy of nation-states is associated with a variety of economic dimensions. Utilizing cluster analysis, we first examined the world system theory assumption to determine if there is a hierarchy of nations. Our analysis established that there is a pecking-order of nations associated with a set of standalized indicator especially economic ones. The cluster analysis included variables utilized in a variety of previous research examining the world system but also included population dimensions. We debated whether we should include per capita energy consumption in the cluster analysis (see Chase-Dunn 1998: 216, 265). If only one variable had been used for developmental level classification, GNP would have undoubtedly been the best one; the results of our cluster analysis fairly well compared to the GNP, but not entirely so. Chase-Dunn (1998 via Wallerstein) implies that there are different kinds of production activities taking place in the core, semi-periphery, and periphery (also see Arrighi and Drangel 1986; Bergesen and Fernandez 1995). Other possible variables suggested by Chase-Dunn (1998: 216) were (1) ratio of GNP to the size of the active work force, (2) level of urbanization, and (3) percent of labor force in agriculture.

Among nations at one level of the hierarchy, there was little change in position regardless of mumber of clusters included greater than three. We ultimately concluded that a six-cluster output appeared to be the best fit (for analytical results, see Map 3.1 and Table 3.1).

As a result of our analysis, we labeled a large number of countries as being at the economic *lower level.*[3]  Chase-Dunn (1998; 338) argues that there is especially a need for data allowing *"differences among peripheral countries"* to become known (italics in original). He believes that there are "extreme periphery" and "external periphery" countries contributing to the outer boundaries of the world system. Substantially similar consistent results were noted for nations classified in the *middle-level* of development, regardless of the number of clusters examined.

*Upper-level* developed nations split into several important clusters when different cluster steps were investigated, with a few nations clustering differently. This appears to confirm Chase-Dunn's observation that there may be hegemonic core powers, other core powers, and second-tier core powers. The results of our analysis implied that two nations (multicentric) form one *upper-upper level* development cluster; for Japan this may not be amazing; however, the inclusion of Switzerland along with Japan in this super level may be surprising (however see Beer 1999; Crenshaw 1992).

Two other clusters formed what appeared to be *upper-level* developed nations. One of these two other clusters of upper-level nations included many European nations, along with Hong Kong, Singapore, and the United States. The placement of the U.S. as not one of the main core nations may be a surprise to some. However, Chase-Dunn (1998: 342), Chase-Dunn and Podobrmik (1985), and Bergesen and Fernandez (1995) argue that the U.S. is a declining hegemonic state. The second cluster consists of a mixture of nations including Australia, Canada, Finland, Italy, Kuwait, and the United Arab Emirates. The cluster

---

[2]  For a discussion of cluster analysis techniques used in this effort, see chapter 2
[3]  A cluster analysis of the vast number of nations at the lower-level of development possibly could reveal some variation among them; such an analysis might result in what Altman (1999) has labeled 'the fourth world – the least developed parts of Africa and Asia.

analysis resulted in two middle level developed nations, one cluster appearing to be at a somewhat lower level than the other one. For our purposes, all other nations were classified at a lower level of development.

Of particular interest in longitudinal analyses are nation-states that have made some upward or downward movement. As an example, we submit that Botswana and Mexico undoubtedly have shown upward movement in developmental level. Other research strengthened the confidence we have in our results (see Korzeniewicz and Moran 1997). However, our analytic results also resulted in several surprises that are in disagreement with some previous research. For example, Rossem (1996: 518) placed in the "upper" core, significantly above other nations Japan, U.S., France, and the Federal Republic of Germany. Our analysis categorized Japan and Switzerland as the premier core nations. Rossem placed Japan in the core but at a lower level than five other nations and Switzerland as the second highest nation in the semi-periphery. In addition, he categorized China as a core nation and India as one of the major semi-periphery nations. Economic growth in China has been the most important variable equalizing world nations from 1950 to 1977 in weighted studies; that is, controlling for population growth (Berry et al. 1983). Remove China from the analysis and there is divergence and rising income inequality. In addition, India, because of its large population affects analytic results.

We concluded that both China and India should be classified as periphery nations. We disagree with Rossem and believe that Firebaugh has the explanation as to why China and India were placed by Rossem higher than in our analysis; that is population per se and/or vast geographic territory do not make for a core or semi-periphery country. Note also that from a different orientation, Evans and Rauch (1999: 763) also place India as a 'developing' country.

## Mexico States Developmental Cluster Analysis

World system theory makes the assumption that there is a hierarchy of nations; we made an additional supposition that the perspective also could be applied to states within Mexico (also see Chase-Dunn 1998: 210). As with nation-states, we assumed that there is a hierarchy of states within a nation – in this instance Mexico -- also associated with a variety of economic dimensions comparable to those for nation-states. In this research we thus transferred the world system theory assumption that there is a hierarchy of nations to the belief that there also is a regime of units within a nation associated with a variety of economic and population factors. Ultimately, the concern is whether or not international globalization processes or a nation's national class structure have greater consequences for its national development (Chase-Dunn 1998: 328). This is a question that we have not yet answered but believe that globalization of the Mexican economy so far has not altered the basic class structure of Mexico. That is, we assumed that there has been regional inequality within Mexico and its cities and that this basic inequality has not been modified.

Accordingly, then, we assume that a Mexican *state* developmental level cluster analysis was necessary to determine if there was a hierarchy of levels within Mexico. The basic postulate of this analysis is that within Mexico there are different developmental levels. The methodological procedure was the same as for the study of nation-state clusters.

Inasmuch as possible, variables utilized in the state level analysis were the same ones used for the nation-states developmental study. For Mexico, several surrogate variables were used because in Mexico data-gathering focuses on production rather than consumption. Results of this Mexican-state cluster analysis were reported in Table 3.2 and Map 3.2.

Our basic assumption of varying development levels of Mexican states was verified using the cluster method. The Federal District and Baja California formed a separate, multicentric, *upper-upper level* development cluster. In contrast to the nation-state analysis, however, four *middle-level* clusters were clearly demarcated. The two *lower level* development clusters buttressed our belief that the cluster analysis reflected contemporary developmental levels in Mexico. The lowest development cluster included states anyone familiar with Mexico would recognize – Chiapas, Oaxaca, and Guerrero. We have not found any other research studies on Mexico making such distinctions.

## Major Mexican Cities Developmental Cluster Analysis

We had already carried out a series of cluster analyses of Mexico Megacity using 30 variables and carried out selected other cluster analyses focusing on specific concerns such as the economy, labor force, and social status (Pick and Butler, 1997; 2000). The cluster analysis for Mexico City utilized variables similar to those for the nation-state and Mexico-state analyses (see Map 3.3). The cluster analysis shows quite clearly that Mexico City has a "traditional urban development core" consisting of a very few area-units in the city. Of the zones identified by cluster analysis, they clearly had substantially different developmental levels. Other aspects of that cluster study demonstrated that Mexico City does not fit the traditional development of cities in the U.S. For example, the poorest areas are located on the outer perimeters of the city. One is tempted to utilize world system theory terminology and label the traditional center as a 'core' area with a plurality of the major transnational and Mexican '500' corporations being located there. Galtung (1980) suggests that there is a periphery of the center (core) and a center of the periphery that fits our analysis quite well. Also attractive, then, is to label outer areas of the metropolitan region as peripheral areas in the context of a core center. Of course, that leaves a number of areas in the metropolis catalogued as semi-periphery.

Of special interest is that an earlier accomplished 1980 factor analysis using a more geographically restricted definition of Mexico City identified essentially similar zones demonstrating that while some changes may have taken place in the 1980s, the major types remained substantially the same (Rubalcava and Schteingart 1987; also see Garza 1987).

As we noted in Chapter 3, at the municipio level, other Mexican cities do not have a sufficient number of municipio units to carry out a cluster analysis. Smaller area data within cities (AGEBs) are available in the Mexico Database but have not yet been studied. Undoubtedly they would show variation similar to that we have observed for Mexico City.

## Mexico's World System Relationships

Our cluster analysis and other analyses have firmly established that contemporary Mexico is in a middle-level of development – the semi-periphery (*World Bank* 1995). A longitudinal analysis of Mexico's developmental level also undoubtedly would have shown Mexico at a lower level of development at earlier dates. Thus, developmental level is not seen as being immutable but subject to change, both upward and downward (see Shannon 1996 for a long-term historical view). However, we do not envision development as occurring in an ordered sequence such as postulated by modernization theory. In contrast, for the short-term we make two assumptions: (1) the most likely happenstance is that there is stability in world system position and (2) that some minimal upward and downward mobility takes place. Over the long-term, however, undoubtedly nations will continue to rise and fall in the hierarchy. Rarely, if ever, has a periphery nation-state become a core state (Chase-Dunn 1998:121). However, a similar conclusion may not be warranted for Mexican states, e.g. in historical context, the state of Baja California appears to have moved from the periphery to the semi-periphery to the core. While we have not examined them yet in this respect, some areas within Mexico City may have moved up in the hierarchy.

Earlier world system research placed Mexico in the periphery (Snyder and Kick 1979: 1110 ff.). However, some world systems research recently placed Mexico in the semi-periphery category (Rossem 1996). So, some changes in Mexico's position have been reported. An important question is whether or not this change in the world system took place simultaneously with other nations or at a different time. Only by separating out developmental level from network changes can this be determined.

In determining Mexico's relationship with other countries of the world, using dimensions analyzed in various chapters in this book, we consistently demonstrated extensive corporate penetration by U.S. and other international corporations into Mexico, but mainly from the U.S. We also confirmed extensive foreign direct investment, export and imports by specific nations, in-bond industry, oil, and tourism. Our research emphasizes the hegemonic nature of Mexico City in Mexico. That is, it clearly has competitive advantage over all other states and cities in Mexico. At the state level, Baja California is challenging and at the city level, clearly Monterrey (especially in manufacturing) and Guadalajara may be considered as "other core" cities.

In this research, since its inception, we argued that the greatest impact on Mexico was its variety of associations with the U.S. Historically over the past several hundred years that affinity has been substantially stronger than with any other nation. Its relationship with the U.S. has included all the "categorical variable" dimensions used by world systems researchers, including arms sales, diplomatic relations, armed interventions, trade, and economic penetration. While these dimensions were not explored in our analysis they are consistent with the influence of the U.S. on Mexico. We pointed out earlier that any analysis ignoring the monumental changes in the relationship between Mexico and the U.S. and that puts them into a binary relationship is flawed from the very beginning.

*Transnational Corporate Penetration*

The research reported in this volume makes evident over and over again, in virtually all sectors examined, there is extensive transnational corporate penetration into Mexico. The vast majority of foreign penetration is of U.S. origin; over half of the foreign capital in Mexico is from the U.S. (*Expansión* various dates). In 1986, 96 of the Mexican '500' corporations were U.S.; of them, 29 percent were prominent in the U.S. 'Fortune 500.' In 1997, of the major 500 entities in Mexico, 22 of the Top 50 were U.S. corporations. With three other foreign enterprises, 50 percent of the Top 50 were non Mexican.

Overall, the concentration of "500" corporations in Mexico increased in the Federal District from 149 in 1986 to 206 in 1993, and further increased by 1997. Clearly, in addition, there was a concentration of both foreign and Mexican corporations in the Federal District (Mexico City). Table 3.4 and Map 3.5 illustrated this concentration in Mexico City in the same two adjoining delegations of – Miguel Hidalgo and Cuauhtemoc, and in two adjoining municipios of Ecatepec and Tlalnepantla in greater Mexico City located outside of the Federal District in the State of Mexico. Thus, as we postulated and demonstrated, there is increasing geographic concentration of major economic enterprises by state, city, and small areas within Mexico City (Pick and Butler 1997).

*Foreign Direct Investment*

Mexico's acceptance of foreign direct investment (FDI) has increased substantially during recent years. Currently there are more substantial FDI inflows to Mexico than in the past (Bleakley 1995; United Nations 1992). At least partially as a result of the 1982 economic crisis in Mexico, Mexico in 1983 extensively liberalized its FDI rules and regulations (UN 1992: 83; also see Pick and Butler 1997, 2000). The result was expansive FDI increases in 1987 and following years. We agree with the United Nations report indicating that Mexico then moved from a 'restrictive high growth' nation into a 'liberal, low growth' nation (UN 1992: 68). The impact of FDI, of course, may be viewed as positive or negative depending upon host country or countries from which FDI originates (see Chase-Dunn 1975: 726).

Increases in FDI undoubtedly influenced the magnitude of industrial restructuring in Mexico, but only in specific sectors. In any case, changes have occurred in nation-states, states within Mexico, cities and small areas within cities in Mexico; thus we corroborated our expectations.

*Exports and Imports*

The magnitude of exports from and imports to Mexico has changed considerably over the years (see Figure 3.1). The balance of imports and exports has been at equilibrium at times, and at other junctures there has been an imbalance in either exports or imports. Further, the countries exported to and imported from also have varied over time (IMF 1979, 1991; Pick and Butler 1997; 2000). These variations reinforce our view that a binary analysis misses much of what is important. While changes in magnitude have been substantial, research reported in this volume constantly reminds us that the U.S. has remained Mexico's main trading partner, dwarfing the trade of all other countries put together. Thus there have been a variety of trends and cycles regarding the relationship of the U.S. to Mexico; these trends and cycles undoubtedly will accelerate in the future. Thus, any networked relationship needs to take into account the historical context and must recognize that a one-way binary relationship misrepresent the direction and magnitude of connections.

*In-Bond Industry (Maquiladoras)*

In Chapter 9 we explored development of the in-bond or maquiladora industry along the U.S. – Mexico border. Alderson (1999) argues that the development of maquiladoras in Mexico was not typical; thus, if he is correct, generalizing beyond our research on such developments may be risky.

Utilizing extensive data we illustrated extent of maquiladora concentrations among border cities, salaries, gender differences, and foreign and domestic components used in the industry. Overwhelmingly, foreign components were used as opposed to Mexican domestic components (also see Pick and Butler 1994).

There has been a relatively consistent rapid growth of the in-bond industry but growth accelerated during 1996 and 1997 as a result of the passage of NAFTA (INEGI 1995). Maquiladoras are almost exclusively foreign owned entities, again with the U.S. dominating the overall industry. An exception to the foreign domination of maquiladoras is the textile industry. Mexico dominates with 79% of textile capital (V. Carrillo 1994). While multifarious countries are involved in other sectors, our analysis demonstrates that the maquiladora industry is fundamentally accommodating U.S. corporations and the U.S. market. In addition, as with other exchanges with the U.S. and the world system, there is great variation in magnitude, direction, and sectors.

The maquila labor force is basically working for minimal wages at lower level jobs; the vast majority of the labor force consists of young women, although this varies somewhat by sector.

In Mexico, transnational corporations' standard manufacturing activities are primarily chemicals, fabricated metals, auto parts, and transportation equipment. However, *maquiladoras* are principally textile and electronic corporations, but in almost every circumstance these activities are dictated primarily by the core nations especially the U.S.

## Privatization and Oil

Driven by core nations and their financial influence on Mexico, during the past few years nationalized enterprises mostly have been privatized. Our examination of Mexico's "500" at several different time periods illustrated that the vast majority of privatization of major enterprises took place prior to 1993. The oil industry in Mexico, however, has remained under national ownership. As with most other relationships of Mexico with other world-states, the oil industry's major crude oil export partner is the U.S., exceeding all other countries (see Table 3.6 and Chapter 8). There also is extensive variation of Pemex's relationships with other states and cities. In particular, oil production and refining are dominated by two states (Tabasco and Veracruz) and occur in a limited number of other states.

## Tourism

As with most other economic aspects in Mexico, tourists entering Mexico by place of origin are dominated by the U.S. – ca. 90 percent. Similarly, over 90 percent of tourists from Mexico have the U.S. as their destination (see Table 3.7 in Chapter 10). Again any analysis that only is concerned with a one-way binary relationship is misleading. In addition, while tourism in both directions is growing with the U.S., Latin American tourists increasingly are not visiting Mexico (Secretaria de Turismo, Banco de Mexico 1992; Pick and Butler 1994).

There are substantial differences in international visitors to Mexico and the destinations of national visitors. In 1990, this variation occurred whether planned, traditional, grand city, interior city, or border cities tourist centers are the focus of the analysis (FONATUR nd; Pick and Butler 1997, 2000). As examples, the planned tourist centers of Cancun and Los Cabos attracted substantially more foreign visitors while the planned tourist centers of Ixtapa and Bahias de Huatulco were more attractive to Mexican tourists. The overall conclusion is that international tourism to Mexico is systematically allied to the core nation-states, markedly to and from the U.S. On the other hand there are substantially different manners with national visitors more likely to visit semi-periphery or periphery states. Like maquiladoras, the tourism domestic work force is low paid in menial jobs.

## Other Flows and Exchanges

Substantial information on other types of flows and exchanges of Mexico with other world nations was presented in other chapters of this book. Other aspects that we have illustrated but still need to be systematically investigated include cartel arrangements, R&D, patent license exchanges, subsidiaries, alliances, etc. More substantial data also need to be presented on domestic flows and exchanges among the states and within cities (see CONAPO 1991; Pick and Butler 1997).

Another aspect of the globalization of the Mexican economy that stood out in the writing of this book is the acceleration of mergers, alliances, and relationships with U.S. and other core-nation transnational corporations. They have occurred in all major economic sectors and are especially prominent in the communications and banking sectors. What this portends for the people of Mexico remains an open question.

Another notable event that we illustrated taking place in Mexico is that several major Mexican corporations are becoming major world players in their own right.

## Concluding Remarks

Analyses reported in this volume clearly support the notion that there is a hierarchy of nation-states. The nation-state analysis resulted in several surprises that did not fit common perceptions or some previous world system research, especially as regards Switzerland, China, and India. While our analysis was cross-sectional, we clearly do not see much future potential for convergence of nations in the world's nation-state hierarchy. We anticipate relative stability in world system classification. Firebaugh's (1999) analysis of nations, when they are weighted by population size, appears to confirm this conclusion from 1960 to 1989. Thus, consistent with his analysis, we forecast existing polarization to remain with insignificant movement upward or downward in the world system hierarchy over the next several decades, excluding traumatic events. Firebaugh's research also has substantial implications for Mexico because he concludes that population growth is a major factor in the distribution of per capita income across nations. This has special impact on Mexico since population projections reveal that over the next fifteen years, approximately one million persons per year will be coming of working age, i.e. ready to move into the labor force (Pick, Butler, and Ramirez 1992).

Our analysis, as we postulated, placed Mexico in the nation-state hierarchy at the middle-level, or using world system terminology, as a semi-periphery nation (also see Rossem 1996). Our application of the theory to units in Mexico – states and municipios – showed its utility for internal nation-state analysis. Thus, we demarcated levels within Mexico and Mexico City that clearly fit common perceptions of Mexico and intersect with world system theory.

We clearly assumed a relationship between the level of development of a nation, in this case Mexico, and its exchanges with other nations. We believe that eventually development and world system research will have to come to grips with the problem of causality. That is, how do nation-state development levels and the world system interact with each other at different times. Does developmental level cause a nation's relationship in the world system or does position in the world system cause developmental level? Or, is there a discursive, feedback system at work?

The little longitudinal research that has been accomplished suggests that nations, both in developmental level and world system position, remain relatively stable across time. Mexico illustrates that some mobility may be occurring. Further, there is research demonstrating that ascendancy and descendancy at the nation-state does in fact occur over longer periods of historical epochs (see Shannon 1996) and may be occurring in the contemporary world (see Korzeniewicz and Moran 1997: 1025 ff.). If so, the proposition that strength begets strength in economic systems needs to be examined more thoroughly. So a key question is under what factors does a country ascend or descend in developmental level in the world system since this apparently is an unusual occurrence? Our belief is, however, that very little change in relative position in the global hierarchy is going to occur over the next 20 years.

In longer-term analyses, we also expect substantial stability within Mexico, both at the state and smaller unit level; that is there may be some upward and downward movement of states and/or municipios in economic level but this movement will be minimal. In fact, at all units of analysis – nation-states, states within a nation, and areas within a state -- our hypothesis is that stability will be the norm.

Altman (1999) argues that on a global scale, technology has helped create a huge gap but that it also can give the poorest nations access to the economic mainstream. Our view is that it is highly unlikely that in the foreseeable future the gap between the "haves" and "have-nots" will be alleviated by technology. Technology – particularly emerging electronic communications – may actually increase the gap between those who now have and those who do not have. Our assumption, in fact, is that technology will provoke increasing inequality at all levels, including nation-states, states within nations, and smaller metropolitan areas within nations and cities.

Finally, we noted that most research has been time bound (see Shannon 1996 for a longer-term view). A longitudinal perspective raises the question of long term, dynamic world system changes and time bound causality. We have undertaken study of shorter duration that focuses on the late twentieth century.

# References

Adelson, Naomi. 1999. "Social Programs: Do They Really Help?" *El Financiero International.* July 26, 1999, p. 5.

Adelson, Naomi. 1999. "Keep on Trucking? Not Yet," *El Financiero International Edition*, October 11.

Afifi, A.A. and Stanley P. Azen. 1979. *Statistical Analysis: A Computer Oriented Approach.* New York: Academic Press.

Alba, Francisco. 1999. "La Migración Mexicana a Estados Unidos: Un Rompacabezas Difícil de Armar." *Este Pais.* Diciembre, pp. 32-37.

Alba Vega, Carlos and Dirk Kruijt. 1995. *La Utilidad de Lo Minúsculo: Informalidad y Microempresa en México, Centroaméria y Los Países Andinos.* Jornadas, 125. Mexico, D.F.: El Colegio de México.

Allen, Michael and John Bussey, "Mexico Feels Pain of Drop in World's Oil Prices," *Wall Street Journal.*, March 12, 1998.

Arrighi, Giovanni and Jessica Drangel. 1986. "The Stratification of the World Economy: An Exploration of the Semi-Peripheral Zone." *Review* 10:9-74.

Astorga, Luis. 1998. "Understanding the Drug Business." *U.S./Mexico Business*, pp. 26-28.

Bacon, David. 1998. "Maquiladora Mayhem." *In These Times*, July 12, 5-6.

Banamex. 1994. "Industrial Concentration," *Review of the Economic Situation in Mexico.* LCC (Nov.-Dec.):452-457.

Banamex. 1998. *México Social.* México, D.F.: División de Estudios Económicos y Sociales, Banco Nacional de México.

Banamex. 1998. "Automotive Industry, 1998-1999," *Review of the Economic Situation in Mexico.* LCC (Nov.), 422-424.

Bancomext. 1996. *Annual Report 1996.* Mexico, D.F.: Bancomext.

Banco de México. 1999. *Informe Annual 1998.* Mexico City: Banco de México.

Barkin, David. 1990. *Distorted Development: Mexico in the World Economy.* Boulder: Westview Press.

Barkin, David. 1992. "The New Shape of the Countryside: Agrarian County-Reform in Mexico." Talk to the Program in Agrarian Studies, Yale University, November 6.

Barnet, Richard J. and Ronald E. Muller. 1974. *Global Reach: The Power of the Multinational Corporations.* New York: Simon and Schuster.

Bath, C. Richard. 1986. "Environmental Issues in the United States-Mexico Borderlands." *Journal of Borderlands Studies* 1(1):49-72.

Becerril, Isabel. 1998. "La Industria Petroquímica, Capaz de Dar Independencia Financiera al País." *El Financiero.* July 3, 1998, p. 12.

Behrman, Jack N. 1972. *The Role of International Companies in Latin American Integration: Autos and Petrochemicals.* Lexington, Mass.: Lexington Books.

Bello, Walden. 1994. *Dark Victory: The United States, Structural Adjustment, and Global Poverty.* London: Pluto Press.

Berman, Paul. 1998. "Labyrinth of Solitude." *New York Times Magazine,* August 2, pp. 50-73.

Bleakely, Fred R. 1995. "Developing World Gets More Investment." *Wall Street Journal, December 15.*

Bleakley, Fred R. 1996. "Foreign Investment by Multinationals Grow 40% in 1995, Lifted by Mergers," *Wall Street Journal,* September 25.

Blomstrom, Magnus. 1988. "Labor Productivity Differences Between Foreign and Domestic Firms in Mexico," *World Development,* 16 (No. 11):1295-1298.

Boadu, Fred O. 1991. "The U.S.-Mexico Free Trade Agreement: Legal Issues for Agriculture." Texas A & M: Texas Agricultural Market Research Center, Report No. IM- 9-91, April.

Boli, John and George M. Thomas. 1997. "World Culture in the World Polity." *American Sociological Review* 62(April): 171-190.

Bollen, Kenneth. 1983. "World System Position, Dependency, and Democracy." *American Sociological Review* 48:468-497.

Bowles, Paul and Brian MacLean. 1996. "Regional Blocs: Can Japan be the Leader?" in Boyer, Robert and Daniel Drache (eds.), *States Against Markets: the Limits of Globalization,* New York and London, Routledge, pp. 155-169.

Boyer, Robert and Daniel Drache . 1996. "Introduction," in Boyer, Robert and Daniel Drache (eds.), *States Against Markets: the Limits of Globalization,* New York and London, Routledge, pp. 1-27.

Bradshaw, York, Young-Jeong Kim, and Bruce London. 1993. "Transnational Economic Linkages, the State, and Dependent Development in South Korea, 1966-1988: A Time Series Analysis." *Social Forces* 72:315-346.

Bromley, Ray. 1978. "The Urban Informal Labor Sector: Why Is It Worth Discussing?" *World Development,* 6 (Nos. 9/10): 1033-1039, September/October

Bruner, Richard. 1998. "Talking About Innovative Tortillas: They Are a Multi-Billion-Dollar Business in the U.S." *El Financiero International.* December 29, 19997-January 4, 1998.

Buckley, Peter J. and Mark Casson. 1976. *The Future of the Multinational Enterprise.* London: The Macmillan Press.

Burke, Garance. 1998. "Commercial Loans are Still a Dead-End Street." *El Financiero International.* April 13-19, page 10.

Burke, Garance. 1998. "Nafta Creates Setbacks For Mexican Agriculture," *El Financiero International Edition,* March 16-22.

Burke, Garance. 1998b. "Changes in Land Tenure Promote Investment," *El Financiero International Edition,* June 8-14

Burke, Garance. "Drought and Forest Fires Strip the Nation," *El Financiero International Edition,* May 18-24.

Burke, Garance. 1998. "Grain Imports Rise As Farmers Look On," *El Financiero International Edition,* September 7-13..

Buswell, Jacqueline. 1998. "Maquiladoras, A Success Story with a Cost." *El Financiero International,* July 13-19, 10.

Butler, Edgar W. 1976. *Urban Sociology.* New York: Harper and Row, Publishers.

Butler, Edgar W., James B. Pick, Hiroshi Fukurai, and Suhas Pavgi. 1987. "Migration to Baja California 1900-1980." The Center for Inter-American and Border Studies, The University of Texas at El Paso." *Research Paper Series,* No. 26, 54 pp.

Butler, Edgar W. and Jorge Bustamante. 1991. *Sucesion Presidencial: The 1988 Mexican Presidential Election.* Boulder, Colorado: Westview Press.

Cabello, Alejandra. 1999. Globalización y Liberación Financieras y La Bolsa Mexicana de Valores. Mexico City, D. F.: Plaza y Valdés S.A. de C.V.

Camacho, Michelle E. Madsen. 1996. "Dissenting Workers and Social Control: A Case Study of the HotelIndustry in Huatulco, Oaxaca." *Human Organization* 55(1):33:40.

Camp, Roderic. 1997. "Educando a Una Elite. El Pasado se Repite?," in Ortega Salazar, Sylvia, David E.Lorey (coords.), *Crisis y Cambio de la Educación Superior en México*, México, D.F.: Limusa Noriega Editores, pp. 55-27.

Carrillo, Jorge V. and Jorge Santibáñez. 1993. "Estructura Ocupacional en Plantas
    Maquiladoras." In Jorge Carrillo V. (coord.), *Condiciones de Empleo y
    Capacitación en las Maquiladoras de Exportación en México*, Tijuana, Mexico,
    Secretaría del Trabajo y Previsión Social and El Colegio de laFrontera Norte, 59-
    133.

Case, Brendan M. 1999. "Tortilla Transformation." *MB*. March, pp. 12-13.

Castells, Manuel and Jeffrey Henderson. 1987. "Techno-economic Restructuring, Socio-
    political Processes and Spatial Transformation: A Global Perspective,"

Castillo, Alejandro. 1998. "Explotar la Maquila." *Expansión*, April 22, 123-124.

Catán, Thomas. 1998. "Made in Mexico." *U.S./Mexico Business*, October, pp. 43-47.

Catao, Luis A.V. 1998. "Mexico and Export-led Growth: the Porfirian Period Revisited."
    22:59-78.

Central Intelligence Agency. 1996. *The World Factbook*. Pittsburgh, Pennsylvania:
    Superindent of Documents.

Centro. 1987. *La Economica Subterranea en Mexico*. Mexico: Editorial Diana, Centro de
    Estudios Economicos del Sector Privado A.C.

Cervero, Robert. 1998. *The Transit Metropolis*. Covelo, California: Island Press.

Chase-Dunn. Christopher. 1975. "The Effects of International Economic Dependence on
    Development and Inequality: A Cross-National Study." *American Sociological
    Review* 40 (December): 720-738.

Chatfield, Christopher and Alexander J. Collins. 1980. *Introduction to Multivariate
    Analysis*. London: Chapman and Hall Ltd.

Chetley, Andy. *The Baby Killer Scandal*. London: War on Want.

Chirot, Daniel and Thomas Hall. 1982. "World-System Theory." *Annual Review of
    Sociology* 8:81-106.

CIA. 1996. *1996 World Factbook*. Washington, D.C.: Central Intelligence Agency.

CIA. 1999. *The World Factbook 1999*. Washington, D.C.: Central Intelligence Agency.

Clancy, Michael J. 1999. "Tourism and Development: Evidence from Mexico." *Annals of
    Tourism Research* 26(1):1-20.

Cockcroft, James D. 1981. "Subordinated Technological Development: The case of
    Mexico," *Research in Social Movements, Conflict, and Change*, 4:253-282.

Cole, William E. and Richard D. Sanders. 1970. *Growth and Change in Mexican Agriculture*. Knoxville, TN: Univ. of Tenn., Center for Business and Economic Research.

Commerce, U.S. Dept. of. 1984. *Biotechnology: High Technology Industries: Profiles and Outlook*. Washington, D.C.: U.S. Department of Commerce.

CONACYT. 1995. *Indicadores de Actividades Científicas y Tecnologicas*. Mexico, D.F.: Consejo Nacional de Ciencia y Tecnología

CONAPO. 1991. *Sistema de Ciudades y Distribución Espacial de la Población en México*. Tomo I.Integración de Resultados de los Estudios de los Subsistemas de Ciudades de México. México, D.F.:Consejo Nacional de Población.

Connor, John M. 1977. *The Market Power of Multinationals: A Quantitative Analysis of U.S.Corporations in Brazil and Mexico*. New York Praeger.

Connor, John M. and Willard F. Mueller. 1977. *Market Power and Profitability of Multinational Corporations in Brazil and Mexico*. Washington, D.C.: U.S. Government Printing Office (Report to the Subcommittee on Foreign Economic Policy).

Corporate Strategy. 1999. "Prodigy/Telmex/Acer: Virtual Symbiosis,"*Business Latin America*, October 4.

Crane, Agnes T. 2000. "Damage Control." *MB*. January/February, page 36.

DCA. 1996. *Directory of Corporate Affiliations: International Public and Private Companies*. New Providence, NJ: A Reed Reference Publishing Co.

De Kadt, Emanuel. 1979. *Tourism: Passport to Development?* Oxford: Oxford University Press.

Departamento de Energia. 1998. Various data and information. Web Site http://www.energia.gob.mx.

Dieussart, Tom. 1999. "Their Way is the Highway," *El Financiero International Edition*, October 11

Dougan, Mattei and John Kasarda (eds.). 1988. *The Metropolis Era*, Vols. 1 and 2. Beverly Hills, California, Sage.

Duncan, Otis Dudley, et al. 1960. *Metropolis and Region*. Baltimore, Maryland: The Johns Hopkins Press.

Dunning, John H. 1981. *International Production and the Multinational Enterprise.*
   Boston: George Allen and Unwin.

Dunning, John H. and Robert D. Pearce. 1981. *The World's Largest Industrial
   Enterprises.* New York: St. Martin's Press.

DuPont México. 1997. "DuPont México con México." Mexico, D.F.: DuPont México

Economic Commission for Latin America and the Caribbean. 1997. *Statistical Yearbook
   for Latin America and the Caribbean.* Economic Commission for Latin America
   and the Caribbean.

Economist Magazine. 1999. "The Americas Shift Toward Private Health Care." *The
   Economist*351 (8118). 1 page.

Economist. 1997. "Poison Across the Rio Grande." *The Economist.* November 15, pp.
   36-37.

EFI Staff. 1998. "Agriculture Suffers Most from Crisis," *El Financiero,* January 19-25.

EFI Staff. 1998a. "Coming Soon, Consumer Satellite Services,"*El Financiero
   International Edition*, August 17-23.

EFI Staff. 1998b. "Telmex Looks to Guatemala, Brazil." *El FinancieroInternational
   Edition*, August 17-23b.

El Financiero Internacional. 1998. "México Pierde Popularidad entre Turistas
   Extranjeros." *ElFinanciero Internacional*, Sept. 21.

El Financiero Internacional. 1998. "Pemex: Ambitious Projects Get Underway." *El
   Financiero Internacional.* March 16-22, p. 13.

El Financiero. 1997. "Representa 10% del PIB La Economía Informal: INEGI." *El
   Financiero*, November29, 1997, p. 11.

El Financiero. *1998.* "Mexico-U.S. Agro Agreements Reached," *El Financiero,* June
   22-28.

El Sector. 1993. *El Sector Informal en Mexico.* Mexico: Secretaria del Trabajo y

ENFES. 1989. "Encuesta Nacional Sobre Fecundidad y Salud, 1987." Columbia,
   Maryland: Institute for Resource Development/Macro Systems Inc.

ENP. 1980. "Encuesta Nacional de Prevalencia el el Uso de Métodos Anticonceptivos,
   1979." Mexico,D.F.: Coordinación del Programa Nacional de Planificación
   Familiar.

Evans, Peter. 1979. "Beyond Center and Periphery: A Comment on the World System
   Approach to the Study of Development." *Sociological Inquiry* 49(4):15-20.

Expansión y Reforma. 1997. "Expande IBM de México Su Planta de Manufactura." *Expansión y Reforma. Suplemento Comercial.* November 17, page 2.

Expansión. 1997. "TLC y Maquiladoras." *Expansión,* October 8.

Expansión. 1996. "Localización Geográfica de las 500." *Expansión,* August.

Expansión. 1999. "Empresa Mex-Tex." *Expansión,* April 28, pp. 10-11.Prevision Social.

Fajnzylber, Fernando and Trinidad Martinez Tarrago. 1976. *Las Empresas Transnacionales.* Mexico: Fondo de Cultura Economica.

Febre Pruneda, Luis. 1999. "Crisis Lurks: Mexican Banks Under Pressure." *El Financiero International.* April 5, page 3.

Fernández-Kelly, María Patricia. 1983. *For We Are Sold, I and My People: Women and Industry on Mexico's Northern Frontier.* Albany: State University of New York Press.

Fernández Nuñez, Joaquín. 1997. "Amor con Barreras." *Expansión.* October 8, pp. 21-36.

Fernández Núñez, Joaquín. 1997. "No Sólo Banca de Segundo Piso." *Expansión.* September 10, 163-168.

Fernández, Raul. 1977. *The United States-Mexico Border.* Notre Dame: Notre Dame University Press.

Fineren, Daniel. 1999. "Transportation Systems in Dire Need of Investiment," *El Financiero International Edition,* October 11.

Firebaugh, Glenn. 1999. "Empires of World Income Inequality." *American Journal of Sociology,* 104(May): 1597-1630.

Flores Escárzaga, Efraín. 1997. "Los Sistemas de Servicios de Salud de Estados Unidos, Canada y México, Ante Los Nuevos Enlaces de la Salud Transnacional: Analisis Comparativo." *Journal of Border Health,* April/May, 2(2):10-26.

FONATUR. Nd. "Secretaria de Turismo, Fondo Nacional de Fomento al Turismo, and Aeropuertos y Servicios Auxiliares Reports," Mexico City, D.F.: FONATUR.

Foote, William Fulbright. 1997. "Mexico City's Street Vendors Have Big Brothers." *The Wall Street Journal.* February 14, p. A15.

Frenk, J. 1993. "La Salud de la Población. Hacia Una Nueva Salud Pública." *Fondo de Cultura Económica.* Vol. 29.

Garza, Gustavo. *El Proceso de Industrialización en la Ciudad de México 1821-1970.* Mexico, D.F.: El Colegio de México, 1985.

Garza, Gustavo. 1987. "Hacia La Superconcentración Industrial en La Ciudad de México," in Gustavo Garza (ed.), *Atlas de las Ciudad de México*, Mexico City, D.F.: Departamento del Distrito Federal y El Colegio de México, pp. 100-102.

Garza, Gustavo. 1987. Distribución de la Industrial en La Ciudad de México 1960-1980," in Gustavo Garza (ed.), *Atlas de las Ciudad de México*, Mexico City, D.F.: Departamento del Distrito Federal y El Colegio de México, pp. 100-102.

Garza, Gustavo (cord.). 1995. *Atlas of Monterrey*. Monterrey: Gobierno del Estado de Nuevo León.

Gellner, Sarah. "Ports Swamped by Sea Trade Boom," *El Financiero International Edition*, October 11.

Garza, Adolfo. 1997. "Pemex Privatization Facing Stiff PRD, PAN Opposition." *The Mexico City News*. October 23, p. 31.

Garza, Gustavo. 1999. "Globalización Económica, Concentración Metropolitana y Políticas Urbanas en México." *Estudios Demográficos y Urbanos*. 14(2):269-311.

Gedicks, Al. 1978. Panel Member: "Hultinational Enterprise in Latin America: An Historical Perspective," in *Multinational Corporations in Latin America: Private Rights - Public Responsibility*, in Donald P. Irish (ed.). Ohio University: Center for International Studies, Series No. 2.

Gellner, Sarah. 1999. "Modernization Boosts Air Cargo," *El Financiero International Edition*, October 11.

Gereffi, Gary A. 1980. " 'Wonder Drugs' and Transnational Corporations in Mexico: An Elaboration and a Limiting-Case Study of Dependency Theory," Unpublished Doctoral Dissertation, Yale University.

Gladwin, Thomas N. and Ingo Walter. 1980. *Multinational Under Fire*. New York: John Wiley and Sons.

Gómez-Dantés, Octavio, Julio Frenk, and Carlos Cruz. 1999. "Commerce in Health Services in North American within the Context of the North American Free Trade Agreement." *Pan American Journal of Public Health*. 1(6):460-465.

Gonzalez, Ariadna. 1998. "Reaching Rural Communities Reaps Little Benefit," *El Financiero International Edition*, August 17-23.

González Lara, Mauricio. 1999. Inversión Extranjera. *Expansión*. April 14-28, pp. 54-65.

Golden, Tim. 2000. "Mexican Tale of Absolute Drug Corruption." *New York Times*, January 8, www.nytimes.com.

References

Golden, Tim. 2000. "Mexican Tale of Absolute Drug Corruption." *New York Times International*. January 8. www.nytimes.com.

Grayson, George W. 1996. "Why Mexican Labor Fights a Petrochemical Selloff," *Wall Street Journal*, June 14.

Grosse, R. 1988. "The Economic Impact of Foreign Direct Investment: A Case Study of Venezuela," *Management International Review*, 28 (No. 4): 63-78.

Grupo Financiero Bancomer. 1996. *Informe Anual*. Mexico, D.F.: Grupo Financiero Bancomer.

Guzmán Reyes, Ilyana. "Tortuosa Apertura Telefónica; La Autoridad, Pausada: Alestra." *El Financiero*, February 4, page 19.

Guenette, Louise. 1999. "Cintra Basks at the Top, Despite Dispute," *El Financiero International Edition*, October 11.

Gutierrez, Elvia. 1997. "Dos Puestos Ambulantes por Cada Establecimiento Formal," *Economica, 4-7*, November 30.

Hartigan, John A. 1975. *Clustering Algorithms*. New York: John Wiley and Sons.

Hartman, John. 1998. "Convergence and Divergence in the World Economy." Paper presented at the Annual Meeting of the International Sociological Association, Montreal.

Heath, John R. 1987. "Constraints on Peasant Maize Production: A Case Study From Michioan," *Mexican Studies/Estudios Mexicanos* 3 (No. 2): 263-286.

Hernández Morón, Leticia. 1999. "Logra Cemex Sus Mejores Márgenes en 10 Años a Marzo." *El Financiero*. April 26, 64.

Hertford, Reed. 1971. *Sources of Change in Mexican Agricultural Production, 1940-65*. Washington, D.C.: U.S. Department of Agriculture, Foreign Agricultural Economic Report No. 73.

Hewlett-Packard de México. "Hewlett-Packard Informa Sobre Los Resultados de Sus Operacions Por El Ejercicio Fiscal 1997." Mexico, D.F.: Hewlett-Packard de México.

Hiernaux Nicolas, Daniel and Manuel Rodríguez Wong. 1990. "Tourism and Absorption of the Labor Force in Mexico." Working Paper 54. Washington, D.C.: Commission for the Study of International Migration and Cooperative Economic Development.

Hill, Charles W. L. 1998. *International Business*. New York: McGraw Hill.

Hirst, Paul and Grahame Thompson. *Globalization in Question.* Cambridge, England: Polity Press.

Howard, Georgina. 1999. "Gigantes Extranjeros Seguirán Fusionanda Bancos Mexicanos." *El Financiero International.* April 26, 1999, p. 10.

Hughes, John A., Peter J. Martin, and W.W. Sharrock. 1995. *Understanding Classical Sociology: Marx,Weber, Durkheim.* London: SAGE Publications.

Humble. 1997. "The Humble Tortilla as a Billion Dollar Business," *US/Mexico Business,* November.
Humphrey, Chris. 1997. "Fueling Mexico's Future." *U.S./Mexico Business.* November, pp. 12-13.

Illeris, Sven. 1996. *The Service Economy: A Geographical Approach.* Chichester, England: John Wiley and Sons.

IMF. 1979 and 1991. *International Financial Statistics Yearbook.* New York: InternationalMonetary Fund.

INEGI. 1985. *Comparaciones Internacionales: Mexico en el Mundo.* Aguascalientes, Mexico: INEGI.

INEGI. 1992. *XI Censo General de Población y Vivienda: Estados Unidos Mexicanos.* Aguascalientes, Mexico: Instituto Nacional de Estadística, Geografía, e Informática.

INEGI. 1993. *Estadisticas Historicas de México.* 2 vols. Aguascalientes, Mexico: Instituto Nacional de Estadística, Geografía, e Informática.

INEGI. 1993. *Niveles de Bienstar en México.* Aguascalientes, Mexico: Instituto Nacional de Estadística, Geografía, e Informática.

INEGI. 1994. *Estadistica Industria Maquiladora de Exportación 1989-1993.* Aguascalientes, Mexico: Instituto Nacional de Estadistica, Gegrafía e Informática.

INEGI. 1994. *XII Censo de Transportes y Communicaciones.* Aguascalientes, Mexico: INEGI.

INEGI. 1995. *Industria Maquiladora de Exportacion.* Aguascalientes, Mexico: Instituto Nacional de Estadistica, Geografia e Informatica.

INEGI. 1995. *XI Censo de Servicios: Servicios Financieros.* Aguascalientes, Mexico: Instituto Nacionalde Estadística, Geografía e Informática

INEGI. 1995. *Industria Maquiladora de Exportacion.* Aguascalientes, Aguascalientes: Instituto Nacionalde Estadistica, Geografia e Informatica.

INEGI. 1996. *Anuario Estadistico del Comercio de los Estados Unidos Mexicanos, 1995.* Aguascalientes: INEGI.

INEGI. 1996. "Encuesta Nacional de Micronegocios, 1994." Aguascalientes, Aguascalientes: INEGI.

INEGI. 1996. *Censos Económicos 1994.* Aguascalientes, Mexico: D.F.: Instituto Nacional de Estadística, Geografía, e Informática.

INEGI. 1997. *Estadistica Industria Maquiladora de Exportación 1991-1996.* Aguascalientes, Mexico: Instituto Nacional de Estadistica, Geografia e Informática.

INEGI. 1997. "Encuesta Nacional de Micronegocios, 1996." Aguascalientes, Aguascalientes: INEGI.

INEGI. 1998. *Cultivos Perennes de Mexico, VII Censo Agropecuario.* Aguascalientes: INEGI.

INEGI. 1998. *La Industria Automotriz en México. Edición 1996.* Aguascalientes, Mexico: Instituto Nacional de Estadística, Geografía, e Informática.

INEGI. Various dates. *Annuarios y Annuarios Estadisticos.* Aguascalientes, Mexico: Instituto Nacionalde Estadistica, Geografia e Informatica.

INEGI. Various dates. *Anuarios y Anuarios Estadisticos.* Aguascalientes, Aguascalientes: InstitutoNacional de Estadistica, Geografia e Informatica.

Inter-Continental Hotels and Resorts. 1999. "Inter-Continental Hotels and Resorts: Corporate Profile June1998." Inter-Continental Hotels and Resorts Website. http://www.interconti.com. April 28, 1999.

International Monetary Fund. 1998. *International Financial Statistical Yearbook.* Volume 51. Washington, D.C.: International Monetary Fund.

Jackman, R.W. 1982. "Dependence on Foreign Investment and Economic Growth in the Third World." *World Politics* 34: 175-196.

Jamar, Christen and Rachel Salaman. 1998. "Mexico's Top 50 Service Firms." *U.S./Mexico Business.* May, pp. 29-39.

Jamar, Christen and Angelo Young. 1999. "NAFTA at 5." *MB* April, pp. 26-34.

Juarez, Antonio. 1979. *Las Corporaciones Transnacionales y Los Trabajores Mexicanos.* Mexico: Siglo Veintiuno Editores.

Kacapyr, Elia. 1998. "Notes from Underground," *American Demographics,* January, pp. 30-31.

Kahn, Jeremy. 1998. "The Fortune Global Five Hundred." *Fortune*, August 3, pp. 130-134, F1-F27.

Kandell, Jonathan. 1988. *La Capital: The Biography of Mexico City*. New York: Random House.

Kanter, Rosabeth M. 1994. "Collaborative Advantage," *Harvard Business Review*, July-August, pp. 96-108.

Kanter, Rosabeth M. 1995. *World Class: Thriving Locally in the Global Economy*. New York: Touchstone.

Kirman, Alan P. and Luigi M. Tomasini. 1969. "A New Look at International Income Inequalities." *Economia Internazionale* 22: 437-461.

Knight-Ridder. 1996. "The Coming Global Food Challenge,: Knight-Ridder Newspapers, November 10.

Knox, Paul and John Agnew. 1997. *The Geography of the World Economy*. 2nd Edition. London: Arnold Publishing.

Korzeniewicz, Roberto P. and Timothy P. Moran. "World-Economic Trends in the Distribution of Income, 1965-1992." *American Journal of Sociology* 102 (January): 1000-1039.

Kennedy, Paul. 1987. *The Rise and Fall of the Great Powers*. New York: Random House.

Krueger, Anne and Aaron Tornell. 1999. "The Role of Bank Restructuring in Recovering from Crises: Mexico 1995-98." Working Paper No. 7042. Cambridge, Massachusetts: National Bureau of Economic Research. March

Lezama, Jose L. 1991. "Ciudad, Mujer, y Conflicto: El Commercio Ambulante en el D.F.," *Estudios Demograficos y Urbanos*, 6 (No. 3): 649-675.

Liverman, Diana M. 1990. "Drought Impacts in Mexico: Climate, Agriculture,Technology, and Land Tenure in Sonora and Puebla." *Annals of the Associationof American Geographers 80 (1): 49-72*.

Long, Veronica. 1993. "Techniques for Socially Sustainable Tourism Development: Lessons from Mexico. In Nelson, J.G., R. Butler, and G. Wall (eds.), *Tourism and Sustainable Development: Monitoring, Planning, Managing*, Heritage Resource Centre Joint Publication Number 1, Waterloo, Canada: Heritage Resource Centre, pp. 201-216.

Longrigg, S.J. 1980. *Major Companies of Brazil, Mexico, and Venezuela: 1980/1981*. London: Graham and Trotman.

Lopez, Ramon, John Nash, and Julie Stanton. 1995. "Adjustment and Poverty in
    Mexican Agriculture: How Farmers' Wealth Affects Supply Response."
    Washington, D.C.: World Bank, No. 1494, August.

Lorey, David. 1993. *The University System: Economic Development in Mexico Since
    1929.* Stanford, California: Stanford University Press.

Lorey, David E. "Education and the Challenges of Mexican Development." *Challenge.*
    38 (2), March-April, 51-56.

Lorey, David E. 1993. *The University System and Economic Development in Mexico
    Since 1929.* Stanford, California: Stanford University Press.

Lota, Louinn. 1999. "NTSB Weighing Mexican Trucks," *Los Angeles Times*, October 22.

Lustig, Nora. 1992. *Mexico: The Remaking of An Economy.* Washington, D.C.: The
    Brookings Institution.

Maloney, William F. 1997. "Labor Market Structure in LDCs: The Time Series Evidence
    on Competing Views," unpublished paper, May 29.

Market Facts of Canada Ltd. 1989. "Pleaseure Travel Markets to North America:
    Mexico." Report prepared for United States Travel and Tourism Administration
    and Tourism Canada. 72 page report. Market Facts of Canada Ltd., June.

Martinez, Fabiola. 1997. "54% de la PEA Vive de un Empleo Informal," *La Jornada*
    March 21.

Martinez, Miraim. 1997. "Coffee Wars Leave a Bitter Taste," *US/Mexico Business,*
    November.

Martinez, Mirian. 1997. "ANDSA On Sale," *Business Mexico,* September.

Martinez, Zaida L. and David A. Ricks. 1989. "Multinational Parent Companies'
    Influence Over Human Resource Decisions of Affiliates: U.S. Firms in Mexico,"
    *Journal of International Business Studies*, 20 (No. 3): 465-487.

Massey, Douglas S. 1998. "March of Folly: U.S. Immigration Policy After NAFTA." *The
    American Prospect.* Vol. 37 (March April), pp. 22-33.

Maurer, Noel. "Banks and Entrepreneurs in Porfirian Mexico: Inside Exploitation or Sound
    Business Strategy?" 1999. *Journal of Latin American Studies* 31:331-361.

McCosh, Dan. 1998. "Maquiladora Rules Should Cut Red Tape." *El Financiero
    International.* June 8 14.

McCosh, Dan. 1999. "Trade Still Rises Five Years Into NAFTA." *El Financierio
    International.* Dec. 28, 1998-January 3, 1999, p. 8.

McKern, Bruce. 1993. "Introduction: Transnational Corporations and the Exploitation of
    Natural Resources," in Bruce Kern (ed.), *Transnational Corporations and the
    Exploitation of Natural Resources*, New York: United Nations Library on
    Transnational Corporations, Vol. 10, p. 33.

McKinlay, Joann D. 1998. "Westcoast Seeks Key Energy Contracts." *El Financiero
    International*. December 29-January 4, p. 15.

Millman, Joel. 1996. "Rail Privatization In Mexico Begins With 3 Bidders," *Wall Street
    Journal*, October1.

Millman, Joel. 1998. "High-Tech Jobs Transfer to Mexico with Surprising Speed." *The
    Wall Street Journal*, April 9, A18.

Moncada, Gerardo. 1997. "Y Se Hizo La Luz." *Expansión*. November 19, pp. 18-33.

Moser, Caroline O.N. 1978. "Informal Sector or Petty Commodity Production: Dualism or
    Dependence in Urban Development?" *World Development,* 6(Nos. 9/10): 1041-
    1064.

Mumme, Stephen P. 1991. "Clearing the Air: Environmental Reform in Mexico."
    *Environment* 33(10):7 30.

Muñoz Valencia, Araceli. 1998. "Men Who Can Make or Break the Economy." *El
    Financiero International*. January 5-11, page 8.

Muñoz Valencia, Araceli. 1998. "Men Who Can Make or Break the Economy." *El
    Financiero International Edition*. January 5-11, p. 8.

Newfarmer, Richard S. 1978. *The International Market Power of Transnational
    Corporations: A Case Study of the Electrical Industry*. New York: United
    Nations, UNCTAD.

Newfarmer, Richard S. and S. Topik. 1992. "Testing Dependency Theory: A Case Study
    of Brazil's Electrical Industry," in Michael Taylor and Nigel Thrift (eds.), *The
    Geography of Multinationals*, New York, St. Martin's Press.

Noin, Daniel. 1996. *Atlas de la Population Mondiale*. Mont-Pellier-Paris: RECLUS - La
    Documentation Francaise.

Nolan, Mary Lee and Sidney Nolan. "The Evolution of Tourism in Twentieth-Century
    Mexico." *Journal of the West*. 27(4):14-25.

Norton, Erle. 1996. "Global Makeover: Alcoa," *Wall Street Journal*, September 26.

Ohmae, Kenichi. 1995. *The End of the Nation State*. London: HarperCollins Publishers.

Ott, M. 1987. "The Growing Share of Services in the U.S. Economy: Degeneration or
    Evolution?" *Review of the Federal Reserve Bank of St. Louis*, June/July, pp. 5-22.

References

Quinones, Sam. 1998. "The Maquiladora Murders." *M.S.,* May/June, pp. 11-16.

Overman, E. Sam. 1995. "Privatization in China, Mexico, and Russia." *Public Productivity and Management Review* 19(1);46:60.

Ozuna, Teofilo and Gary W. Williams. 1993. "The Environment and U.S.-Mexico Agricultural Trade." Texas A & M: Texas Agricultural Market Research Center, Report No. IM 3-93, July.

Pick, James B. and Edgar W. Butler. 1994. *The Mexico Handbook: Economic and Demographic Maps and Statistics.* Boulder, Colorado: Westview.

Peacock, Walter, Greg Hoover, and Charles Killian. 1988. "Divergence and Convergence in International Development: A Decomposition Analysis of Inequality in the World System." *American Sociological Review* 53: 838-852.

Pemex. 1992. *PEMEX Statisticall Yearbook 1992.* Mexico City: PEMEX.

Pemex. 1998. Web Site. Various data.

Perez, Gonzalez Lourdes. 1997. "Dos Puestos Ambulantes por Cada Establecimento Formal," *Economia,* 5, November 30.

Perrucci, Robert. 1994. *Japanese Auto Transplants in the Heartland: Corporatism and Community.* New York: Aldine de Gruyter.

Petrella, Riccardo. 1996. "Globalization and Internationalization," in Boyer, Robert and Daniel Drache (eds.), *States Against Markets: the Limits of Globalization,* New York and London, Routledge, pp. 62-83.

Philpott, Tom. 1999. "Social Ills: Programs Founder as Poverty Rises." *El Financiero International.* July 26, 1999, p. 3.

Pick, James B., Edgar W. Butler, and Elisabeth Lanzer. 1989. *Atlas of Mexico.* Boulder, Colorado: Westview Press.

Pick, James B., Edgar W. Butler, and Raul Gonzalez Ramirez. 1992. "Projection of the Mexican National Labor Force, 1980-2005." *Social Biology* 40(3-4):161-190.

Pick, James B. and Edgar W. Butler. 1994. *The Mexico Handbook.* Boulder, Colorado: Westview Press.

Pick, James B. and Skye Stephenson-Glade. 1994. "The NAFTA Agreement and Labor Force Projections: Implications for the Border Region." *Journal of Borderlands Studies* 9(1):69-99.

Pick, James B. and Edgar W. Butler. 1996. "Application of Cluster Analysis in the Study of urban Growth and Differentiation." *Proceedings of the American Statistical Association, Social Statistics Section*, Alexandria, Virginia, American Statistical Association, pp. 62-67.

Pick, James, Edgar W. Butler, and W. James Hettrick. 1996. "An Economic Geographic Information Systems for the Mexico City Metropolis." *URISA '96 Proceedings*, Urban Regional and Information Systems Association.

Pick, James B. and Edgar W. Butler. 1997. *Mexico Megacity*. Boulder, Colorado: Westview Press.

Pick, James B. and Edgar W. Butler. 1998. "Demographic, Social, and Economic Effects on Mexican Causes of Death in 1990." *Social Biology* 45(3-4).

Pick, James B., Nanda Viswanathan, W. James Hettrick, and Elliott Ellsworth. 1999. "A Geo-Statistical Analysis of Binationality in the U.S.-Mexico Border Twin Cities." *Proceedings of the American Statistical Association*, Section on Statistical Graphics.

Pick, James B., Edgar W. Butler, and Raul Gonzalez Ramirez. "Projection of the Mexican National Labor Force, 1980-2005." *Social Biology* 40(3-4):161-190.

Pick, James B., Nanda Viswanathan, W. James Hettrick, and Elliott Elllsworth. 1999. "Spatial and Cluster Analyses of Urban Patterns and Binational Commonalities in the Mexicali and Imperial County Twin Metropolitan Region." *Proceedings Of American Statistical Association, Section on Statistical Graphics*, in press.

Pick, James B., W. James Hettrick, Nanda Viswanathan, and Elliott Elllsworth. 2000a. "Cooperative Binational Geographical Information Systems: A Design Framework and Example for International Border Cities. *GITM Conference Proceedings*, in press.

Pick, James B., W. James Hettrick, Nanda Viswanathan, and Elliott Elllsworth. 2000b. "Intra-Censal Geographical Information Systesms: Application to Binational Border Cities." *Proceedings of European Conference on Information Systems*, in press.

Pick, James B., Swapan Nag, and Edgar W. Butler. "A Cluster Analysis Approach to Marketing Research in the Borderlands Region of Mexico." In Kuklan, Hooshang, Joan Anderson, and Denise Dimon (eds.), *1988 BALAS Proceedings*, Business Association of Latin American Studies, pp. 19-25.

Poole, Claire. 1998. "Eyes on the Prize." *U.S./Mexico Business*. May, pp. 12-13.

Poole, Claire. 1998. "Oil Wars." *Latin Trade*. August, p. 27.

Poole, Claire. 1998. "The Honeymoon is Over." *U.S./Mexico Business*. July/August, pp. 12-14.

Population Reference Bureau. 1990-93, 1998. "World Population Data Sheet." Washington, D.C.: Population Reference Bureau.

Potts, Malcolm. 2000. "The Unmet Need for Family Planning." *Scientific American* 282(1);88-93.

Portes, Alejandro. 1985. "The Informal Sector and the World Economy: Notes on the Structure of Subsidized Labour," in Timberlake, Michael (ed.), *Urbanization in the World-Economy*, New York, Academic Press, pp. 53-62.

Portes, Alejandro. 1987. "Making It Underground: Comparative Material on the Informal Sector in Western Market Economies," *American Journal of Sociology* 93(1):30-61.

Portes, Alejandro and Saskia Sassen-Koob. "Making It Underground: Comparative Material on the Informal Sector in Western Market Economies." *American Journal of Sociology* 93(1):30-61.

Portes, Alejandro and Richard Schauffler. 1993. "Competing Perspectives on the Latin American Informal Sector." *Population and Development Review* 19:33-60.

Presidencia. Ca. 1990. "Mexico and the Current World Transformation." Mexico: Presidency of Mexico.

Rabell, Cecilia, Marta Mier, and Teran Rocha. 1986. "El Descenso de la Mortalidad en México de 1940 a 1980." *Estudios Demograficos y Urbanos* 1(1): 39-92.

Rebello Pinal, Herminio. 1998. "67% of Micro Businesses are in the Informal Economy." *El Financiero International*. June 8-14, p. 18.

Ramirez Tamayo, Zacarías. 1997. "El Espejismo Renovado." *Expansión*. October 8, pp. 38-47.

Ramírez Yáñez, Jaime. 1999. "Tortilla Flats: Big Makers Squeeze Small Ones." *El Financiero International*. June 7, p. 17.

Rossem, Ronan Van. 1996. "The World System Paradigm as General Theory of Development: A Cross-National Test." *American Sociological Review* 61 (June): 508-527.

Rubalcava, Rosa Maria and Martha Schteingart. 1987. "Diferenciación Socioespacial Intraurbana en la Area Metropolitana de al Ciudad de Mexico." *Estudios Sociologicos* 9 (also in *Atlas de la Ciudad de México*. Mexico City: Departmento del Distrito Federal y El Colegio de Mexico, pp. 108-115.

Rubinson, Richard. 1976. "The World-Economy and the Distribution of Income Within States: A Cross-National Study." *American Sociological Review* 41 (August): 638-659.

Rudino, Lourdes E. 1998. "EL PIB Agropecuario Atraviesa por el Ano Mas Negro de su Historia: CAN," *El Financiero* May 28.

Ruiz, Yolanda. "La Pobreza de Progresa." *Expansión.* June 7-21, pp. 63-68.

Rymer-Zavala, Jenny. 1998. "Fresh Produce Farmers Seek Big U.S. Sales," *El Financiero International Edition, 13, May 18-24.*

Rymer-Zavala, J. and C. Benavides. 1998. "Tourism Fights Against Bad Publicity." *El Financiero International*, August 17-23, p. 7.

Safa, Helen. 1987. "Urbanization, the Informal Economy and State Policy in Latin America." In Smith, Michael and Joe Feagin (eds.), *The Capitalist City: Global Restructuring and Community Politics*, New York, Basil Blackwell, pp. 252-272.

Salaman, Rachel. 1997. "Bitter Sweeteners," *US/Mexico Business,* October.

Sanderson, Steven E., 1986. *The Transformation of Mexican Agriculture.* Princeton, NJ: Princeton University Press.

Saravi, Gonzalo A. 1996. "Marginalidad e informalidad: Aportaciones y Dificultadas de la Perspectiva de al Informalidad," *Estudios Sociologicos*, 14: 435-452.

Sassen, Saskia. 1991. *The Global City: New York, London, Tokyo.* Princeton: Princeton University Press.

Sassen, Saskia. 1994. *Cities in a World Economy.* Thousand Oaks, California: Pine Forge Press.

Shannon, Thomas R. 1996. *An Introduction to the World-System Perspective.* Boulder, Colorado: Westview Press (2nd edition).

Saunders, Peter. 1985. "Space, the City, and Urban Sociology," in *Social Relations and Spatial Structures*, Derek Gregory and John Urry (eds.), London: Macmillan, pp. 67-89.

Schneider, Ben R. 1990. *The Politics of Privatization in Brazil and Mexico: Variations on a Statist Theme.* New York: Columbia University and New York University Consortium.

Schulthies, B. Kris and Gary W. Williams. 1992. "U.S.-Mexico Agricultural Trade and Mexican Agriculture: Linkages and Prospects Under a Free Trade Agreement." Texas A & M: Texas Agricultural Market Research Center, Report No. IM-6-92, July.

Scott, Ian. 1982. *Urban and Spatial Development in Mexico.* Baltimore: The John Hopkins University Press.

Scott, Allen J. 1988. *Metropolis: From the Division of Labor to Urban Form.* Berkeley: University of California Press.

Schott, Thomas. "Models of Dyadic and Individual Components of a Social Relation: Applications to International Trade." *Journal of Mathematical Sociology 12: 225-249.*

SECOFI. 1995. "Todo Lo Que Usted Quería Saber Sobre la Industria Maquiladora de Exportación." Mexico, D.F.: Subsecretaria de Comercio Exterior e Inversión Extranjera. 27 pp.

Secretaría del Trabajo y Previsión Social. 1995. *Tendencias de la Estructura Económica y el Sector Informal en México, 1988-1993.* Cuaderno del Trabajo Número 10. Mexcio, D.F.: Secretaría del Trabajo y Previsión Social, 186 pp.

Secretaria de Energía. 1998. Secretaria de Energía Website. http://www.energia.gob.mx, August 9, 1998.

SEDUSOL. 1996. "Programa Para Superar La Pobreza, 1995-2000, México." Mexico, D.F.: SEDUSOLl.

Seguros Comercial América. 1997. "Presentación Financiera de Seguros Comercial América, S.S. de C.V." Monterrey, Mexico: Seguros Comercial América.

Seguros Comercial America. 1998. "Financial Strength" and "Our Products." Seguros Comercial America Website. http://www.segcoam.com.mx. July 15, 1998.

Senzek, Alva. 1998. "Mixed Outlook for Agriculture," *El Financiero International Edition,* August 18-17.

Senzek, Alva. 1998b. "Agricultural Barrier to EU Accord," *El Financiero International Edition,* August 17-23.

Shannon, Thomas R. 1996. *An Introduction to the World-System Perspective.* Boulder, CO: Westview Press (2nd edition).

Shannon, Thomas R. 1996. *An Introduction to the World-System Perspective.* 2nd Ed. Boulder, Colorado: Westview/HarperCollins.

Shields, David. 1997. "Oil: Global Privatization Inevitable." *The Mexico City News,* October 10.

Shields, David. 1998. "Sustainability of Oil Output is Questioned." *El Financiero International,* January 12-18.

Shields, David. 1998. "Doubts on Natural Gas Availability." *El Financiero International,* May 25-31, 1998, p. 8.

Shields, David. 1998. "Sin Efecto Las Normas Ecológicas para Disminuir Infición de Pemex." *El Financiero.* March 10, page 23.

Shields, David. 1998. "Sustainability of Oil Output is Questioned." *El Financiero International.* January 12-18, page 6.

Shields, David. 1999. "Energy Privatization Stalls." *El Financiero International.* February 22-28, page 1.

Smith, David and Roger Nemeth. 1990. "Dependent Urbanization in the Contemporary Semi-Periphery: Deepening the Analogy," in Drakakis-Smith, David (ed.), *Economic Growth and Urbanization in Developing Areas,* London, Routledge, pp. 8-36.

Smith, David, and Douglas White. 1992. "Structure and Dynamics of the Global Economy: Network Analysis of International Trade, 1965-1980. *Social Forces* 70:857-893.

Smith, David, and Su-Hoon Lee. 1990. "Limits on a Semi-Peripheral Success Story: State Dependent Development and Prospects for South Korean Democratization," in Martin, W. (ed.), *Semi-Peripheral States in the World-Economy*, New York, Greenwood.

Smith, David A. 1996. *Third World Cities in Global Perspective: The Political Economy of Uneven Urbanization.* Boulder, Colorado: Westview/Harper Collins.

Smith, David A. 1996. *Third World Cities in Global Perspectives.* Boulder, Colorado: Westview Press.

Smith, James F. 1998. "Salsa and Chips." *Los Angeles Times*, March 8, pp. D1, D15, D18.

Smith, James F. 1998. "U.S. Phone Giants, Telmex Do Battle Over Long-Distance," *Los Angeles Times*, March 3.

Snyder, David and Edward L. Kick. 1979. "Structural Position in the World System and Economic Growth, 1955-1970: A Multiple-Network Analysis of Transnational Interactions." *American Journal of Sociology* 84 (5):1096-1126.

Solis Perez, Marlene Celia. 1995. "El Comercio en la Via Publica: Una Forma de Lucha Social?" Masters Thesis in Urban Development. February. 106 pp.

Spain, Patrick J. and James R. Talbot. 1996. *Hoover's Handbook of World Business, 1995-1996.*

SPSS. 1998. *SPSS 8.0.* Chicago, Illinois: SPSS Inc.

Stavenhagen, Rodolfo. 1986. "Collective Agriculture and Capitalism in Mexico," in
    Modern Mexico." *State, Economy, and Social Conflict*, Nora Hamilton and
    Timothy F. Harding (eds.), Beverly Hills, CA: Sage.

Steinmetz, Greg and Tara Parker-Pope. 1996. "All Over the Map," *Wall Street Journal*,
    September 26.

Stoddard, Ellwyn R. 1987. *Maquila: Assembly Plants in Northern Mexico*. El Paso: Texas
    Western Press.

Sutter, Mary. 1997. "Advanced Chemistry: Exports and Local Sales Add up to Potent
    Formula for DuPont Mexico." *Business Mexico Special Edition*, pp. 70-71.

Teichman, Judith A. 1988. *Policymaking in Mexico: From Boom to Crisis*. Boston: Allen
    and Unwin.

"Television Espanola, Grupo Televisa Seek Digital-TV Alliance," *Wall Street Journal*,
    September 5, 1996.

The Economist. 1997. "Back on the Pitch: Business in Latin America." Special Survey.
    *The Economist*. Dec. 6, 1997.

Thomson, Adam and Sally Bower. October 1997. "Telecom Boom," *Latin Trade*.

Toro, María Celia. 1998. "The Political Repercussions of Drug Trafficking in Mexico." In
    Joyce, Elizabeth and Carlos Malamud, *Latin America and the Multinational Drug
    Trade*, pp. 132-145.

Unikel, Luis et al. 1976. *El Desarrollo Urbano de México: Diagnostico e Implications
    Futuras*. Mexico: El Colegio de Mexico.

Unikel, Luis. 1977. "Urbanization in Mexico: Process, Implications, Policies, and
    Prospects," in Goldstein, Sidney and David F. Sly (eds.), *Patterns of
    Urbanizaiton: Comparative Country Studies*. Dolhain, Belgium: Ordina Editions,
    pp. 465-568.

UNESCO. 1998. *World Education Report 1998*. Paris, France: UNESCO Publishing.

U.N. 1985. *Environmental Aspects of the Activities of Transnational Corporations: A
    Survey*. New York: United Nations.

UN. 1987. *Global Report on Human Settlements*. Oxford: Oxford University Press.

U.N. 1989. *Mexico*. New York: United Nations.

UN. 1990. *Statistical Yearbook for Latin America and the Caribbean*. New York: United
    Nations Commission for Latin America and the Caribbean.

U.N. 1990. *Transnational Corporations and the Transfer of New and Emerging Technologies to Developing Countries.* New York; United Nations.

U.N. 1992. *World Investment Report 1992: Transnational Corporations as Engines of Growth.* New York: Untied Nations.

U.N. 1992. *Foreign Direct Investment and Industrial Restructuring in Mexico.* New York: United Nations, Series A, No.18.

U.N. 1993. *Transnational Corporations and Regional Economic Integration.* New York: United Nations Library on Transnational Corporations, Vol. 9.

U.N. 1993. *Transnational Corporations and the Exploitation of Natural Resources.* New York: United Nations Library on Transnational Corporations, Vol. 10.

U.N. 1993. *Transnational Corporations in Services.* New York: United Nations Library on Transnational Corporations, Vol. 12.

U.N. 1993. *Transnational Corporations from Developing Countries: Impact on Their Home Countries.* New York: United Nations.

U.N. 1994. *World Investment Report: Transnational Corporations, Employment and the Workplace.* New York: United Nations.

UN. 1997. *Statistical Yearbook for Latin America and the Caribbean.* New York: United Nations Commission for Latin America and the Caribbean.

United Nations. 1997. *Trade and Development Report, 1997.* Pub. No. 3.97.II.D.8. New York: United Nations.

UNICEF. 1996. *II Censos de los Ninos y Ninas de la Calle, Ciudad de Mexico.* Mexico: UNICEF, DIF, DDF.

U.S. State Department. 1999. Background Notes: Mexico. Washington, D.C.: Bureau of Western Hemisphere Affairs, U.S. Department of State. From website http://www.statae.gov/www/background_notes. March 26, 2000.

U.S. Mexico Business. 1997. "The Humble Tortilla as a Billion Dollar Business." *U.S./Mexico Business*, November, p. 54.

U.S. Energy Information Administration. 1997. "Venezuela." Web Site. Dated September, 1997.

U.S. Energy Information Administration. 1998. "Mexico." Web Site. Dated May, 1998.

U.S. Energy Information Administration. 1998. "United States of America." Web Site. http://www.eia.doe.gov/emeu, Dated April 14, 1998.

U.S. Energy Information Agency. 1999. "International Energy Data." Website http://www.eia.doe.gov/emeu, Dated February 19.

Valladolid Chavez, Luis Felipe. 1995. "Privatization of Mexican Ejidos: The Implications of the New Article 27." *95 McNair Journal.*

Van Den Berghe. 1994. *The Quest for the Other: Ethnic Tourism in San Cristóbal, Mexico.* Seattle: University of Washington Press.

Van Den Berghe. 1995. "Marketing Mayas: Ethnic Tourism Promotion in Mexico." *Annals of Tourism Research.* 22(3):568-588.

Vaupel, James W. and Joan P. Curman. 1973. *The World's Multinational Enterprises.* Boston: Harvard University, Division of Research, Graduate School of Business Administration.

Vernon, Raymond. 1977. "Storm Over the Multinationals: Problems and Prospects," *Foreign Affairs* 55 (No. 2):243-262.

Vernon, Raymond. 1963. *The Dilemma of Mexico's Development: The Roles of the Private and Public Sectors.* Cambridge, Massachusetts: Harvard University Press.

Viswanathan, Nanda K., James B. Pick, W. James Hettrick, and Elliott Ellsworth. 1999. "An Analysis of Binationalism in the Twin Metropolitan Areas of San Diego, California, and Tijuana, Mexico." Unpublished manuscript.

Wall Street Journal. 1996. "The Global Giants," *Wall Street Journal*, September 26.

Wallach, Lori and Michelle Sforza. 1999. "NAFTA at 5." *The Nation*, p. 7.

Wallerstein, Immanuel. 1974. *The Modern World-System.* Vol. 1. New York: Academic Press.

Wallerstein, Immanuel. 1976. "Semi-peripheral Countries and the Contemporary World Crisis." *Theory and Society* 3(4):461-484.

Wallerstein, Immanuel. 1980. *The Modern World-System.* Vol. 2. New York: Academic Press.

Wallerstein, Immanuel. 1989. *The Modern World-System.* Vol. 3. New York: Academic Press.

Ward, Kathryn. 1993. Reconceptualizing World System Theory to Include Women," in England, P., *Theory on Feminism/Feminism on Theory*, New York: Aldine de Gruyter, pp. 43-68.

Watts, H.D. 1980. *The Large Industrial Enterprise.* London: Croom Helm.

Weston, J. Fred. 1975. *Large Corporations in a Changing Society*. New York: New York University Press.

Whetten, Nathan L. 1948. *Rural Mexico*. Chicago: University of Chicago Press.

Wills, Rick. 1998. "Working Women: Evaluating Progress," *El Financiero, May 25-31*.

Wolfe, Alvin W. 1977. "The Supernational Organization of Production: An Evolutionary Perspective," *Current Anthropology*, 18 (December): 615-635.

World Bank. 1995. *World Development Indicators 1995*. Washington, D.C.: The World Bank.

World Bank. 1997. *World Development Report 1997*. Washington, D.C.: The World Bank.

World Bank. 1995. *World Development Report 1995: Workers in an Integrating World.* Oxford: Oxford University Press.

WFS. 1980. "The Mexican Fertility Survey, 1976-1977: A Summary of Findings." Voorburg, Netherlands: International Statistical Institute.

World Bank. 1997. *World Development Report*. New York: Oxford University Press.

World Tourism Organization. 1997. "Tourism Highlights 1997." Madrid, Spain: World Tourism Organization. 30 pages.

World Tourism Organization. 1998. *Tourism Market Trends, Americas, 1988-1997*. Madrid, Spain: World Tourism Organization.

Wright, Harry K. 1971. *Foreign Enterprise in Mexico: Laws and Policies*. Chapel Hill: University of North Carolina Press.

Wright, Jeff. 1997. "For Sale for Better or for Worse," *Business Mexico*. October, pp. 8-13,37.

Zellner, Mike. 1995. " A Tortillazos Limpios," *AmericaEconomia*, No. 92, Febrero.

Zepeda Miramontes, Eduardo. 1996. "El TLC y La Industrialización en la Frontera Norte de México," in Carlos Pallán Figueroa, James W. Wilkie, and Jesus Arroyo Alejandre (eds.), *México y las Américas. Memorias de la VIII Conferencia Anuies-Profmex*, Mexico, D.F., Asociación Nacional de Universidades e Instituciones de Educación Superior, pp. 402-413.

# Index